Macmillan Computer Science Series

Consulting Editor
Professor F.H. Sumner, University of Manchester

S.T. Allworth and R.N. Zobel, *Introduction to Real-time Software Design, second edition*
Ian O. Angell and Gareth Griffith, *High-resolution Computer Graphics Using FORTRAN 77*
Ian O. Angell and Gareth Griffith, *High-resolution Computer Graphics Using Pascal*
M. Azmoodeh, *Abstract Data Types and Algorithms*
C. Bamford and P. Curran, *Data Structures, Files and Databases*
Philip Barker, *Author Languages for CAL*
A.N. Barrett and A.L. Mackay, *Spatial Structure and the Microcomputer*
R.E. Berry, B.A.E. Meekings and M.D. Soren, *A Book on C, second edition*
P. Beynon-Davies, *Information Systems Development*
G.M. Birtwistle, *Discrete Event Modelling on Simula*
B.G. Blundell and C.N. Daskalakis, *Using and Administering an Apollo Network*
B.G. Blundell, C.N. Daskalakis, N.A.E. Heyes and T.P. Hopkins, *An Introductory Guide to Silvar Lisco and Hilo Simulators*
T.B. Boffey, *Graph Theory in Operations Research*
Richard Bornat, *Understanding and Writing Compilers*
Linda E.M. Brackenbury, *Design of VLSI Systems — A Practical Introduction*
G.R. Brookes and A.J. Stewart, *Introduction to occam 2 on the Transputer*
J.K. Buckle, *Software Configuration Management*
W.D. Burnham and A.R. Hall, *Prolog Programming and Applications*
P.C. Capon and P.J. Jinks, *Compiler Engineering Using Pascal*
J.C. Cluley, *Interfacing to Microprocessors*
J.C. Cluley, *Introduction to Low-Level Programming for Microprocessors*
Robert Cole, *Computer Communications, second edition*
Derek Coleman, *A Structured Programming Approach to Data*
Andrew J.T. Colin, *Fundamentals of Computer Science*
Andrew J.T. Colin, *Programming and Problem-solving in Algol 68*
S.M. Deen, *Fundamentals of Data Base Systems*
S.M. Deen, *Principles and Practice of Database Systems*
C. Delannoy, *Turbo Pascal Programming*
Tim Denvir, *Introduction to Discrete Mathematics for Software Engineering*
D. England *et al.*, *A Sun User's Guide*
K.C.E. Gee, *Introduction to Local Area Computer Networks*
J.B. Gosling, *Design of Arithmetic Units for Digital Computers*
M.G. Hartley, M. Healey and P.G. Depledge, *Mini and Microcomputer Systems*
Roger Hutty, *Z80 Assembly Language Programming for Students*
Roland N. Ibbett and Nigel P. Topham, *Architecture of High Performance Computers, Volume I*
Roland N. Ibbett and Nigel P. Topham, *Architecture of High Performance Computers, Volume II*
Patrick Jaulent, *The 68000 – Hardware and Software*
P. Jaulent, L. Baticle and P. Pillot, *68020–30 Microprocessors and their Coprocessors*
J.M. King and J.P. Pardoe, *Program Design Using JSP — A Practical Introduction*
E.V. Krishnamurthy, *Introductory Theory of Computer Science*
V.P. Lane, *Security of Computer Based Information Systems*
Graham Lee, *From Hardware to Software — An Introduction To Computers*

(continued overleaf)

Understanding and Writing Compilers

A do-it-yourself guide

Richard Bornat

Department of Computer Science and Statistics,
Queen Mary College,
University of London

MACMILLAN

First published 1979
Reprinted 1981, 1982 (twice), 1984 (twice), 1985, 1986 (twice),
1989, 1990

Published by
MACMILLAN EDUCATION LTD
Houndmills, Basingstoke, Hampshire RG21 2XS
and London
Companies and representatives
throughout the world

Printed in Hong Kong

ISBN 0–333–21732–2

Contents

Contents

Introduction

In the past compiler writers and designers seemed to form an elite group within computing science, set apart by their esoteric knowledge and their ability to produce large, important system programs which really worked. The admiration of the computing public, whether it was once deserved or not, is no longer merited now that the principles of programming-language implementation are so well understood. Compiler-writing is no longer a mystery.

This book attempts to explain and demystify the principles of compiler writing so that you can go out and build a working compiler of your own. There is enough detail in this book for you to build a compiler for quite a complicated language - certainly PASCAL, perhaps ALGOL 68 or SIMULA 67 - but it doesn't attempt an encyclopaedic coverage of the field. It is intended more as an introduction to compiler-writing and a do-it-yourself kit for the compiler-writer, giving enough detail for you to understand the principles of the subject, than as a survey of past history or present horizons. The principles of interpretation are close enough to those of compilation for chapter 19 to give a simple introduction to interpreter writing.

The method of treatment and the relative amount of attention given to various topics in this book reflects my own views about the relative importance of those topics. There is a separate section on run-time support, less attention is paid than is perhaps usual to the topic of parsing or syntax analysis and the discussion of translation is totally oriented to tree-walking. I have presented the subject in this way for both practical and educational reasons. First, the object code instruction sequences which implement run-time support are more important in practice than is usually recognised. It is differences in run-time mechanisms, as much as or more than anything else, which distinguish one language from another - say SIMULA 67 from ALGOL 68, POP-2 from ALGOL 60 - and the efficiency of run-time support code fragments is crucial to the efficiency of the object program. Second, I believe it is more important to give a _practical_ description of syntax analysis in a book which is intended for the

practical compiler-writer than to give a more formal and complete
introduction to the topic. The syntax analysis mechanisms chosen
for illustration in section IV are selected for their practical
relevance. Of the three mechanisms presented, the 'one-track' and
'operator-precedence' mechanisms are now rather old-fashioned but
are still quite adequate to the task of parsing popular modern
languages. Finally, my insistence on tree-walking as the best
means of translation is both because it makes explanation of
translation algorithms much easier and enables me to bring out the
topic of 'crucial code fragments' which forms so much of the life
of the professional compiler writer; also in my experience it is a
practical way in which both novice and expert can quickly build a
working translator containing the minimum number of errors.

Throughout the book I have emphasised the fact that the task of
compilation can be divided into separate <u>modular</u> sub-tasks. It is
largely the identification of and emphasis on this essential
modularity that has clarified the subject. Emphasis on modular
design also helps me to avoid discussing every known technique for
each of the tasks - if you know what the task is, one or two good
ways to accomplish it and how to recognise another good way if
somebody shows you one, then you are on the way to becoming a
capable compiler writer.

Throughout the book I have emphasised the need for the compiler
to provide a service to its users. It seems to me that the demands
of system or compiler efficiency are too often given precedence
over the justifiable demands of the user who wants understandable
error reports, accurate and reliable object code or strict
adherence to an industry standard. The same goes, I believe, for
the demands of small compiler size or simplicity of construction.
A good compiler can be acceptably efficient and reasonably small
yet still provide a good user service. Indeed I believe that the
well-designed compiler will out-perform the 'efficient' special-
purpose construction, but even if it isn't so the compiler writer
should stand by the principle that machines are provided to save
<u>human</u> time and effort. A few seconds of machine time which saves
minutes (or more often hours) of human time is machine time well
spent!

Host, Object and Source Language in Examples

In the examples throughout the book most algorithms are written in
a version of the language BCPL, details of which are briefly
explained in appendix A. Some example algorithms are in PASCAL: I
would have used PASCAL more extensively were it not for the fact
that its lack of block structure, lack of conditional expressions
and lack of a simple 'union-type' convention forces an obscure
programming style. BCPL's advantage is that it is untyped and
that therefore the examples can show the bare bones of an
algorithm without too much unnecessary hedging round of type
declarations. At the same time this is a drawback: BCPL's lack of

data structure declarations makes it difficult to explain some fairly simple algorithms. Early examples give some explanation of the data structures which are manipulated by the algorithms: it is worth pointing out that in every case the values which are manipulated are <u>pointers</u> to record-structures rather than the structures themselves.

Appendix B explains the assembly code which is used to illustrate the operation of the translation algorithms in sections II and III. It is the code of a single-address, multi-register single-segment-addressing machine. Throughout the book there is an emphasis on the machine-independence of compiler design and the fact that details of the object machine's instruction set don't affect the design of the compiler. Nevertheless it is useful, when discussing translation algorithms, to illustrate the code of an example object machine in order to show the advantages of good design of code fragments.

With the present explosion in the use of microprocessors interest in compiling has re-emerged, particularly interest in compiling system-programming languages. The problems of compiler-writing for small machines are mainly to do with producing compact object code: the examples presented in this book are not directly oriented towards this purpose but may be readily adapted to it. The desire to produce a very small compiler, as opposed to a small object program, should be curbed until you properly understand the principles of compiler design (when perhaps the desire will go away!)

The source language which is used to illustrate syntax analysis and translation algorithms has a variable syntax and semantics, floating somewhere in the space between BCPL, ALGOL 60, ALGOL 68 and PASCAL. Some attention is given to the detailed difficulties which arise in writing a compiler for each of these languages. I didn't wish to limit the discussion to those features displayed by any particular language, however, nor to get bogged down in the details of that language. Most examples therefore relate to the general difficulties of compiling any language which includes recursive procedures, block-structuring, dynamic arrays, pointer variables, and so on.

Acknowledgements

I'm enormously indebted to all the people who have argued with me about compilers and compiling over the years, lectured to me, listened to me, corrected me and generally helped me develop the ideas I present in this book. Many of the good ideas are those of my mentors. Thanks especially to Jeff Rohl for helping me in my first steps and encouraging me to develop my ideas as far as they have gone: thanks also to Bernard Sufrin for so many invaluable discussions about the best way to build and to explain compilers. Thanks to my colleagues at the University of Essex - Bruce

Anderson, Mike Brady, Tony Brooker, Mike Foster, Pete Gardner, Pat
Hayes, John Laski, Bob Wielinga and all the students who listened
to earlier versions of this book in the form of lectures.

This book was type-set on a DEC PDP-11/40 and printed using a
Diablo printer. Thanks to the denizens of the Queen Mary College
Computer Systems Laboratory for allowing me to use the machine so
heavily and especially to George Coulouris, Jon Rowson, Ben Salama
and Harold Thimbleby for leading me through the intricacies of the
local software.

Section I
Modular Organisation
of Compilers

Compilers, at first appearance, seem to display a bewildering variety of organisation: there are single-pass compilers, multi-pass compilers, optimising compilers, load-and-go compilers, interactive compilers and so on and on. Luckily for the compiler-writer, all these apparently different forms can be seen as variations on a simple theme. All compilers perform the same collection of tasks and apparent variations come about because the tasks are put together in slightly different ways or because certain of the tasks are given more emphasis than others in some variations. Below the surface the theme is constant - all compilers perform the same sequence of essential tasks <u>in the same order</u> and by and large the optional tasks which they may perform have a fixed position in the sequence as well.

It's this underlying regularity of organisation which makes it possible to describe the principles of compiler writing in a space as small as this book, because the question of the organisation of the compiler as a whole can be separated from the questions of the design of its sub-sections. Each of the sub-tasks, and the various algorithms for carrying it out, can then be studied in relative isolation. In addition the regularity makes compiler writing largely source-language independent: though to the novice it might seem that a COBOL compiler would differ enormously from a PASCAL compiler I shall show that it isn't so. Perhaps even more surprising is that the problems of compiler writing are largely object-machine independent as well. Both source language and object machine affect only details of compiler construction, whilst the overall organisation remains fixed. Once you have understood the principles of compiler design, most of the details fall naturally into place.

Of the chapters in this section, chapter 1 discusses the organisation of compilation as a sequence of phases, each carried out by a separate module of the compiler, and gives brief examples of the operation of each phase. Chapter 2 gives a more detailed introduction to the principles of translation and justifies the use of a tree-walking translation mechanism. Chapter 3 gives an introduction to the principles of syntax analysis. Chapter 4 discusses lexical analysis and loading: apart from a discussion of lexical analysis grammars in chapter 15 and a discussion of symbol-table building algorithms in chapter 8, both of these rather simple topics are then ignored for the rest of the book.

Later sections expand the treatment which is given in this section. Section II concentrates on translation and code optimisation, section III on the code which performs run-time support functions such as stack handling during a procedure call, section IV deals with syntax analysis and section V treats the allied topics of interpretation (as distinct from compilation) of source programs and the run-time debugging of compiled programs.

I discuss these topics in this order because I believe that it is useful to understand mechanisms of translation before mechanisms of syntax analysis, even though syntax analysis occurs before translation when a program is compiled. Translation, with code optimisation, is probably the most interesting phase of compilation to the active compiler-writer. The novice needs some instruction in the mechanisms of syntax analysis - but it comes much easier if you've seen the requirements of a translator first. In that way you can see why a syntax analyser is necessary and why it must produce the kind of output that it does. Also, having seen the powers and limitations of simple translation, you're in a better position to assess the importance (or unimportance) of code optimisation.

1 Phases and Passes

The most obvious overall task of a compiler is to read a program in one language - the 'source' program in the 'source' language - and to translate it to produce an equivalent program in another language - the 'object' program in the 'object' language. The object language is usually the machine language of a computer, or something close to it, and the source program is usually in a 'high-level' language such as FORTRAN, PASCAL, ALGOL 68, SIMULA 67 or BCPL, because translation from high-level language to machine language is the practical problem which compilers exist to solve. Compilers can be written to translate from any kind of programming language into any other, however, with varying degrees of efficiency of the resulting object program.

Another part of the compiler's overall task, just as important but too often neglected, is that the compiler must check that the source program makes some kind of sense and, when it doesn't seem to make sense, must produce a description of the problem (an error report) so that the programmer can correct the program. I'll return to dicuss the tasks of error detection and reporting later in this chapter.

Before describing how the overall tasks are split up into sub-tasks it's worth discussing the ways in which the sub-sections of a compiler can be combined to make a complete compiler. The overall activity of compilation can be divided into a sequence of <u>phases,</u> during each of which one of the sub-tasks is carried out. As emphasised in the introduction to this section, all compilers perform the same sub-tasks in the same sequence, and therefore all compilers consist of the same sequence of phases. Conceptually each phase transforms the program fragment-by-fragment, taking as input a fragment of some representation of the source program and producing as output a fragment of some other, transformed, representation. Because the transformation is fragment-by-fragment it is possible to choose how the phases are linked. If each separate fragment goes through all the phases before compilation of the next fragment starts we have a <u>single-pass</u> compiler, because all of the source program is compiled in a single pass over the source text. Conversely, if the entire program goes through each one of the phases before any of it is presented to the next phase we have a <u>multi-pass</u> compiler, because each phase performs a separate pass over the program. Clearly if there are **N** phases, you can organise the compiler into anything from 1 to **N** passes.

Thus every compiler must be multi-<u>phase</u>, but it may or may not be multi-<u>pass</u>. Logically the phases must be joined together in the same order no matter how many passes are employed, so that it might not seem to matter whether this book concentrates on multi-pass or single-pass organisation. In practice, however, the multi-pass organisation is simpler to describe and to understand because the interface between the phases is so much more straightforward. Indeed for some languages - ALGOL 60 is a prominent example - it is difficult to construct an effective single-pass compiler at all and therefore the multi-pass organisation is also more generally useful.

It is often believed that multi-pass compilation is inherently less efficient than single-pass. This is simply untrue: since in any compiler each fragment must be processed by the same sequence of phases, a single-pass compiler must perform the same amount of work as a multi-pass compiler. Suppose, however, that each pass of a multi-pass compiler were to write its output into a disc file (or any backing store file) from which the next pass had to read it in again. Such a multi-pass compiler would indeed be less efficient than a single-pass compiler which didn't use backing store but the inefficiency would be caused by the overhead of input and output between passes.

A multi-pass compiler which stores the output of each pass in the main computer memory will certainly be no slower than a single-pass compiler. On a modern computer the only disadvantage of multi-pass compilation is that it may use quite a lot of space to store the output of the various passes. Nowadays computer memories (for everything but the smallest micro-processors!) are large enough for this minor drawback to be overwhelmed by the enormous advantages of clarity of design, and consequent ease of construction, of a multi-pass compiler. For most of the rest of this book I describe a compiler organised in two passes, which is an effective compromise between economy of space and clarity of organisation. In the discussion of compilation algorithms, however, it is usually simplest to imagine that each of the phases in a compiler always performs a separate pass over the program.

Tasks and Sub-tasks

Figure 1.1 shows a coarse breakdown of the overall compilation task (I deal with the parallel task of error processing separately below). A compiler must first <u>analyse</u> a program to see what its

intended effect is. The result of this analysis will be a
representation of the program which is adequate for later
<u>translation</u> into the object language. As I show below and in
chapter 2, this representation is a structure which shows how the
separate fragments of program inter-relate. It splits naturally
into two parts:

(i) the 'parse tree' which shows the structure of the
program text - how the fragments of program join together
to make up larger fragments, how those join to make still
larger fragments and so on.

(ii) the 'symbol table' which provides a correlation between
all the different occurrences of each name throughout the
program and hence provides a link between each name and
its declaration, whether implicit or explicit, in the
source text.

These two information structures are the most important milestones
in the compilation process. Compilation as a whole is an activity
which first builds up information structures which describe how
the program may be broken into fragments and how these fragments
inter-relate, then extracts from these structures the information
which is required in order to translate the program.

Neither analysis nor translation is yet a simple enough sub-
task to describe individually. Figure 1.2 shows a more detailed
breakdown into sub-tasks. The figure shows clearly the
hierarchical-sequential nature of the compiling process: each of
the sub-tasks is entrusted to a particular phase and the phases
don't overlap at all[1]. Capital letters (e.g. LEXICAL ANALYSIS)
indicate a phase or sub-task, lower case letters (e.g. **parse
tree**) an information structure or an intermediate program
representation.

The arrangement of phases in figure 1.2 is partly determined by
the nature of the compiling task but is also partly conventional.
In particular the LEXICAL ANALYSIS phase is present for
convenience' sake and the fact that the compiler's output is most
commonly presented to a LOAD phase before execution is equally a

```
source      ANALYSE    |analysed|  TRANSLATE   object
program  ------------>| program |-------------->  program
```

Figure 1.1 Coarse structure of compilation

---

1 There are some minor exceptions to this rule when compiling
  rather old languages such as FORTRAN. These exceptions have
  been eliminated in most modern languages.

matter of convenience.

Consider the LEXICAL ANALYSIS phase: it has been found convenient to include a phase, immediately before SYNTAX ANALYSIS, which partitions the characters of the source program into 'items', roughly analogous to words and punctuation marks in natural languages. This not only makes the design of the syntax analyser easier, but also it happens that almost all of those sections of the compiler whose speed of operation is important fall into the READ and LEXICAL ANALYSIS phases. Thus the task of improving the compiler's operating efficiency can be reduced to the task of improving the efficiency of the relatively simple input phases and in the rest of the compiler it is possible to ignore the demands of speed of operation in order to concentrate on clarity of design and construction.

Consider next the LOAD phase shown in figure 1.2. If the source program is split into sections which are compiled separately to produce separate sections of object code, it is necessary eventually to use a loader program to combine all the separate code sections into a complete executable program. At the same time the loader can automatically incorporate sections of code from a separate code library. People find the facility to split their program into sections convenient, so the loader

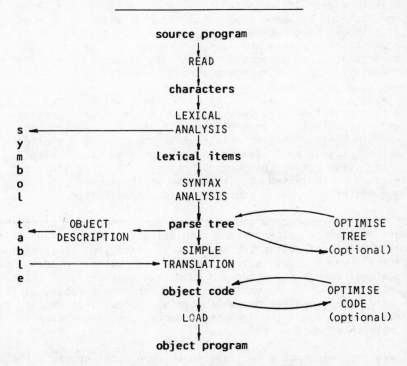

Figure 1.2 Finer structure of compilation

increases human efficiency although in terms of machine utilisation alone it can be more efficient to compile the entire program in one piece and to avoid the loading overhead entirely. At any rate the compiler may, but need not, output code in 'loadable' form as the compiler-writer wishes.

I discuss the input and output phases (READ, LEXICAL ANALYSIS and LOAD in figure 1.2) together with the question of code output formats in chapter 4, so as to separate these matters from the more central and more important phases of analysis, translation and optimisation which occupy most of this book.

Translation and Optimisation

Two of the phases in figure 1.2 are marked as optional - OPTIMISE TREE and OPTIMISE CODE. They are included in the figure because they are so important and so frequently included (or desired by the user if they are not included!). In order to explain the breakdown of the diagram at this point it's necessary to distinguish between 'simple translation' and 'optimisation' in general

Simple translation takes a representation of a fragment of the source program and produces an equivalent fragment of object code. It doesn't take much account of the interaction between fragments, except insofar as it must do in order to produce correct code, but it may be quite sophisticated in the way in which it selects the particular code fragment which it generates as the translation of each source program construct.

Optimisation takes a wider view of the program: it looks at a representation of a larger section of the source program and reorganises the fragments within it, or improves the way in which they interface, so as to produce a shorter object program or a faster object program than simple translation could produce. Sometimes it is possible to produce an optimised object program which is both shorter and faster than one produced by simple translation.

It's not possible to draw a hard line between the two approaches because it's not clear when sophisticated simple translation becomes primitive optimisation. Some so-called 'optimising' compilers would be better viewed as rather good simple translators: many straightforward compilers include some element of optimisation. True optimisations, for the purposes of this book, are those translations which exploit peculiarities of the control flow specified in the source program. Chapter 10 discusses this topic more fully.

There are essentially two ways in which a compiler can optimise a program - i.e. produce a better-than-simple translation

(i) It can include a phase which alters the source program algorithm in such a way that subsequent simple translation can produce the desired effect. This is shown as OPTIMISE TREE in figure 1.2: essentially it replaces the source program's algorithm with another which has the same effect but which can be translated into more efficient code.

(ii) It can include a phase which modifies the code produced by simple translation in order to increase the efficiency of the object program. This is shown as OPTIMISE CODE in figure 1.2: this phase looks mainly at the ways in which the code fragments interface with each other.

These two approaches can be equivalent in their effect and sometimes compilers employ both. The OPTIMISE TREE technique is the more machine-independent of the two and is perhaps potentially the more powerful.

Object Descriptions in the Symbol Table

The names used in a program are merely used to identify run-time objects of one kind or another - variables, arrays, records, procedures, labels and so on. Apart from the needs of debugging, the source program names used are completely arbitrary and the object program operates entirely upon the run-time objects without taking any account of the names which originally introduced them. In order to keep track of the association between names and run-time objects, the compiler must keep a table (the symbol table in figure 1.2) in which it stores against each name a description of the run-time object which that name denotes. The translator uses this table to replace each occurrence of a name by a reference to the corresponding run-time object.

As names are encountered in the source program they are inserted into the symbol table by the lexical analyser (more discussion of this in chapters 4 and 8) but information about the associated run-time object can only be inserted after the program has been syntactically analysed. Names are 'declared' either implicitly (e.g. in FORTRAN) or explicitly (most other languages!). In general the declarative information must be processed before any statement using the name can be translated. Thus correlation of names with run-time objects must precede translation, but must of course follow syntax analysis in which the declarative information is recognised. So there is only one time in the compilation process at which such correlation is possible - hence the OBJECT DESCRIPTION phase in figure 1.2 falls between syntax analysis and simple translation or optimisation.

Run-time Support

Much of the object program consists of instructions which carry out the tasks of calculation, assignment, comparison, etc. which

are specified in the source program. However there are also
sections of the source program whose task is <u>run-time support</u> of
various kinds. Two important tasks of run-time support are to
implement the storage and register manipulations necessary for the
execution of a procedure call[1] (discussed in detail throughout
section III) and the maintenance of 'heap' storage systems
(touched on in chapter 14). The efficiency of the run-time
support fragments in the object program ought to be a major
concern of the compiler writer: users will present programs for
compilation which are based on highly efficient algorithms and
will be justifiably annoyed if the object program is inefficient
purely because of the operation of run-time support code fragments
'behind the scenes'.

The most important task of the run-time support fragments is to
maintain the <u>Activation Record Structure</u>. When a procedure call is
executed a <u>procedure activation</u> is created, which exists until the
corresponding procedure return is executed.   In non-recursive

---

```
program: begin integer a,b;
            ....
            procedure A(x) real x;
            begin real y;
                .... B('a'); ....
            end;

            procedure B(u) character u;
            begin string v;
                .... A(3.7); ....
            end;

            .... A(1.0); ....
        end
```

After outer block calls A, which calls B,
  which calls A again:

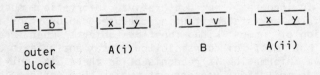

outer   A(i)   B   A(ii)
block

Figure 1.3 Activation Record Structure in a simple program

---

1 Throughout this book I use the word 'procedure' to include the
word 'function' - a function is merely a procedure which
computes and returns a result. So far as run-time support is
concerned, functions and procedures are almost identical.

languages such as FORTRAN only one activation at most can ever
exist for each procedure but in languages which permit recursion
there may be several activations in existence, each in a different
stage of execution of a single procedure body and each with its
private storage and private copy of the arguments with which it
was called. Each of these activations can be described by a data
structure - in a recursive programming language the data structure
is an 'activation record', 'data frame' or 'stack frame' stored on
a stack - and the linkages between these data structures define
the Activation Record Structure. Figure 1.3 shows a simple example
of the structure which can result.

The maintenance of the Activation Record Structure in an
implementation of a recursive programming language is an important
'overhead' cost in the execution of the object program. By
prohibiting recursion, languages such as FORTRAN reduce the
overhead cost but the discussion in section III shows how careful
design of code fragments can minimise or even eliminate the
efficiency gap between recursive and non-recursive languages.
Even recursive languages must restrict the manipulation of some
values in the object program in order to allow the Activation
Record Structure to be kept in a stack: chapter 14 discusses the
way in which the necessary restrictions can be applied in an
implementation of ALGOL 68 and touches on the implementation of
SIMULA 67, which can avoid the imposition of such restrictions
because it doesn't use a data-frame stack.

Source Program Errors

"Any fool can write a compiler for correct source programs"
(J.S. Rohl 1972)

People write programs and people make mistakes. They often need
help in order to correct their mistakes and sometimes a compiler
can provide it. Compiler designers too often seem to place
'helping people' rather low down on their scale of priorities,
well below 'compiler efficiency', 'object program efficiency' and
'source language facilities'. My opinion is that this order of
priorities is wrong-headed but I hope to demonstrate in this book
that it is unnecessary as well. There is no conflict in practice
between, on the one hand, the goal of providing help with errors
in source programs and, on the other hand, the goal of providing a
compiler which is efficient and which produces efficient object
programs.

A compiler has two basic tasks to perform in connection with
source programs which contain errors:

(i) Compile-time error processing:
    The compiler must somehow provide information to a
    programmer who has submitted a program which cannot be
    compiled. The information must, as far as possible, give

an explanation of why the program cannot be compiled and
if possible make suggestions as to how the error might be
corrected.

(ii) Error-checking code:
Many programs, though syntactically correct, specify
impossible sequences of operations when they are executed.
Some object program errors (e.g. arithmetic overflow) may
be detected by the object machine's hardware but probably
many others will not be. In order to detect run-time
errors which are not covered by hardware checks the
compiler must produce object code fragments which check
whether a run-time error has occurred each time they are
run. An example is the array-bound check: it is common for
a compiler to generate code for an array access which
checks the validity of the array subscript each time an
access is made.

In either case error processing can be divided into three separate
activities: error <u>detection</u>, error <u>reporting</u> and error <u>recovery</u>.

First consider compile-time errors: chapter 3 and section IV
show that compile-time error detection is an automatic consequence
of the normal compilation process. This implies that detection of
errors cannot affect the speed of operation of a compiler;
therefore the (imaginary super-human) user who always writes
correct programs is not affected by the vagaries of ordinary
mortals, at least so far as speed of compilation is concerned.
Once an error has been detected in the source program the
programmer is no longer concerned simply with how rapidly the
compiler translates but rather with how quickly the error can be
removed from the program. A small amount of computer time spent in
error reporting and recovery is well spent if it saves human time
and effort. Of course a compiler which includes a great deal of
error reporting and recovery facilities will be larger than one
that contains only a small amount and so there is some penalty in
terms of space occupied, but the extra space and the few fractions
of a second of computer time spent in producing a readable error
report are surely worthwhile if they save minutes (or perhaps
hours!) of human effort.

Similar considerations apply to run-time error-handling. In
this case error-detection can be expensive - the code fragments
which repeatedly check for error will inevitably slow down the
execution of the object program - but the bulk of the error
processing code will be concerned with error reporting and error
recovery and so will only be activated when an error has already
been detected. It's outside the scope of this book to debate
when, if ever, the programmer should ask the compiler to omit
error checking code so as to save execution time and object
program space - at any rate the compiler should always give the
option that it can be included.

Chapter 20 discusses run-time error handling in detail. I include run-time error checking as a task of the compiler, rather than of the operating system or of some other separate program, because the design of object code fragments must take into account the needs of run-time error-checking and error-reporting. Furthermore the compiler designer must consider the production, at compile-time, of information structures which will be used by a run-time debugger to provide error reports related to the original source program. The requirements of run-time error processing can have a major influence on the detail design of object code fragments.

Figure 1.2 doesn't include any mention of error processing but in reality it is a part of the task of _every_ phase of compilation. I shall return again and again in later chapters to the question of how the various phases may be designed to produce readable and understandable error reports.

Two-pass Compilation

Most compilers that aren't single-pass use only two passes rather than the four or five implied by the structure of figure 1.2. Using two passes is a popular compromise between generality and the somewhat demanding space requirements of a true multi-pass compiler. The two-pass organisation essentially follows figure 1.1 - there is an analysis pass and a translation pass. The analysis pass includes the READ, LEXICAL ANALYSIS and SYNTAX ANALYSIS phases. In order to combine these phases into a single pass it is conventional to make READ a subroutine of LEXICAL ANALYSIS and LEXICAL ANALYSIS a subroutine of SYNTAX ANALYSIS - as chapter 4 shows, this isn't very difficult. The translation pass usually consists of a SIMPLE TRANSLATION phase only.

The two-pass organisation seems to leave out the OBJECT DESCRIPTION phase entirely and in a two pass compiler this phase is rather difficult to include as a separate entity. Object description is usually carried out piecemeal during one or other (or both) of the passes. Perhaps most convenient is to perform all object description during the translation pass: every time the translator encounters a section of the tree that may contain declarative information it must be processed by the object description phase, which creates symbol table descriptors based on any declarations contained in that section of the tree, before it can be translated into object code. The examples in sections II and III show algorithms in which the object description phase is a subroutine of the translation phase, called each time the translator encounters a 'procedure declaration' node or a 'block' node in the parse tree.

An Example of Compilation

In the rest of this chapter I show, very briefly, the action of some of the phases of compilation taking as example input the program of figure 1.4. First of all the characters of the program are read in, then these characters are lexically analysed into separate items. Some of the items will represent source program

```
begin integer a; real b;
    a := 1; b := 1.2;
    a := b+1;
    print(a*2)
end
```

Figure 1.4 Example program

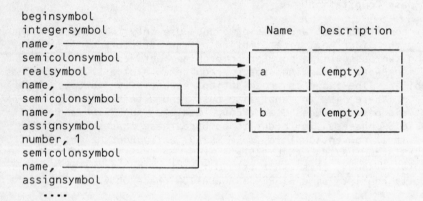

Figure 1.5 Part of the output from the lexical analyser

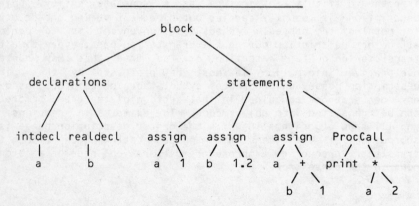

Figure 1.6 Output from the syntax analyser

identifiers and will include a pointer to the symbol table[1].
Figure 1.5 shows part of the results of lexical analysis: in most

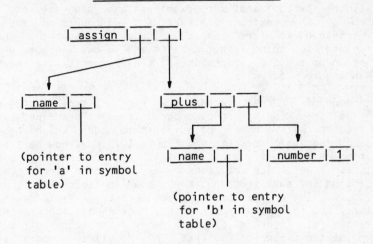

(pointer to entry
for 'a' in symbol
table)

(pointer to entry
for 'b' in symbol
table)

Figure 1.7 Data structure representation of a tree

Name	Descriptor
a	variable, **integer,** address #1
b	variable, **real,** address #2
print	procedure, one **integer** argument address from loader

Figure 1.8 Symbol table descriptors

```
LOAD   1, address #2
fADDn  1, 1.0
FIX    1,
STORE  1, address #1
```

Figure 1.9 Possible machine (assembly) code output

---

1 The item which represents a number may also contain a pointer
  to a table which contains a representation of the number. For
  simplicity figures 1.5 and 1.6 show the value of the number as
  part of the lexical item itself.

languages subdivision of the input into items can be performed without regard to the context in which the name occurs.

Next, the syntax analyser examines the sequence of items produced by the lexical analyser and discovers how the items relate together to form 'phrase' fragments, how the phrases inter-relate to form larger phrases and so on. The most general description of these relationships of the fragments is a tree, as shown in figure 1.6.

Each node of the tree includes a <u>tag</u> or <u>type</u> field which identifies the kind of source program fragment described by that node, together with a number of pointers to nodes which describe the subphrases which make it up. Figure 1.7 shows how part of the tree shown in figure 1.6 might actually be represented as a data structure. There are of course a number of different ways of representing the same tree, and that shown in figure 1.7 is merely an example. There are as many different ways of drawing the structure, and throughout most of this book I shall show trees in the manner of figure 1.6. The only significant differences between the two picturings is that, in the first, nodes aren't shown as sequences of boxes and names aren't shown as pointers to the symbol table. Figure 1.7 is perhaps more faithful to reality, so it should be borne in mind whenever you encounter a simplified representation like that in figure 1.6.

After syntax analysis, the object description phase takes the tree and the symbol table entries produced by the lexical analyser. It analyses the declarative nodes in the tree, producing descriptive information in the symbol table as shown in figure 1.8. Standard procedures, such as 'print', may receive a default declaration before translation: figure 1.8 shows a possible entry in the symbol table. Note that, since the tree contains a pointer to the symbol table in each node which contains a reference to an identifier, neither object description phase nor translator need search the symbol table but need merely to follow the pointer to the relevant entry.

After the object description phase has filled in the descriptors in the symbol table, a simple translation phase can take the tree of figure 1.7 together with the symbol table of figure 1.8 and produce an instruction sequence[1] like that shown in figure 1.9.

The addresses used in the instructions need finally to be relocated by the loader. Suppose that, when the program is loaded into store, its memory cell space starts at address 23. Then the first line of figure 1.9 would be converted into 'LOAD 1, 24' and

---

1 See appendix B for a brief description of the assembly code
  instructions used in this and other examples.

the last line into 'STORE 1, 23'.

Optimisation of the object code in this case could produce an enormous improvement in its execution efficiency. The total effect of the program is to print the number '4'. By looking at the way in which the values of variables are used throughout the program and by deferring translation of assignment statements until their result is required - in this case they are never required - an optimisation phase could reduce the program just to the single statement 'print(4)'. Optimisation is a mighty sledgehammer designed for bigger nuts than this example, of course, and it is always an issue whether the expense of optimisation is worth it: in the case of figure 1.4 it would certainly cost more to optimise the program than it would to run it!

Summary

The underlying organisation of compilers is simple and modular. This chapter discusses how the various phases cooperate so that later chapters can concentrate on the separate phases in isolation.

Input and lexical analysis is discussed in chapters 4 and 8; syntax analysis in chapters 3, 16, 17 and 18; object description in chapter 8; translation in chapters 5, 6, 7 and 9; optimisation in chapter 10; loading in chapter 4; run-time support in chapters 11, 12, 13 and 14; run-time debugging in chapter 20.

2 Introduction to Translation

The most important task that a compiler performs is to translate a program from one language into another - from source language to object language. Simple translation is a mechanism which takes a representation of a fragment of the source program and produces an equivalent fragment in the object language - a code fragment which, when executed by the object machine, will perform the operations specified by the original source fragment.

Since the object program produced by a simple translator consists of a sequence of relatively independent object code fragments, it will be less efficient than one produced by a mechanism which pays some attention to the context in which each fragment must operate. Optimisation is a mechanism which exists to cover up the mistakes of simple translation: it translates larger sections of program than the simple translator does, in an attempt to reduce the object code inefficiencies caused by poor interfacing of code fragments.

In order to be able to produce object code phrases the translator must have access to a symbol table which provides a mapping from source program names to the run-time objects which they denote. This table is built by the lexical analyser (see chapters 4 and 8) which correlates the various occurrences of each name throughout the program. The mapping to run-time objects is provided by the object description phase (see chapter 8) which processes declarative information from the source program to associate each identifier in the symbol table with a description of a run-time object.

This chapter introduces the notion of a 'tree-walking' translator, which I believe is a mechanism that is not only easy to construct but which can readily and reliably produce efficient object code fragments. Such a translator consists of a number of mutually recursive procedures, each of which is capable of translating one kind of source program fragment and each of which can generate a variety of different kinds of object code fragments

depending on the detailed structure of the source fragment which
is presented to it.

Because the process of translation depends on the selection at
each point of one of a number of possible code fragments
translators tend to be voluminous but, since the selection of a
fragment is fairly simple and generating the instructions is very
straightforward, they tend to run very rapidly.   A   simple
translator will usually use less than 15% of the machine time used
by all phases of the compiler together, but will make up more than
50% of the compiler's own source code.

Phrases and Trees

In this chapter I introduce the technical term phrase, which is
used to describe a logically complete fragment of source program.
Statements, for example, are phrases; so are expressions. Phrases

---

Statement:
  if hour*60+minute=1050 **or** tired **then** leave(workplace)

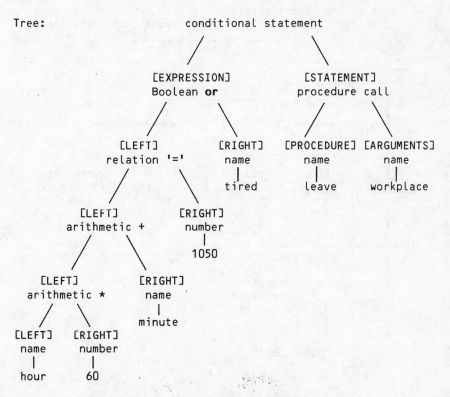

Figure 2.1 Tree describing a simple statement

are either 'atomic' - e.g. a name, a number - or are made up of sub-phrases - e.g. a statement may have a sub-phrase which is an expression, the statement itself may be a sub-phrase of a block which is a sub-phrase of a procedure declaration, and so on. In this chapter the largest phrase shown in the examples is an expression or a simple structured statement. In a multi-pass compiler the unit of translation is the entire program - at least at the topmost level - but a single page isn't large enough to show the necessary trees!

The state of the art in programming language translation is now, and will remain for some time, that a program can only be translated if it is first analysed to find how the phrases inter-relate: then the translator can consider each phrase in turn. The result of the analysis shows how the program (the phrase being translated) can be divided into sub-phrases and shows how these sub-phrases inter-relate to make up the entire phrase. For each sub-phrase the description shows how it is divided into sub-sub-phrases and how they are inter-related. The description continues to show the subdivision of phrases in this way until the atomic phrases - the items of the source text - are reached.

The most general representation of the results of such an analysis is a tree like that in figure 2.1. The lines are

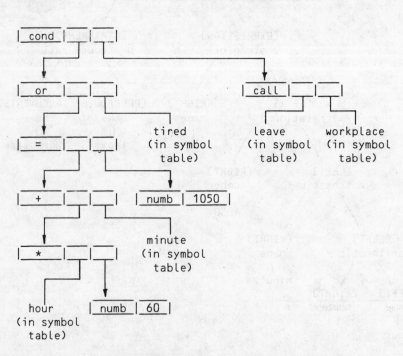

Figure 2.2 Data-structure representation of the tree

branches, the place where branches start and finish are <u>nodes</u>. The topmost node of the tree is its <u>root</u> - the tree is conventionally drawn 'upside down'. Nodes which don't divide into branches are <u>leaves</u> and represent the atomic items of the source program. Each phrase of the source program is represented by a separate node of the tree. To translate a phrase it is merely necessary to concentrate on one node and, if it has sub-nodes, to translate its sub-nodes as well.

Figure 2.2 shows a possible data-structure representation of the tree of figure 2.1 using record-vectors and pointers. Many other representations are possible - for example one in which each pointer is represented by a subscript of a large integer vector. The tree structure, no matter how it is represented, gives the translator the information it needs in order to translate the statement - it shows which phrases are related, and how they are related. From the source statement it isn't immediately obvious what the object program should do. Should it, for example, evaluate 'hour*60'? Must it evaluate 'minute=1050'? What about '1050 **or** tired'? A glance at the tree gives the answers - only the first is represented by a node because analysis has shown it to be a phrase of the program.

In order to be able to translate a phrase of a program it is <u>essential</u> to know what kind of phrase it is, what its sub-phrases are and how they are inter-related. There can be non-tree-like representations of the necessary information, but the tree holds and displays the information in its most accessible and useful form. In addition it emphasises the essentially recursive nature of translation - a nature which is somewhat hidden, but not denied, in so-called 'linear' representations.

Tree Walking

It's extremely easy to translate - generate code for - a phrase if you know how to generate code for its sub-phrases. Figures 2.3a and 2.3b show some sample procedures which translate in this way. Each procedure translates a phrase by generating a single instruction, or a short sequence of instructions, which links together the code fragments that are the translation of its sub-phrases. Only for indivisible phrases (leaf nodes) is it necessary to know how to translate the entire phrase. In order to generate code for a sub-phrase, all the translator needs to do is to look at the type of phrase it is - the 'tag' or 'type' field of the tree node - and to call the relevant translation procedure.

Figure 2.4 shows the code produced by these procedures when presented with the tree of figure 2.1. (The figures don't show the translation procedure which handles the procedure call node, or the code produced - section III deals with this topic.) Starting at the root of the tree, the translator works downwards. It's essentially a recursive process - one operand of a '+' node may be another '+' node or may contain a '+' node, for example. Since the process is recursive it's trivially easy to translate structured statements like the conditional statement which might at first seem the hardest to translate. Imagine how straightforward it is to translate a PASCAL compound statement or an ALGOL 68 serial clause!

The most important thing to note about figure 2.4 is that the code would <u>work</u> if it was given to the object machine to execute. Tree walking is a powerful technique precisely because it is easy to design procedures like those in figures 2.3a and 2.3b which really will generate accurate code. The object code produced by

---

1: Conditional statement
    1a: call procedure which generates code to load
        value of expression part into register 1
    1b: invent a label #Lf
    1c: generate **JUMPFALSE 1, #Lf**
    1d: call procedure which generates code to carry
        out statement part
    1e: generate **#Lf:**

2: Boolean **or** (result to be in register k)
    2a: call procedure which generates code to load
        value of left operand into register k
    2b: call procedure which generates code to load
        value of right operand into register k+1
    2c: generate **ORr k, k+1**

3: Relation '=' (result to be in register k)
    3a: call procedure which generates code to load
        value of left operand into register k+1
    3b: call procedure which generates code to load
        value of right operand into register k+2
    3c: generate **LOADn   k, TRUE**
            SKIPEQr k+1, k+2
            LOADn   k, FALSE

4: arithmetic + (result to be in register k)
    Exactly as for Boolean **or**, except that the final
        instruction is **ADDr k, k+1.**

5: arithmetic '*' (result to be in register k)
    Exactly as for Boolean **or**, except that the final
        instruction is **MULTr k, k+1.**

Figure 2.3a Translation procedures for non-leaf nodes

these procedures isn't optimal by any means, but it's relatively trivial to change the procedures to improve it. Each procedure is a separate module: although figure 2.3a doesn't include all of the standard programming language expression operators, it wouldn't be necessary to make any changes to the existing set when new node-translating procedures are added.

Linear Tree Representations

Before describing how to improve the code produced by the

6: name (value to be loaded into register k)
      generate **LOAD k,** <run-time address of variable
      denoted by name>

7: number (value to be loaded into register k)
      if value is small enough then
            generate **LOADn k,** <value of number>
      else generate **LOAD k,** <run-time address where
      value will be found>

Figure 2.3b Translation procedures for leaf nodes

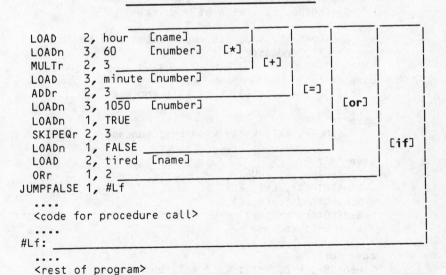

```
LOAD       2, hour    [name]                  |    |     |     |     |
LOADn      3, 60      [number]    [*] |        |    |     |     |
MULTr      2, 3 _____| [+] |   |    |     |     |
LOAD       3, minute [number]                  |    |     |     |
ADDr       2, 3 _____| [=] |    |     |     |
LOADn      3, 1050    [number]                 | [or] |    |     |
LOADn      1, TRUE                             |      |    |     |
SKIPEQr    2, 3                                |      |    |     |
LOADn      1, FALSE _____|   |      | [if] |   |
LOAD       2, tired  [name]                           |      |   |
ORr        1, 2 _____|      |   |
JUMPFALSE  1, #Lf                                            |   |
   ....
   <code for procedure call>
   ....
#Lf: _____|
   ....
   <rest of program>
```

Figure 2.4 Code produced by the translation procedures

    hour, 60, *, minute, +, 1050, =, tired, **or**

Figure 2.5 Linearised expression

translation procedures of figure 2.3 it is necessary to dispose of
a   red   herring   -   'Reverse   Polish'   or   'postfix   string'
representation.   The collection of procedures in figures 2.3a   and
2.3b   describe   a   <u>tree   walk</u> - a process which visits the nodes of
the tree in a particular, predetermined order. If the nodes of the
expression   part of the tree of figure 2.1 are written out in just
the order in which   the   tree   walker   would   visit   them   then   a
translator   can   walk   them with a non-recursive algorithm. Figure
2.5 shows the nodes of the tree from figure 2.1, written   out   in
the order in which they are visited by the tree walker.

Considering only the string   which   represents   the   expression
part   of the tree in figure 2.1, it is possible to define a simple
iterative procedure which generates code for it: figure 2.6   shows

----

```
k := 1  /* k records next free register */
until end-of-string do
 { switchon current-element into
    { case name:
        Gen(LOAD, k, <address of variable>)
        k := k+1; endcase

      case number:
        if number is small enough then
          Gen(LOADn, k, <value of number>)
        else
          Gen(LOAD, k, <address where value will be found>)
        k := k+1; endcase

      case '+':
        Gen(ADDr, k-2, k-1); k := k-1; endcase

      case '*':
        Gen(MULTr, k-2, k-1); k := k-1; endcase

      case '=':
        Gen(LOADn, k, TRUE)
        Gen(SKIPEQr, k-1, k-2)
        Gen(LOADn, k, FALSE)
        Gen(LOADr, k-2, k)
        k := k-1; endcase

      case 'or':
        Gen(ORr, k-2, k-1); k := k-1; endcase

      default: CompilerFail("invalid element in string")
    }
   current-element := next-element
 }
```

Figure 2.6 Linear string walker

a possible algorithm. There is a slight difficulty with the '='
node, which is in effect 'visited' twice in the tree walk, once to
reserve the register which will hold TRUE or FALSE and once to
actually generate the instructions which carry out the comparison.
In the case of a simple Reverse Polish string the operator appears
only once, so that the code for the '=' node must move the
computed value into its intended register — the 'extra
instruction' shown in figure 2.7.

The string walking algorithm uses a stack of registers, so its
status as 'non-recursive' is in doubt anyway. Note that it is
impossible to vary the way in which the tree is walked, according
to some code generation strategy, after the string has been
generated. Use of a postfix string representation of the source
program merely freezes the compiler into a particular kind of tree
walk. Although the string-walking algorithm could be improved
quite easily in some ways (e.g. avoiding 'LOAD, ADDr' instructions
in sequence) most of the improvements which are introduced below
and discussed in detail in later chapters involve changing the way
the tree is walked and so are impossible (or at best extremely
difficult) using any linear representation.

Improving the Tree Walker

Once you have a working translator, you are in business as a
compiler-writer. Using tree walking will get you to this point
faster. It will also help you to get farther and faster along the
road to better code than any ad hoc solution could.

Improving the efficiency of the code produced by a tree-walking
translator means looking at the code fragments generated by one or
more of the procedures and deciding that the procedure's strategy
was weak, or that it should look out for that particular source
construct and generate a specially selected code fragment for it.
The various possibilities are summarised in figure 2.8. It's hard
to decide where tactics shade into strategy: figure 2.9 shows an

```
LOAD     1, hour
LOADn    2, 60
MULTr    1, 2
LOAD     2, minute
ADDr     1, 2
LOADn    2, 1050
LOADn    3, TRUE
SKIPEQr  1, 2
LOADn    1, FALSE
LOADr    1, 3      /* extra instruction */
LOAD     2, tired
ORr      1, 2
```

Figure 2.7 Code produced by the linear string walker

improved arithmetic '+' procedure. This procedure saves an instruction and a register when the right operand is a leaf: I would classify this as a tactical manoeuvre. Using this procedure the first three instructions of figure 2.4 would be compressed into two and, if a similar improvement were made to the procedures which translate '=' and **or** nodes, the translator would produce the code shown in figure 2.10 for the example expression. This code is a considerable improvement over that of figure 2.4 - it uses two rather than three registers, seven rather than eleven instructions - and it was reached by making simple and modular

---

(i) Generate special code for a node with a special local property (tactics).

(ii) Alter the way the tree is walked when a node has a particular general property (strategy).

(iii) Modify the tree before it is walked (optimise the tree).

(iv) Modify the code which was generated, after the tree walk has finished (optimise the code).

Figure 2.8 Tactics and strategy

```
4: arithmetic '+' (result to be in register k)
   4a: generate code to calculate value of left operand
       in register k
   4b: if right operand is a name then
           4b1: generate ADD k, <address of variable>
       else if right operand is a number then
           4b2: generate ADDn k, <value of number>
                or ADD k, <place where value will be found>
       else
           4b3a: generate code to calculate value of
                 right operand in register k+1
           4b3b: generate ADDr k, k+1
```

Figure 2.9 Improved translation of binary operation nodes

```
LOAD      2, hour
MULTn     2, 60
ADD       2, minute
LOADn     1, TRUE
SKIPEQn   2, 1050
LOADn     1, FALSE
OR        1, tired
```

Figure 2.10 Code produced by improved translator

changes to the procedures of the translator. Chapter 5 shows that much more can be done about the code generated for arithmetic operator nodes, and chapter 6 shows that quite a different approach is possible for Boolean operation nodes.

Improvements like that in figure 2.9 can also be made to the iterative string-walking procedure. Strategic alterations are far more difficult, however, since a linear representation doesn't allow the translator to take account of the structure of an expression.

Some further tactical possibilities are shown in figure 2.11. These are 'sub-optimisations' because the code which is generated for a particular source fragment doesn't depend on the control context within which the object code fragment will operate. True optimisations take account of this context and consider, for example, whether there are any registers which already hold the values of variables, whose contents can be used to avoid an

---

1: Statement: a := 0   Tree: assign
                                    /   \
                                   a   0

```
        Normal code:                Optimised code:
          LOADn 1, 0                   STOZ  , a
          STORE 1, a
```

2: Statement: b := b+<anything>   Tree: assign
                                          /   \
                                         b   +
                                               / \
                                              b   <anything>

```
        Normal code:                Optimised code:
          LOAD  1, <anything>          LOAD   1, <anything>
          ADD   1, b                   ADDST  1, b
          STORE 1, b
```

3: Statement: c := c+1   Tree: assign
                                      /   \
                                     c   +
                                           / \
                                          c   1

```
        Good code:                  Better code:
          LOADn 1, 1                   INCST   , c
          ADDST 1, c
```

Figure 2.11 Some simple sub-optimisations

Program: **for** i = 1 **to** 100 **do**
          begin
             x := 0.5 * sqrt(y+z);
             a[i] := x;
             b[i] := y;
             ....
          end

Tree: program

... ... for ... ...

i 1 100 compound

x:=... a[i]:=x b[i]:=y ...

Altered tree: program

... ... x:=... for ... ...

i 1 100 compound

a[i]:=x b[i]:=y ...

Figure 2.12 Moving code out of a loop

Program:
     a := b+1;
     c := a

Original code:
     LOAD   1, b
     ADDn   1, 1
     STORE 1, a (possibly unnecessary)
     LOAD   1, a (certainly unnecessary)
     STORE 1, c (possibly unnecessary)

Figure 2.13 Removing unnecessary instructions

unnecessary LOAD instruction. To generate this code, the procedure for assignment nodes must look for nodes with a particular special property and generate a special code fragment for them. The number of possible tactical improvements is enormous and the translator should implement only those tactics which are cost-effective – i.e. where the improvement in object program efficiency is sufficient to justify the cost of recognising the tactical situation and also the frequency with which the situation arises is sufficient to justify checking each possible node in the tree.

Modifying the tree and modifying the code (cases iii and iv in figure 2.8) are examples of optimisation techniques. Case iii is illustrated by 'code motion' out of a loop to reduce the number of times a fixed calculation is carried out (figure 2.12) and case iv by 'register remembering' to eliminate unnecessary LOAD and STORE instructions (figure 2.13). Code modification can be done after translation has finished or, perhaps better, as a sort of filter on the code proposed by the translator as it generates it.

Using the Symbol Table Descriptors

The symbol table is built by the lexical analyser in order to correlate the various occurrences of each particular source program name. The object description phase inserts into the symbol table against each name a descriptor which gives information about the run-time object which is denoted by that name, determined by the declarations in which the name appears.

The descriptor not only distinguishes between different kinds of objects – variables, arrays, procedures – but also in a

---

1. INTEGER + INTEGER

         LOAD   n, a
         ADD   n, b

2. REAL + INTEGER

         LOAD   n, a
         LOAD   n+1, b
         FLOATr n+1,
         fADDr   n,   n+1

3. REAL + COMPLEX

         LOAD   n,   a
         ADD   n,   breal
         LOAD   n+1, bimag

Figure 2.14 Code for various type combinations

compiler for an algebraic language the descriptor will give the
type of the run-time object. Figure 2.14 shows some possible code
fragments for combinations of FORTRAN's INTEGER, REAL and COMPLEX
types in an arithmetic '+' node each of whose sub-nodes is an
arithmetic variable name. As well as recording the type and kind
of the object, the descriptor must contain the (possibly
relocatable) store address of the run-time object so that the a's
and b's in the instructions of figure 2.14 can be replaced by the
proper run-time addresses.

In languages with more complex data structures, such as COBOL,
PL/1, ALGOL 68 or SIMULA 67, the descriptor structure will not be
a simple description of an object but rather a description of a
run-time structure. In the case of COBOL, the ADD CORRESPONDING
statement provides the most obvious example - the descriptor for
HEAD-OFFICE and that for NORTH-OFFICE in figure 2.15 must give the
underlying hierarchical structure so that the translator can
generate code for the necessary sequence of simple ADD statements.
In such a case, the tree obviously extends into the symbol table.

Statement: ADD CORRESPONDING NORTH-OFFICE TO HEAD-OFFICE

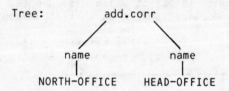

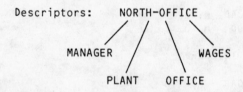

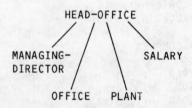

Figure 2.15 Symbol table which contains structure

Translation Error Handling

A translation error report is generated when a source fragment
appears to be of the correct superficial form, but for some reason
can't be translated. Some obvious causes of this are undeclared
names, names whose descriptor types don't match the required
context and so on. Figure 2.16 gives some examples. These errors
are almost all discovered by checking the tree against the
contents of the symbol table. They are all <u>syntactic</u> errors –
semantic errors happen at run-time.

---

1. Operands of a node are of wrong type

   Statement: **if** a **then** x := b+1

   Tree:

   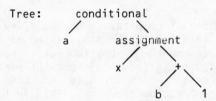

   Symbol Table: a is a **real** variable
                 b is a **Boolean** variable

2. Name not declared – so its descriptor is empty

   e.g. name 'x' not declared in example above

3. Ambiguous data name (COBOL)

   Statement: MOVE PLANT TO PLANT

   Symbol Table: as in figure 2.15 above.

4. Invalid combination of phrases

   Statement: **if** u=v=0 **then** ....

   Tree:

   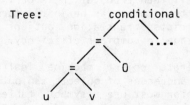

Figure 2.16 Some kinds of error detected in translation

Case 4 of figure 2.16 can come about when the syntax analyser doesn't check every syntactic rule as the tree is built. This form of error corresponds to syntactic rules of the form 'a phrase X cannot be a subphrase of a phrase Y'. Such errors are easier to detect and to report upon during translation than during syntax analysis - see the discussion in chapters 5 and 17.

Translation error detection <u>does</u> <u>not</u> <u>slow</u> <u>down</u> the translator. Since the types of operands must be checked in order to select a code fragment, type combination errors will be detected automatically. Since the descriptor must be used to translate a leaf name, the lack of information will be detected automatically. Since the translator must search the COBOL hierarchy to distinguish between different data objects, lack of distinction will be detected automatically. Since it must investigate the types of subphrase nodes in order to select the appropriate code fragment, invalid combinations will be detected automatically - and so on.

Error reporting in any phase of compilation should always be in source language terms and the translation phase is no exception. It is possible to use the tree and the symbol table to produce a version of the source statement, although without the particular arrangement of newlines and spaces which was used in the source program to lay the statement out on the page. This fact is the basis for the existence of 'pretty printers', which take the parse tree and from it produce a judiciously laid out version of the source program.

Error recovery during translation is simple - forget about the error, assume that the node was correctly translated and carry on. Of course a faulty program should not be run and some action such as deleting the translator's output should be taken to ensure that it the program isn't loaded and executed. Error correction during translation is more than usually dangerous and is rarely attempted.

Summary

Translation takes a source program, fragment by fragment, and produces corresponding fragments of object program. The relationships between fragments define a tree, and if the input to the translator is the tree itself then translation is particularly straightforward. Input to the translator can be in the form of a string but this merely restricts translation options without giving any corresponding advantage in compiler efficiency.

In order to be able to generate object machine instructions which refer to the run-time addresses of objects manipulated by the object program, the translator must use a symbol table which contains information about those objects including type, kind, run-time address, etc. The names are inserted in the table by the lexical analyser as they are encountered in the source program and the descriptors are filled in by the object description phase before translation commences.

Because the interfacing and relative positioning of code fragments in the linear sequence of object machine instructions can affect efficiency, a pure tree-walking translator will not generate entirely optimal code. Code optimisation attempts to overcome these deficiencies and is discussed in chapter 10. A tree-walking translator may however be designed so that the fragment it generates for a node depends on the immediate context of the node and the particular characteristics of the node itself. In this way a sophisticated simple translation phase may reduce the need for optimisation, perhaps even to the point at which it is no longer cost-effective.

Sections II and III concentrate on the translation of particular source program fragments, giving attention to the actual machine instructions which a tree walker might generate for each of them. Certain nodes are 'crucial' in that the code fragments generated as their translation will have a major effect on the speed and size of the object program. Concentration on such crucial code fragments can be enormously productive and may largely make the difference between a good translator and one which is merely effective. The major advantage of tree walking as a translation technique, outweighing all others, is that incremental development and incremental improvement of the translator is possible. In this way both novice and expert can produce a good, working, translator faster than with any other technique.

3 Introduction to Syntax Analysis

If the task of translation is to go from the tree to the object code, then the task of analysis must be to go from source program to tree. Lexical analysis, as chapter 4 shows, discovers how the input characters are grouped into items and the task of syntax analysis is to discover the way in which the items link together into phrases, the phrases link into larger phrases and so on. The output of the syntax analyser must be a tree or some equivalent representation such as a sequence of 'triples' or 'quadruples'[1] or a postfix string. It's convenient to divide up the description of syntax analysis into two parts: first to describe how to <u>recognise</u> a phrase and second how to <u>output</u> a tree node which describes that phrase. It turns out that the recognition technique used, of which there are many, doesn't affect and is not affected by considerations of how to produce analysis output.

Syntax analysis is a well-understood topic, by which I mean that serious theoretical analysis has <u>proved</u> that certain approaches must work given certain properties of the source language. Thus designing a syntax analyser is mostly a matter of picking a technique and following the rules which tell how to produce an analyser based on that technique. This chapter gives a brief introduction to the principles of syntax analysis so that the intensive treatment of translation which follows in sections II and III can rely on some background understanding. It illustrates two of the techniques which are dealt with in more detail in section IV - top-down one-track analysis, which is discussed in chapter 16, and operator-precedence analysis, which is discussed in chapter 17. Chapter 18 deals with the technique known as LR analysis, which isn't introduced in this chapter.

---

1 A 'triple' consists of an operator and two operands, a 'quadruple' is an operator and three operands. In effect each of these representations shows the tree viewed from underneath - see figure 3.10.

Building a syntax analyser which can process 'correct' programs is pretty trivial - it is just a matter of constructing an analyser which is based on the syntax description of a language, by blindly following the rules associated with one of the well-known syntax analysis techniques. Real live users don't always submit syntactically correct programs: they often make mistakes and the true tasks of the analyser include recognising, reporting upon and recovering from the consequences of those mistakes. Error handling is by no means well understood and therefore a major difficulty when building a syntax analyser is to provide reasonable behaviour in the face of all the source program errors

---

FORTRAN

A logical IF statement is of the form
        IF (e) s
where 'e' is a logical expression and 's' is any statement except a DO statement or another logical IF .....

A logical expression is a logical term or a construct of the form
        logical expression .OR. logical term

A logical term ......

COBOL
                                      | identifier-1 |
COMPUTE identifier- [ROUNDED] = | literal |
                                      | arithmetic-expression |
          [; ON SIZE ERROR imperative-statement]

Arithmetic expressions are data-names, identifiers or numeric literals or a sequence of ....

ALGOL 60

<for statement> ::= <for clause> <statement>
                    | <label>: <for statement>
<for clause> ::= **for** <variable> := <for list> **do**
<for list> ::= ......

PASCAL

<procedure heading> ::= **procedure** <identifier> ;
        | **procedure** <identifier> (<formal parameter section>
                    { ; <formal parameter section> }) ;

Figure 3.1 Sample syntax definitions

which may eventually arise.

Language Descriptions (Grammars)

Programming language descriptions all fall naturally into two parts

1. A description of the <u>syntax</u> of the language which details the 'superficial form' of a program, laying down rules of punctuation and showing how a program may be built up out of items and characters.

2. A description of the <u>semantics</u> of the language, which defines the actions which a processor[1] will carry out when presented with a (correct) program in the language.

Part 1 of the description itself breaks into two further parts

1a: <u>Short-range</u> syntax
How particular phrases must be written in terms of the sub-phrases they must contain and how these sub-phrases must be separated by punctuation items.

1b: <u>Long-range</u> syntax
How the various uses of a name (an identifier) in a program must be correlated in terms of consistency between declaration and use.

The breakdown into short- and long-range syntax can always be made, even in languages such as ALGOL 60, whose description categorises long-range syntax (wrongly, in my view) under the heading of 'semantics'. The definition of ALGOL 68 mixes together short- and long-range syntax in a single formal description - see the discussion of 'two-level grammars' in chapter 15.

Syntax analysis is concerned simply with the rules of short-range syntax. Long-range syntax can be investigated only after the superficial form of the tree is known, when the context in which each name is used has been discovered. The object description phase can then process the declarative sections of the parse tree, writing symbol table descriptors which convey information about the kind of object denoted by each name. Finally the translator, in attempting to make use of information about the run-time object which a name has been declared to denote, can effectively check the long-range syntax rules.

Figure 3.1 shows some fragments of the syntax of FORTRAN, COBOL, ALGOL 60 and PASCAL. Note that each of these syntax

---

1 The object machine is the processor in the case of a compiled program.

descriptions describes a tree structure like that used in chapter 2 - each gives the form of a source language phrase in terms of the sub-phrases it may contain, the form of the sub-phrases in terms of sub-sub-phrases, and so on. Syntax analysis merely consists of searching for patterns of phrases in the source text. Obviously it is necessary to find the small phrases (those made up of single items) first, then to find patterns involving small phrases which combine into a larger phrase, but different analysis mechanisms use different methods of searching for and detecting the phrases.

---

1. <Boolean expression> ::= <Boolean term>
            | <Boolean expression> **or** <Boolean term>

2. <Boolean expression> ::= <Boolean term>
            | <Boolean term> **or** <Boolean expression>

3. A Boolean expression is a Boolean term or a sequence of Boolean terms separated by the **or** operator.
4. A Boolean expression is a Boolean variable, a Boolean constant, a Boolean function call, a relational expression or a construct of the form
      Boolean-expression Boolean-operator Boolean-expression
   The Boolean operators are, in increasing order of priority, **or**, ...

Figure 3.2 Alternative descriptions of expressions

```
<statement> ::= <number> : <statement> | begin <compound>
        | goto <number> | <identifier> := <expression>
        | <identifier> ( <expression> )
        | if <B-expression> then <statement>

<compound> ::= <statement> end | <statement> ; <compound>

<expression> ::= <B-expression> | <A-expression>

<A-expression> ::= <A1> | <A-expression> + <A1>
              | <A-expression> - <A1>
<A1> ::= <A2> | <A1> * <A2> | <A1> / <A2>
<A2> ::= <identifier> | <number>

<B-expression> ::= <B1> | <B-expression> or <B1>
<B1> ::= <B2> | <B1> and <B2>
<B2> ::= <identifier> | true | false
              | <A-expression> = <A-expression>
```

Figure 3.3 Grammar of a simple language

It isn't necessary to stick to the syntax rules laid down in the definition of a language provided that you can invent some equivalent rules which cover all the programs defined by the original. Figure 3.2 shows some alternative descriptions of the syntax of part of a typical programming language expression: mechanisms of constructing syntax analysers largely depend on either choosing the right kind of description or else changing an inconvenient description into the right form.

Figure 3.3 shows a short-range syntax description (a _grammar_) for a very simple language related to ALGOL 60 or PASCAL, written in the BNF notation used for the definition of those languages. Just like the descriptions in figure 3.1, it details the _phrase structure_ of the language. A distinction can be drawn between 'bottom-up' and 'top-down' syntax analysis[1] of programs in this language

> _Bottom-up_ analysis looks for patterns in the input which correspond to phrases in the grammar. The grammar shows how items can be combined into phrases, how phrases and items can be combined into larger phrases. The analyser therefore replaces first simple patterns of items by a single phrase-description (a pointer to a tree node), then more complex patterns of items and phrase-descriptions by a phrase-description, until the entire input has been compressed into a description of a <statement> phrase.

> _Top-down_ analysis assumes that the input will be a <statement>. The grammar shows how a <statement> phrase can be built up of sub-phrases, and to find a statement the analyser merely searches for each of the sub-phrases in turn. To find a sub-phrase the analyser searches for each of its (sub-)sub-phrases, and so on until the search is reduced to a matter of searching for a single item, which it looks for in the input.

This may sound rather complicated but in practice it's quite straightforward. In this chapter I describe simplified versions of the bottom-up and top-down mechanisms which are discussed more fully in chapters 17 and 16 respectively.

Bottom-up Analysis of Expressions

As a schoolchild I was taught that when calculating the value of an arithmetic 'sum', certain operators were more important than others and had to be considered first. The rule was more or less

---

1 The LR mechanism described in chapter 18 has elements of both bottom-up and top-down analysis: however for the purposes of introduction it is reasonable to consider top-down and bottom-up as distinct analysis mechanisms.

Calculate bracketed expressions first; multiply or divide before adding or subtracting; always work from left to right.

This principle can be harnessed to determine the structure of expressions in a programming language. Each operator is given a <u>priority</u> which can be deduced from the grammar. Figure 3.4 gives the priorities of the operators in the grammar shown in figure 3.3. The higher the number the higher the priority - the significance of the zero-priority 'empty' operator will emerge later.

The first example algorithm can be understood by analogy with a simple railway network, shown in figure 3.5. The algorithm moves identifiers directly from input to output and moves operators from input to output via the 'siding'. At each step it can decide to move an item from input to output, from siding to output, from input to siding or else it can halt. The algorithm is shown in figure 3.6, in a pseudo BCPL notation. It converts an expression at the input into a postfix or Reverse Polish string at the output. Figure 3.7 shows the algorithm in operation on an expression[1] very like that used in chapter 2 - note that the

Operator	Priority
*,/	5
+,-	4
=	3
and	2
or	1
empty	0

Figure 3.4 Priorities of operators

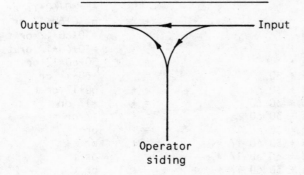

Figure 3.5 Shunting analogy

---

[1] The identifiers in this example have been abbreviated to save space on the page.

'siding' is in effect a stack. This algorithm is capable of detecting certain syntax errors - if the input was 'a*+-b' or '13 a' it would refuse to analyse it.

```
while input is not empty do
  { /* read an operand */
    if input is not an identifier or a number then
      Error("operand expected")
    else move input to output;

    /* inspect the input operator */
    if input is not an operator or empty then
      Error("operator expected")
    else
    while priority(siding) >= priority(input)
          and siding is not empty do
      move siding to output;

    /* read in the operator */
    if input is not empty then
      move input to siding
  }
```

Figure 3.6 Converting expressions to postfix strings

	Output	Siding	Input
1			h*60+m=30+60*17 **or** t
1a	h		*60+m=30+60*17 **or** t
1b	h	*	60+m=30+60*17 **or** t
2	h 60	*	+m=30+60*17 **or** t
2a	h 60 *		+m=30+60*17 **or** t
2b	h 60 *	+	m=30+60*17 **or** t
3	h 60 * m	+	=30+60*17 **or** t
3a	h 60 * m +		=30+60*17 **or** t
3b	h 60 * m +	=	30+60*17 **or** t
4	h 60 * m + 30	=	+60*17 **or** t
4a	h 60 * m + 30	= +	60*17 **or** t
5	h 60 * m + 30 60	= +	*17 **or** t
5a	h 60 * m + 30 60	= + *	17 **or** t
6	h 60 * m + 30 60 17	= + *	**or** t
6a	h 60 * m + 30 60 17 *	= +	**or** t
6b	h 60 * m + 30 60 17 * +	= +	**or** t
6c	h 60 * m + 30 60 17 * + =		**or** t
6d	h 60 * m + 30 60 17 * + =	**or**	t
7	h 60 * m + 30 60 17 * + = t	**or**	
7a	h 60 * m + 30 60 17 * + = t **or**		

Figure 3.7 Operation of the postfix analyser

The discussion in chapter 2 shows, however, that the postfix string which this analysis algorithm produces is an unsuitable description of the program so far as translation is concerned. Happily, it is simple to do something about it: any analysis mechanism can produce any description of the tree you like. Figure 3.8 shows an algorithm which uses two stacks (sidings) to produce a representation of the program in the form of 'triples', each of which contains an operator and two operands. The procedures 'pushRand' and 'popRand' maintain a stack of operands: 'pushRator' and 'popRator' a similar stack of operators.

The triples produced by this analyser, illustrated in figure 3.9, could be seen as a form of pseudo-assembly code: first multiply h by 60, leaving the result in register 1; next add register 1 and m, leaving the result in register 2; next multiply 17 by 60, leaving the result in register 3, and so on. It is just as easy to see the triples as a form of tree in which '#1' is a pointer to the node labelled '1'. The root of the tree is the last triple produced: figure 3.10 shows the output of the algorithm viewed from this standpoint.

```
Tnumber := 0; /* initialise triple number */

while input is not empty do
 { /* put an operand on the stack */
   if input is not an identifier or a number then
     Error("operand expected")
   else { pushRand(input); read(input) }

   /* inspect input operator */
   if input is not an operator or empty then
     Error("operator expected")
   else
   while priority(topRator) >= priority(input) &
               topRator \= empty do
   { let op2 = popRand()
     let op1 = popRand()
     let opr = popRator()

     Tnumber := Tnumber+1;
     move ("Tnumber, opr, op1, op2") to output;

     pushRand(Tnumber); /* put triple number on stack */
   }

   /* read operator */
   if input is not empty then
     { pushRator(input); read(input) }
 }
```

Figure 3.8 Converting expressions to triples

```
     opeRands          opeRators              Input

1                                             h*60+m=30+60*17 or t
1a  h                                         *60+m=30+60*17 or t
1b  h                    *                    60+m=30+60*17 or t
2   h 60                 *                    +m=30+60*17 or t
2a  #1                                        +m=30+60*17 or t
2b  #1                   +                    m=30+60*17 or t
3   #1 m                 +                    =30+60*17 or t
3a  #2                                        =30+60*17 or t
3b  #2                   =                    30+60*17 or t
4   #2 30                =                    +60*17 or t
4a  #2 30                = +                  60*17 or t
5   #2 30 60             = +                  *17 or t
5a  #2 30 60             = + *                17 or t
6   #2 30 60 17          = + *                or t
6a  #2 30 #3             = +                  or t
6b  #2 #4                =                    or t
6c  #5                                        or t
6d  #5                   or                   t
7   #5 t                 or
7a  #6
```

```
          Output
      #1:  *     h  60
      #2:  +    #1   m
      #3:  *    60  17
      #4:  +    30  #3
      #5:  =    #2  #4
      #6:  or  #5   t
```

Figure 3.9 Operation of the triple analyser

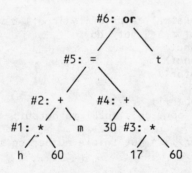

Figure 3.10 Triples viewed as a tree

Given a means of producing a tree node by combining a tag and several pointers or other values, it is possible to build the tree directly. Figure 3.11 shows an algorithm which builds a tree in this way - it uses the 'node' procedure discussed below in this chapter and the 'LexAnalyse' procedure discussed in chapter 4. Thus it is possible to produce the tree structure which is required for the translation of an expression using a simple algorithm and a set of numerical priorities of operators.

The expression grammar of figure 3.6 is extremely simple, however: it doesn't include unary operators, bracketed expressions, function calls or array references. Chapter 17 shows how the operator-precedence algorithm can be developed to handle real programming language expression grammars, how to calculate the priorities and how to handle syntax errors.

```
let ParseExpression() = valof
{ let nodep = empty
  let nextop, topop = empty, empty

  while lexitem=identifier | lexitem=number do
  { /* push item onto operand stack and read next item */
    pushRand(node(lexitem, lexvalue))
    Lexanalyse()

    /* compare stack and input */
    nextop := (IsOperator(lexitem) -> lexitem, empty)

    while priority(topop) >= priority(nextop) &
          topop \= empty do
    { let opr2 = popRand()
      let opr1 = popRand()

      pushRand(node(topop, opr1, opr2))
      topop := popRator()
    }

    /* push operator on stack */
    pushRator(topop); topop := nextop
    if topop\=empty then LexAnalyse()
  }

  if topop \= empty then
    Error("operand expected")
  else resultis popRand()
}
```

Figure 3.11 Building an expression tree

Top-down Analysis of Statements

The technique illustrated in figures 3.7, 3.8 and 3.11 can also be
applied to the analysis of statements. It isn't very suitable for
the purpose because it has poor error-recognition properties, and
I therefore illustrate a different technique which can handle the
syntax of a <statement> given in figure 3.3. Figures 3.12 and
3.13 show the procedures of a top-down analyser based on that
grammar. To recognise a statement it looks at the output of the
lexical analyser, to recognise a phrase it calls a procedure. In
particular, to recognise an expression it can call the bottom-up
procedure of figure 3.11. Although the grammar differentiates
between <B-expression>s and <A-expression>s, this analyser makes
no attempt to tell the difference or to act upon it and is happy
to accept a statement such as

if a+**true**=**false then** b := a=a-1

Chapter 5 shows how the translator could check that a sub-tree, of
an 'IfStat' node say, is of the right type and thereby could
handle such errors.

The procedures in figures 3.12 and 3.13 are interesting in that
the error messages which they generate are highly specific to the
context in which the error occurs. Whereas the bottom-up
analysers illustrated above could only produce one or two not very
informative error reports, the top-down analyser can go some way
towards explaining the symptoms of an error - there is a bracket
missing here, a colon missing there, an unexpected item at the
beginning of a statement, and so on. In this simple example, the
analysis stops at the first syntax error but a real analyser would
attempt to <u>recover</u> from a syntax error and continue to process the
input.

It is worth noting that none of the algorithms in this chapter
takes any notice of the 'type' (**real, integer, Boolean,** etc.) of
an identifier, a constant or an expression. A syntax analyser
<u>never</u> needs to consider the effects of the declaration of
identifiers, even when the grammar says it should: such matters
are best left to the translator. Indeed for many source languages
it is impossible to check the type of an expression until after
the entire source program has been syntax analysed, for example
because of mutually-recursive procedures.

Sometimes the grammar may seem to require the syntax analyser
to look at the type of an identifier: for example in FORTRAN the
expression

A(2,B+1,1)

could be either an 'array element reference' or a 'function
reference' depending on declaration of the name 'A'. There are all

```
let ParseStatement() = valof
{ let item, value = lexitem, lexvalue

  switchon lexitem into
  { case number: LexAnalyse()
      if lexitem \= ':' then
        Error("':' expected after numeric label")
      else
      { LexAnalyse();
        resultis node(LabelStat, value, ParseStatement())
      }

    case beginsymbol: LexAnalyse();
    resultis ParseCompound() /* figure 3.13 */

    case gotosymbol: LexAnalyse()
      if lexitem \= number then
        Error("number expected after 'goto'")
      else
      { let nodep = node(GotoStat, lexvalue)
        LexAnalyse(); resultis nodep
      }

    case ifsymbol: LexAnalyse()
    { let expr = ParseExpression() /* figure 3.11 */

      if lexitem \= thensymbol then
        Error("'then' expected in conditional statement)
      else
      { LexAnalyse()
        resultis node(IfStat, expr, ParseStatement())
      }
    }

    case identifier:
    { let name = node(lexitem, lexvalue)

      LexAnalyse()
      if lexitem=assignsymbol then
      { LexAnalyse()
        resultis node(AssignStat, name, ParseExpression())
      }
      elsf lexitem='(' then
      { ... handle procedure call ... }
      else Error("':=' or '(' expected after identifier")
    }

    default: Error("unrecognisable statement")
  }
}
```

Figure 3.12 Analysing a statement 'top-down'

sorts of rules which apply to array element references – they mustn't have more than three subscript expressions, the expressions can only take a restricted form and must all be INTEGER type. It is unnecessary and difficult to check this information during syntax analysis, whereas the translator can do it very simply and straightforwardly.

Building a Node of the Tree

The translation and analysis procedures in this book almost all operate with a tree structure which they manipulate via <u>pointers</u> to nodes of the tree: these pointers are the results of analysis procedures and the arguments to translation procedures. Although it would be possible to use a generalised 'heap' storage mechanism to allocate space for the nodes of the tree, it isn't necessary to

---

```
let ParseCompound() = valof
{ let first = ParseStatement()

  if lexitem = endsymbol then
  { LexAnalyse()
    resultis first
  }
  elsf lexitem = ';' then
  { LexAnalyse()
    resultis node(CompoundList, first, ParseCompound())
  }
  else
    Error("semicolon or 'end' expected after statement")
}
```

Figure 3.13 Analysing a compound statement

```
let node(tag, p1, p2, p3, p4, p5, p6, p7, p8) = valof
{ let nodep = bottom /* first free word in array */
  let count = NumberOfArgs()
  let pointer = @tag /* address of first argument */

  /* allocate space for new node and check limit */
  bottom := bottom+count
  if bottom>=top then CompilerFail("tree space exhausted")

  /* copy arguments into new node */
  for i = 0 to count-1 do nodep!i := pointer!i

  /* return pointer to node */
  resultis nodep
}
```

Figure 3.14 Allocating space for a node of the tree

do so since the compiler uses the tree in a highly predictable way. In particular it never releases single nodes of the tree: at the start of compilation there are no nodes allocated and at the end the entire tree can be discarded. A very simple mechanism can therefore be used to create tree nodes within a large array of words or characters.

Figure 3.14 shows a procedure in BCPL which manipulates an array of words to allocate space for nodes of a tree. A global variable 'bottom' initially points to the first location in the array, 'top' points to the first location after the array. The 'node' procedure copies its arguments into the locations pointed to by 'bottom' and allocates the space by incrementing the value of 'bottom'. Subsequent calls to the 'node' procedure will allocate space farther along the array, as the example in figure 3.15 shows.

Exactly the same free-space allocation mechanism can be used for all sorts of other purposes in the compiler. Chapter 4 shows why the lexical analyser may wish to use it to build lists of identifiers with similar 'hash addresses' in the symbol table. The space for the symbol table descriptors built by the object description phase (see chapter 8) can be taken from the same array. It is even possible to use the 'top' variable to implement a temporary stack on which to store, for example, the various components of a node which are being accumulated by a top-down or LR syntax analyser - see chapters 16 and 18.

It is convenient if all the space requirements of the compiler are met from a single area in this way. If the compiler were to

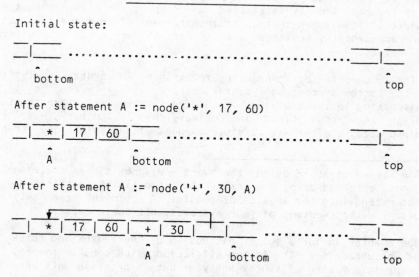

Figure 3.15 Building a node

contain several different data spaces then the differing
characteristics of source programs would ensure that it is
impossible to achieve a correct balance: inevitably one of the
spaces would become exhausted when others were still relatively
empty. Meeting all requirements for space from a single data area
means that you never have to worry about balancing differing space
requirements.

Syntax Error Handling

Error detection in syntax analysis is an automatic by-product of
the normal analysis mechanism. An error is detected when the input
doesn't conform to the short-range syntax rules - i.e. when the
analyser can't discover any phrase structure for the input.
Producing a report on the error[1] means inventing an error message
which you hope will indicate something about the cause of the
error. Error recovery is essential if the compiler is not to give
up after the first error - it must attempt to make some sense of
the rest of the program.

   Recovery from syntax errors always involves a measure of error
correction, even if it only means deleting a faulty phrase from
the program. Accurate error correction is difficult in many
situations and therefore error recovery often gives rise to so-
called secondary error reports - reports about situations which
would not be erroneous if the primary error was corrected by the
user. Secondary error reports are often produced, for example,
when the compiler finds a punctuation error in a declaration.
Subsequent occurrences of identifiers which appeared in the faulty
declaration will each cause an 'undeclared identifier' error
report. A secondary error report can also occur after the
compiler has wrongly attempted to correct a syntax error, for
example if it assumes that a particular item of punctuation has
been accidentally omitted when in fact the error has some other
explanation.

   The fundamental error-handling requirement in syntax analysis
is to catch short-range syntax errors as early as possible.
Backtracking in the analyser, which occurs when it attempts to
analyse the input first in one way, then in another[2], must be
avoided because after all possible avenues of analysis have been

---

1 I've tried to avoid using the word 'diagnosis' in talking
  about error handling - a compiler's capabilities certainly do
  not extend into the area of diagnosis. A compiler can only
  describe the symptoms of your mistakes, not their causes.

2 See chapter 16 for a fuller discussion of the causes and cures
  of backtracking. It is an affliction which can, in theory,
  occur in any kind of syntax analyser but in practice only very
  old-fashioned top-down analysers are prone to it.

explored it is impossible to tell which of them were cul-de-sacs
and which contained the error. Some short-range syntax errors such
as 'relational operator follows relational operator', which have
to do with checking the validity of the subphrases of a node after
the node has been built, are better handled by the translator
along with the long-range errors such as those to do with the type
of an expression, undeclared or misdeclared names and so on.

In many situations a top-down analyser can predict with
absolute certainty the next item. Thus, for example, if the top-
down analyser of figure 3.14 is halfway through the analysis of a
conditional statement, the absence of a **then** symbol can be
reported accurately - see figure 3.16. (The error report should
always be in plain language: a computer should not oblige a human

---

1.   ... if i<0 goto 3; ...
              ^

      'then' expected in conditional statement

2.   ... if i<0 thon goto 3; ...
              ^   ^
              a   b
      a: 'then' missing in conditional statement
      b: ':=' or '(' expected after identifier

Figure 3.16 Error reporting and error correction

---

1.   a := f+-2
                 ^

    bottom-up: invalid input sequence ('-' follows '+')
    top-down: operand expected

2.   if u=v=b-1=0 then ...
                 ^

    bottom-up: invalid sequence of operators
    top-down: logical operator expected

Figure 3.17 Syntax errors in expressions

---

1.   a = a+1;
            ^

    '= found where ':=' expected

2.   a := (-b+sqrt(b^2-4*a*c)/(2*a);
                                     ^

    right bracket missing

Figure 3.18 Error correction

to look up an error number in a manual!) If the lexical analyser
produces a listing of the program line by line then the error
report can indicate the position of analysis at which the error
was detected.

After the error report has been produced the analyser must
attempt to recover and to continue to process the rest of the
source program, in order to find as many syntax errors as possible
in a single compilation run. The simplest form of recovery is to
find the end of the current phrase and to proceed as if a valid
phrase had been present: thus in figure 3.16 the analyser might
search for the next semicolon or **end** symbol. More sophisticated
error-recovery mechanisms might look at the current symbol to see
if it is one which can continue the analysis. In case 1 of figure
3.16, for example, the analyser might 'correct' the error by
assuming that a **then** symbol is missing. In case 2, however, this
error recovery strategy will cause a rather confusing secondary
error report since the analyser will decide that the name 'thon'
starts a statement, that therefore a **then** symbol is missing, and
will proceed to search for the rest of an assignment or a
procedure call statement.

The top-down mechanism is good at error handling only in
situations where the results of analysis up to the current
position determine the identity of the next symbol with very high
probability. Such a technique is less useful in processing
expressions, where almost any item may follow any other no matter
what stage the phrase recognition has reached. Error handling in
this situation can.hardly progress beyond the stage of reporting
that an invalid sequence of items has been detected or that two
incompatible operators have been found - see figure 3.17. In each
case I give the kind of error message that can be produced by a
bottom-up or top-down analyser. Neither technique gives a
particularly good report in either situation. It is worth re-
emphasising that an error like that in case 2 of figure 3.17 can
and should be left for the translator to detect and report upon.

Error recovery is always necessary and always involves some
element of error correction. True error correction is sometimes
possible but, as case 2 of figure 3.16 shows, it can be dangerous.
Figure 3.18 shows an example situation in which error correction
is possible - a top-down analyser might recognise the common
mistake of putting an '=' symbol in an assignment statement when a
':=' symbol is what is required. Case 2 in figure 3.18 shows why
accurate error correction requires understanding of the program.
On reading the expression the syntax analyser would discover that
it contains more left brackets than right - if the analyser
corrects the error by inserting a right bracket then it may choose
the wrong position for insertion. This in turn may cause
secondary errors in the translator because of invalid combinations
of different types of operands in the expression. There are nine
distinct places in the expression at which the missing bracket

might be inserted and whilst every algebra student knows that it goes after the 'c', no compiler ever does!

Error recovery without proper error correction is usually brutally simple. The analyser searches for some item in the input which makes sense in the present context and ignores the section of program in which the error was detected. In a top-down analyser this means returning a pointer to a dummy node as the result of an analysis procedure, in a bottom-up analyser it means inserting a dummy phrase marker in the stack. In either case the fact that a fragment of the program is effectively ignored may cause secondary errors - in particular if the fragment contained any declarative information then it will not be recorded in the symbol table by the object description phase, and thus there will be secondary long-range error reports produced by the translation phase.

Summary

The process of analysis is one of recognition coupled with output of a record of what was recognised. Output may be in the form of a tree structure - which is what the analyser discovers in every case - or it may be a linearised form of the tree. The form of output chosen does not affect the recognition process, nor (vice-versa) does the mechanism of recognition constrain the form of output.

Top-down analysis works by recursive search for the subphrases of a phrase, bottom-up analysis by finding patterns which match phrase descriptions.

Syntax error handling does not impose any overhead on the process of analysis in that the speed of compilation of a correct program is not altered by any amount of error detection; error reporting requires care if the messages are to be meaningful to anyone but the compiler-writer; error recovery may cause secondary errors; error correction is tempting in certain situations but can be dangerous in that it may lead to a torrent of secondary error reports.

4 Lexical Analysis and Loading

It's worthwhile to dispose of the simplest and least interesting phases of compiling as early as possible, so as to be able to concentrate in the rest of the book on the more difficult and interesting topics of syntax analysis, translation and code optimisation. The processes of input to and output from a compiler are fairly straightforward. There are simple techniques used to implement these activities and it is on these that I concentrate in this chapter.

The input phases are worth detailed consideration (despite the fact that they are rather straightforward, even boring!) because of their effect on the compiler's efficiency. It is common to find that more than 50% of the compiler's time is spent in the reader and lexical analyser, although these phases will typically take up less than 10% of the source code of the compiler. The reason for this is that the input phases compress a great many input characters into a small number of items: although the processing of each character should take only a few instructions the overall cost is overwhelming. Other, later, phases process the more compact representation of the source program which is produced by the lexical analyser.

Both input and output phases convert between different representations of the program

- the input phases convert from a representation of the source program suitable for humans to read, into a representation suitable for automatic analysis

- the output phases convert from a representation of the object program produced by automatic translation into a representation suitable for another program to read or otherwise interpret.

The input transformation is from characters to symbolic items in the store of the machine, the output transformation from some internal symbolic form into 'relocatable binary' (for a loader to read) or 'absolute binary' (for a machine to interpret). This chapter considers the two transformations in turn.

Reading the Source Program

The original form of the source program, so far as the compiler is concerned, is a collection of physically-detectable disturbances in an input device, such as holes in a card, key depressions on a terminal or patterns of polarisation on a magnetic surface. So far as the syntax analysis phase is concerned, the input is a sequence of 'items', 'atoms' or 'tokens'. The task of the input phases is to convert between these two very different representations. In so doing, the program goes through three distinct transformations, shown in figure 4.1. The item code will be a superset of the standard character code since, for example, ':' is an item and a character, ':=' is an item but not a single character.

Thankfully the conversion between device code and standard character code is nowadays normally regarded as the responsibility of the operating system, but on older systems where this is not so, or when exotic input devices are provided for the purposes of program input, the compiler will have to include a section of code for each input device type which converts the code for that device into a standard form. An example of this is the so-called 'line reconstruction' facility, provided in many University of Manchester compilers over the years. This enables users with backspacing and underlining input devices to construct programs in an ALGOL-like language which contain underlined keywords. It's essential that if the line typed looks right to the user then it must be read correctly, no matter how strange the sequence of space, backspace and underline characters that was typed to construct it. Thus when the input line appears to contain 'end', the reader phase must pass the sequence of characters 'underlined e', 'underlined n', 'underlined d' to the lexical analyser no matter in what order the backspace and underline characters were used to move the carriage to produce that visual appearance. The technique also requires that the lexical analyser must accept a superset of the machine's basic character codes.

Tasks i and ii in figure 4.1, then, are the responsibility of the reader phase and are easily delegated to a standard subroutine or even to the operating system so that in practice the reader is hardly regarded as a part of the compiler. However lexical

---

```
  (i) Physical disturbances    -> device-dependent code
 (ii) Device-dependent code    -> standard character code
(iii) Standard character code  -> internal item code
```

Figure 4.1 Transformations of the source program on input

analysis will be more efficient if a complete line of input is read into a buffer, which is then scanned linearly, than if the reader subroutine is called to provide a single character each time the lexical analyser requires one. Line-by-line input also means that the reader can produce a line-by-line program listing which is useful in the production of syntax error reports, as chapter 3 shows. Even when the compiler doesn't produce a listing the contents of the line buffer provide an essential part of every syntax error message, giving the user a visual clue to the location of the error.

Macro processing may involve switching the reader phase from source-file to source-file, or from source-file to a copy of a macro body in the memory. Source-file switching is a particularly useful feature: when writing a program it is often convenient to be able to write a macro command such as **'include** decls' where the file 'decls' contains some standard declarations or some other text which should be spliced into the program at the point where the **include** macro occurs. It's best if the lexical analyser maintains a stack of input 'streams' since the file 'decls' may itself utilise the **include** macro. Other macro processing is usually also item based, and consists of replacing one item or item sequence with another item sequence. It therefore goes on after stage iii in figure 4.1, at the interface between lexical analysis and syntax analysis.

Characters to items

In a two-pass compiler the lexical analysis phase is commonly implemented as a subroutine of the syntax analysis phase, so task iii in figure 4.1 must be the kind of task which can be delegated to a subroutine. This implies that the lexical analyser cannot use information about previous items, or information about the current syntactic context, to determine which items it should encounter: all the necessary information must come from the characters of the item itself.

The definition of the syntax of a programming language always gives the syntax of an item in a manner which is independent of the context in which it occurs[1], and the form of programs, statements, expressions and other constituents of the language in terms of the items and phrases which they may contain. In effect the lexical analysis phase consists of those parts of the syntax analyser whose task is to recognise items by recognising the characters which form their internal structure.

---

1 In old (obsolescent?) languages such as FORTRAN or COBOL it is necessary to establish a context before an item can reliably be recognised. Such languages require a prescan to accomplish 'statement identification' before analysis can begin: more modern languages do not fall into this trap.

The definition of the syntax of items - the 'micro-syntax' of the language - will define the form of an item in such a way that it can be recognised by the fact that it starts with a particular character, or one of a class of characters such as a number or a letter, and then either consists of a particular sequence of characters or else follows a simple set of rules which determine, for each subsequent character, whether it forms part of the item or not. Descriptions of the way items may be written are usually like those shown in figure 4.2.

Item description in terms of simple sequences of characters makes it possible to write a lexical analyser which only needs to look at the current character in the input stream in order to decide what to do next. This character may itself be a simple-item (e.g. a comma), it may start a simple-item (e.g. the ':' character starts the ':=' item) or it may start an item which is a member of a 'class' of items such as an identifier, a number or a string. There is some discussion in chapter 15 of the theory of lexical analysis grammars: in this chapter I show only the practical results.

Once a character which makes up a simple-item has been read and recognised there is little more for the lexical analyser to do, though in some cases the character read may be the first character of more than one simple-item - e.g. in SIMULA-67 the character ':' signals the start of

```
the <assign> item        ':='
the <ref-assign> item     ':-'
the <colon> item         ':'
```

and in such cases the item definition is so designed that the analyser can separate the simple-items merely by reading the next character and deciding what to do. If the character which is read can start a class-item then the lexical analyser must read characters and follow the micro-syntax rules to determine whether each succeeding character is part of the item or not.

Figure 4.4 shows part of a lexical analyser which accepts numbers of the form shown in figure 4.3 (see chapter 15 for a discussion about the properties of this syntax description). The analyser produces three strings 'ipart', 'fpart' and 'epart', representing the integer part, fractional part and exponent part

---

```
an <itemX> is the sequence of characters   ABCD
an <itemY> is the character  E
an <itemZ> starts with the characters  F,G,H, ... or
   K and may be continued with any one of the
   characters L,M, ... X,Y
```

Figure 4.2 Simple lexical syntax description

of a number. Most working lexical analysers convert numbers into their eventual run-time representation as they are read in, although there are arguments against this - see the discussion below.

Another way of describing the actions of figure 4.4, often used in 'compiler factories' where programmers need to be able to generate lexical analysers automatically, is to use a state-transition table, as illustrated in figure 4.5. Each row of the table represents an input character, each column a state of the analyser. Each square contains an <action,new-state> pair: the action which must be performed if that character is read in that analyser state, and the new state which the analyser should then take up. Figure 4.5 shows four rows of a possible table.

Efficiency of the input phases

The input phases take up so much of the overall compilation effort precisely because they have to handle so much data. It is common to place a single statement on a single line, for example - the lexical analyser then has to compress many characters into a very few items. For example, if a card contains the statement

        IDX3 := 76.3;

four items are represented by eighty characters. Thus the input phases have a great deal of processing to do but, as later chapters will show, the syntax analysis and translation of a four-item statement is relatively simple and rapid.

In fact it's convenient that the potential inefficiencies of a compiler are concentrated in the input phases. These phases are extremely simple in operation and relatively small (a lexical analyser should be no more than about four pages in a system programming language) so that you can profitably spend time and effort in speeding up the lexical analysis algorithm or even speeding up the actual instruction sequence which it executes. It is, of course, possible in theory that you might write a syntax analyser which was so inefficient that it became the inner loop of the compiler, but the remedy is obvious in practice!

```
<integer> ::= <digit> | <integer><digit>
<real> ::= <integer>.<integer> | .<integer>
<number> ::= <integer> | <real> | <real>E<integer>
                       | <integer>E<integer>
```

Figure 4.3 Syntax of numbers

```
let LexAnalyse() be
{ let ipart, fpart, epart = empty, empty, empty

   switchon char into
    { case '0' .. '9':
       { /* read integer part */
         while '0'<=char<='9' do
          { ipart := ipart ++ char; readch(@char) }
         if char = '.' then
          { readch(@char)
            if '0'<=char<='9' then goto point
            else Error("digit expected after point")
          }
         elsf char = 'E' then goto exponent
         else { lexitem := integernumber;
                lexvalue := ipart; return
              }
       }

      case '.':
        { readch(@char)
          if 0<=char<=9 then
          { /* read fractional part */
   point:   while '0'<=char<='9' do
             { fpart := fpart ++ char; readch(@char) }
            if char = 'E' then
            { /* read exponent */
   exponent: readch(@char)
               unless '0'<=char<='9'
                 Error("digit expected in exponent")
               while '0'<=char<='9' do
                 { epart := epart ++ char; readch(@char) }
            }
            lexitem := realnumber
            lexvalue := node(ipart, fpart, epart)
            return
          }
          else { lexitem := '.'; return }
        }

      case ':' .. /* distinguish ':' and ':=' */
      case 'A'..'Z', 'a'..'z': .. /* read identifier */
      .....
    }
}
```

Figure 4.4 Lexical Analyser in program form

Representing an item

The task of the input phases is to communicate results to the
later phases and in a true multi-pass implementation to produce a
sequence of items from the original sequence of characters. The
first of the later phases - the syntax analyser - is interested to
know whether a simple-item or a class-item has been discovered.
For simple-items it needs to know which item has been found (these
items are like punctuation in natural languages) and for class-
items (like words in natural language) which member of which class
has been found in order that this information can be inserted into
the tree. It is essential to realise, though, that in order to
recognise a phrase the syntax analyser should be concerned only
with the identity of the punctuation-items which it contains and
the class-type of other items - the form of a phrase is not
affected by the magnitude of numbers, the content of strings or
the identity of names.

There are many ways in which an item description may be
communicated to the syntax analyser. In the syntax analysis
examples in this book I use a convention which you may find

	S	I	F0	F1	F2	E1	E2
0..9:	1,I	3,I	5,F2	5,F2	5,F2	6,E2	6,E2
'.':	2,F0	4,F1	9,exit	error	8,exit	error	8,exit
'E':	....	4,E1	9,exit	error	4,E1	error	8,exit
other:	....	7,exit	9,exit	error	8,exit	error	8,exit

```
action #1: ipart,fpart,epart := empty,empty,empty
action #2: ipart,fpart,epart := empty, empty,empty
           readch(@char)
action #3: ipart:=ipart++char; readch(@char)
action #4: readch(@char)
action #5: fpart:=fpart++char; readch(@char)
action #6: epart:=epart++char; readch(@char)
action #7: lexitem := integernumber
           lexvalue := ipart; return
action #8: lexitem := realnumber
           lexvalue := node(ipart, fpart, epart)
           return
action #9: lexitem := '.'; return
```

Figure 4.5 Lexical Analyser in table form

convenient. The item-code takes a particular value for each individual simple-item and for each class-type (identifiers, numbers, strings etc.). The lexical analyser constructs a two-part representation for each item:

1. (lexitem) - the item-code
2. (lexvalue) - a further value identifying a class-item

Syntax analysis can proceed by inspecting only the item-code and the phases after syntax analysis can use the further value to distinguish between different members of a class.

For certain class-items - numbers or strings, for example - a compiler will often use the run-time representation of the item as the 'further value' in the item description. However there are good reasons to use an item description which is close to the original source form and to leave all matters of translation between source forms and run-time representations as a task of the translator. The argument in favour of this technique is that all compile-time error reports can then refer to the characters of the original source program item and that the compiler is made more 'portable' (more practically machine-independent). To change such a compiler so that it produces code for a different object machine it is only necessary to change some parts of the translation phases while the lexical analyser can remain unchanged. The counter-argument is that the run-time representation of a number, say, will usually be more compact than the original sequence of characters of the source item. The saving in space may mean that you prefer to discount the advantages of modularity of construction of the compiler and to store numbers internally in their run-time representation.

Identifiers and keywords

All items, including class-items such as numbers, identifiers and strings, may be recognised by techniques like those of figures 4.4 and 4.5. For identifiers, however, there remains the problem of representing an identifier-item.

If the translator is interested in identifiers at all it is only for the purpose of noticing that the same identifier is used in several places in the program. Obviously we may take a program which contains the identifier ABC but not the identifier XYZ, change ABC to XYZ throughout, and have no effect on the final translation. A reasonable description of an identifier, so far as the translator is concerned, is that it is the same as another identifier which occurs elsewhere in the program.

This leads fairly naturally to the notion that there should be a table of identifiers which have been encountered so far in the lexical analysis of the program, and the 'further value' in the case of an identifier-item should be a pointer to the relevant entry in this table. The table is variously called the <u>symbol</u> <u>table</u>, <u>name</u> <u>table</u> or <u>cross-reference</u> <u>table</u>. As each identifier is read, the lexical analyser must look it up in the table, adding it as a new entry if it has not previously been encountered. The 'further value' of the item description is then a pointer to the old entry, if one existed, or to the new entry if one was created. Chapter 8 discusses in some detail both the construction of the table and the contents of the object descriptors which it contains.

An additional task of the lexical analyser, in many language implementations, is to distinguish between 'keywords' (or 'reserved words') and normal identifiers. In such implementations certain items such as EEGIN or END, though visibly conforming to the syntax rules for the construction of an identifier, are to be regarded as simple-items - in effect these 'keywords' are simply rather large punctuation marks. In such a case the lexical analyser must distinguish a pseudo-identifier-item from an actual identifier-item once it has recognised the characters which make up the item. I describe ways in which this might be done efficiently, once again using the symbol table, in chapter 8.

Detecting lexical errors

The lexical analyser can be entrusted with very few error processing tasks, although certain very simple punctuation errors may be detected during lexical analysis. For example, the definition of the syntax of a class item may be such that it is possible to make a lexical punctuation error - thus in ALGOL 60 a <number> may not end with a '.' character. An error may also be detected when the lexical analyser converts a number into its run-time representation as it is encountered in the source program: as it does so the lexical analyser should test for overflow or underflow caused by conversion of a number outside the object machine's limits of representation. I don't believe that a language should impose limits on the maximum length of identifiers or string constants, but if such limits are imposed then the lexical analyser must police the restriction.

In many languages comments can be included anywhere in the source program, enclosed between opening and closing comment symbols such as '/*' and '*/'. It is convenient for syntax analysis if comments are removed, or 'stripped', by the lexical analyser. In so doing the lexical analyser should be alert for signs that the closing comment symbol has been omitted - signs such as the occurrence of a semicolon, a 'keyword' or an opening comment symbol in the text of the comment. The latter situation almost certainly indicates an error, the others less certainly. In each of these cases the lexical analyser should produce a 'warning' report to indicate to the user that something may be wrong with the program.

The lexical analyser itself cannot detect spelling errors. Spelling errors can only be suspected, and spelling correction invoked, when the syntax analyser finds a keyword where an identifier is expected (or vice-versa) or when the translator encounters an undeclared or mis-declared identifier in the parse tree.

When the language implementation demands that keywords should be enclosed in escape characters, for example

        'BEGIN' 'REAL' X;

it is possible to detect the omission of an escape character. In the UMRCC ALGOL 60 compiler this was done with some success. Keywords were enclosed in 'prime' characters as illustrated above: if the characters following a prime formed a keyword then the lexical analyser checked that a closing prime was present; if these characters didn't form a keyword then a reverse scan of the characters before the prime catered for the possibility that an opening prime had been omitted. The technique requires a pre-scan of the input to detect keywords before searching for identifiers – in effect, a two-phase lexical analyser! I wouldn't recommend the technique, though, precisely because it finds so many mistakes in programs: users make far fewer mistakes when they are allowed to input keywords as pseudo-identifiers, separated from the subsequent item by a space or a punctuation character.

Certain error-handling tasks should not be entrusted to the lexical analyser. These include checking the context in which an item occurs and, in particular, checking the symbol-table descriptor when an identifier is read so as to distinguish between 'undeclared' and 'declared' identifiers. The lexical analyser must not be expected to detect the difference between, say, a label identifier and any other kind of identifier merely because that would seem to help in later syntax analysis. It is invariably true that when syntax error processing is entrusted to the lexical analyser, confusing error messages result because it cannot know enough about the syntactic context in which it is operating.

Tricks of implementation

If the lexical analyser is to be a subroutine of the syntax analyser, there is one slight difficulty which should be revealed to the novice: the lexical analyser must necessarily read the character after each class-item (number, identifier, string, etc.) in order to see that it isn't part of the class-item itself. Where a character may be a simple-item or start an item – e.g. the ':' character may be an item or may start the ':=' item – the lexical analyser must read the next character to distinguish the two possibilities. When the lexical analyser comes to read the next item it must be aware of whether the next character has already been read or not. In order to build a straightforward and clear

lexical analysis subroutine, an effective solution to this problem
is to ensure that it <u>always</u> reads in the first character of the
next item, even after single-character simple-items (commas,
semicolons, ...). Note that the difficulty doesn't arise in a true
multi-pass implementation: note also that it doesn't arise if the
lexical analyser and syntax analyser are coroutines (parallel
processes) rather than one a subroutine of the other.

   I can't leave discussion of lexical analysis without pointing
out that restricting the maximum length of an identifier (e.g. to
six characters, eight characters or even two hundred and fifty six
characters) makes the lexical analyser more complex than it need
be. To allow long identifiers it is merely necessary to delete the
part of the lexical analyser which checks the length of the
identifier: the simplest solution to the pseudo-problem of 'over-
long' identifiers is to allow them to be of any length. Few users
will have the patience to type an identifier too long to fit into
the computer's store!

Output for a Loader

Many language implementations allow the user to construct a
program in separate sections which may be compiled separately but
which are intended to be combined into an entire program when they
are about to be run. The program which combines the sections in
this way is variously called a <u>linking loader</u>, <u>linkage editor</u> or a
<u>consolidator</u>: I have called it a <u>loader</u> in this book.

   The output from a compiler in such an implementation must be
designed so that it can be processed by the loader. The loader
itself will probably be used by more than one compiler so the
forms it can accept will not always be exactly those which a
compiler-writer might need for the most effective loading of a
particular language.

   Broadly speaking the tasks of a loader may be classified under
three headings:

1. Joining the separate sections of a program to make a
   complete program (<u>linking</u>).

2. Assembling the code for a single section into a form
   suitable for execution (<u>relocation and fixup</u>).

3. Preparing for run-time debugging.

I consider these tasks in sequence and show how the requirements
of the loader influence the operation of the compiler and allow
the translator to shuffle off some of the tasks it would otherwise
have to carry out itself.

Linking program sections

It's convenient to be able to refer, in one section of the source program, to an object defined in another section merely by mentioning an external name of that object. Thus the source program can contain a call to procedure 'fred' in a section other than that which contains the procedure declaration. In such cases the translator can't produce machine instructions to call 'fred' immediately, since such instructions would have to include the run-time address of 'fred' – which cannot be known until the section which contains 'fred' is loaded into the store. Therefore it must generate a sequence of incompletely specified instructions, interspersed with requests to the loader to insert pieces that are missing. Figure 4.6 shows an example. Conversely, when processing a procedure declaration the translator will have to insert information which tells the loader about the values (addresses in this case) which are to be associated with particular external names. Figure 4.7 shows an example.

A similar technique allows for communication of the addresses of particular memory cells, important constants, addresses of labels and so on. If a program contains references to external objects which aren't defined in any of its sections the loader can search a library of precompiled sections (a subroutine library) to find the definition of any undefined symbols. Note that neither the translator nor the loader need have any prior knowledge of the library's contents.

Relocating a program section

Since the object program will consist of several sections combined into a single address space the translator cannot know the eventual run-time addresses of the instructions which it generates

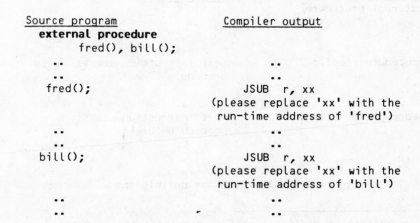

Figure 4.6 Loader linkage requests

when translating a section nor even the eventual run-time addresses of the data objects which are declared in it. It must generate code assuming that the section is to be loaded into the store starting at some fixed address (say location 0 or location 200 or any pre-arranged address) and the loader must 'relocate' the instructions when the section is actually loaded into the computer memory. The translator must necessarily indicate any part of an instruction which refers to another instruction, so that it may be correctly relocated. For example, suppose instructions were generated starting at notional location 0 and the section is in fact loaded into store starting at location 343[1]. Then 'JUMP , 200' has to be relocated as 'JUMP , 543', 'JSUB 1, 242' becomes 'JSUB 1, 585' and so on. This mechanism of 'relocation' has given its name to the output from the compiler to the loader - 'relocatable binary'.

References to data objects which aren't held on a stack (see chapter 11) must also be relocated. Many loaders use two separate relocation counters, one for instructions and one for memory cells: in this way the data cells (which may be overwritten) can be separated from program instructions and constants (which should be write-protected). Thus the translator must not only indicate which addresses should be relocated but also by what mechanism they should be relocated - to which program area they refer.

Fixup of label values

It would be possible for a translator to prepare all the output for a single program section before sending it to the loader. In practice, however, the translator produces a stream of instructions and loader commands because the loader can take over

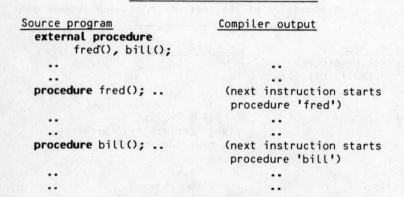

Source program	Compiler output
external procedure	
fred(), bill();	
..	..
..	..
procedure fred(); ..	(next instruction starts procedure 'fred')
..	..
..	..
procedure bill(); ..	(next instruction starts procedure 'bill')
..	..
..	..

Figure 4.7 Loader linkage definitions

1 This number is in decimal notation as are all the numbers in this book Octal, binary and hexadecimal are for machines!

some of the task of joining together the separate pieces of code within a section. The classic problem of intra-section linkage is provided by the FORTRAN 'GOTO': how can a GOTO statement whose label has not yet been processed be translated when the object code address of the labelled statement is unknown? In more modern languages, though use of the **goto** statement is declining, the problem remains because of the need to translate structured statements like the **while,** as illustrated in figure 4.8. In such a case it is necessary to produce a JUMPFALSE statement before its destination address is known. The loader can help with this task, often called 'label fixup', if the translator includes commands in the instruction sequence which inform the loader about each instruction which must be fixed-up and of the destination address when it is known: it is likely that several instructions may refer to the same destination.

One solution is to use symbolic names in the loader commands, as in figure 4.8 - another is to use a 'fixup chain', as illustrated in figure 4.9, if the object machine instructions are large enough to hold a store address. In this latter technique, each instruction which refers to a destination contains the address of the previous instruction which referred to that destination. In the example three instructions refer to the final destination. When the address of the destination is known, the loader can move back down the chain, setting the address held in each instruction to the destination address (in this case 400). More complex fixups are possible, for example allowing the translator to ask the loader to compute expressions involving the values of addresses.

Run-time debugging and the loader

I mention run-time debugging in this chapter in order to emphasise that the task of a compiler is not merely to generate a more-or-

---

while <expression> **do** <statement>

    may be translated as

        (define labela)   /* definition for loader */
            ...
    {code to evaluate <expression> in register 1}
            ...
        JUMPFALSE 1, labelb   /* request to fixup */
            ...
    {code to perform <statement>}
          ..
        JUMP , labela   /* request to fixup */
        (define labelb)   /* definition for loader */

   Figure 4.8 Forward references to instructions

less literal translation of a program, but is also to assist in all stages of debugging of the algorithm. It is desirable at run-time that there should be some structure available which gives information about the relationship between the machine-code instructions of the object program and the fragments of the source program which they represent. The structure might be a compressed (or expanded) version of the compiler's symbol table, or it might be a structure specially designed for the task. The purpose of this structure is to enable run-time error reports to be 'decompiled' into reports about the original source program fragment which produced the error.

The run-time information structure must provide an extensive cross-reference between source program and the run-time program. It should, for example, give the names and run-time code addresses of all source-language procedures, and perhaps also a line-number/run-time-address directory so that panic dumps and other debugging aids, discussed in chapter 20, can report the state of the object program in terms of the original source program. It should give names and object code addresses of all 'static' memory cells. It should give the stack-offsets of all 'dynamic' memory cells and their source-language names. This topic is discussed further in chapter 20, where I also discuss the design of a debugger program that is capable of using all this information.

Loaders and system efficiency

In the mid-1960s so-called 'in-core'[1] compilers became popular in university computing centres, which have to process large numbers of somewhat trivial programs submitted by students who are learning to program. It was found that general-purpose compilers couldn't process such a workload efficiently, in part because they

---

```
address 123:     JUMP , 0
                   ...
                   ...
address 233:     JUMP , 123
                   ...
                   ...
address 256:     JUMP , 233
                   ...
                   ...
address 400:     (please fixup the chain
                 which starts at address 256)
```

Figure 4.9 Address chains in fixup

---

1 In the days before semiconductor memories, 'core' = 'core store' = 'memory'.

process a program in sections and use a loader. The system activity which is required to load a program is quite significant: the loader must be made ready to run; it must find and read all the separate object code files which make up the program; it must find and search through at least one subroutine library. So far as the computing centre director is concerned, the major problem is the 'real time' or 'elapsed time' overhead of loading a program, and for a small program this can be much larger than that required to compile the program. Even the 'CPU time' or 'mill time' required to load a program is comparable with that required to compile it. In-core compilers avoid the loader overhead by producing executable object code and running it as a subroutine of the compiler, providing linkage to only a small standard number of subroutines which are also in effect compiler subroutines. In this way the 'throughput' of student programs can be increased enormously, which both improves the service to student users and releases an important proportion of machine resources to do other work.

The in-core compiler is a technological fix which improves computer efficiency but computer efficiency isn't all of the story: computers after all are supposed to help people by relieving them of unnecessary tasks. Although the in-core compiler may provide adequate facilities for the student programmer, use of a loader enables other programmers to split a large, unwieldy program into manageable sections, to establish libraries of useful procedures and so on. This makes programming easier and hence makes programmers more productive. If similar facilities can be provided efficiently without a loader then a loader isn't required: if not then, as far as is possible in a world of limited resources, the requirements of computer system efficiency should be placed second to those of human efficiency.

Error detection in the loader

If a program contains more than one definition of a particular external symbol - more than one declaration of a procedure, for example - or if an external symbol isn't defined anywhere in the program or in the library, then the loader must signal an error. It helps if the loader gives the name of each file in which a symbol is defined, in the case of a multiply-defined symbol, or from which its value was requested, for undefined symbols, since a high proportion of these errors will be caused by simple spelling mistakes.

Most implementations of block-structured languages which allow the program to be split into sections demand that each section contain a dummy declaration of every procedure which is called in that section but not declared within it. If there is no proper declaration of the procedure anywhere in the program or in the library then the loader will signal an error: if there is a declaration then it ought to check that each dummy declaration

corresponds to the real declaration in number, type and kind of
parameters and in the type of result returned by the procedure.
If the loader doesn't check this then the run-time support
fragments should do so - see below and chapter 12. Unfortunately
too few language implementations impose such a check before the
program runs and either include run-time checks, which have a
disastrous effect on program efficiency, or no checks at all,
which means that inconsistent declarations cause unexplained run-
time errors.

After the Loader

After the loader has done its work and the object program begins
to run the run-time support sections of the object program take
over. Before the object code fragments which specify calculation,
input and output can operate a run-time environment must be set
up: pointers to the stack must be initialised, storage allocated
for the heap, input and output buffers acquired and so on. These
tasks can't easily be delegated to the loader - unless it's a
special loader used by a single compiler - but they can easily be
carried out by standard subroutines which the loader automatically
extracts from the subroutine library and inserts into every object
program.

   In an implementation of a recursive language which uses a
stack, or any more general storage management system, references
to data objects cannot be fixed up by the loader but must be made
via some pointer which indicates a position in a stack of 'data
frames'. These data frames make up the Activation Record Structure
introduced in chapter 1. Section III contains detailed discussion
of object code fragments that manipulate the Activation Record
Structure and maintain the pointers which indicate data frames
within it.

Summary

The input and output phases of a compiler aren't hard to write or
hard to design. The input phases have to be efficient because
their speed essentially determines the speed of the entire
compiler. They can be written as subroutines of the analysis phase
because of the simplicity of their task.

   The translator can take advantage of the existence of a linking
and relocating loader to allow it to compile a program in
sections, to output partially-assembled instructions and to insert
program-wide debugging information.

Section II
Translation and Crucial
Code Fragments

Translation and code optimisation are the compilation tasks which professional compiler-writers enjoy thinking and talking about most. Given a statement or some other fragment of program, discussion centres around the eventual machine instructions which ought to be generated as its translation and how a translator might be written that could effectively generate those instructions. Certain kinds of program fragments are usually regarded as more important than others because they are the sort of operations that occur often in programs or because they occur often at the centre of the program's inner loop. Such a fragment as

$$x := x+1$$

would usually be accepted as an important fragment, worthy of special attention by the compiler writer, whereas

$$x := sin(y)^2 + cos(y)^2$$

might not. I'd say that if you write the second you deserve the code you get, although in theory it might be optimally compiled as if you'd written 'x := 1.0'.

The problem is to design a translator that will generate the best possible code for important source fragments and correct code for all other possible fragments. The technique of tree walking allows even the novice to approach this ideal, because it makes it easy to build a translator which gives correct, but sub-optimal, code for all cases, then later to improve the translator by giving special attention to the translation of important code fragments. Chapter 2 shows how a tree walking translator can be built to give correct and fairly efficient translations of some specific fragments: in this section I show how this technique can be used to give as good results as any other mechanism of simple translation.

Amongst the important program fragments will usually be found those shown in figure II.1. The calculation of arithmetic values is included in this list because practically everything you write in a program involves an expression - if only the calculation of

---

Calculation of an arithmetic value   (chapter 5)
Conditional transfer of control   (chapter 6)
Data structure access   (chapter 9)
Procedure call and return   (chapter 11)
Argument passing   (chapter 12)
Access to a variable   (chapter 13)
Stack addressing (environment link or display vector)
                                     (chapter 13)

Figure II.1   Some crucial code fragments

the value of a single variable. Many of the others are included because history has proved that compilers can easily generate disastrous code for these program fragments if their designers don't take care. Truly these are <u>crucial</u> source program fragments and the quality of the code fragments which you choose to generate from them will be crucial for both the speed of execution of the object program and the number of instructions included in it.

In this section, chapter 5 concentrates on code for arithmetic expressions. Chapter 6 deals with the generation of code which is used - e.g. in an **if** statement - to select between alternative paths of execution. Chapter 7 shows how the procedures which translate expressions can be used in the translation of statements and declarations. Chapter 8 deals with the building of the symbol table and the descriptors which it contains. Chapter 9 discusses code for data structure access. Chapter 10 discusses the principles of code optimisation and queries its cost-effectiveness.

At first sight it is perhaps surprising that figure II.1 quotes the loading of the value of a variable as a crucial code fragment. In this section I assume for the most part that the value of a variable can always be accessed by a single instruction, but section III and, in particular, chapter 13 shows that this is not so and that the code which accesses the memory is perhaps the most crucial code fragment of all!

Communication between Translation Procedures

In this section and in section III the translation mechanism illustrated is based on the use of 'switch' procedures which select an appropriate translation procedure for a tree node: TranArithExpr in chapter 5, TranBoolExpr in chapter 6, TranStatement and TranDecl in chapter 7. Each of these procedures looks at the 'type' field of a node, which contains an integer uniquely identifying the type of the node, and calls the relevant procedure.

Although it would be possible to use a single switch procedure for all kinds of node, the use of separate procedures enables the translator to check some contextual errors - for example an arithmetic expression node presented to TranBoolExpr indicates the use of an arithmetic expression in a Boolean context - which chapter 3 and section IV argue should be checked by the translator rather than the syntax analyser. Each switch procedure accepts only a limited range of node-types: this makes the compiler as a whole more 'self-checking' since the switch procedures in effect partially check the structure of the tree which is built by the syntax analyser.

Node format

The translation procedures almost invariably have a parameter
'nodep', the value of which is a pointer to a tree node. Each node
contains an identification field or 'tag field' called 'type' and
several other fields, which in most cases contain pointers to
other tree nodes. The value held in the 'type' field defines the
node-type. Nodes of different types have different collections of
fields with different names - e.g. the pointer fields of a binary
arithmetic operation node are called 'left' and 'right', a
conditional statement node contains pointer fields called 'test',
'thenstat' and 'elsestat', the symbol table descriptor of a
variable will contain a field called 'address', and so on.   The
expression 'nodep.x' accesses the field 'x' in the node pointed to
by 'nodep'.

5 Translating Arithmetic Expressions

Figure 5.1 shows an example arithmetic expression which might appear anywhere in a typical program - say on the right-hand side of an assignment statement - together with the parse tree which describes its structure. It also shows the object code which is the best translation of this expression - 'best', that is, if the expression is considered in isolation. The example shows the point from which a compiler-writers' discussion will start - what translation algorithm will generate this 'best' code in practice?

The first step in the solution of this problem is to devise a translator that will generate correct code for every arithmetical fragment: the tree-walking mechanism of chapter 2 will certainly do so. In figure 5.1 and in the examples below I assume that the object program must calculate the value of an expression in some register or other, in order that the value may be stored, passed as an argument, compared with another value, etc. It's simplest also if I assume that registers 1,2, ... (up to some maximum register number 'maxreg') are available for the calculation of

---

Expression: minutes + hours*60

Tree:
```
              +
            /   \
      minutes    *
                / \
            hours   60
```

'Best' code: LOAD 1, hours
                MULTn 1, 60
                ADD   1, minutes

Figure 5.1 A simple example expression

expressions. Figure 5.2 shows TranArithExpr and TranBinOp
procedures which, when given the tree of figure 5.1 and the
register number '1', will produce the code shown in figure 5.3.

These procedures, for all their faults, generate code which
would <u>work</u> if you ran it. As a compiler writer, I find that
correctness of code is more important than efficiency of
execution. Inefficient object programs are annoying, but
incorrectly translated object programs are useless! It wouldn't
be reasonable, however, to accept the code generated by the
procedures in figure 5.2 since it is so clearly possible to do
better. To reiterate the lesson of chapter 2: a tree-walking
translator can be improved by choosing strategies and tactics
according to the characteristics of the node being translated.

If I incorporate the improvements sketched in chapter 2, the
TranBinOp procedure of figure 5.2 becomes the procedure of figure
5.4. This procedure shows two major improvements. First, it
notices when the second sub-node is a name or a number, and in

```
let TranArithExpr(nodep, regno) be
 switchon nodep.type into
  { case '+':      TranBinOp(ADD, nodep, regno); endcase
    case '-':      TranBinOp(SUB, nodep, regno); endcase
    case '*':      TranBinOp(MULT, nodep, regno); endcase
    case '/':      TranBinOp(DIV, nodep, regno); endcase

        ...

    case name:
         Gen(LOAD, regno, nodep.descriptor.address); endcase
    case number:
         Gen(LOADn, regno, nodep.value); endcase

    default: CompilerFail("invalid node in TranArithExpr")
  }

let TranBinOp(op, nodep, regno) be
 { TranArithExpr(nodep.left, regno)
   TranArithExpr(nodep.right, regno+1)
   Gen(op++'r', regno, regno+1) /* change XXX to XXXr */
 }
```

Figure 5.2 Straightforward translation procedures

```
          LOAD  1, minutes
          LOAD  2, hours
          LOADn 3, 60
          MULTr 2, 3
          ADDr  1, 2
```

Figure 5.3 Straightforward object code

this case it calls TranLeaf, which generates only one instruction
rather than two. Second, it notices when the left-hand sub-node
is a name or a number and the right-hand sub-node is a more
complicated expression and in this case it reverses the order of
translation. The first improvement saves registers and
instructions in many cases

```
         LOAD n, alpha              LOAD n, alpha
         LOAD n+1, beta   becomes   ADD  n, beta
         ADDr n, n+1
```

and the second improvement allows this technique to become
effective in more situations, when the original expression is
'leaf op <expr>' and could have been more efficiently written
'<expr> op leaf'. Given the tree of figure 5.1, the TranBinOp
procedure of figure 5.4 will generate exactly the 'best' possible
code sequence. Although it isn't possible to do better in this
particular case, I show below how a similar mechanism can be

_____

```
let TranBinOp(op, nodep, regno) be
{ let first, second = nodep.left, nodep.right

  /* test for <leaf> op <non-leaf> */
  if IsLeaf(first) & not IsLeaf(second) then
  { /* interchange and reverse the operation */
    first, second := nodep.right, nodep.left
    op := reverse(op) /* changes SUB to xSUB */
  }

  TranArithExpr(first, regno)
  if IsLeaf(second) then
    TranLeaf(op, second, regno)
  else
  { TranArithExpr(second, regno+1)
    Gen(op++'r', regno, regno+1)
  }
}

let IsLeaf(nodep) = (nodep.type=name | nodep.type=number)

let TranLeaf(op, nodep, regno) be
 switchon nodep.type into
 { case name:
       Gen(op, regno, nodep.descriptor.address); endcase
   case number:
       Gen(op++'n', regno, nodep.value); endcase

   default: CompilerFail("invalid arg. to TranLeaf")
 }
```

Figure 5.4 First improved translation procedure

developed which can be applied in more complicated situations.

Reverse Operations

Strictly speaking the translator can't always reverse the order of node evaluation - 'a-b' is not the same as 'b-a'. If it reverses the order of evaluation of a '-' node, therefore, it must generate a different subtract instruction - a so-called 'reverse subtract'. Prefix 'x'[1] denotes a reverse instruction, so whereas 'SUB reg,store' means "reg:=reg-store", 'xSUB reg,store' means "reg:=store-reg". This is the reason for the statement 'op:=reverse(op)' in figure 5.4. While the xADD and xMULT instructions are indistinguishable from ADD and MULT, unfortunately not every machine has a complete set of reverse instructions. Reverse divide or reverse subtract is often missing, for example.

Reverse operations are important only when the machine doesn't have a complete set of 'reversed' instructions. In the absence of proper instructions, the reverse operation can take many more instructions than the forward variant. Figure 5.5 shows some example code for a machine without a reverse integer divide (xDIV) instruction - code (a) shows a solution which uses no more registers than necessary (but uses three instructions to carry out the division); code (b) shows a solution which performs the operation without reversing (using 'only' two instructions for the divide yet occupying an extra register during computation of the right-hand operand); code (c) uses an extra register instead of a store location yet then must either leave the result in the 'wrong' register or must include an extra instruction to transfer it to the correct register; code (d) uses the minimum of registers by directing the right hand operand to another register[2]; code (e) is only possible if the xDIV instruction is available.

Figure 5.5 shows that reverse operations are occasionally expensive, and that therefore they should be avoided whenever possible. I show below that in many cases it is difficult to avoid reverse operations, particularly when there aren't enough registers available to calculate the value of a complicated expression.

---

1 I use 'x' rather than 'r' to avoid confusion between, say, xSUB (reverse subtract) and SUBr (subtract between two registers).

2 I leave it as an exercise for the reader to discover the modifications required to the TranBinOp procedure, as developed in this chapter, which would allow it to generate case (d) from figure 5.5.

Register Dumping

Although the TranBinOp procedure of figure 5.4 reduces the number
of registers required to calculate the value of an expression, it
assumes that there are always a sufficient number available, no
matter how complicated the expression. Even on multi-register
machines this may not be so - some of the registers may be devoted
to other purposes as chapter 11 shows - and on a machine with only
one or two registers it is vitally important to use a translation
algorithm which doesn't demand an infinite supply of registers.
It is easy to invent an expression which uses all the available
registers: if an expression contains a function call, for example,
it is reasonable to assume (see below) that it requires all the
registers no matter how many there are available. Minimising the
number of registers required in order to evaluate an expression is
an issue whether the object machine has only one register or has
thirty-two or even (as on ATLAS of fond memory) one hundred and
twenty-eight.

Consider, for example, the expression shown in figure 5.6.
Figure 5.7 shows the code which would be produced by the TranBinOp
algorithm, as developed so far, when given this rather involved
expression. The code is acceptable provided the machine has three
registers available: if there are only two then it seems that the
translator must generate instructions which 'dump' the value held
in one of the registers during evaluation of the expression. It's
complicated to describe a register-dumping scheme and I won't

---

Source: i/<expr>
         (result to be in register n)

Tree: /
                         /   \
                       i   <expr>

Possible code:
a: <expr> -> register n   d: <expr> -> register m
   STORE   n, #t1   LOAD   n, i
   LOAD   n, i   DIVr   n, m
   DIV   n, #t1

b: LOAD   n, i   e: <expr> -> register n
   <expr> -> register m   xDIV   n, i
   DIVr   n, m

c: <expr> -> register n
   LOAD   m, i
   DIVr   m, n
  ?(LOADr n, m)

Figure 5.5 The cost of a reverse divide operation

attempt to give one in detail here.

It would require quite a lot of modification to make the procedure of figure 5.4 dump registers. First it would need a table of 'registers in use', filled in by the TranArithExpr procedure each time it generates an instruction which loads a value into a register and altered by TranBinOp when that value is no longer required.   Second, if a procedure is called with a 'regno' which is too large (register 3 when there are only registers 1 and 2, say) the procedure must dump one of the registers currently in use and perform the operation in that dumped register. Third, each procedure must return as its result the number of the register in which the operation was actually performed - because of register dumping this may not be the same as the argument 'regno'. The section of the TranBinOp procedure which handles '<expr> **op** <expr>' nodes, in which neither operand is a leaf, must take account of the fact that something which it loads into a register may be dumped later. Part of a possible procedure is shown in figure 5.8.

Expression: a*b / ((c*d-e*f) / (g+h))

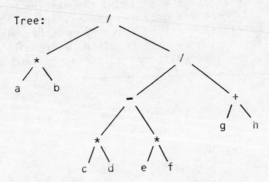

Figure 5.6 A more complicated example expression

```
Code:    LOAD   1, a
         MULT   1, b      /* r1 := a*b */
         LOAD   2, c
         MULT   2, d      /* r2 := c*d */
         LOAD   3, e
         MULT   3, f      /* r3 := e*f */
         SUBr   2, 3      /* r2 := c*d-e*f */
         LOAD   3, g
         ADD    3, h      /* r3 := g+h */
         DIVr   2, 3      /* r2 := (c*d-e*f)/(g+h) */
         DIVr   1, 2      /* r1 := a*b/((c*d-e*f)/(g+h)) */
```

Figure 5.7 Code from the tree of figure 5.6

The trouble with this procedure is that it may dump the 'wrong' register. Figure 5.9 shows the effect of dumping the 'wrong' register (l.h. column) compared to the 'right' register (r.h.column). Note that the two different dumping strategies produce the final answer in different registers[1]. The dumping instructions are marked '*', the corresponding reverse operations with '!'. Note that the more dumping that goes on, the more reverse operations are required and the longer and slower the object program. Remember also that reverse operations may be more expensive than the forward variant, as illustrated in figure 5.5.

```
{ let firstreg = TranArithExpr(first, regno)
  let secondreg = TranArithExpr(second, regno+1)

  if dumped(firstreg) then
  { Gen(reverse(op), secondreg, placedumped(firstreg))
    resultis secondreg
  }
  else
  { Gen(op++'r', firstreg, secondreg)
    resultis firstreg
  }
}
```

Figure 5.8 Dealing with dumped registers

```
    'Wrong' register:              'Right' register:
        LOAD  1, a                     LOAD  1, a
        MULT  1, b                     MULT  1, b
        LOAD  2, c                     LOAD  2, c
        MULT  2, d                     MULT  2, d
    *   STORE 2, #t1               *   STORE 1, #t1
        LOAD  2, e                     LOAD  1, e
        MULT  2, f                     MULT  1, f
    !   xSUB  2, #t1                   SUBr  2, 1
    *   STORE 2, #t2                   LOAD  1, g
        LOAD  2, g                     ADD   1, h
        ADD   2, h                     DIVr  2, 1
    !   xDIV  2, #t2             !     xDIV  2, #t1
        DIVr  1, 2
```

Figure 5.9 Dumping 'right' and 'wrong' registers

---

[1] In some cases - e.g. where the value of an expression is to form the result of a function - it may be important that the value is actually loaded into a particular register, so there is more to this problem than appears at first sight.

If the translation algorithm is to generate the code shown in the right-hand column of figure 5.9, it must always dump the register whose next use is farthest away in the list of machine instructions. This is easy enough to decide in simple cases like that in figure 5.6, but in general it needs proper flow analysis of the program and flow analysis isn't simple translation - it's optimisation. In any case, there is a better answer to the problem of register dumping in the shape of the tree-weighting algorithm developed below.

When a program uses temporary 'dump' locations - e.g. #t1 in figure 5.9 - they can be allocated to run-time memory locations in the same way as other variables (see chapter 8). It's tempting, on a machine with a hardware stack, to use the stack for dump locations but it's usually inefficient and always unnecessary.

Tree Weighting

The translation algorithm which has been developed so far in this chapter has been strong on tactics in certain simple situations, but weak on strategy in cases where the tactics don't directly apply. If we consider once more the tree of figure 5.6, there is a sequence of instructions, shown in figure 5.10, which uses only two registers. It is possible to design an algorithm which extends the mechanism of figure 5.5 to handle the trees of both figure 5.1 and figure 5.6 and which can generate 'best' code in either case.

If you look closely at the tree of figure 5.6 and the instruction sequence of figure 5.10 you can see how the code can be derived: confronted with a choice between two expression sub-nodes, the translator should generate code for the more complicated sub-node (the one which uses the most registers) first. This minimises the number of registers: suppose the left subnode uses a maximum of L registers during its evaluation and the right subnode uses a maximum of R registers, then

```
        LOAD   1, c
        MULT   1, d      /* r1 := c*d */
        LOAD   2, e
        MULT   2, f      /* r2 := e*f */
        SUBr   1, 2      /* r1 := c*d-e*f */
        LOAD   2, g
        ADD    2, h      /* r2 := g+h */
        DIVr   1, 2      /* r1 := (c*d-e*f)/(g+h) */
        LOAD   2, a
        MULT   2, b      /* r2 := a*b */
      ! xDIVr  1, 2      /* r1 := a*b/((c*d-e*f)/(g+h)) */
```

Figure 5.10 Alternative code for the tree of figure 5.6

- if the object program evaluates the left subnode first, it will need L registers to do so, then one register to hold the result while the the right subnode is evaluated - i.e. overall it will use maximum(L,R+1) registers

- if it evaluates the right subnode first it will use maximum(R,L+1) registers

Thus if L is bigger than R the left subnode should be evaluated first - the object code fragment will then need only L registers to evaluate the whole node - and vice versa if L is less than R, the right subnode should be evaluated first. If L and R are equal, the order doesn't matter and the object code will use one more register than is required for either of the subnodes. Figure 5.11 shows a BCPL algorithm which calculates the 'weight' of a node - the minimum number of registers that will be needed to calculate the value of the expression represented by that node. This procedure assumes that the subnodes of a particular node will always be evaluated in the optimal order. It gives leaf nodes a zero weighting because when only one subnode is a leaf then the other subnode should be evaluated first: where both subnodes are leaves then it takes only one register to evaluate the expression represented by the node.

If every node in the tree of figure 5.6 is tagged with its weight by this procedure the result will be a weighted tree, shown in figure 5.12. A minor change to TranBinOp will enable it to translate the weighted tree into the 'ideal' code shown in figure 5.10, assuming that there are enough registers available to do so. The new TranBinOp algorithm is shown in figure 5.13. This algorithm reduces the need for register dumping by minimising the number of registers used to evaluate an expression.

The TranBinOp procedure shown in figure 5.13 also allows for the fact that the object machine has a limited number of registers for expression evaluation. Any node which requires the maximum number of registers will be weighted at 'maxreg' by the procedure of figure 5.11. Recursively, any node which contains such a

---

```
let weight(nodep) = valof
{ if IsLeaf(nodep) then nodep.nregs := 0
  else
    { let L = weight(nodep.left)
      let R = weight(nodep.right)
      nodep.nregs := (L>R -> L, R>L -> R,
                      L=maxregs -> maxregs, L+1)
    }
  resultis nodep.nregs
}
```

Figure 5.11 Producing the weighted tree

maximal subnode will itself be weighted with 'maxreg' and therefore the entire expression tree will be a maximal tree. If TranBinOp translates such a tree, there are two possibilities

a. Only one subtree is maximal: in this case it will select the maximal subtree for translation first and therefore

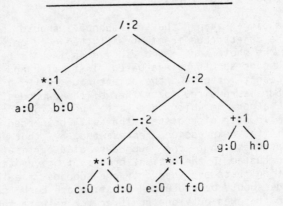

Figure 5.12 The weighted tree

```
let TranBinOp(op, nodep, regno) be
{ let first, second = nodep.left, nodep.right

  if first.nregs<second.nregs then
  { /* interchange operands, reverse operator */
    first, second := nodep.right, nodep.left
    op := reverse(op)
  }

  TranArithExpr(first, regno)

  if IsLeaf(second) then
    TranLeaf(op, second, regno)
  elsf second.nregs=maxregs then
  { let temp = dumpreg(regno) /* dump first operand */

    /* re-use same register and reverse the operation */
    TranArithExpr(second, regno)
    Gen(reverse(op), regno, temp)
  }
  else /* no need to dump unless 'second' is maximal! */
  { TranArithExpr(second, regno+1)
    Gen(op++'r', regno, regno+1)
  }
}
```

Figure 5.13 Translating the weighted tree

there is no register to dump.

b. Both subtrees are maximal: in this case it must generate
code which dumps the register that holds the value of the
first subtree before the second subtree is evaluated.

In either case the code which is generated for a maximal subtree
will be executed when there are no values in the registers which
ought to be dumped: by induction when any maximal node is
translated there is no need to dump unless both its subnodes are
maximal. It is impossible, of course, to eliminate the dump
instruction by reversing the order of evaluation since both
subnodes require all the registers.

Avoiding Reverse Operations

The tree-walking algorithm now looks remarkably powerful - it
never seems to make a wrong step so far as register dumping is
concerned. Now, however, for a rather clever improvement. The
TranBinOp procedure has access to information not only about the
weight of the subnodes but also about the kind of operation (ADD,
SUB, etc.) required for calculation of the overall value of a
node. Notice that it has to produce a reverse operation (xDIV,
xSUB etc.) if it reverses the order of evaluation of the subnodes.
Notice also that it must reverse the operation when it is forced
to dump a register because both subnodes are maximal. As figure
5.5 shows, reverse operations are occasionally expensive, and
unnecessary expense should be avoided whenever possible. The
tree-walking mechanism makes it simple to do so!

The TranBinOp procedure takes a strategic decision when it
reverses the order of evaluation of the subnodes to minimise the
number of registers used during evaluation of the node. Each
reversal saves one register and the question of strategy is to
decide in exactly what circumstances reversal should occur.
First, if the register saved forces the translator later on to
generate a sequence of instructions so as to simulate a reverse
operation - a reverse divide on a machine without an xDIV, for
example - it might be better to perform the forward operation and
not to bother about the number of registers used. Second, when
both subnodes are maximal then dumping must occur anyway and the
operation will be reversed - if the order of evaluation of the
subnodes is reversed initially then the eventual operation
performed will be 'reverse(reverse(op))', which is the original
forward operation!

TranBinOp can discover when the operation it is considering is
'reversible' (has a reverse instruction in the object machine), so
it can almost always avoid having to simulate reverse operations
by using the strategy of figure 5.14. The strategy is: if the
operation is reversible (has a hardware reverse instruction)
always interchange when the second operand is heavier; if the

operation isn't reversible then interchange only if there aren't enough free registers to evaluate the operands in the normal order: however if both operands are maximal and the operation isn't reversible then always interchange (the eventual operation generated will be reverse(reverse(op)), which is the forward operation).

Although the final TranBinOp procedure which combines figures 5.13 and figure 5.14 is by no means perfect, this extended example demonstrates the power of the tree-walking technique as a means of generating object code which is both accurate and efficient. Since the translator has available at every point all of the information about the fragment it is translating, it can take an informed decision about how to handle it. The discussion so far has said nothing about the way in which a code fragment should be interfaced with those which will precede and follow it in the object program - that is discussed in chapter 10, under the heading of code optimisation - but for simple translation, fragment by fragment, tree walking is definitely the easiest way to produce acceptable object code for crucial code fragments.

The algorithm of figures 5.13 and 5.14 might be further improved in various different ways and there are criteria other than speed of execution by which we might wish to judge the quality of the object code. On a microprocessor, for example, users are likely to require short code sequences even at the expense of object code speed. One area where speed and code size conflict is in the code to do with function and procedure calls, discussed below and in chapter 11. It is certainly possible to produce a tree-walking translator which uses tactics and strategy to minimise the number of instructions in the object program: the algorithm presented so far already does so in the limited area of arithmetic expression code.

Function Calls and Register Dumping

In the object program each source program procedure is represented by a sequence of machine instructions. These instructions are

---

```
  let wfirst,wsecond = first.nregs, second.nregs

  if (hasreverse(op) -> wsecond>wfirst,
          (wsecond>wfirst & nfreeregs()-1<wsecond) |
          wfirst=wsecond=maxregs)
    then
      { first, second := nodep.right, nodep.left
        op := reverse(op)
      }
    ....
```

Figure 5.14 Node-reversal strategy

'called' by sections of the object program which are compiled versions of function call source program fragments. As chapter 11 shows, it takes much more than a single JSUB instruction to call a procedure or function - but that needn't detain us here, because the difficulty with function calls in expressions is that they influence register dumping.

The code for a function can be called from many different contexts and must return to as many different contexts in the object program. Clearly it would be foolish to leave values in some of the registers, to call the function and expect that the function will not touch those registers - this would be impossible with a recursive function in any case. Either all of the registers must be dumped at the start of the function and reloaded at the end - which will slow the object program since they must <u>all</u> be dumped and reloaded on <u>every</u> function call, no matter how many are actually in use - or else the code for any expression which contains a function call must ensure that there are no registers in use when the function call is executed. Dumping all registers on function entry and reloading on exit might produce a shorter object program because it shortens the function call sequence (which may be included many times in the object program) at the expense of the code for the function itself (which only appears once) and for that reason might be preferred in a compiler for a mini- or micro-computer.

The tree weighting mechanism of figure 5.11 and the TranBinOp translation procedure of figure 5.13 can be used to produce fast code which contains the minimum number of register dumping instructions, merely by regarding each function call as a 'maximal' subnode of the tree. Any node above the function call

Expression: x*y + f(x)/g(y)

Tree:

```
                        +:max
                       /      \
             *:1              /:max
            /   \            /      \
         x:0    y:0     f(x):max    g(y):max
```

Code: <call g(y)>
          STORE 1, #t1   /* dump value of g(y) */
          <call f(x)>
          DIV   1, #t1   /* r1 := f(x)/g(y) */
          LOAD 2, x
          MULT 2, y   /* r2 := x*y */
          ADDr 1, 2   /* r1 := f(x)/g(y)+x*y */

Figure 5.15 An expression involving two function calls

node will also be maximally weighted by the procedure of figure
5.11. So if a tree contains two function-call nodes, the question
of register dumping and of avoiding reverse operations must
necessarily arise. Therefore the worst-case situation, in which
TranBinOp must decide whether to interchange the order of two
maximal subnodes or not, arises more often in practice than you
might otherwise have supposed.

I assume that all functions return their results in the same
standard register. This fits simply into the tree-weighting
technique as described so far if the function returns its value in
register 1 (or whatever register is the 'bottom' of the register
vector). Thus the TranBinOp procedure of figures 5.13 and 5.14
would produce compact code for the expression of figure 5.15,
using the reversal strategy of figure 5.14 to re-order the
function calls for a machine without an xDIV instruction.

Other Forms of the Tree

Everything that has been said so far relates to the translation of
binary nodes – each node defining an operation and two subnodes.
It's perhaps natural to think of an expression like that in figure
5.16 as a multiple sum rather than a recursive structure – as an
n-ary tree rather than binary. Several operations which are
difficult on the binary tree are easy on the n-ary. One useful
trick, for example, is to evaluate expressions involving constants
at compile time – thus 'x+2*3' can be translated as if it was
written as 'x+6'. A preliminary tree-walk, similar to the 'weight'
procedure of figure 5.10, can discover subtrees which contain only
constants and replace them by a node which shows their overall
value. It is rather harder to discover from a binary tree that an
expression like that in figure 5.16 is amenable to the same
treatment. The example expression can be seen to be equivalent to
'a+b+3': using the n-ary tree it is simple to sort out the
constant sub-nodes and recognise that the expression contains

---

Expression: a+1+b+2

Figure 5.16 Binary and n-ary node structures

constant values that might be combined at compile time.

The node-reversal mechanism discussed above will only affect the value of an expression when a function called from the expression has a side-effect on a value used elsewhere in the expression. In such a case the order of evaluation of the expression would be important and it is to help the compiler-writer that most language definitions outlaw such an expression. (Programs often contain Boolean expressions whose order of evaluation is important: their translation is discussed in chapter 6.) Sorting the subnodes of an n-ary node, however, can be numerically disastrous. If you evaluate the expression 'a-b+c-d', with a=b=10^12, c=d=0.1, using floating point arithmetic on a machine with less than 12 digits accuracy and working from left to right, the answer is '0.0'. If you evaluate 'a+c-b-d', with the same values and again working from left to right the answer this time is '-0.1'. Thus re-ordering the sub-nodes in an n-ary node is a technique which must be used with care, like all techniques which border on optimisation.

Combinations of Arithmetic Types

Many languages which permit the kind of expression whose translation is discussed in this chapter also use a variety of compile-time types - **real, integer, character,** and so on. This at once puts a burden of error handling on the translator and means that it must become more voluminous than ever (though not more complicated).

The 'type' of a node depends on the 'types' of its subnodes and the operation which must be carried out. Some prohibited combinations of types and operators will be classified as compile-time errors[1] - e.g. in FORTRAN, REAL*LOGICAL, COMPLEX**COMPLEX, etc. - whilst those type combinations which are permitted will require individual treatment. The type is easily found recursively, either by a preliminary tree-walk or at the same time as the instructions which compute the value are being generated. Using a preliminary tree-walk can help if, for example, the choice of a code fragment depends on the order of evaluation of the subnodes.

The TranBinOp procedure must look at the types of the left and right subnodes of an expression to select a code fragment on the basis of the type combination revealed. In figure 5.17 the source language allows only **real, integer** and **Boolean** variables, and on the object machine all arithmetic instructions have a floating

---

1 These errors are sometimes wrongly called 'semantic' errors. They're really long-range sytactic errors. True semantic errors arise when a program asks for an impossible sequence of operations at run-time.

point variant. In this strange language **integer** + **real** is **integer**, **real** + **integer** is **real**. I assume that each node in the expression tree contains an 'atype' field which records its arithmetic type and that constant nodes and symbol table descriptors have an appropriate value stored in their 'atype' field. The last few lines in figure 5.17 illustrate how the translator can detect type-combination errors and how easy it is to write a 'self-checking' translator.

The fact that translators can easily carry out type processing, and can as a side effect check type validity in hierarchies of nodes, allows the syntax analyser to avoid any type checking even when, as with Boolean/arithmetic types in ALGOL 60, the syntax specifies permissible combinations of operations. Thus the <u>translator</u> can easily detect that '(a=b)*(c=d)' is an invalid

```
let TranBinOp(op, nodep, regno) = valof
{ let first, second = nodep.left, nodep.right

    /* node reversal, etc. omitted to clarify algorithm */
    TranArithExpr(first, regno)
    TranArithExpr(second, regno+1)
    op := op++'r'

    { let Ltype = first.atype
      let Rtype = second.atype

      if Ltype=Rtype then
      { Gen((Ltype=INT -> op, 'f'++op), regno, regno+1)
        nodep.atype := Ltype
      }
      elsf Ltype=INT & Rtype=REAL then
      { /* convert second operand to INT type */
        Gen(FIXr, regno+1, 0); Gen(op, regno, regno+1)
        nodep.atype := INT
      }
      elsf Ltype=REAL & Rtype=INT then
      { /* convert second operand to REAL type */
        Gen(FLOATr, regno+1, 0); Gen('f'++op, regno, regno+1)
        nodep.atype := REAL
      }
    - elsf Ltype=BOOL | Rtype=BOOL then
      { Error("Boolean expression in arithmetic context")
        nodep.atype := INT /* avoid secondary error */
      }
      else
        CompilerFail("garbaged types in TranBinOp", nodep)
    }
}
```

Figure 5.17 Translating with mixed arithmetic types

expression, if the language definition makes it so. The translator's diagnostic, which could describe the error as an invalid combination of types, is close to my intuition about the kind of misunderstanding on the part of the user which might lead to the inclusion of such a construct in a program. The message that would be produced if a syntax analyser detected the error - 'invalid sequence of operators' or 'logical operation expected' (see chapter 3 and section IV) isn't nearly so helpful.

Allowing a complicated type structure in expressions, then, merely means that the tree-walking translator must check for and individually process each valid type combination. The translator becomes more voluminous, though not more complicated. If the type structure is really intricate, as it is in COBOL or PL/1, it may be more economical to use a lookup matrix to detail the actions required for each operation rather than to code them explicitly as in figure 5.17.

Summary

This chapter demonstrates the power of tree-walking techniques to generate remarkably good code from a tree which represents an arithmetic expression. It shows the strength of the design technique set out in chapter 3 - first produce a general mechanism which can translate the most general form of a particular kind of node, refine it to work better if the node has a particular structure, refine it still further if there are any special cases worthy of consideration.

The power of the tree-walking technique comes not from the quality of the final code - code like that illustrated in this chapter can be produced in a number of different ways - but from the technique of structured refinement. If the translator never progresses beyond the stage in which it uses the most general mechanism it is still usable as a translator. It cannot be too strongly emphasised that a correct but sub-optimal translator is infinitely preferable to one which produces excellent code in almost every case yet breaks down whenever presented with a novel situation. I don't claim that tree walking eliminates such bugs but I do claim that it minimises them. Once the general mechanism is working you can move on to refine any crucial code fragments which are seriously sub-optimal, and using tree walking means that this refinement doesn't disturb any other sections of your translator, which go on operating just as they did before.

Later chapters show how the tree-walking mechanism can handle other kinds of node, but it is perhaps in the area of expression evaluation, as demonstrated in this chapter and the next, that it is at its most impressive.

6 Translating Boolean Expressions

It's possible to treat Boolean expressions in exactly the same way as arithmetic expressions - generate instructions to evaluate the subnodes, generate an instruction (or a sequence of instructions) to combine the Boolean values. Thus Boolean **and** and Boolean **or** operations can be translated using the TranBinOp procedure of chapter 5 with the machine instructions AND and OR. However Boolean expressions more often than not appear as the conditional test in an **if** or a **while** statement and, as a result, are used more as sections of program which select between alternative paths of computation than as algebraic expressions which compute a truth value. Most good compilers therefore try to generate 'jumping' code for Boolean expressions in these contexts. First of all, however, it is necessary to demonstrate the code fragments which are required when Boolean expressions are regarded as value-calculating mechanisms.

Evaluating a Relational Expression

Primary constituents of Boolean expressions can be constants, variables, elements of data structures or the results of function calls, just as in the case of an arithmetic expression. Relational expressions, however, are a little different and require special treatment since the object code fragment must usually execute a 'test' instruction to discover the result of a comparison. In this chapter I use the SKIP family of instructions to test the truth of a relation such as '<' or '='.

Consider the expression 'a<b', in the context 'x := a<b'. Here 'x' is a Boolean variable, which should contain **true** or **false** after the statement has been executed. The expression 'a<b' is then a means of calculating the value **true** or the value **false**. Figure 6.1 shows a translation procedure for relational expression nodes which can generate code to do this, together with the code generated as a result of giving it the operation 'LT', a pointer to the tree for 'a<b' and the register number 1. The code isn't ideal for its purpose - some modifications to TranBinOp would be

needed to generate the 'LOADn 1, TRUE' instruction immediately before the 'SKIPxx' instruction, so that a register isn't occupied unnecessarily whilst the operands are evaluated. Minor improvements apart, though, the procedure does deliver an acceptable code sequence for situations in which the result of the relational comparison is to be treated as a manipulable value.

Figure 6.2 shows a different context in which the expression might appear, with the 'ideal' code for that situation compared with the code which would be produced using the translation procedure of figure 6.1. Once again the question is - what algorithm will generate the ideal code in this situation and others like it?

Boolean or Conditional Operators?

The Boolean connectives are unusual operators in that it is often unnatural to regard a Boolean expression as a combination of

```
let TranRelation(op, nodep, regno) be
{ Gen(LOADn, regno, TRUE)
  TranBinOp('SKIP'++op, nodep, regno+1)
  Gen(LOADn, regno, FALSE)
}
```

Tree: . <

```
        a              b
```

```
Code:   LOADn    1, TRUE
        LOAD     2, a
        SKIPLT   2, b
        LOADn    1, FALSE
```

Figure 6.1 Computing the value of a relational expression

Statement: **if** a<b **then** <statement>

```
Simple code:                    'Best' code:
    LOADn     1, TRUE               LOAD    1, a
    LOAD      2, a                  SKIPLT  1, b
    SKIPLT    2, b                  JUMP      , labela
    LOADn     1, FALSE           {<statement>}
    JUMPFALSE 1, labela          labela:
    {<statement>}
labela:
```

Figure 6.2 Relational expression in a conditional context

simple values. The expression

$$i<=n \ \& \ A[i]<0$$

for example can naturally be regarded as a section of program
whose operation is as follows

- if the value of 'i' is greater than the value of 'n' the
  answer is **false**;
- otherwise, if 'i' is not greater than 'n' compare A[i]
  and 0 to find the value of the expression.

Such an interpretation of a Boolean operation can lead to highly
efficient code: however its effect is not at all the same as the
'algebraic' interpretation of the same expression. The
interpretation above would make the value of the expression **false**
whenever 'i>n': however in ALGOL 60, whose language definition
treats the Boolean **and** as an algebraic operator, the expression
would produce a run-time error if the upper bound of A is 'n' and
i>n.

It's often very convenient, though, to give a conditional
interpretation to at least some of the Boolean connectives.
Figure 6.3 shows the conditional definitions of the operators **and**,
or and **not**. Restated in English these definitions mean: if the
first operand of an **and** operator is false, the expression is

---

```
E1 and E2   means   E1 -> E2, false
E1 or E2    means   E1 -> true, E2
not E       means   E  -> false, true
```

Figure 6.3 Conditional interpretation of Boolean operators

Statement: **if** (i<0 **or** j>100) **and** (k<0 **or** n>50) **then** S;

```
Code:     LOAD      1, i
          JUMPLT    1, labela
          LOAD      1, j
          SKIPGTn   1, 100
          JUMP       , labelfalse
labela:   LOAD      1, k
          JUMPLT    1, labeltrue
          LOAD      1, n
          SKIPGTn   1, 50
          JUMP       , labelfalse
labeltrue:
          {code for statement S}
labelfalse:
```

Figure 6.4 The conditional interpretation in action

false; if the first operand of an **or** is true, the expression is true; the **not** operator merely reverses the sense of the interpretation of its operand. This gives some nice 'ideal' code for Boolean expressions used in conditional statements, as shown in figure 6.4. This rather attractive code is surprisingly easy to produce.

The code shown in figure 6.4 evaluates a Boolean expression without ever storing its value. The value of the expression is represented by a position in the code fragment and JUMP instructions are used to terminate evaluation whenever the value of a part of the expression or the whole expression becomes clear. The 'jumping code' sequence shown in figure 6.4 is not only shorter than that which would be generated if the expression was evaluated by combining truth-values but also the maximum number of instructions which can be executed is much less than in a comparable algebraic evaluation. A strict algebraic interpretation would execute between 15 and 17 instructions, depending upon whether the SKIP instructions were successful or not, while the code of figure 6.4 would execute between 4 and 9 instructions to distinguish between 'labeltrue' and 'labelfalse'. Although expressions which include Boolean variables and function calls can sometimes require longer code sequences when using the 'jumping code' mechanism, the number of instructions executed will on average be smaller than when using an algebraic evaluation mechanism.

Jumping Code for Boolean Expressions

For simplicity I assume in this chapter that there are two separate translation procedures which translate a Boolean operation node in each of the contexts in which it can occur - either in a value-calculating context or as the test expression inside a conditional statement. I show how to generate jumping code for the conditional case and leave the extension of this technique to the value case as an exercise.

The basic mechanism which I describe uses symbolic labels invented by the compiler, references to which are fixed-up by the loader as described in chapter 4. The procedure 'newlabel' invents a unique label which can be used in JUMP instructions: the procedure 'define' informs the loader that the address associated with a particular label is that of the next instruction to be generated. It would be as easy and probably more efficient to use 'fixup chains' as described in chapter 4, but the algorithms are more readable using invented labels.

In jumping code which is the translation of a Boolean expression in a conditional context, three kinds of control transfer are possible, always initiated by the evaluation of a Boolean primary such as a relational expression, a variable or a Boolean function call. A transfer can be caused by the evaluation

of a relational expression (via the JUMP instruction which follows
the SKIP) or by a JUMPFALSE or JUMPTRUE which follows the
evaluation of a Boolean variable, a Boolean array references, or a
Boolean function call. Code for Boolean operations, conditional
expressions and conditional statements is generated by defining
labels to which these JUMP instructions can transfer control.

During evaluation of a Boolean expression there are three
possible control paths: either the value of the expression is
prematurely **true** (e.g. midway through an **or** node) or it is
prematurely **false** (e.g. midway through an **and** node) or control
simply leaves the expression in the normal way (e.g. when the
SKIP instruction at the end of a relational expression skips over
the JUMP). The code for most nodes will use only one or two of the
possible kinds of control transfer: for example the relational
node will use only one of the exit control paths for the JUMP
instruction.

Each translation procedure, then, is given three extra
arguments. The first (Tlabel) represents the control path to be
taken when the expression turns out to have the value **true**, the
second (Flabel) represents the control path to be taken when the
expression turns out to be **false** and the last (nojump) is either
'true' or 'false', indicating that if evaluation of the node
doesn't cause a transfer of control to either Tlabel or Flabel,
the code fragment must ensure that the value is **true** or **false**
respectively.

Figure 6.5 shows how these parameters can be used in a
TranIfStatement procedure to generate code for a conditional
statement with two sub-statements. The effect of the use of the
'Tlabel', 'Flabel' and 'nojump' arguments is that control arrives
at '%Lt' if the expression in the **if** statement turns out to be
true, at '%Lf' if it turns out to be **false**. The additional label
called 'Endlabel' serves only as the address in the JUMP
instruction which comes between 'thenpart' and 'elsepart', and
transfers control to '%Le' when the execution of 'thenpart' is
complete. Addresses %Lt and %Lf aren't known when the relevant
JUMP instructions are generated in the 'test part' of the
statement, which is why the procedures pass around labels rather
than relocatable object code addresses. The example assumes the
existence of a procedure 'TranBoolExpr' which, rather like
TranArithExpr in chapter 5, selects the relevant translation
procedure for a Boolean node in a conditional context – parts of
this procedure are shown in figure 6.9.

By using tree walking and manipulating the chains and the
'nojump' condition it is possible to generate very attractive code
indeed. The technique isn't as complex as it might at first
appear – it will become clearer, I hope, as you progress through
the example procedures.

```
let TranIfStat(nodep) be
{ let Tlabel, Flabel, Endlabel =
               newlabel(), newlabel(), newlabel()

  /* code for expression may 'fall through'
   * when value is true
   */
  TranBoolExpr(nodep.test, 1, Tlabel, Flabel, 'true')

  /* Make any jumps to 'Tlabel' arrive at
   * the start of the statement after then
   */
  define(Tlabel)
  TranStatement(nodep.thenstat)

  /* after execution of 'thenstat', jump over
   * the rest of the statement
   */
  Gen(JUMP, 0, Endlabel)

  /* make any jumps to 'Flabel' arrive at
   * the start of the statement after else
   */
  define(Flabel)
  TranStatement(nodep.elsestat)

  define(Endlabel)
}
```

Code Layout:

Figure 6.5 Jumping code for a conditional statement

Relational expressions

Figure 6.6 shows a TranRelation procedure which implements the jumping code mechanism for relational operators. This procedure has been created by refinement of a simple technique. This simple technique would always generate a 'SKIPop' instruction followed by a JUMP instruction. The sense of the SKIP instruction is varied according to the argument 'nojump'. If 'nojump' is 'true' then the SKIP should take place (and the JUMP will thereby be avoided) when the relation holds between the values of the subnodes. If 'nojump' is 'false' then the sense of the SKIP instruction is inverted to skip if the relation doesn't hold.

The first refinement is to notice when one of the subnodes is the constant zero, in which case the SKIP and JUMP instructions can be combined. It is illustrated in figure 6.7, which shows the code generated for 'a<0' before and after refinement. The second refinement reverses the order of comparison if the second operand is the constant zero. Note that there is a difference between 'reverse(op)', which just reverses the order of the comparison and thus changes, say, 'LT' into 'GT', and 'inverse(op)' which changes the sense of the comparison and converts 'LT' into 'GE' since whenever a<b is true, a>=b is false. The fragments which would be produced by figure 6.6 can be recognised in the 'ideal' code of figure 6.4.

```
let TranRelation(op, nodep, regno, Tlabel, Flabel, nojump) be
{ let first, second = nodep.left, nodep.right
  let destination = (nojump='true' -> Flabel, Tlabel)

  if zeroconst(first) then
  { /* convert 0<a into a>0 */
    first, second := nodep.right, nodep.left
    op  = reverse(op)
  }

  if zeroconst(second) then
  { let jumpop = JUMP++(nojump='false' -> op, inverse(op))

    TranArithExpr(first, regno)
    Gen(jumpop, regno, destination)
  }
  else
  { let skipop = SKIP++(nojump='true' -> op, inverse(op))

    TranBinOp(skipop, nodep, regno)
    Gen(JUMP, 0, destination)
  }
}
```

Figure 6.6 Generating jumping code for relationals

Binary Boolean operators

Having shown how to generate jumping code for a primary
constituent of a Boolean expression, it is necessary to show how
tree walking handles combinations of simple nodes. Figure 6.8
illustrates the procedure for logical **and**. The procedure for
logical **or** is very similar, the procedure for logical **not** should
be obvious as soon as you understand figure 6.8 and I leave the
construction of both procedures as exercises (that for **not** is
particularly simple). The register number argument 'regno' is
required in the TranRelation procedure and when generating code
for Boolean variables - see figure 6.9.

Code for 'a<0' before refinement:

```
nojump means true              nojump means false
   LOAD   1, a                    LOAD   1, a
   SKIPLTn 1, 0                   SKIPGEn 1, 0
   JUMP    , <Flabel>             JUMP    , <Tlabel>
```

Code for 'a<0' after refinement:

```
nojump means true              nojump means false
   LOAD   1, a                    LOAD   1, a
   JUMPGE  1, <Flabel>            JUMPLT  1, <Tlabel>
```

Figure 6.7 Jumping code produced for relationals

```
let TranAnd(nodep, regno, Tlabel, Flabel, nojump) be
{ let secondpart = newlabel()

   /* generate code for the first operand which transfers
    * to 'secondpart' if that operand is true, to
    * 'Flabel' if that operand is false (because then
    * the whole node is false) and, if it falls through
    * to evaluate the second operand, only does so when
    * the first operand is true
    */
   TranBoolExpr(nodep.left, regno, secondpart, Flabel, 'true')

   /* if control reaches it, the second operand gives
    * the final value of the expression
    */
   define(secondpart)
   TranBoolExpr(nodep.right, regno, Tlabel, Flabel, nojump)
}
```

Figure 6.8 Generating jumping code for Boolean operator

This procedure depends on the conditional interpretation of the
and operator, set out in figure 6.3. The code fragment generated
as the translation of the first operand of the **and** operator
transfers control to 'Flabel' if it is found to be **false** but
either jumps to 'secondpart' or exits in the normal way if the
value is **true**. If the second operand is evaluated at all,
therefore, the value of the first operand must be **true** and this
part of the expression must be translated in exactly the way
prescribed for the expression as a whole. Given a similar
procedure for **or**, it is simple to produce the 'ideal' code of

---

```
let TranBoolExpr(nodep, regno, Tlabel, Flabel, nojump) be
{ switchon nodep.type into
  { case 'and':
      TranAnd(nodep, regno, Tlabel, Flabel, nojump); endcase

    case 'or':
      TranOr(nodep, regno, Tlabel, Flabel, nojump); endcase

    case 'not':
      TranNot(nodep, regno, Tlabel, Flabel, nojump); endcase

    case '<':
      TranRelation(LT, nodep, regno, Tlabel, Flabel, nojump)
      endcase

    case '<=':
      TranRelation(LE, nodep, regno, Tlabel, Flabel, nojump)
      endcase

    ....

    case name, FuncCall, VecAccess, (etc.):
      TranArithExpr(nodep, regno)
      if nojump='true' then Gen(JUMPFALSE, regno, Flabel)
      else Gen(JUMPTRUE, regno, Tlabel)
      endcase

    case 'true':
      if nojump\='true' then Gen(JUMP, 0, Tlabel)
      endcase

    case 'false':
      if nojump\='false' then Gen(JUMP, 0, Flabel)
      endcase

    default: CompilerFail("invalid node in TranBoolExpr")
  }
}
```

Figure 6.9 Part of the TranBoolExpr procedure

figure 6.4.   Note that reversing the order of translation of subnodes is inappropriate when considering Boolean operators in this
way because the order of evaluation of the nodes affects the
meaning of the expression. The expression 'a>0 & (4/a)<2' has not
at all the same meaning as '(4/a)<2 & a>0' when using the jumping
code mechanism, since when the value of 'a' is zero the former
will evaluate to **false** yet the latter will produce a run-time
error.

Boolean variables and constants

Figure 6.9 shows part of the TranBoolExpr procedure, including the
part which translates leaf nodes. The case of name nodes is pretty
obvious - load the value and jump according to the value loaded -
but the case of Boolean constants is a little more surprising.
When generating jumping code for a constant, if no jump will be
interpreted as the same value as the constant, then there is no
need to generate any code at all!

Conditional expressions

It is possible to use the jumping code mechanism developed so far
to generate efficient code for conditional expressions. If the
expression occurs in a context in which its value is required, the

---

```
Source: test -> firstexpr, secondexpr

let TranCondExpr(nodep, regno, Tlabel, Flabel, nojump) be
{ let Lt, Lf = newlabel(), newlabel()

  TranBoolExpr(nodep.test, regno, Lt, Lf, 'true')

  /* if the test in the conditional expression evaluates to
   * true, evaluate the expression after the arrow
   */
  define(Lt)
  TranBoolExpr(nodep.firstexpr, regno, Tlabel, Flabel, nojump)

  /* and if control exits from that expression, execute
   * a jump to either Tlabel or Flabel
   */
  Gen(JUMP, 0, (nojump='true' -> Tlabel, Flabel))

  /* if the test is false, evaluate the expression
   * after the comma
   */
  define(Lf)
  TranBoolExpr(nodep.secondexpr, regno, Tlabel, Flabel, nojump)
}
```

Figure 6.10 Jumping code when no value is required

translation procedure would be similar to the procedure which
translates a conditional statement, shown in figure 6.5 above.
Where a conditional expression is used in a conditional context,
the procedure might be as shown in figure 6.10. It would be easy
to incorporate both approaches into a single procedure which was
informed of the context and selected its strategy accordingly - I
haven't done so here in the interests of clarity.

Summary

This chapter demonstrates the clarity with which quite complicated
translation algorithms can be expressed in terms of tree walking.
By applying a simple mechanism recursively to every node of a
Boolean expression, it is possible to produce code which executes
a minimum of instructions in order to discover if the expression
has the value **true** or the value **false**.

The mechanisms presented in chapter 5 and in this chapter form
a solid base for the development of a translator. An enormous
proportion of the object code fragments are concerned with
calculation of values and with selecting paths of control through
the program. If efficient code fragments can be generated for
these crucial source program fragments and for the related
fragments which perform data structure access (chapter 9), non-
local data access and procedure call (section III) then an
acceptably efficient object program is assured.

7 Translating Statements and Declarations

Chapters 5 and 6 show the tree-walking mechanism to its best advantage, working on the translation of source program constructs whose efficient implementation is crucial to the efficiency of the object program. Code fragments for statements are rarely so crucial, particularly when the expressions which they contain are efficiently translated. This chapter therefore shows example procedures which translate statements by linking together the code fragments discussed in chapters 5, 6 and 9 and in section III.

Most declarations in a program translate into sections of code. Various chapters below discuss the translation of different declarations: record and array declarations are discussed in chapters 9 and 11, procedure declarations throughout section III. This chapter shows how the translation of a block or a procedure declaration links statement and declaration fragments together into a complete program.

Assignment Statement

Chapter 5 shows how to translate an arithmetic expression and chapter 9 shows how to generate code which calculates the address of an element of an array. Figure 7.1 shows 'TranAssignStat' and 'TranAddress' procedures which use these techniques in translating an assignment statement. I assume (see chapter 9) that the 'TranVecAccess' procedure assigns values to two global variables 'Address' and 'Modifier' whose values can be used in the STORE instruction. To simplify the TranAssignStat procedure I haven't shown the actions which it must carry out when evaluation of the left-hand-side expression requires all the registers and I have assumed a source language which permits the right-hand-side expression to be evaluated before the left-hand-side.

Figure 7.2 shows samples of the code which this procedure would generate. It recognises an assignment statement whose right-hand-side expression is the constant zero and generates a special code fragment for it: it would be fairly simple to make the

```
let TranAssignStat(nodep) be
{ let lhs, rhs = nodep.left, nodep.right
  let rhszero = false

  /* if rhs is zero, don't evaluate it */
  if ZeroConst(rhs) then rhszero := true
  else TranArithExpr(rhs, 1)

  /* store value in object denoted by lhs */
  TranAddress(lhs, 2)
  if rhszero then Gen(STOZ, 0, Address, Modifier)
  else Gen(STORE, 1, Address, Modifier)
}

let TranAddress(nodep, regno) be
  if nodep.type=name then
    Address, Modifier := nodep.descriptor.address, 0
  elsf nodep.type=VecAccess then
    TranVecAccess(nodep, regno) /* see chapter 9 */
  else
    CompilerFail("invalid node in TranAddress")
```

Figure 7.1 Translating an assignment statement

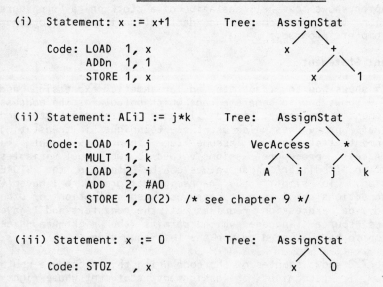

(i)   Statement: x := x+1   Tree: AssignStat

      Code: LOAD 1, x   x   +
            ADDn 1, 1
            STORE 1, x   x   1

(ii) Statement: A[i] := j*k   Tree: AssignStat

      Code: LOAD 1, j   VecAccess   *
            MULT 1, k   /   \   /   \
            LOAD 2, i   A   i   j   k
            ADD   2, #A0
            STORE 1, 0(2) /* see chapter 9 */

(iii) Statement: x := 0   Tree: AssignStat

      Code: STOZ , x   x   0

Figure 7.2 Code for some assignment statements

procedure recognise the other sub-optimisations illustrated in figure 2.11. Even without such improvements, the code produced by TranAssignStat is quite respectable. The discussion of TranVecAccess in chapter 9, however, shows some deficiencies in the code which is produced for an assignment statement such as

$$A[i-1] := A[i+5]$$

which makes more than one access to a vector: it would require the code optimisation techniques discussed in chapter 10 to make any significant improvement in this case.

'While' Statement

Figure 6.5 in chapter 6 shows how to translate a conditional (**if-then-else**) statement given a TranBoolExpr procedure which generates 'jumping code' for the expression part of the statement. Exactly the same mechanism can be used in translating a conditional iteration statement: figure 7.3 shows a 'TranWhileStat' procedure which does just this. Figure 7.4 shows the unremarkable code which it generates.

Figure 7.3 also shows, together with the TranLoopStat procedure of figure 7.5, how the use of global variables 'LoopLabel' and 'BreakLabel' can implement the BCPL **loop** and **break** statements, which allow premature repetition and termination of the iterative

---

```
let TranWhileStat(nodep) be
{ let Restart, Lt, Lf = newlabel(), newlabel(), newlabel()
  let OldLoop, OldBreak = LoopLabel, BreakLabel

  define(Restart) /* 'Restart' is beginning of expression */
  TranBoolExpr(nodep.expr, 1, Lt, Lf, 'true')

  /* execute statement if expression is true
   * allow loop and break statements within it
   * jump to re-evaluate expression afterwards
   */
  LoopLabel, BreakLabel := Restart, Lf
  define(Lt)
  TranStatement(nodep.stat)
  Gen(JUMP, 0, Restart)

  /* avoid execution of statement when expression is false
   * reset loop and break indicators
   */
  LoopLabel, BreakLabel := OldLoop, OldBreak
  define(Lf)
}
```

Figure 7.3 Translating a 'while' statement

statement within which they are contained. A **loop** statement will
transfer control to the label 'Restart' which re-evaluates the
expression, a **break** statement to the label 'Lf' which provides
exit from the **while** statement as a whole. By saving the values of
these variables and resetting them after the statement has been
translated, TranWhileStat allows the use of **loop** and **break**
statements in nested loops. The code for the escape statements is
a single JUMP instruction - it can be so simple because of the
mechanism used to handle the BCPL stack, discussed in chapter 14.

```
Statement: while a>b | x<y do <statement S>

Code:    %R: LOAD    1, a
             SKIPGT  1, b
             JUMP      , %t
             LOAD    1, x
             SKIPLT  1, y
             JUMP      , %f
         %t:  ....
             <code for statement S>
             ....
             JUMP      , %R
         %f:  ....
```

Figure 7.4 Code generated for a 'while' statement

```
let TranLoopStat(nodep) be TranEscape(LoopLabel)

let TranBreakStat(nodep) be TranEscape(BreakLabel)

let TranEscape(label) be
  if label=empty then
    Error("escape statement occurs outside loop")
  else
    Gen(JUMP, 0, label)
```

Figure 7.5 Translating 'break' and 'loop' statements

```
let TranStatement(nodep) be
  switchon nodep.type into
  { case AssignStat: TranAssignStat(nodep); endcase
    case WhileStat:  TranWhileStat(nodep); endcase
    case ForStat:    TranForStat(nodep); endcase
    case GoToStat:   TranGotoStat(nodep); endcase
         ....
    default: CompilerFail("invalid node in TranStatement")
  }
```

Figure 7.6 Part of the TranStatement procedure

The 'TranStatement' procedure, part of which is shown in figure 7.6, is a 'switch' procedure like TranArithExpr in chapter 5 or TranBoolExpr in chapter 6. It merely inspects the 'type' field of a statement node and calls the relevant statement-translating procedure.

BCPL 'for' Statement

The code fragment which represents a **for** statement is very similar to that of a **while** statement in that it contains code for a sub-

---

```
let TranForStat(nodep) be
{ let Stat, Increment = newlabel(), newlabel()
  let Test, Fin = newlabel(), newlabel()
  let var, initial = nodep.first, nodep.second
  let final, incr = nodep.third, nodep.fourth

  /* declare the variable for the duration of the loop */
  DeclareVariable(var)

  /* assign initial value to variable */
  TranArithExpr(initial, 1)
  Gen(STORE, 1, var.descriptor.address)
  Gen(JUMP, 0, Test)

  /* generate code for sub-statement */
  define(Stat)
  TranStatement(nodep.fifth)

  /* increment variable - value '1' is assumed
   * if increment expression is absent
   */
  define(Increment)
  if incr=empty | (incr.type=number & incr.value=1) then
    Gen(INCRST, 0, var.descriptor.address)
  else
   { TranArithExpr(incr, 1)
     Gen(ADDST, 1, var.descriptor.address)
   }

  /* test for end of iteration */
  define(Test)
  TranArithExpr(final, 1)
  Gen(SKIPLT, 1, var.descriptor.address)
  Gen(JUMP, 0, Stat)

  /* remove the descriptor of the variable */
  UnDeclareVariable(var)
}
```

Figure 7.7 Translating a 'for' statement

statement and code fragments which control the iterative execution of the sub-statement. The controlling fragments can be arranged before or after the sub-statement: in the 'TranForStat' procedure shown in figure 7.7 I have chosen to put them partly before the sub-statement and partly after it.

The semantics of the BCPL **for** statement are such that the 'increment' and 'final value' expressions are evaluated only once, before the first statement of the sub-statement: for simplicity the procedure shown in figure 7.7 produces code in which each of these expressions is evaluated each time round the loop. Also for simplicity I have omitted the manipulation of 'LoopLabel' and

---

Statement: **for** count = a+13 **to** 20 **do** <statement S>

Tree: ForStat

          [var]   [initial] [final] [incr] [statement]
          count   +   20   <S>
                    / \
                   a   13

          Code: LOAD   1, a
                   ADDn   1, 13
                   STORE   1, count
                   JUMP   , %T
            %S: ....
                   <code for statement S>
                   ....
            %I: INCRST   , count
            %T: LOADn   1, 20
                   SKIPLT 1, count
                   JUMP   , %S
            %F: ....

Figure 7.8 Code for a 'for' statement

Statement: **for** i = 1 **to** 20 **do** <statement S1>

Code: LOADn   1, 20
         STORE   1, i
  %S: ....
         <code for statement S1>
         ....
  %I: DECSKP   , i   /* decrement and skip if zero */
         JUMP   , %S
  %F: ....

Figure 7.9 Counting code for a 'for' statement

'BreakLabel' which is required to allow the use of **loop** and **break** statements within a **for** statement: **loop** would transfer to the label 'Increment', **break** to the label 'Fin'. The procedure is faithful to the BCPL definition, though, in that the controlling variable in the loop is declared at the beginning of the loop and 'undeclared' after the loop: this is the purpose of the 'DeclareVariable' and 'UnDeclareVariable' procedure calls in figure 7.7.

Figure 7.8 shows the code which would be produced by this procedure, given a sample statement. The only attempt which it makes to produce efficient code is to notice when the 'increment' expression is absent or has the value 1, and then to generate only one instruction which increments the value of the controlling variable, rather than two. This code is neither remarkably good nor remarkably bad. It is always worthwhile to study the instruction set of the object machine closely, to see whether any improvements can be made to the code fragments generated - even a single instruction saved can noticeably improve the speed of the object program.

Code optimisation can improve the execution of the loop by moving code out of it. If the value of the controlling variable is never used inside the loop then the repetitive fragments can be replaced by fragments which merely count the number of times the loop is executed - see figure 7.9. When the initial value, final value and increment expressions are constants then a combination of the 'counting' code of figure 7.9 and the standard technique illustrated in figure 7.8 can provide some minor savings in execution time.

FORTRAN 'DO' Statement

The translation of a DO loop is hardly different to that of a **for** statement. However the syntax of FORTRAN allows the user to make errors, an example of which is shown in figure 7.10, which are impossible using **for** statements and **begin-end** bracketing. Although it is possible to build a translator which works directly from the unstructured list of statements which defines a FORTRAN DO loop its operation is confusing and I therefore assume that the

---

```
    DO 1 I = 1,10
    <S1>
    <S2>
    DO 2 J = 3,25
    <S3>
  1 <S4>
    <S5>
  2 <S6>
```

Figure 7.10 Impermissible nesting of DO loops

syntax analyser builds a tree for the DO loop like that shown in figure 7.11.

The FORTRAN 66 standard imposed various restrictions on the execution of DO loops, almost universally applied in FORTRAN compilers then and since. Each of the initial value, final value and increment expressions must be an integer variable or a constant: if a variable, then the program must not alter the value of that variable during execution of the loop. The initial value of the controlling variable must not be greater than its final value, and the program must not alter the value of the controlling variable during execution of the loop. FORTRAN compilers are entitled to assume that the program obeys these restrictions and can exploit them to produce very efficient code for the loop - see

```
Source: DO 1 I = 1, 20
           <S1>
           <S2>
           ....
         1 <Sn>
```

Tree: DoLoop

     [var] [initial] [final] [incr] [stats]
       I   1   20   Compound

                              <S1> <S2> ... <Sn>

Figure 7.11 Structured description of DO loop

```
Source: DO 23 I = J1, J2
           <S1>
           <S2>
           ....
        23 <Sn>

Code:    LOAD    1, J1
         STORE   1, I
    %S: <code for statement S1>
        <code for statement S2>
         ...
    23: <code for statement Sn>
         INCRST  , I
         LOAD    1, J2
         SKIPLT 1, I
         JUMP    , %S
```

Figure 7.12 Code for a DO loop

figure 7.12 - but in so doing they perpetuate all sorts of FORTRAN idiosyncracies (the code shown in figure 7.12, for example, substantiates the myth that a FORTRAN DO loop is always executed once, no matter what the values of initial and final expressions in the DO statement). I don't show the procedure which translates a DO loop, since it is so similar to that shown in figure 7.7 which translates the BCPL **for** statement.

The use of a tree and a recursive tree-walking translator makes the translation of a 'nest' of DOs, shown in figure 7.13, quite trivial and straightforward. To translate the program from a linear list of statements is much more confusing: it means keeping lists of DO-terminating labels, checking that loops are properly nested and ensuring that, when several loops share the same terminating label, the code fragment which controls iteration of the <u>last</u> DO loop encountered comes <u>first</u> in the object program.

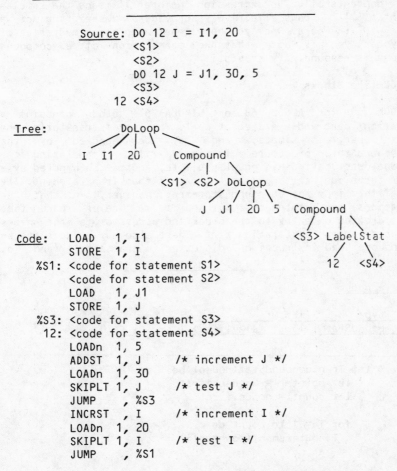

Figure 7.13 Code for nested DO loops

When using a tree the hierarchical structure of the program is revealed and the translator can make use of it. The example of the DC loop shows how much easier it is to compile a language which has structured statements than one which, like FORTRAN, COBOL or assembly code, linearises the few control structures which it possesses.

Compound Statements

A compound statement is a list or collection of statements. It can be represented by a list data-structure or by an n-ary node: figure 7.14 shows a procedure which handles an n-ary node. The node contains, in the field 'first', a count of the number of pointer fields held in the node: the 'TranCompoundStat' procedure takes each of these pointers and passes it to TranStatement for translation. The operator '@' means 'address of', the operator '!' means 'contents of'. The expression 'pointer!i' means the same as '!(pointer+i)' and thus effectively provides subscripting of a pointer to the node. Once you have penetrated these mysteries of BCPL syntax, you will agree that the translation of a compound statement is resoundingly trivial!

ALGOL-60-like Blocks

An ALGOL 60 (or ALGOL 68 or SIMULA 67) block contains a declaration part and a statement part. The job of translating the statement part is simple, and may be handled by the TranCompoundStat procedure of figure 7.14. Translating the individual declarations is equally simple, and may be handled by a similar technique, calling TranDecl rather than TranStatement. The block differs from the compound statement, however, in that the declarations and statements within it may refer to run-time objects created on entry to the block and accessed via the names introduced in the declaration part. There also may be some stack-handling overhead instructions, discussed in chapters 11 and 13,

---

Example node:

```
 _____type_____first_____ _____ _____        _____
|  CompoundStat  |  10  |  <s1>  |  <s2>  |  ....  |  <s10>  |
```

```
    let TranCompoundStat(nodep) be
    { let pointer = @nodep.first
      let count = nodep.first

      for i = 1 to count do
        TranStatement(pointer!i)
    }
```

Figure 7.14 Translating a compound statement

which must be executed on entry to and exit from a block.

Figure 7.15 shows a procedure which translates an ALGOL-60-like block. The 'declare' procedure is the object description phase discussed in chapters 1 and·8: it creates descriptors for each of the run-time objects denoted by the names introduced in the declaration part, it checks that a name isn't declared twice in the block and it links the descriptors into the symbol table. The procedure 'declarelabels' does the same for any labels declared in the statement part of the block. The 'undeclare' and 'undeclarelabels' procedures remove all these descriptors after the block has been translated. This object-description mechanism will produce the ALGOL 60 'scope' effect in which the body of a procedure declared in a particular block can contain references to any other procedure, data object or label declared in the block: in particular this makes it very simple to declare (and to translate!) mutually-recursive procedures.

The 'enter' and 'leave' procedures called from the TranBlock procedure generate the block entry and exit overhead instructions discussed in chapter 13. I assume that the TranDecl procedure, which is a 'switch' procedure like TranStatement, TranArithExpr and TranBoolExpr, generates code for every declaration which requires it. Array declarations, for example, may require code to allocate space for the array - see chapter 11 - pointer variable declarations may require code which initialises the pointer to 'empty' - see chapters 9 and 14 - and procedure declarations translate into a sequence of code which represents the body of the

---

```
let TranBlock(nodep) be
{ let declpart, statpart = nodep.first, nodep.second

    /* set up symbol table and generate entry overhead */
    declare(declpart); declarelabels(statpart)
    enter(nodep)

    /* translate declarations */
    { let pointer, count = @declpart.first, declpart.first

        for i = 1 to count do TranDecl(pointer!i)
    }

    /* translate statements */
    TranCompoundStat(statpart)

    /* generate exit overhead, reset symbol table */
    leave(nodep)
    undeclarelabels(statpart); undeclare(declpart)
}
```

Figure 7.15 Translating an ALGOL 60 block

procedure - see below and section III.

Procedure Declarations

A procedure declaration has three parts: a name, a heading and a

---

```
let TranProcDecl(nodep) be
{ let name, heading, body =
                        nodep.first, nodep.second, nodep.third
  let Exit, Endbody = newlabel(), newlabel()
  let OldExit = EndLabel

  /* jump round procedure body on entry to block */
  Gen(JUMP, 0, Endbody)

  /* set up symbol table, tell the loader the address
   * of the procedure and generate entry overhead
   */
  declare(heading); define(name.descriptor.address)
  prologue(nodep)

  /* set up ExitLabel for return and resultis
   * statements and translate the body
   */
  ExitLabel := Exit; TranStatement(body)

  /* define destination of return and resultis
   * statements and generate exit overhead
   */
  define(Exit); epilogue(nodep)

  /* reset ExitLabel and symbol table, define
   * destination of JUMP instruction above
   */
  ExitLabel := OldExit; undeclare(heading)
  define(Endbody)
}
```

Figure 7.16 Translating a procedure declaration

```
let TranReturnStat() be
  if ExitLabel=empty then Error("not inside procedure body")
  else Gen(JUMP, 0, ExitLabel)

let TranResultisStat(nodep) be
{ TranArithExpr(nodep.first, 1)
  TranReturnStat()
}
```

body. The heading gives the names of the parameters and specifications of their types, kinds, and so on. The body, in a block-structured language, is a single statement - which may of course be a block· or a compound statement. Just as in the translation of a block, descriptors for the parameter objects must be linked into the symbol table before the body is translated and removed afterwards.

The TranProcDecl procedure of figure 7.16 shows the translation of a procedure declaration. It informs the loader of the address of the procedure (I assume that the translator is using the symbolic-label technique discussed in chapter 4) and generates a JUMP instruction which ensures that the procedure body is not executed as part of the declaration sequence, but only when called from the body of the block in which it is declared. The 'prologue' and 'epilogue' procedures generate the procedure entry and exit overhead instructions discussed in section III. The global variable 'ExitLabel' can be used in JUMP instructions generated as the translation of **return** and **resultis** statements, in exactly the same way as the **loop** and **break** statements are handled in figure 7.11 above. Figure 7.17 shows example procedures.

Summary

This chapter includes example procedures which translate a range of important statement and declaration nodes. In each case the tree-walking technique allows the construction of a simple, straightforward and transparent translation procedure which generates accurate and reliable code. In many cases it would be relatively simple to improve the operation of the procedure to cater specially for nodes with special characteristics. The structured statements of modern languages are no harder to translate than the linear statements of an old-fashioned language such as FORTRAN or COBOL.

Other chapters add to the treatment given in this chapter. Section III as a whole deals with the code for procedure call/return and block entry/exit. Chapter 9 discusses the code for array and record declaration and access. Chapter 10 looks again at the code generated both for iterative statements and for the statements which they contain.

8 Creating and Using the Symbol Table

Chapters 1 and 4 justify the existence of a table which is used by the lexical analyser to correlate multiple occurrences of a single name and is used by the translation phases to convert occurrences of source program names into references to run-time objects. This table is called the <u>symbol table</u> in this book: it is sometimes called a 'cross-reference table' a 'name table' or an 'identifier table'. It is used by all the phases from lexical analysis to translation and, as chapter 20 shows, it may be used at run-time to help debug the program. The word 'table' is misleading since the information may be stored in a list-structure, a tree, or in any other kind of data structure.

It is fair to say that the symbol table is central to the operation of the compiler. In particular it is important that the lexical analyser finds names in the table as rapidly as possible, because each name or keyword it encounters in the source text requires it to search the symbol table. The translation phases use the information in the symbol table to produce an error report when a name is used incorrectly and therefore the design of the table will also affect the error reporting capabilities of the compiler.

The symbol table contains a collection of <name,descriptor> pairs. The first element of the pair contains the characters of the name itself: it is used by the lexical analyser to recognise repeated occurrences of the name and is included in error reports about program fragments which contain an occurrence of that name. The second element of the pair is an object-descriptor (or a collection of object-descriptors) which contains all the information so far collected about the run-time object (or objects) which a particular name has been declared to denote. As shown below, it is common for a single name to correspond to several object-descriptors. In many languages a name may be declared to denote a constant or a 'type' and in such a case the descriptor will describe that constant or type, rather than a run-time object.

Table Lookup

The task of the lexical analyser, confronted with the characters of a particular name, is to indicate to the syntax analyser that such an item has been encountered and to construct a unique identification of the item, which can be inserted into the tree and used by later phases to record and to access information about the run-time object (or objects) which that name denotes. This task can be conveniently performed if the lexical analyser converts every occurrence of each name into a pointer to the unique symbol table entry for that particular name. The pointer can be included in the tree and used by the object-description and translation phases to insert and access information about the object denoted by the name.

Programs are mostly made up of names and keywords so the lexical analyser will spend a great proportion of its time in searching the symbol table. In practice, provided the rest of the lexical analyser is coded efficiently, this activity can be one of those which determines the overall speed of the compiler and therefore the table lookup algorithm must be made as efficient as possible. The recipe for success is simple and easy to follow: for speed use hash addressing, for speed and ease of construction use hash addressing with chaining. I describe each of these mechanisms below: first, however, I discuss some simpler techniques of table lookup in order to make the superiority of the hash addressing mechanism doubly clear.

Figure 8.1 shows a general characterisation of the table-lookup problem. The major measure of efficiency is the <u>number of accesses</u> which are required to find a name in the table - the number of times the program goes round the **while** loop - and a subsidiary measure is the cost of adding a new name to the table.

```
let TableSearch(item) = valof
{ let entry = ... first entry ...

    /* look for previous occurrence of name */
    while entry\=empty do
      if entry.namepart = item then resultis entry
      else entry := ... next entry ...

    /* name is not in table - create new entry */
    entry := ... new entry ...
    entry.namepart := item
    entry.descriptor := empty
    resultis entry
}
```

Figure 8.1 The table-lookup problem

Sequential lookup

Sequential lookup is the first, most obvious and worst available technique. The first entry examined is T_0, the next is T_1, the next T_2, and so on. In a table of **N** names, the sequential lookup algorithm will, on average, make about **N**/2 accesses to find a name which is already in the table. In the 1950s and early 1960s people actually wrote compilers which used sequential lookup and which were amazingly slow in operation. In some cases it was found that a change to a hash-addressing mechanism speeded up the compiler as a whole by a factor of 10 or more!

Binary chop

If the names in a sequential table are ordered in some way, so that by comparing two names the lexical analyser can tell which comes first in the order, it is possible to produce a simple lookup algorithm which is faster than sequential lookup, although not as fast as hash addressing. Alphabetic ordering is commonly used, because it corresponds to the numerical ordering of character codes on most computers.

Figure 8.2 shows a 'binary chop' table lookup algorithm. Given a collection of names like that in figure 8.3, the algorithm will find the name i5 in only four accesses. The 't_i', 'm_i' and 'b_i' markers in figure 8.3 refer to the positions of the 'top', 'middle' and 'bottom' pointers during the ith access to the table. Binary chop is much better than sequential lookup and simple algebra shows that on average it takes about $(\ln_2 N - 1)$ accesses to search a table of **N** names.

```
let BinaryChopSearch(item) = valof
 { let bottom, top = 0, N

   while bottom<=top do
    { let middle = (bottom+top)/2
      let midentry = T+middle

      if midentry.namepart=item then resultis midentry
      elsf midentry.namepart<item then bottom := middle+1
      else top := middle-1
    }

   /* name is not in table - insert a new entry */
     ....
 }
```

Figure 8.2 Table lookup by binary chop

Name tree

Although the binary chop algorithm has relatively good lookup
performance, it is useless in practice because of the necessity to
insert new names into the table from time to time. If the lexical
analyser inserts the name i5a into the table of figure 8.3, for
example, it must move entries i1-i4 or i6-i15 to make room for the
new entry. A different representation of the table - the 'name
tree' illustrated in figure 8.4 - allows the binary chop mechanism
to be used as a practical technique. In this representation of the
table each name is stored together with two pointers: one to a
sub-tree of names earlier in the order, the other to a sub-tree of
names later in the order. The algorithm shown in figure 8.5 uses
these pointers to search the name tree.

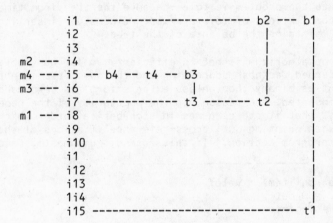

Figure 8.3 Searching by binary chop

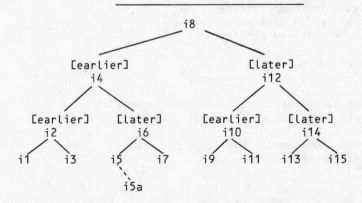

Figure 8.4 Name tree representation of an ordered table

With this representation of an ordered table, insertion of a name is extremely simple. When the chosen sub-tree is empty the algorithm creates a new entry and puts a pointer to it in the relevant node. For example, when searching for i5a in the tree of figure 8.4 the 'later' sub-tree of the name i5 will be found to be empty and therefore the 'later' pointer of i5 will be made to point to a new entry which contains the new name.

A perfectly balanced name tree would generate exactly the same sequence of comparisons as the ordered table and the binary chop algorithm. The tree is very rarely perfectly balanced, however, and when using an algorithm like that in figure 8.5, which inserts names into the table in the order in which they are encountered, it is possible to produce a table which is extremely unbalanced. Suppose, for example, that the names used in a source program occur in alphabetical order - then the name tree created by this algorithm will behave just as badly as a sequential table! The only solution to the problem is to re-balance the tree from time to time during compilation, or to use a more expensive insertion algorithm which maintains the balance of the tree.

The binary chop algorithm is not as efficient, so far as table lookup is concerned, as hash addressing and the name tree is not even as efficient as binary chop unless extra effort is expended when names are inserted. One reason for the popularity of the name tree mechanism is that it stores names in alphabetical order which can be useful when printing out 'cross-reference' listings of the names used in a program section. If this form of diagnostic aid

---

```
let NametreeSearch(item) = valof
{ let pointer = @root
  let entry = !pointer

  while entry\=empty do
  { if entry.namepart=item then resultis entry
    elsf entry.namepart<item then
      pointer := @entry.earlier
    else pointer := @entry.later

    entry := !pointer
  }

  /* name is not in tree: insert new entry with
   * empty 'descriptor', 'earlier' and 'later' fields
   */
  entry := node(name,item,empty,empty,empty);
  !pointer := entry
  resultis entry
}
```

Figure 8.5 Name-tree lookup algorithm

is to be used - and it has only dubious advantages in my opinion -
it would be better to use hash addressing during compilation of a
program, because of its speed, and to create a name tree at the
end of compilation in order to produce the cross-reference
listing.

Hash Addressing

It is possible to reduce the number of accesses required to find a
name to a minimum by using 'hash addressing'. The number of
accesses can easily be reduced to about four or five in a table of
a few hundred names and at this level the speed of the lookup
algorithm will no longer dominate the inner loop of the lexical
analyser.

The hash addressing mechanism works by selecting a 'first
entry' which depends on the characters of the item being searched
for in the table. If each possible name had a different 'first
entry' value then it would take only a single access to find it in
the table. However the number of possible names is enormous: even
in FORTRAN, which allows only up to six characters in a name,
there are more than a thousand million possible names and if the
implementation allows names of any length then the number is
effectively infinite. Given a symbol table of restricted size
many names in any source program will correspond to the same
'first entry' and collisions, which involve different names with
the same hash key, are therefore inevitable. Different mechanisms
handle such collisions in different ways: either by re-hashing or
by chaining.

In any hash-addressing technique the first step is to calculate
the 'first entry' address - the so-called hash key - from the
characters of the input item. The computation must be
deterministic and repeatable since it must produce the same hash
key for a particular item on each occurrence of that item. Some

---

A: Compute a number **H** from the characters of the item
   e.g. take the sum of the character codes
       or the sum of the words of the string which
           represents the item
       or the first word of the string
       etc.

B: From **H** compute a key (a table address) **K** which is
   modulo table size **N**
   e.g. (if **N** is prime) compute **H** rem **N**
       or (if $N=2^1$) square **H** and take 'i' bits
           from the result
       etc.

Figure 8.6 Computing a hash key

techniques for computing the key are shown in figure 8.6: a good
hash key computation will produce a value which depends on every
character in the item and on their order and will produce each
possible key with approximately equal frequency.   It is also
important that the key computation should be fairly simple, since
it must be carried out each time a name or a keyword is
encountered in the input.

It is simple to devise a key computation which works well given
a random distribution of names, but in practice the names in a
source program are not randomly invented. Programmers tend to use
names which differ only in the last few characters - for example
'processaword' and 'processachar' and often use very short names -
for example 'x', 'x1' and 'x1a'. It is important, therefore, to
test the performance of the key computation algorithm on some real
source programs. It is impossible to produce a perfect
distribution on every source program and you should not worry
unless examination of the symbol table shows some really serious
imbalance in the distribution of keys across the possible entries.

Re-hashing after a collision

Step B in figure 8.6 ensures that many names will correspond to
each possible hash key. The 're-hashing' mechanism handles the
resulting collisions, when the entry selected contains not the
item being searched for but some other item which has the same
hash key, by computing new keys K_1, K_2, etc. until either the item
is found or an empty entry is encountered. Figure 8.7 shows some
re-hashing mechanisms.

The aim in designing a re-hashing mechanism is to avoid
clustering. Figure 8.8 illustrates the clustering that can occur
when the linear re-hash mechanism is used. I assume in this
example that the entries arrive in alphabetical order. Names i2
and i3 have the same hash key: i2 arrives first and finds an empty
entry; i3 must fill the next entry in the table. The same thing
happens with i4 and i5. When i6 is encountered it collides with i5
even though the two names have different hash keys. The chain of
entries which includes i4 and i5 has clustered together with the
chain which includes i6. The number of entries in the cluster is
the sum of those in the separate chains and it will increase
rapidly as entries are added and the cluster extends to engulf
other chains.

The problem of clustering has nothing to do with the
distribution of hash keys over the available table addresses.
People have thought that it was, and have tried to separate the
chains by using the add-a-prime re-hash mechanism illustrated in
figure 8.7: the only effect is to cause clustering between chains
that are 'prime' entries apart rather than one entry apart. (The
clustering isn't so obvious to the eye when the table is
inspected, but it's there just the same!) In fact clustering will

occur in any re-hashing mechanism when the computation of the next
key depends only on the value of the current key, since then if
two chains contain the same key they must form a cluster.

The solution to the problem of clustering, so far as the re-
hashing mechanism is concerned, is to select the next key
depending on both the value of the current key and on the route by
which this key was reached. Then two chains which touch will
immediately separate since they cannot have arrived at the same
entry by exactly the same route. The add-the-hash mechanism adds
the value of the original key, which is different for each chain:
the quadratic re-hash mechanism increases the offset of the next

---

[all keys are modulo table size **N**]

a. $K_{n+1} = K_n + 1$ (linear re-hash)

b. $K_{n+1} = K_n + prime$ (add-a-prime re-hash)

c. $K_{n+1} = K_n + K_0$ (add-the-hash re-hash)

d. $K_n = 0.5n^2 + n + K_0$ (quadratic re-hash)

$[K_{n+1} = K_n + 2n + 1$ - i.e.
$K_1 = K_0 + 1$
$K_2 = K_1 + 3$
$K_3 = K_2 + 5$
        etc.]

Figure 8.7 Re-hashing mechanisms

```
                   name       descriptor
   i1 ------> |    i1    |             |

             ....

  12, i3 --> |    12    |             |
             |    i3    |             |

             ....

  i4, i5 --> |    i4    |             |
  i6 ------> |    i5    |             |
             |    i6    |             |

             ....
```

Figure 8.8 Clustering after linear re-hash

entry on each step of the search (each of these mechanisms requires that the table size is a prime number.) Of the two, quadratic re-hash gives the better anti-clustering performance.

There has been much analysis of the performance of hash addressing mechanisms given different re-hashing algorithms, mostly motivated by a desire to produce efficient lexical analysers. I believe that the effort is misguided, so far as compiler writing is concerned, because any re-hashing mechanism gives poor performance when the table is nearly full. No matter how cleverly you separate the chains to avoid clustering, if there are only a few empty entries in the table it will take a great number of accesses to find them! If re-hashing is used in a lexical analyser, therefore, it is necessary for the sake of efficiency to rebuild the table when it gets more than about 80% full. Rebuilding the table is a necessary function of a compiler which uses this hashing mechanism, since otherwise it could not compile a source program section which contains more names than there are table entries.

Chaining to avoid clustering

There is a simple solution which eliminates clustering and the need to rebuild the table: it works by storing a pointer in each table entry to a <u>chain</u> (a list) of entries with that particular hash key. Each element in the chain contains a pointer to the next element, or 'empty' if it is the last entry in the chain. To find an entry in the table the hash key is computed as before: if the table entry is empty a new chain is created, otherwise the chain pointed to by that entry is searched. If the item is not found in the chain, a new element is created using the same allocation mechanism as that for tree nodes (see chapter 3) and inserted into the chain. Figure 8.9 shows the table which would be created given the names shown in figure 8.8.

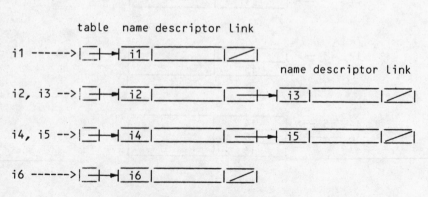

Figure 8.9 Chained hash table

The hash chaining mechanism is simple and provides good lookup performance. If a source program contains more names than there are entries in the table, the performance of the algorithm just falls off linearly, depending on the ratio of entries to names. The overhead of storing a single pointer together with each name is very slight and, I believe, worthwhile because of the advantages which it brings. Although each symbol table entry must carry the overhead of a pointer to other entries with the same hash key, each element in the hash table itself is only a single pointer and the number of entries in the hash table can be relatively small. Thus the actual amount of extra space occupied by the chained data structure, compared with that occupied when re-hashing is used, can be very small indeed.

Keywords in the symbol table

In many language implementations a 'keyword' or 'reserved word' such as **begin** can be written in exactly the same way as any source program name. The lexical analyser, on encountering a keyword, must recognise it and produce an item-description which records it as a simple-item (see chapter 4). It would be disappointing if the efficiency of the table lookup mechanism was wasted because every name which is encountered was first checked against a list of keywords before the symbol table is searched. A better mechanism is to store keywords in the symbol table, with their entries marked to show that they are not source program names and to show the item-code by which an occurrence of that keyword should be signalled to the syntax analyser. A uniform lookup mechanism can then find names in the symbol table and simultaneously distinguish between names and keywords.

A keyword is just a large punctuation mark and despite the fact that it may be stored in the symbol table it is important that the lexical analyser produces an item-code as the internal representation of a keyword. To represent a keyword by a pointer to the symbol table would be wrong because it would obscure the operation of the syntax analyser and tie it to a particular external representation of that keyword.

The keywords should be 'pre-hashed' into the symbol table each time the compiler runs, using the same lookup algorithm as is used to search for names in the table. The execution cost of this is minute, and it ensures that at the beginning of every compilation the symbol table is set up correctly no matter what changes are made to the lookup algorithm from time to time. It is certainly worth checking that the hash algorithm produces an even spread of keywords across the table: it would be unfortunate if several keywords were to have the same hash key.

Tables of constants

It may be worthwhile to keep a table of constants (strings, numbers) encountered in the source program, searched in the same way as the symbol table and indexed according to the value of the constant. The translator can use this table to avoid generating multiple copies of the same constant in the object code. (I once saw this trick described as 'constant Nationalisation': I think it should have been 'constant Rationalisation', but I prefer the misprint!)

Object Descriptions in the Symbol Table

Figure 8.10 shows the information which is required in general to describe a run-time object. A descriptor is created when the object-description phase processes a declaration. The 'kind' 'type' and 'accessing information' entries are determined by the details of the particular declaration. The 'run-time address' is set up by the object-description phase as discussed below. In compilers for many languages object-descriptors may be linked together in various ways. The descriptor of a procedure, for example, will contain a pointer to a descriptor for each of the parameters of that procedure, which may also be accessible via the entry for the name of that parameter. It is common for a single name to correspond to more than one descriptor: for this and other reasons the 'descriptor' field in the symbol table entry will normally be a pointer to a list of descriptor-records rather than the descriptor-record itself.

In simple languages the 'type' field of a descriptor[1] can be an integer which identifies one of a small fixed number of types. Where the source language allows the user to invent new types this field must contain a pointer to a type-descriptor, which might for example define the layout of a particular record-type. (Chapter 9 shows an example of the kind of symbol table layout that might

---

   (i) Kind of object (variable, array, procedure etc.)
  (ii) Type of object
 (iii) Run-time address of object
 (iv) Accessing information
      e.g. (for an array) dimensionality, bounds
           (for a procedure) list of parameter descriptors
           (for COBOL or PL/1 variables) hierarchical
                    qualification pointers
      (etc.)

Figure 8.10 Contents of a symbol table descriptor

---

1 Not to be confused with the 'type' field which identifies a tree node.

result.) In a compiler for such a language the descriptors in the symbol table will not all describe run-time objects: however I shall stick to the term 'object description' because it identifies the main task of the phase.

It is worth emphasising once more that none of the information shown in figure 8.10 is of interest to the syntax analyser. If the analysis of a fragment of program - its division into sub-fragments - were to depend on the declaration of names in the source program then the user would find the language awfully confusing to use. Even though object-description may be carried out as a subroutine of the syntax analyser in a two-pass compiler, the information held in the descriptor is only of interest in translation.

Once a fragment has been analysed to produce a tree, though, the interpretation which is placed upon it - its translation into object code - depends crucially on the contents of the symbol table descriptors associated with the names within that fragment: this may extend, as it does in ALGOL 68, to the interpretation of some names as additional operators in the language. The contents of the descriptor are used by the translator both to check the validity of a use of the name and also to generate instructions which access the run-time object denoted by that name.

Assigning addresses to data objects

Variable names denote run-time memory cells. Data-structure names denote run-time collections of memory cells. The main task of the object-description phase, for these kinds of names, is to insert a run-time address in the symbol table descriptor with which they are associated. This enables the translation phases to generate instructions which will refer to the relevant cell or collections of cells, merely by mentioning the run-time address.

The fundamental principle of compile-time storage allocation is the data frame. Each logical subdivision of a program which may contain a declaration - a procedure, a subroutine, a block[1] - possesses its own particular data frame. The object-description phase can tell which data frame any memory cell or data-structure belongs to. By allocating data objects to consecutive locations within the data frame as their declarations are processed, it can determine the relative position of a data object - its offset - within the data frame. Use of a 'dope vector' to access a variable-sized object - see chapters 9 and 11 - means that the object-description phase can assign a fixed address within the

---

1 Chapter 13 shows how it is possible to allocate data frames only to procedures and not to blocks, in order to maximise the efficiency of run-time storage access. I ignore this mechanism in this chapter.

data frame even to variable-sized data structures such as ALGOL 60's 'dynamic arrays'.

In the case of 'statically allocated' data objects which are not stored on a stack - which includes every data object in languages such as FORTRAN and COBOL - there is little more to do. The translator can include the offset within the data frame in the address part of any instruction which accesses the object and can request the loader to relocate the instruction (see chapter 4) by adding the run-time address of the data frame. In FORTRAN, for example, all run-time addresses are either calculated from the base address of a particular COMMON area or from the base of the data frame which is allocated for memory cells local to the current program unit. In COBOL, so far as data frames are concerned, the matter is even easier since there is only one program section which may declare data structures.

Section III shows that there is little more to do even for objects held in data frames on the run-time stack. At run-time there will be a number of pointers into the stack, each of which will point to the base of a particular data frame. To implement an access to a particular data object the translator will, if necessary, generate instructions which move the pointers so that one of them points to the relevant data frame, followed by an instruction which accesses the object by using that pointer together with the offset which is recorded in its symbol table descriptor.

In every case, therefore, the information <data frame, offset> is sufficient for the needs of the translation phases. In the case of a single-cell data object the information makes up the address of the cell itself: in the case of a multi-cell object it may be the address of the first cell of the object or, as in the case of an array or vector discussed in chapters 9 and 11, the address of the first cell of a 'dope vector' which will at run-time contain information about the data object itself. In the translation algorithms in this section and in section III I have used the notation 'nodep.descriptor.address' as a shorthand to indicate the use by the translator of the data frame and offset information stored in the symbol table descriptor.

Assigning addresses to labels and procedures

The run-time address associated with a label or a procedure cannot be calculated in the same way as that of a data object. However the descriptor must still contain run-time address information. The problem is that the source program may include a so-called forward reference to the object - a reference which appears in the source text before the position at which the label or procedure is declared. When this occurs, the translator must process the reference to the object before the instructions which it labels (or the procedure body which it denotes) have been translated and therefore before the run-time address of the object can be determined.

In a two-pass compiler the section of program which contains a label or procedure declaration will be processed by the object-description phase before it is translated. During translation of the program section the symbol table descriptor will record the fact that the object in question is a label or a procedure, but will not record its address. The translator must use one of the 'fixup' mechanisms discussed in chapter 4: it can shift the burden entirely onto the loader by handling forward references via specially invented symbolic labels or it can use 'fixup chains' to handle all forward references. Another solution is to allocate an extra memory cell and to generate instructions which refer to the label or procedure indirectly via that cell. When the run-time address is known, the translator can issue loader commands to initialise the contents of the cell.

Single Names with Multiple Descriptors

Figure 8.10 shows that in the case of a procedure or a structured data object the descriptor which is associated with a name may contain pointers to other descriptors. Descriptors will also be interlinked when a single name is used to identify more than one run-time object. In block-structured languages, for example, a name may be used at different points in the program to refer to different objects. In COBOL and in PL/1 a name may be used to refer to several objects at the same point in the program and uses of the name must be 'qualified' to select one of the possible objects. A similar possibility arises, discussed in chapter 9, when a name may be used to select different fields in different types of record at the same point in the program.

For the purposes of lexical analysis, however, there can only be a single symbol table entry for each individual name and therefore it is inevitable that there may be several object descriptors held in each symbol table entry. The task of the translator is to discover which of the available descriptors is to be used when a name occurs in a fragment of the source program. In this chapter I discuss the 'hierarchical qualification' facility in COBOL and a symbol table mechanism which provides the scope effects required in block-structured languages.

Hierarchical qualification in COBOL

The hierarchical qualification facility in COBOL and PL/1 makes it necessary to have more than one descriptor associated with a name and necessary also to inter-link the descriptors which describe the fields of a data structure. Names may be declared to denote single objects or collections of objects: each element in a collection can itself be a collection, so that the organisation of elements within a data structure is hierarchical. If a name is used within the program only to denote a particular data object or collection of objects it can be used 'unqualified': if it is used to denote more than one object or collection of objects it must be qualified as

<child> OF <ancestor>
or
<child> OF <ancestor> OF <older ancestor>
etc.

where 'ancestor' is any name in the hierarchy above the child.

Figure 8.11 shows a symbol table structure in which there is a field in a data structure named ACCESS which has sub-fields YEAR, MONTH and DAY, and another field called CREATION which has fields called DAY, MONTH and YEAR. Each descriptor points back to its parent descriptor so that the hierarchy can be traced 'upwards': each descriptor points to the name with which it is associated so that the ancestor can be identified. A simple matching algorithm

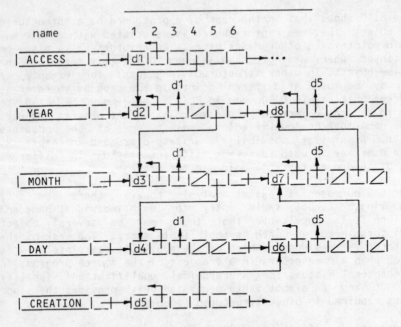

Entry 1: object description
2: pointer back to symbol table entry
3: upward hierarchy pointer (parent)
4: downward hierarchy pointer (eldest child)
5: sideways hierarchy pointer (younger sibling)
6: descriptor chain

Figure 8.11 Symbol table for hierarchical qualification

can now decide that 'DAY OF CREATION' refers to the object described by descriptor d6 in figure 8.11, that 'DAY OF ACCESS' refers to the object described by descriptor d4, but that unqualified 'DAY' is ambiguous and therefore an error.

The COBOL hierarchy can be used in two directions: the statement 'MOVE CORRESPONDING ACCESS TO CREATION' must be translated so that the value held in the object described by d2 is moved to the object described by d8, d3 to d7 and d4 to d6. Each collection descriptor has therefore to indicate its sub-fields - a standard computer-science trick to do this is to make each collection descriptor point to the descriptor of its first sub-field and to make each sub-field descriptor point to its neighbour. In this way arbitrarily large collections may be pointed to with a fixed-size descriptor: entries 4 and 5 in the structure shown in figure 8.11 do just this.

Block-structuring and scope

In block-structured languages such as ALGOL 60, ALGOL 68, PASCAL or PL/1 a single name can refer to different objects in different blocks of the program. The translator must discover which of the various possible objects is intended by noting the context in which the name occurs. The simplest technique is to maintain a list of descriptors in each symbol table entry and to manipulate the list during translation so that the descriptor at the front of the list is always the currently relevant one. All that is required is to collect together the descriptors for a block or procedure (or whatever program section can declare objects). Just before translation of the section commences, each of these descriptors is inserted at the front of the relevant descriptor list; when translation of the section is over, each descriptor can be removed from its list. This is the function of the 'declare' and 'undeclare' procedures called from TranBlock and TranProcDecl in chapter 7.

To remove the descriptors after a block has been translated it is possible to trace through all the declarations in the block and to remove the first descriptor associated with each name declared there. An alternative mechanism is to link together all the descriptors for the names declared in a block as they are created and to use this link to remove the names at the end of the block - as with the COBOL descriptors above, the mechanism requires that each descriptor contain a pointer to the symbol table entry with which it is associated. There are a variety of other possible techniques. If the descriptors are to be used to create a run-time debugging table (see chapter 20) then it may be necessary to preserve them after they have been unlinked from the symbol table entry.

Whichever method is used, the effect is the same, and figure 8.12 shows the way in which the descriptor list would change

during the translation of a sample ALGOL 68 program. Note that
this mechanism ensures that whenever the name denotes no object at
all the descriptor list is empty - which is the situation
recognised by the translator when it produces an error report
'undeclared identifier X'. In effect each descriptor list mimics
the operation of a separate descriptor stack.

Summary

The symbol table is used to correlate the separate occurrences of
a name during compilation of a program. Because the lexical
analyser must search the table each time it encounters a name or
keyword in the source program, it should be searched by a 'hash
addressing' technique for maximum efficiency. It's convenient to
use the symbol table to recognise keywords. It may be useful to
build a similar table which correlates multiple uses of particular

---

```
begin co (i) in the outer block X is undeclared oc
      ...
      begin int X;
            ... co (ii) in block 1 X is an int oc
            begin real X;
                  ... co (iii) in block 2 X is a real oc
            end;
            ... co (iv) X is an int again oc
            begin bool X;
                  ... co (v) in block 3 X is a bool oc
            end;
            ... co (vi) and once again an int oc
      end;
      ... co (vii) back in the outer block and undeclared oc
      begin string X;
            ... co (viii) in block 4 X is a string oc
      end;
      ... co (ix) and finally X is undeclared* again oc
end;
```

State of descriptor list:

(i)	after program **begin:**	empty
(ii)	after block 1 **begin:**	D1(**int**)
(iii)	after block 2 **begin:**	D2(**real**), D1(**int**)
(iv)	after block 2 **end:**	D1(**int**)
(v)	after block 3 **begin:**	D3(**bool**), D1(**int**)
(vi)	after block 3 **end:**	D1(**int**)
(vii)	after block 1 **end:**	empty
(viii)	after block 4 **begin:**	D4(**string**)
(ix)	after block 4 **end:**	empty

Figure 8.12 Block-structure effects in the symbol table

constants in the source program.

The descriptors held in the symbol table give information about the run-time objects which source program names denote. An important component of this information is the run-time address of an object. By keeping track of locations within a data frame the object description phase can assign addresses to all data objects: the translator or the loader can assign addresses to labels and procedures. The information in a descriptor is inserted when a declaration is processed by the object-description phase and is used by the translation phases both to check the validity of use of the name and to generate the instructions which will manipulate the run-time object.

In many languages a name may describe more than one object in the program. The descriptors associated with a name will reflect the language structures that give rise to them - in COBOL a hierarchy, in ALGOL 60 a list or stack of descriptors.

9 Accessing an Element of a Data Structure

Compiled languages usually have one or more of the kinds of data structures discussed in this chapter. <u>Records</u> are like the nodes of the parse tree used in the examples of this book - multi-element objects which contain a collection of values, some of which may be pointers to other such objects. Accessing an element of a record, via the name of that element, is relatively efficient and may be compile-time checked for validity.

<u>Vectors</u> and <u>arrays</u> are random-access storage areas indexed according to the value of a subscript expression; accessing an element of an array involves calculation of the address of that element, which may be an expensive activity. Much effort can usefully be expended on making array access less expensive and I describe two alternative mechanisms of address calculation.

In this chapter I discuss the code fragments which implement data structure access without showing example translation procedures in every case. I show a translation procedure which generates fairly straightforward code for a vector access and one which generates code for a PASCAL-like record access: for the other examples it would be tedious to display translation procedures which had only minor differences from these two.

The code fragments discussed in this chapter are as crucial as those discussed elsewhere. This chapter shows the tree-walking translation mechanism at its worst, however, because in translating a source program fragment which makes multiple reference to a data structure element, a tree walker cannot easily prevent unnecessary re-calculation of the address of that element in the object code.

Accessing an Element of a Vector

The symbol table descriptor of an array will give its dimensionality, the bounds of each dimension if they are known at compile-time, and its address within a particular data frame.

This address, in a compiler for a language which allows 'dynamic arrays', will normally be that of a fixed-size <u>dope vector</u> which at run-time will contain the address of the actual elements of the array together with information about its dimensionality and its actual bounds.

I consider first the case of a vector, which in programming language terms is just a single-dimension array. The 'dope vector' will contain at run-time three items of information

  #V0 - the address of the element V[0] (note that this address may be outside the bounds of the space allocated to the elements of the vector, for example if it is declared as V[2:24]).

  #V1 - the lower bound given in the declaration of the vector.

  #V2 - the upper bound given in the declaration of the vector.

The latter two pieces of information are useful for the purposes of run-time error detection and may also be used when the vector is passed as an argument in a procedure call (see chapter 13). Chapter 11 shows how the 'dope vector' can be set up at block entry: figure 9.1 shows a 'TranVecAccess' procedure which generates code that uses the contents of the 'dope vector' to access an element of the vector proper. The procedure assigns values to two global variables 'Address' and 'Modifier' which can

---

```
let TranVecAccess(nodep, regno) be
{ let vecname, subscript = nodep.left, nodep.right
  let vecdescr = vecname.descriptor

  if vecdescr=empty then
    Error("undeclared name", vecname)
  elsf vecdescr.kind \= vector then
    Error("not a vector name", vecname)

  if subscript.kind=number then
  { Gen(LOAD, regno, vecdescr.address)
    Address := subscript.value; Modifier := regno
  }
  else
  { TranArithExpr(subscript, regno)
    Gen(ADD, regno, vecdescr.address)
    Address := 0; Modifier := regno
  }
}
```

Figure 9.1 Translating accesses to a vector element

be used in the generation of instructions by the calling procedure. Thus TranAssignStat (chapter 7) can insert these values into a STORE instruction, a procedure called by TranArithExpr (chapter 5) or TranBoolExpr (chapter 6) could use them in a LOAD, ADD, MULT (or whatever) instruction.

Figure 9.2 shows how the code produced by TranVecAccess would be used in code for expressions and assignment statements. Code (a) shows how an element of the vector can be accessed in the most general case and code (b) shows the slightly more efficient code fragment which is used to access a constant-subscript element. Code (c) shows how disappointing the code can be in some cases (code optimisation could do something about this code).

Figure 9.3 shows the code which could be produced if TranVecAccess catered specially for cases in which the subscript was <expr>+<constant> or <expr>-<constant>. However in this example it is in fact unnecessary to recalculate the address of V[i] and code optimisation might exploit this to produce a more efficient code fragment. The optimised code that could be produced is shown in the right-hand-column of figure 9.3: although a tree-walker might be designed to produce this code for the example shown it would fail to produce optimal code in general.

```
(a) Source: V[i] := x          (c) Source: V[i-1] := V[i+1]

    Code: LOAD  1, x               Code: LOAD  1, i
          LOAD  2, i                     ADDn  1, 1
          ADD   2, #V0                   ADD   1, #V0
          STORE 1, 0(2)                  LOAD  1, 0(1)
                                         LOAD  2, i
(b) Source: V[3] := y                    SUBn  2, 1
                                         ADD   2, #V0
    Code: LOAD  1, y                     STORE 1, 0(2)
          LOAD  2, #V0
          STORE 1, 3(2)
```

Figure 9.2 Code to access a vector

```
Source: V[i-1] := V[i+1]

Simply translated:                 'Optimised':
        LOAD  1, i                     LOAD  1, i
        ADD   1, #V0                   ADD   1, #V0
        LOAD  1, 1(1)                  LOAD  2, 1(1)
        LOAD  2, i                     STORE 2, -1(1)
        ADD   2, #V0
        STORE 1, -1(2)
```

Figure 9.3 Improved vector access code

The procedure of figure 9.1 assumes that each element of a vector occupies a single memory cell. When accessing a vector of multi-cell objects (ALGOL 68 **struct**s, PASCAL **record**s, FORTRAN COMPLEX variables) or parti-cell objects (characters or bits) it is necessary to adjust the subscript by multiplying, dividing or shifting to produce the correct offset from the base of the array. Every element of a vector must occupy the same number of memory cells as every other element, and the size is known at compile-time, so the computation of an address can be fairly efficient, at least in the case of a vector of multi-cell objects. It is worth exploiting any bit- or byte-addressing instructions which the object machine may possess to access a vector of parti-cell elements: if there are no such instructions then perhaps it is best to store each element of the vector in a separate cell to preserve accessing efficiency.

Fixed-size vectors

In an implementation of a recursive programming language, access to the dope vector must be via an index register which points to the base of a particular data frame (see chapter 11). Thus it is impossible to combine the 'ADD' and 'STORE' instructions in the code fragments which access elements of the vector, shown in figures 9.2 and 9.3, unless the object machine has 'double indexing' instructions. However in some source languages the size of a vector must be fixed at compile-time - notably this is so in PASCAL, in FORTRAN and in most system-programming languages - and in such a case access to a constant-subscript element of a vector can be made more efficient. The actual position of the vector elements in the data frame can be fixed by the object-description phase and therefore the address of a vector element with a constant subscript can be determined by the translator.

In the case of fixed-size vectors held in 'static' storage - all vectors in FORTRAN - it is possible to go further still towards efficient vector access. The address of the first element of the vector is a constant and can be included in the LOAD or STORE (or whatever) instruction which accesses the vector. Figure

---

(a) Source: V(I) = X

```
Code: LOAD  1, X
      LOAD  2, I
      STORE 1, <#V-1>(2)
```

(b) Source: V(3) = Y

```
Code: LOAD  1, Y
      STORE 1, <#V+2>
```

(c) Source: V(I-1) = V(I+1)

```
Code: LOAD  1, I
      LOAD  1, #V(1)
      LOAD  2, I
      STORE 1, <#V-2>(2)
```

Figure 9.4 Code to access a FORTRAN vector

9.4 shows the code that can be produced: '#V' is the address of vector element V(1). The fact that this code is possible for FORTRAN on most machines, but not for more modern languages, shows that machine design lags behind language design. The ICL 2900 series machines have instructions which both access an element of a data frame on the stack and allow modification via an index register at the same time - this allows efficient access to a vector in a recursive programming language.

Run-time checks on vector access

Code like that shown in figures 9.2, 9.3 or 9.4 is dangerous! When the value of a subscript expression is accidentally outside the bounds of of the vector the effects are unpredictable. If the object program attempts to assign a value to such a non-existent vector element it may overwrite the contents of other data structures or even the instructions of the program. A few machines have instructions which simultaneously access the vector and check that the subscript is within bounds, but on most machines it is necessary to include instructions in the vector accessing code which check the validity of each subscript as it is used. Constant-subscript accesses to a fixed size vector can be checked at compile-time: all other accesses need a run-time check.

   Figure 9.5 shows code which checks access to a vector. The error-checking code executes two SKIP instructions, which is about a one-third increase in the cost of execution of the statement. Checking the bounds of vector and array access is an inherently expensive business and for this reason most compilers make its inclusion optional. It is worth remarking that in the absence of instructions to the contrary the compiler should always include run-time checks on vector access (together with as many other diagnostic aids as it can) and it should oblige experienced users to request the exclusion of run-time checks. It is the novice who needs the assistance which this code can give, but the novice who doesn't know how to ask for it!

```
Source: V[i*j] := z

Code: LOAD  1, z
      LOAD  2, i
      MULT  2, J
      ADD   2, #V0
        SKIPLT 2, #V1    /* check against lower bound */
        SKIPLE 2, #V2    /* and against upper bound */
        JSUB   L, error-in-vector-subscript
      STORE 1, 0(2)
```

Figure 9.5 Checking the bounds of vector access

Vectors as arguments in a procedure call

The 'dope vector' discussed above contains all the information necessary to access a vector: therefore in the case of a vector passed as an argument in a procedure call the 'argument information' discussed in chapter 12 should be the dope vector, or perhaps a pointer to it so that the called procedure can make a copy in its own data space. Access to the parameter vector from the called procedure is then no less efficient than access to a local vector. In the case of an ALGOL 60 vector passed by value, the called procedure must copy the elements of the argument vector into its own data frame and then create a new dope vector which addresses the copy.

An element of a vector is a simple data object. When passed as a 'value' argument, it should be treated as if it appeared on the right-hand-side of an assignment statement and should be processed by the TranArithExpr procedure of chapter 5; when passed as a 'reference' or 'address' argument it should be processed by the TranAddress procedure of chapter 7.

Accessing an Element of an Array

When an array has more than one dimension the code to access an element within it must be more complicated. The use of an index or address-modifier register in an instruction provides hardware assistance with vector access (for FORTRAN vectors at least) but few machines have instructions which can do the job directly for multi-dimensional arrays. The two access mechanisms most frequently used are multiplicative subscript calculation - obligatory in the case of FORTRAN programs - and indirect access via pre-calculated vectors of addresses, in Britain often called 'Iliffe vectors'. Multiplicative access can be more expensive to execute than Iliffe vector access, but the latter may impose an overhead on block entry when the address vectors must be initialised.

Multiplicative subscript calculation

The definition of FORTRAN 66 includes a mechanism of subscript calculation which effectively converts access to an element of a multi-dimensional arrays into access to a vector which contains the same number of elements

to access $A(I,J,K)$ after a declaration DIMENSION $A(d1,d2,d3)$ calculate a subscript S:

$$S = (K-1)*d1*d2 + (J-1)*d1 + I$$

Furthermore the language definition declares that only the magnitude of the subscript S counts, not the magnitudes of the individual subscript expressions I, J and K - it is valid to

access A(-10, -10, 100000) if the calculation of S finishes within
the bounds (1:d1*d2*d3) of the notional vector!

Calculating the subscript is an expensive business but there is
some room for manoeuvre, given the restricted forms of permitted
subscript expressions in FORTRAN, by exploiting simple algebra. In

---

```
Source:        DIMENSION A(10,20,5)
               ....
               A(I,J,K) = X
               ....

Calculation:   S = (K-1)*d1*d2 + (J-1)*d1 + I
                 = (K*d2+J)*d1+I - (d2*d1+d1)
                 = (K*20+J)*10+I - 210

Code:  LOAD   1, X
       LOAD   2, K
       MULTn  2, 20
       ADD    2, J
       MULTn  2, 10
       ADD    2, I
         SKIPLTn 2, 211    /* check (lower bound + 210) */
         SKIPLEn 2, 1210   /* check (upper bound + 210) */
         JSUB    L, error-in-array-access
       STORE   1, <#A-211>(2)
```

Figure 9.6 Code which accesses a FORTRAN array

```
Source:        DIMENSION A(10,20,5)
               ....
               A(I+1, J-4, K+2) = Z
               ....

Calculation:   S = (K+2-1)*d2*d1 + (J-4-1)*d1 + I+1
                 = (K*d2+J)*d1+I + (d2*d1-5*d1+1)
                 = (K*20+J)*10+I + 151

Code:  LOAD   1, Z
       LOAD   2, K
       MULTn  2, 20
       ADD    2, J
       MULTn  2, 10
       ADD    2, I
         SKIPLTn 2, -150 /* check (lower bound - 151) */
         SKIPLEn 2, 849  /* check (upper bound - 151) */
         JSUB    2, error-in-array-access
       STORE   1, <#A+150>(2)
```

Figure 9.7 Simplifying FORTRAN array subscript calculation

most situations the best technique of subscript calculation is that given in figure 9.6 together with the code which exploits it ('#A' is the address of element A(1,1,1) of the array). The procedure which generates this code is not shown - it isn't very different from the TranVecAccess procedure shown above. The FORTRAN 66 language definition requires the object program to check only the overall validity of the subscript calculated during the array access and not the validity of the subscript expressions which make it up. Error-checking code for a FORTRAN array, also shown in figure 9.6, is then very similar to the vector-access case shown in figure 9.5.

FORTRAN subscripts are restricted in form, and this restriction can lead to efficient access to elements of an array in many cases. Figure 9.7 shows an example: similar code can be generated for access to fixed-size arrays in any language.

The multiplicative mechanism can by used to access elements of an array in a language other than FORTRAN. If the 'dope vector' for an array contains the address of element A[0,0,...0] then the need for algebraic juggling is reduced (note once again that this element may not lie within the bounds of the array and this may give difficulty if its notional address turns out to be outside the bounds of the object program's data store). The dope vector which describes a three-dimensional array could be laid out as shown in figure 9.8: code to access an element of the array could then be as shown in figure 9.9.

The overhead of checking the validity of each individual subscript expression is enormous - in figure 9.9 it more than doubles the length of the code fragment which accesses an element of an array. The expense could be reduced a little if the information in the dope vector were slightly re-organised, but a practical compromise may be to adopt the FORTRAN solution and only check that the final subscript is within bounds. If the dope vector contains additional elements

```
#AL = (#A1l*#A1s)+(#A2l*#A2s)+#A3l
#AU = (#A1u*#A1s)+(#A2u*#A2s)+#A3u
```

then the overall calculation can be checked with only two instructions. This form of check will not detect every run-time

---

#A0 - the address of A[0,0,0]
#A1l - the lower bound of the first dimension of the array
#A1u - the upper bound of the first dimension of the array
#A1s - the size of the first dimension - i.e. (#A1u-#A1l+1)
#A2l, #A2u, #A2s - information about the second dimension
#A3l, #A3u, #A3s - information about the third dimension

Figure 9.8 Dope vector for a three-dimensional array

error but will at least mean that an invalid subscript in an access to the array cannot cause accidental damage to any other data structures in the memory.

Non-multiplicative array address calculation.

An array need not be treated as a random-access 'plane' or 'cube' which contains individual memory cells, addressed by an expensive address-calculation algorithm. Since most object machines provide vector addressing in hardware, via address modification registers,

---

Source: A[i,j,k] := x

With full error-checking:
```
     LOAD  1, x
     LOAD  2, i
      SKIPLT  2, #A1l
      SKIPLE  2, #A1u
      JSUB   L, error...
     MULT  2, #A1s
      LOAD   3, j
      SKIPLT  3, #A2l
      SKIPLE  3, #A2u
      JSUB   L, error...
    ADDr  2, 3
     MULT  2, #A2s
      LOAD   3, k
      SKIPLT  3, #A3l
      SKIPLE  3, #A3u
      JSUB   L, error...
    ADDr  2, 3
    ADD   2, #AO
    STORE 1, 0(2)
```

With minimal error-checking:
```
     LOAD  1, x
     LOAD  2, i
     MULT  2, #A1s
     ADD   2, j
     MULT  2, #A2s
     ADD   2, k
      SKIPLT  2, #AL
      SKIPLE  2, #AU
      JSUB   L, error...
     ADD   2, #AO
     STORE 1, 0(2)
```

Figure 9.9 Access to a three-dimensional array

Declaration: **array** AI[1:n,0:m]

Address
Vector   Array

Figure 9.10 Addressing vectors (Iliffe vectors)

it's profitable to think of an array in a different light, as a hierarchical structure of vectors. A two-dimensional (rectangular) array, for example, can be thought of as a vector of vectors. In figure 9.10 the vertical column is an addressing (Iliffe) vector, each element of which contains a pointer to element [0] of a particular row-vector. In the same way, a three-dimensional array can be thought of as a vector of two dimensional arrays — i.e. a vector of vectors of vectors. This would be represented as a vector of pointers to column vectors, each element of each column vector containing a pointer to a row vector. In general an n-dimensional array can be seen as a vector of (n-1)-dimensional arrays, each of which is a vector of (n-2) dimensional arrays, and so on.

Suppose that the dope vector for the array AI shown in figure 9.10 contains a pointer to element [0] of the addressing vector and that each element of the addressing vector contains a pointer to element [0] of its row-vector: then the code to access an element of AI can be as shown in figure 9.11. On a machine with a relatively slow MULT instruction (or no MULT instruction at all!) this code will be significantly faster than the multiplicative calculation of figure 9.9.

The addressing vector mechanism could regard an array as a structure of column-vectors or a structure of row-vectors with equal facility. The row-vector arrangement is more convenient in practice because of the conventional way in which iterative access to an array is usually written in programs which use arrays — figure 9.12 shows an example. When translating such a source program it is possible to calculate the row-address once per iteration of the outer loop, and to use vector-addressing of the row throughout the inner loop. This is an optimisation technique, of course, and chapter 10 discusses a similar technique which

---

```
Statement: AI[i,j] := a

Code:   LOAD    1, a
        LOAD    2, #AI0 /* address of Iliffe vector */
        ADD     2, i    /* address of element i */
        LOAD    2, 0(2) /* address of row-vector i[0] */
        ADD     2, j    /* address of AI[i,j] */
        STORE   1, 0(2)
```

Figure 9.11 Non-multiplicative array access

```
for i := ...... do
   for j := ....... do
      A[i,j] := .....;
```

Figure 9.12 Row-addressing of arrays

optimises multiplicative array addressing, in effect converting it
into Iliffe-vector addressing!

For fixed-size arrays it is possible to share the addressing
vectors between different procedure activations, and therefore to
initialise them at load-time, provided that the final address
calculated is an offset relative to the start of the array rather
than an absolute pointer. Then on every entry to the block which
declares an array the data frame can contain a pointer to the
addressing vector, with no additional run-time overhead required
to set it up. For dynamic arrays, whose dimensions are determined
on each block entry, the savings of Iliffe-vector address
calculation should be weighed against the cost of setting up the
addressing vector each time the object program enters the block in
which the array is declared. So far as I know, there has been no
experimental or statistical analysis performed to determine
whether multiplicative or addressing vector addressing is superior
overall. I suspect the addressing vector mechanism would be
superior on machines (such as microprocessors) which don't have a
fast MULT instruction.

Error checking code can be just as in the multiplicative case
of figure 9.9, and once again it might be reasonable to check only
the finally computed subscript for validity. It is possible to
arrive at a correct address by accident (e.g. if some other word
in the machine, addressed by a wildly inaccurate subscript,
happens to contain a valid address) but it's so unlikely that it's
reasonable to neglect that possibility.

Record Data Structures

Historically, languages which included array or vector data
structures were invented before languages which include record
structures. Record declarations and record accesses are just as
easy to translate as array declarations or accesses, however, so
age isn't a guide to simplicity. Essentially a record is
represented by a fixed-size vector - usually a small vector, too.
A record variable denotes an instance of such a record-vector,
which is stored in a data frame and addressed in the same way as
other data objects. A pointer variable contains a pointer to such
a record-vector: the pointer is stored in a memory cell within a
data frame like any other variable but the record-vector may be
stored in the 'heap' or in another data frame.

All accesses to the record-vector use constant subscripts: this
gives great efficiency. The only drawback of record processing,
so far as object program efficiency goes, is that free use of
pointers to record-vectors may mean that the space from which the
record-vectors are allocated must be garbage collected. There is
some discussion of this problem, and of some different solutions
to it, in chapter 14.

Record-type declarations

A record-type declaration like that in figure 9.13 declares the
number of elements, the name and the type of each element which
will appear in any instance of a record-vector of that type. This
information must be processed by the object-description phase and
stored in the symbol-table descriptor against the type-name. The
record-type declaration doesn't generate any code, unlike an array
or procedure declaration, and it doesn't allocate any space within
the data frame, unlike a variable declaration. The field-names in
the record-type declaration are used, in effect, to select a
constant subscript in an access to the record-vector of that type
and the types associated with the field-names are used to check
the validity of every access or update of the record-vector.

Declaration: **record** bintree tag : **integer;**
                        left, right: ^bintree

       end

Record layout:

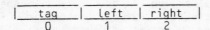

Figure 9.13 Declaration of a record-type

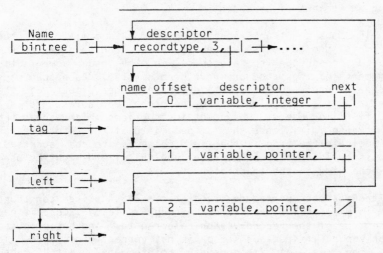

Figure 9.14 Symbol-table layout for type declaration

---

        var local : bintree;
            nodep : ^bintree;

Figure 9.15 Declaring record- and pointer-variables

Figure 9.14 illustrates the symbol table layout which might result from the declaration of figure 9.13. The descriptor for 'bintree' indicates that it is a record-type, gives the number of cells in an instance of a 'bintree' record[1] and contains a pointer to a list of field-descriptors. Each field-descriptor points to the relevant field-identifier (note that the field-identifier does not contain a pointer to the field-descriptor), defines the offset within the record-vector at which that field starts, and gives a description of the type of the field. The type description is used in the translation of accesses to the record-vector. In the case of figure 9.14, two of the field-descriptors point back to the parent record-type descriptor to indicate the type of the field.

Figure 9.15 shows a sample declaration of a PASCAL record- and pointer-variable. A declaration of a record-variable (a PASCAL **record,** an ALGOL 68 **struct**) allocates space within the data frame for an instance of the record-vector: the address of the first cell in the record-vector can be stored in the descriptor of the record-variable. A declaration of a pointer-variable (PASCAL ^**record,** ALGOL **ref struct**) allocates space sufficient to hold the address of a record-vector. If the language implementation includes garbage-collection of an off-stack 'heap' of record-vectors it is essential that the pointer is initialised to some recognisable 'empty' value: it is desirable to do this anyway, since it removes some potential for object program error.

Accessing an element of a record

Figure 9.16 shows a 'TranRecAccess' procedure, similar to the TranVecAccess procedure shown above, which translates a PASCAL-like record access node (to save space on the page some self-checking parts of the procedure have been omitted). Each such node specifies a record-value and a field-name: the effect of the procedure is to assign values to the global variables 'Address' and 'Modifier' for use in subsequent instructions which access the record. It also initialises the 'atype' field of the record-access node to indicate the type of the field which is to be accessed: the discussion in chapter 5 indicates how this field might be used for type-checking in the translator.

The TranRecAccess procedure translates a PASCAL-like construct of the form '<rec>.<field>' or '<recp>^.<field>'. Once it has found the type of the record-vector referred to - and has produced an error report if <rec> or <recp> is not correctly declared - it searches the list of field-names, pointed to by the type-

---

1 In this chapter I make the assumption that every element of a record-vector occupies a single memory cell. This is to simplify the discussion and the examples, but in practice it is easy to handle multi-cell or parti-cell elements of a record.

descriptor, to find the name <field>. (Note that this mechanism does not require a pointer from field-name to field-descriptor and therefore allows a single name to be used as a field-name in many different record-types without difficulty.) Once the relevant field has been located the Address and Modifier values are set up:

```
let TranRecAccess(nodep, regno) be
{ let rec, field = nodep.left, nodep.right
  let recdesc, typedesc = empty, empty

  /* find record type */
  if rec.type=name then /* <rec>.<field> */
   { recdesc := rec.descriptor
     if recdesc=empty then Error("undeclared name",rec)
     elsf recdesc.kind\=recordvariable then
       Error("not a record variable name", rec)
     else typedesc := recdesc.type
   }
  elsf rec.type=pointer then /* <rec>^.<field> */
   { recdesc := rec.first.descriptor
     if recdesc=empty then Error("undeclared name", rec.first)
     elsf recdesc.kind\=pointervariable then
       Error("not a pointer variable",rec.first)
     else typedesc := recdesc.type
   }
  else CompilerFail("bad RecAccess node")

  /* find field offset and type */
  { let fieldlist = typedesc.fields

    while fieldlist\=empty & fieldlist.name\=field do
        fieldlist := fieldlist.next
    if fieldlist=empty then Error("name not field name", field)

    if recdesc.kind=recordvariable then
     { Address := recdesc.address+fieldlist.offset
       Modifier := 0
     }
    else
     { Gen(LOAD, regno, recdesc.address)
       Gen(SKIPNEa, regno, EMPTY)
       Gen(JSUB  L, empty-pointer-error)
       Address := fieldlist.offset; Modifier := regno
     }

    /* record the source-language type of the field */
    nodep.atype := fieldlist.type
  }
}
```

Figure 9.16 Translating access to a record-vector

in the case of an access via a pointer-variable the pointer is
first loaded into a register and, in this procedure, instructions
are included to check that the value isn't 'empty'.

Figure 9.17 shows some of the code which TranRecAccess would
produce, given the declarations in figure 9.15. Note in
particular how efficient access to an element of a record-variable
can be. Figure 9.18 shows example source fragments which

```
Source:    local.tag := nodep^.tag + 1

Code:    LOAD    1, nodep
         SKIPNEa 1, EMPTY
         JSUB    L, empty-pointer-error
         LOAD    1, 0(1)
         ADDn    1, 1
         STORE   1, local  /* local.tag is first cell */
```

Figure 9.17 Code for access to an element of a record

```
local.tag := empty
          /* invalid - tag is integer field */
local.tag := local.tag+5       /* valid */
local.left := nodep^.right      /* valid */
nodep^.right := local.tag + local.left
          /* invalid - addition of pointer and integer */
local.right := new bintree(0, empty, nodep^left)
          /* valid */
local.left := new bintree(empty, empty, empty)
          /* invalid - tag must be an integer */
nodep^.left := new other(1, e, f)
          /* invalid - wrong type of pointer */
```

Figure 9.18 Checking validity of record access

```
Source: nodep := new bintree(1, empty, empty)

Code:    LOADn   1, 3
         JSUB    L, allocate-space
                 /* result is a pointer in register 1 */
         LOADn   2, 1
         STORE   2, 0(1)
         LOADa   2, EMPTY
         STORE   2, 1(1)
         LOADa   2, EMPTY /* unnecessary! */
         STORE   2, 2(1)
         STORE   1, nodep
```

Figure 9.19 Creating an instance of a record

illustrate the way in which the 'atype' field set up by this procedure could be used to check type-validity of access to every field of a record. The **new** construct creates a record-vector on the 'heap' (in the pseudo-PASCAL of this example) and produces a pointer to the vector: the initial values provided are essentially assigned to the fields of the record. Figure 9.19 shows code which might create the pointer and assign values to the fields of the record-vector. The inefficiency involved in reloading the value **empty** is avoidable, but in practice it is just the sort of inefficiency that might be produced by a tree-walking simple translator.

Union types and variant records

It is essential, in most record-processing programs, that a pointer in a record be allowed to refer to one of a number of different types of record-vector. ALGOL 68 allows this with 'union' types, PASCAL with 'variant records'.

The union-type mechanism requires the use of 'conformity clauses'. When accessing a union-type value, the user must provide an expression which selects one of a number of sections of source program, depending on the actual type of the value. Each of the individual sections can then be translated as if the value is of a particular type within the union. The representation of a union-type object must obviously contain information about its type, and the space allocated for such an object must be large enough to hold the largest kind of object within the union.

The variant-record mechanism is less elegant. Each record in PASCAL may contain a number of variant-fields, whose values determine the layout of the record-vector. It is possible even to assign a value to a variant-field but I know of no PASCAL implementation which would thereupon reorganise the contents of the record-vector, as it should if such an assignment were properly implemented. Access to a field of a record with variant-fields would require, if strictly interpreted, a run-time check on the values of the variant-fields to ensure that the access is valid: once again I know of no PASCAL implementation which does this.

Summary

The code fragments which perform data structure accessing are crucial to the efficiency of the object program because they so often appear in the inner loop of the source program. In many numerical analysis programs, for example, the efficiency of array access is the most important factor in determining the efficiency of the object program and in a system program the efficiency of vector and record access can be just as important.

Vector accessing is fairly cheap, array accessing relatively expensive. Record accessing is cheapest of all. While setting up the data space for a dynamic array at block entry time it is necessary to set up a dope vector to aid multiplicative addressing and possible at the same time to set up an addressing vector (Iliffe vector) structure to aid non-multiplicative access.

The unnecessary re-calculation of the address of an element of a data structure in the code generated by a tree-walking simple translator can often produce disappointing inefficiencies. However the treatment in this chapter, in chapters 5, 6 and 7 and in section III emphasises the value of tree-walking as an implementation technique which encourages the compiler writer to generate <u>accurate</u> code in the first instance and then allows incremental refinement of individual procedures to improve the quality of local fragments of code. The code optimisation techniques discussed in chapter 10 may be useful to reduce unnecessary object program activity associated with data structure access.

10 Code Optimisation

In this book I argue that for a modern, well-designed programming language a compiler which includes a tree-walking simple translation phase can produce acceptable object code, particularly when careful attention is paid to the 'crucial code fragments' discussed in chapters 5, 6, 7 and 9 and in section III. No matter how carefully the individual code fragments are designed, though, the code produced by such a compiler can rarely be 'optimal' and it is always easy to spot redundant instructions in the object program or to think of ways in which a particular source construct could be better translated in a particular setting. Code optimisation techniques attempt systematically to reduce the disparity between the code produced by a compiler and the code which might be generated by a very careful hand-translation of the source program. The simpler techniques, discussed in this chapter, merely re-order and merge code fragments which might be produced by simple translation, but more advanced techniques can go so far as to replace the source program's algorithm with a more efficient algorithm of equivalent effect.

Optimisation mechanisms vary not only in their effectiveness but also in the cost of their application. Unusually heavy optimisation of a program can easily double or triple its compilation time. Just where to draw the line between useful and wasteful mechanisms is a matter of taste, but most compiler-writers believe that in practice a few straightforward optimisation techniques can produce most of the effect that is required at a fraction of the cost of application of more advanced and more powerful techniques. Knuth, in an empirical investigation of programs actually submitted to a computing service (Knuth,1971), supported this intuition by showing how the mechanisms of 'constant folding', 'global register allocation', 'deferred storage' and 'code motion out of loops' could at relatively low cost provide quite substantial improvements in the efficiency of most object programs. This chapter accordingly discusses only these simple mechanisms (and because this book is in part a do-it-yourself aid to the construction of a simple compiler it discusses only the principles of the techniques rather than their detailed implementation). In the same paper Knuth showed how more powerful mechanisms could produce dramatic effects on the efficiency of programs, but at a much higher cost because each mechanism was applicable to only a small proportion of real-life programs.

Simple translation depends on the hierarchical relationship between source program fragments, expressed as a tree. Code optimisation mechanisms depend also upon the control flow between source program fragments, best expressed as a 'thread' from node to node of the tree. Wulf et al. (Wulf et al.,1973) give a detailed description of an optimiser which works in this way. This chapter gives only a brief description of optimisation mechanisms and in many cases the examples show a linearised form of the program - it is worth remembering the advantages of the threaded tree representation, however, and I give in figure 10.4 below an example which illustrates it.

In practice there is a continuum of translation mechanisms from the simplest transliteration mechanism discussed in chapter 2 to the most sophisticated optimisation mechanisms; nevertheless in figure 10.1 I have tried to draw a line between 'sub-optimisation' and 'optimisation' proper. I have classified as a sub-optimisation every technique which relates to the translation of a single expression, considered in isolation from the code fragments which surround it. Most language definitions (with the notable exception of ALGOL 60) state that a programmer cannot rely on the order of evaluation of operands or the order of performance of operations within an expression and therefore even a simple translator can impose any convenient order it wishes. True optimisations, for the

---

Sub-optimisations
      constant expression evaluation at compile-time
      expression re-ordering
      local register allocation
      common sub-expression recognition
      jumping code for Booleans

True Optimisations
      constant folding
      code motion
      redundant code elimination
      global register allocation
            - deferred storage
            - index optimisation
      loop optimisation
      strength reduction
      peephole optimisation

Figure 10.1 Sub-optimisation and optimisation techniques

purposes of this book, are those translation mechanisms which take account of the <u>control context</u> within which a code fragment will operate - i.e. the effects of code fragments which are executed before it and after it.

Language restrictions and accurate optimisation

A powerful argument against the use of code optimisation techniques is the undeniable fact that rather too many optimising compilers often produce an invalid translation of the source program - i.e. an object program which doesn't produce the effect specified by the source program. Sometimes this is unavoidable, and in such cases it may be necessary to alter the language definition to make it clear that certain restrictions apply to source programs, but frequently it arises because of the nature of the process of optimisation.

A simple translator produces a range of code fragments, each of which is either always right or always wrong. During debugging of the compiler it is relatively easy to detect errors in the translator which cause it to consistently produce inaccurate code and this makes it very easy to debug a tree-walking translator[1]. Optimisation isn't like that: it rejects a transparent translation in favour of one which exploits peculiarities of the source program's algorithm and the details of control flow in the object program. Quite glaring errors of translation can be made which only show up in programs with a particular pattern of control flow, or which exercise a feature of the optimised code which is rarely used. Many optimising compilers, for example, have implemented multiplication and division by a power of 2 by using 'shift' instructions, which is normally valid except for the case of division when the operand has the value '-1' (Steele,1977). That is almost a simple translation error, but in other cases it is common to find that an optimising compiler will produce an incorrect translation given a particular version of the source program yet a correct translation when some trivial alteration is made, such as interchanging the order of a couple of assignment statements.

Such problems arise when a particular code optimisation technique can only validly be employed given certain properties of the object program. When the compiler-writer has failed to check the validity of application of a technique, or has made an

---

1 Every compiler-writer has the experience of finding translation bugs after the compiler has been operating apparently perfectly for months - bugs which, it often seems, ought to have affected most users of the compiler but didn't! The time does arrive, though, when you can be fairly confident that there are no more such bugs to be found in a simple translator.

ineffective attempt to check it, there is a bug in the compiler. Often, though, the necessary properties of the object program are impossible to check at compile-time. In such a case it may be necessary to define the semantics of the source language in such a way that optimisation is permitted and that users are warned of the possible anomalous effects of code optimisation on some programs. The language definition must, in effect, prohibit source programs which specify one form of processor behaviour when translated transparently but another behaviour when 'optimised'.

Examples of the restrictions that are applied are the following (paraphrased from the FORTRAN 66 definition)

(i) No function call may alter the value of any other element in the statement in which it occurs.

(ii) If textually identical function calls appear within a single statement then each evaluation must produce the same result and the function must be written so that the net side-effect is the same no matter how many of the function calls are actually executed.

(iii) If a single memory cell can be referred to in a fragment of source program by more than one name then alteration of the value of that cell via one of the names may not immediately alter its value when referred to by any of the other names.

Restriction (i) is an extension of that which allows node-reversal in an expression by demanding that 'X+F(X)' must produce the same value as 'F(X)+X'. Restriction (ii) demands that 'RAND(I)/RAND(I)' must always evaluate to '1.0' (which is suprising to the user when RAND is a pseudo-random number function!) and allows the compiler to evaluate 'common sub-expressions' in a statement only once rather than many times. Restriction (iii) implies that the program fragment

```
I = Z+1
J = Z*I
A(J) = A(I)
```

is invalid if I and J can ever refer to the same memory cell, and is imposed to allow the compiler to hold INTEGER values in registers rather than in the memory.

The restrictions above are specific to FORTRAN, but similar restrictions can be applied in any language. Some implementations of PASCAL, for example, go further and demand that no function may produce any side-effects whatsoever. In any language in which a memory cell can be simultaneously referred to by more than one name - say via a parameter name and a global variable name in a block-structured language - some version of restriction (iii) must be applied.

By their very nature such restrictions are uncheckable at compile-time (given the design of conventional programming languages) and even partial checks can prove impossibly expensive: the compiler must therefore generate code which assumes that the restrictions have been obeyed. The naive user will not usually fully understand the purpose or the effect of the restrictions, however, and even the most sophisticated programmer will sometimes make a mistake. As a result it's a common experience that a program which runs apparently 'correctly' when given a simple translation will produce very different results when optimised. The effect is to increase the average effort required to debug a program and, as I argue below and in section V, the cost of debugging may be greater than the cost of executing the unoptimised program throughout its useful life. Which leads me to ask the question –

Is optimisation cost-effective?

In section V I argue that the cost of developing a program – debugging it and bringing it to the point where it can perform a useful service – can be comparable with, and often greater than, the cost of running the same program on a computer throughout its useful life. Therefore for many programs it is doubtful whether optimisation is really worthwhile, especially since it typically increases the cost of development by increasing compilation times and by producing obscure execution bugs. Only when the extra cost of optimisation, measured in both machine time and human effort, is outweighed by the gain in execution time is optimisation of a program worthwhile.

The cost-effectiveness of optimisation can be increased by only optimising part of the program. Every object program has an 'inner loop' within which it spends the majority of its time and for most programs this inner loop is represented by less than 20% of the source code. If the inner loop can be recognised and isolated and if the code produced by an optimiser is loader-compatible with that produced by a simple translator it can be worthwhile to optimise the inner loop alone. Finding the inner loop isn't easy and often it is in an unexpected area of the source program – that of a compiler, for example, is usually the section of the lexical analyser which reads a single character. With hardware assistance it is possible to identify the inner loop in any object program.

I argue below that much of the demand for optimisation comes from users who are using an inappropriate programming language – who are using FORTRAN when a more efficient algorithm could easily be specified in PASCAL or ALGOL 68, say – and that in some cases modern hardware designs can make some optimisations irrelevant. Also the cost of hardware is falling and it may simply be cheaper to buy a new processor or a new installation than to invest in, or to write, an optimising compiler and to invest the effort which is required to optimise existing programs. Buying a new machine is an optimisation technique which optimises everything, including the operating system and any compilers which it supports!

It should be emphasised that 'cost' is a measure which applies everywhere and not just in a commercial environment. In a university, for example, the cost of program development can be seen in the fact that people sit at computer terminals debugging programs when they ought to be sitting at their desks writing about their research results and also in the fact that university computers are continuously overloaded with users who are compiling, testing and re-testing their programs. The university computing environment is admittedly an extreme example, but in such an environment it is fair to say that if optimisation increases the cost of program development then it makes it harder for everybody else to get any work done on the computer!

The case against optimisation is not as clear-cut as I have tried to make it. Wulf et al. (Wulf et al.,1973) argue in favour of the optimisation of system programs such as compilers and operating systems, which are nowadays written almost universally in a 'high level' system programming language such as BCPL, BLISS or C and which should be optimised since they are in almost constant use. They also point out that the benefits of optimisation come when other people have optimised their programs - then their use of the machine is less and there is more for you! Furthermore there will always be programs which can only run with difficulty on the largest and most powerful machine available and which must therefore be optimised[1]. There will always be programs just too large or just too slow to perform some particular function, which optimisation can make into useful tools.

I can't dismiss optimisation as totally unnecessary in a world of limited resources, but I do claim that much of the optimisation which goes on could be eliminated if users changed to a different language and perhaps to a different machine. Many people are still unaware of how insignificant a proportion of the cost of programming is the machine time required to run the program - if they were to measure the true cost of optimisation against its undoubted benefits then they might use it less frequently.

Net Effect and Order of Computation

The net effect of a program can be said to be the total change which is produced by executing the program, ignoring the detailed

---

[1] Some famous current examples are those programs which aid weather forecasting by simulating atmospheric circulation and which, rumour has it, can only just run faster than the real thing.

mechanism by which that change is brought about. Optimisation mechanisms concentrate on producing an object program which has the same net effect as that specified by the source program, but which may not produce it by exactly the same means. The net effect of the example program discussed in chapter 1, for example, is to print the digit '4' and it might seem reasonable to translate it into any object program which will produce that effect, perhaps by using the mechanisms of constant folding and deferred storage discussed below.

Figure 10.2 illustrates the notion of net effect with two examples. Example (i) shows how difficult it can be to discover what the net effect of a program is: an optimising compiler might easily discover that j1, j2 and j3 had constant values but might not discover that the loop sets each successive element of the

---

```
(i) A foolish way to zero a vector:
    begin array Z[1:20]; integer i, j1, j2, j3;
        j3 := 20; j1 := (j2+2)/10; j2 := j1-1;
        Z[1] := 0.0;
        for i := j1 step j2 until j3 do
            Z[i] := Z[i-1] * ln(cos(i)+1.14);
        ....
    end

(ii) An ineffective attempt to measure object program speed:
        ....
        start := runtime()
        for i := 1 to 10000 do x := 0
        finish := runtime()
        print("time for assignment statement",
                            (finish-start)/10000);
```

Figure 10.2 Net effect of computation

Source: a := x-3; b := x*2; c := x**3; x := a+b*c;

initial order: x-3, a:=, x*2, b:=, x**3, c:=, a+b*c, x:=.

essential order: x-3 (#1)   x*2 (#2)   x**3 (#3)

                            #1+#2*#3 (#4)

        a:= (#5)   x:= (#6)   c:= (#7)   b:=(#8)

Figure 10.3 Initial and essential orders of events

vector Z to zero, and thus that the computation of ln(cos(...).)
is never required. Example (ii) shows how optimisation can
occasionally produce hilarious effects: the assignment statement
'x:=0' can be moved outside the loop, the empty loop deleted and
the assignment statement itself deleted since the value of 'x' is
never utilised. The entire program then measures one ten-
thousandth part of the time between one call of the system
procedure 'runtime' and another!

Joking apart, all optimisations consider the net effect first
of a small fragment of object program, then of progressively
larger fragments, building up perhaps to the translation of a
fragment as large as an entire procedure body and eventually
producing a translation which preserves the net effect specified
by the source program without necessarily following the precise
details of its algorithm. Geschke (Geschke,1972) points out that
such a translation depends on the recognition of the essential
order of computation events out of the initial order specified by
the user's program. Figure 10.3 shows an example of the difference
between initial and essential order of events.

The essential order shows the absence of any ordering between
many computations. In the example of figure 10.3 events #1, #2 and
#3 can occur in any order provided that they all occur before
event #4. Events #5, #6, #7 and #8 can likewise occur in any order
provided that in each case the assignment follows the relevant
event #1, #2, #3 or #4. It is the absence of an essential ordering
between many events which makes optimisation possible: the
optimiser can re-organise the computation freely provided that the
actual order of events obeys the constraints of the essential
order. Every optimisation mechanism discussed in this chapter
depends on this insight and on the manipulation of redundancies in
the object program which it reveals. The essential order of
computation can be envisaged as a collection of threads running
through the tree, and optimisation as a process of linearisation
which preserves continuity of every thread and produces efficient
translation by merging portions of different threads.

Basic blocks, regions and structured statements

The smallest unit of a program which can be optimised is a basic
block[1]: a collection of statements which can only be entered at
the beginning and which doesn't contain any intermediate labels,
procedure or function calls. Within a basic block the initial
order of events is obvious and linear. Provided that when control
leaves the basic block the net effect which has been produced is
that specified by the source program, the user has no way of

---

1 The terminology 'basic block' comes from FORTRAN and has
nothing whatsoever to do with block-structuring.

telling whether the program has been optimised or not[1]. Therefore
the optimiser can generate code which produces that net effect in
any way it wishes - naturally the aim is to produce the net effect
with the minimum of run-time effort!

Since the initial order of events within the basic block is
linear and predictable, optimisation can include simple techniques
which note the effect of assignment statements in the symbol table
descriptors of variables - the 'constant folding' and 'deferred
storage' mechanisms discussed below, for example - and which move

---

```
        Source: a := 3;
                if a<b then { x := a; y := x-1 }
                else { x := a; y := x+1 }
                a := 0; x := 0

Initial order:              a := 3
                              a<b

        x := a                      x := a
        y := x-1                    y := x+1

                          a := 0
                          x := 0


Optimised order:              3<b
              y := 2                  y := 3

                        a := 0
                        x := 0
```

Figure 10.4 Structured statements and code motion

```
Unstructured program:            With explicit iteration:
  loop: <S1>                       { <S1>; <S2>; b := next(b) }
        <S2>                          repeatwhile f(b)
      b := next(b)
      if f(b) then goto loop
```

Figure 10.5 Iterative statements and important regions

---

1 That is, provided that the source program obeys all the
  restrictions imposed on programs by the language definition.
  If it does not, the result of optimisation may not be so
  obviously beneficial.

code fragments implicitly within the basic block rather than explicitly.

The end of a basic block is signalled by a labelled statement, a procedure or a function call. In principle control can arrive at a label from any number of different control contexts and therefore simple optimisations must be abandoned when a label is encountered - constant values must be forgotten, deferred STORE instructions generated, and so on. Likewise the effects of a procedure call can be far-reaching and simple optimisations must be abandoned before the procedure is called. Nevertheless the optimisation of a basic block can be very effective, for example when it eliminates the re-calculation of an array element address.

With extra effort it is possible to analyse the ways in which control is passed between the basic blocks of the program, to discover the regions of the source program. Analysis of a basic block will reveal fragments which can be moved between the blocks of a region and thus the range and effectiveness of optimisation can be increased. The structured statements of a modern programming language provide the optimiser with ready-made regions: figure 10.4 shows how code motion between basic blocks can be effective in the optimisation of a conditional statement. It would be simple to discover the structure of the region given a threaded tree, less simple if the representation of the program was a linear one using compiler-generated labels and JUMPs.

Code motion between basic blocks within a region is made possible by the recognition of the essential order of computation of code fragments. Fragments which have no essential predecessor in the basic block may be moved into the preceding basic blocks of the region, fragments which have no essential successor into the following ones. Code motion is particularly effective in the case of a loop, because code within the loop will probably be executed many times while code outside will be executed perhaps only once. Figure 10.5 illustrates the advantages of explicit iterative statements: it is obvious that optimisation of the body of a **repeatwhile** statement may have quite an effect on the efficiency of the object program, but it can be difficult to discover the effective loops in an unstructured program. Structured statements are easier to translate than their unstructured equivalent, as chapter 7 demonstrates: figure 10.5 shows that they are easier to optimise as well!

Optimisation within a Basic Block

I discuss below four techniques which can be used to improve the code which is the translation of a basic block: constant folding, deferred storage, global register allocation and redundant code elimination. Each of them uses the mechanism of marking the symbol table descriptor of a variable to show the effect of the evaluation of expressions and the execution of assignment and other statements. Although it is possible to carry out each of these mechanisms in parallel with simple translation, as a sort of filter on the object code proposed by a tree-walker, I have chosen to show them as a separate translation activity. Each of the mechanisms must be abandoned at the end of a basic block, unless the control flow within a region has been fully analysed. Although code motion between basic blocks, and in particular code motion out of loops, can have the most dramatic effects on program efficiency, the optimisation of basic blocks should not be ignored. Just as the design of crucial code fragments is the basis of good simple translation, so the optimisation of basic blocks is the basis of effective optimisation.

Constant folding

A possible sub-optimisation is to evaluate at compile time those fragments of expressions which contain only constants. This reduces the size of the object program and increases its speed. It is reasonable for a user to write an expression which contains only constants and might more 'efficiently' have been written as a constant value, since constant expressions increase the readability and reliability of the source program. The BCPL expression 'x **bitand** 2^10' obviously selects a particular bit within a word: the expression 'x **bitand** 1048' does not, but it isn't obvious that it doesn't and it is possible to write the second when intending the effect of the first.

The reduction in the size of the object program can be quite impressive if the value of the test expression in a conditional statement has a constant value - for example if the test expression in a **while** statement has the value **false** then the entire statement can be deleted. Once again this is a legitimate programming technique, exploited by users of BCPL compilers everywhere, which allows sections of code useful for debugging to be deleted from the program merely by alteration of a few 'manifest-constant' declarations.

A similar technique, known as <u>constant folding</u>, can be applied to sequences of statements. If the translator keeps a record in the symbol table descriptor of each variable which is assigned a constant value within a basic block, many more fragments of program can be evaluated at compile-time. Figure 10.6 gives an example of a basic block in which this is especially effective. The initial code shown contains 14 instructions, of which the object program would execute either 6 or 13 instructions and make either 10 or 23 store accesses[1], depending on whether the JUMP

---

1 The number of store accesses made by a code fragment may be a more useful measure of execution efficiency than the number of instructions executed. I have assumed that each instruction executed causes one store access to read the instruction

instruction is executed or not. The code after constant folding is smaller and faster: it executes only 5 or 8 instructions and makes only 8 or 13 store accesses. Of all optimisation techniques, constant folding is the one which may most obviously be carried out 'on the fly' in parallel with the activity of a simple translator.

Deferred storage

The tree weighting algorithm of chapter 5 minimises local register usage inside expressions. The registers which it saves are useful for various purposes. Holding a value in a register rather than in the store, for example, reduces the number of store accesses in the object program: 'LOADr rx,ry' takes only a single store access to read the instruction while 'LOAD rx,y' takes an additional access to read the value of y.

If the right hand side of an assignment statement which assigns a value to a variable is evaluated normally, but the STORE instruction is not generated until the last possible moment (e.g. at the end of the basic block), it may be possible to reduce store accesses and to eliminate some instructions as well. As with the

---

```
Source: b := 0; a := 3
        if u>=b then
        { x := b+64*a; y := x+2^a }

Initial code:          After constant folding:
    STOZ     , b          STOZ      , b   /* note b=0 */
    LOADn  1, 3           LOADn  1, 3
    STORE  1, a           STORE  1, a   /* note a=3 */
    LOAD   1, u           LOAD   1, u
    SKIPGE 1, b           JUMPLT 1, %e   /* using b=0 */
    JUMP     , %e         LOADn  1, 192 /* 0+64*3 = 192 */
    LOAD   1, a           STORE  1, x   /* note x=192 */
    MULTn  1, 64          LOADn  1, 200 /* 192+2^3 = 200 */
    ADD    1, b           STORE  1, y   /* note y=200 */
    STORE  1, x     %e:   ...
    LOADn  1, 2           /* now forget values of x and y */
    ASHIFT 1, a
    ADD    1, x
    STORE  1, y
%e:  ...
```

Figure 10.6 Constant folding to perform operations at compile-time

---

itself, and instructions which reference an operand in store make a further store access. On simple machines the speed of the store is a limiting factor on the speed of object program execution.

constant folding mechanism the translator marks the descriptor of
the variable, this time to show that its value is currently held
in a register rather than in its allocated store location. This
deferred storage optimisation may totally eliminate the STORE
operation if there is a later assignment to the same variable
before the end of the basic block.

Figure 10.7 shows an example of the technique. The initial code
includes 9 instructions and makes 17 store accesses: the code
after deferred storage optimisation has only 7 instructions and
makes only 11 store accesses. Note that the order of computation
no longer follows the initial order specified by the source
program and that one STORE instruction has been eliminated.

Global register allocation

Deferred storage is one of many mechanisms which make use of the
global allocation of values to registers rather than to storage
locations (the tree-weighting mechanism of chapter 5 performed
local register allocation within a single expression). The
difficulty in implementing any mechanism of register allocation is
clearly one of register deallocation, since there will almost
always be more candidate values than available registers. There is
no easy solution to this problem - dumping registers on the basis
of frequency of use in the code fragments generated so far is
wrong, since dumping should be determined by the use which the
program will make of the registers in the code fragments yet to
come. In general an analysis of the future history of the object
program is required, which can show the effect of dumping each of
the candidate registers: the translator can then choose to dump a
register so as to cause the minimum of disruption and
inefficiency. In practice it may not matter much which register
is dumped on a multi-register machine since the value can be
reloaded in a single instruction.

```
Source: a := x; b := a+3; c := b-a; .... a := 0; ....

Initial code:          After deferred storage optimisation:
    LOAD   1, x            LOAD   1, x      /* a, x in reg. 1 */
    STORE  1, a            LOADn  2, 3(1)   /* b in reg. 2 */
    LOAD   1, a            LOADr  3, 2
    ADDn   1, 3            SUBr   3, 1      /* c in reg. 3 */
    STORE  1, b            ...
    LOAD   1, b            (no code)        /* note a=0 */
    SUB    1, a            ...
    STORE  1, c            STOZ     , a
    ...                    STORE  2, b
    STOZ     , a           STORE  3, c
    ...
```

Figure 10.7 Deferred storage of registers

When global register allocation is used the descriptor for every variable whose value is being held in a register must state the fact, and the translator must keep a table of 'registers in use', for use when deallocating registers and for generating all the deferred STORE instructions at the end of a basic block or a region.

Redundant code elimination

One of the techniques listed as a sub-optimisation in figure 10.1 is 'common sub-expression recognition'. If an expression tree contains two identical nodes it may be worthwhile to evaluate the node only once and to use that value twice during the evaluation of the expression. It is easy to recognise common nodes as the tree is built: the syntax analyser must keep a table of nodes and look up each node in the table as it is created. Each node in an

---

```
let node(type, p1, p2, p3, p4, p5, p6, p7, p8) = valof
 { let nodep = bottom
   let count = NumberOfArgs()
   let pointer = @type

   /* build node as in chapter 3:
    * first field is 'type', second is 'count'
    */
   if bottom+count+1>top then
     CompilerFail("no more space for tree nodes")

   nodep!0 := type; nodep!1 := 1 /* occurs once */
   for i = 1 to count-1 do
     nodep!(i+1) := pointer!i

   /* look up or insert in table of nodes - procedure
    * returns pointer to new or old copy
    */
   { let entryp = LookupNode(nodep)

     if entryp\=nodep then /* copy exists */
     { entryp.count +:= 1
       /* reduce occurrence count of sub-nodes */
       for i = 2 to count do
         (entryp!i).count -:= 1;
     }
     else /* allocate space */
        bottom := bottom+count+1

     resultis entryp
   }
 }
```

Figure 10.8 Recognising common nodes

expression tree must now contain a 'count' field which records the number of references to that node. Figure 10.8 shows a version of the 'node' procedure introduced in chapter 3, which looks up each node in a hash-addressed table as it is created and returns a pointer to a copy if one exists. To avoid confusion, the table must be emptied before analysis of an expression.

The tree-weighting algorithm of chapter 5 would need extensive modification to take account of common sub-expression optimisation. The number of registers used in a sub-node depends on whether it contains a node which occurs elsewhere in the tree and on whether that node will translate into the first, the last or an intermediate use of the sub-expression in the final object code sequence. The algorithm is involved and I won't include it here.

The same node-building technique can recognise nodes which occur more than once in the program as a whole, rather than merely within a single expression. If such a node represents the value of an expression whose value is used several times within a basic block, evaluating it once and using its value several times will eliminate redundant code from the object program. Implementation of the mechanism requires a technique which can determine when an expression requires re-evaluation. A simple technique which does just this keeps an 'event number' which is incremented each time an assignment or procedure call is translated. The symbol table descriptor of each variable records the event number which was set during translation of the last assignment statement that would alter its value. The 'event number' of a common sub-expression is the largest event number amongst those recorded for the variables within it. By recording the event number of a common sub-expression when its value is first calculated, and recomputing the event number when its value is next required, it is possible to detect whether the expression must be re-evaluated.

It is necessary to be very careful about expressions which contain function calls or references to data structures. In the absence of information about the side-effects of a function (either from analysis of the function body or from user directions such as PL/1's NORMAL/ABNORMAL function specification) it is inadvisable to regard an expression which contains a function call as a candidate for redundant code elimination.

Redundant code elimination can be very effective when combined with global register allocation, particularly when the common sub-expression is an array subscript expression. As the discussion in chapter 9 shows, calculating and re-calculating the address of an array element can be very expensive. If the same or a similar subscript is used repeatedly within a basic block then expensive recalculation can profitably be avoided.

Peephole optimisation

When all optimisations which can be regarded as transformations on the source program have been performed, the object program consists of a linear sequence of instructions. Peephole optimisation looks at the object code in an attempt to detect obvious local inefficiencies. Many optimisations which can be seen as manipulations of the essential order of computation can also be achieved by repeated application of different peephole optimisations, as Wulf et al. (Wulf et al.,1973) show.

Peephole optimisation is a last resort, applied when all other methods have done their best. Figure 10.9 shows how peephole optimisation can eliminate STORE and LOAD instructions: however figure 10.6 shows that a more thoughtful approach can have still more dramatic effects.

Loops and Code Motion

Loops are easily identified regions of the program which will

```
LOAD  n, <address>
STORE n, <address> (unnecessary instruction)

STORE n, <address>
LOAD  n, <address> (unnecessary instruction)
```

Figure 10.9 Peephole optimisation

```
Source program:
    DIMENSION A(5,40,50)
    ....
    DO 1 I = 1, 5
    DO 1 J = 1, 40
    DO 1 K = 1, 50
    ....
    A(I,J,K) = <expression>
    ....
  1 CONTINUE

Unoptimised code for the innermost loop:
    DO 1 K = 1, 50
    ....
    r1 := <expression>
    r2 := (K*40+J)*5+I
    A[r2] := r1
    ....
  1 CONTINUE
```

Figure 10.10 A program with nested loops

probably be executed many times. If code can be removed from a
loop, the effect on the efficiency of the object program will
therefore be greater than if code is removed from the program
outside a loop. If code is merely moved outside the loop, the
effect will be nearly as great. There are often loops within loops
within loops (....) in which case optimisations applied to the
inner loop of a 'nest' of loops will be extremely effective.
Optimisation of a nest of loops proceeds inside out — first the
inner loop of the nest is optimised and in particular as much code
as possible is moved out of this loop into the loop which encloses
it. The process is repeated with the surrounding loop and as much
code as possible is moved into the loop which surrounds it in
turn. It is possible eventually that some code may migrate from
the inner loop right out of the nest entirely.

I discuss below an extended example to illustrate the power of
code optimisation applied to loops. Most code optimisation in
practice is performed with FORTRAN programs, so the example is
that of a DO loop. DO loops often contain array accesses, which
involve expensive multiplication as chapter 9 shows, so that
special techniques have been developed to move as much of the
relevant code out of as many loops as possible. Figures 10.10 to
10.13 show the effects of the process at various stages.
Initially the code for the inner loop, shown diagrammatically in
figure 10.10, performs 200 000 multiplications and 200 000
additions merely in accessing the elements·of the array: this in
itself will be a major activity of the loop and I therefore show
below how this access can be optimised. In particular I
concentrate on the elimination of MULT instructions in the inner
loop, since multiplication operations tend to be more expensive
than additions.

Loop-invariant code

The first step in the optimisation of a loop is to remove so-
called <u>loop-invariant code</u> — calculations which involve quantities
that don't seem to alter during the execution of the loop body.
Detection of loop-invariance involves the essential order of
computation: informally stated, a fragment of code is loop-

```
        t1 := J*5+ I
        t2 := 40*5
        DO 1 K = 1, 50
            ....
        r1 := <expression>
        r2 := K*t2+t1
        A[r2] := r1
            ....
    1 CONTINUE
```

Figure 10.11 Inner loop after loop-invariant code motion

invariant if it has no predecessors in the essential order and
would have no predecessors if placed at the end of the loop. In
the example of figure 10.10 neither J nor I is altered during the
loop - in fact this may be assumed since both J and I are the
controlling variables of enclosing loops. After loop-invariant
code has been moved, the code which accesses an element of the
array appears as in figure 10.11. Already optimisation has
removed one multiplication and one addition operation from the
loop, almost doubling the speed of array access.

Strength reduction

It is often profitable to replace a 'strong' operator by a
'weaker' one which is cheaper to perform. Thus 'x^2' can be
translated as 'x*x', 'x*2' as 'x+x' or even 'x shifted left one
position'. In the case of a loop which involves a multiplicative
array address calculation, it may be possible in some cases to
convert the multiplication into repeated addition. The calculation
of the array address in terms of the value of the variable K in
figure 10.11 can be seen to be a polynomial of degree 1: the
difference between successive terms is just the value of 't2'.
Strength reduction uses this relationship to produce the code
shown in figure 10.12. Note that optimisation has removed all
mention of K from the inner loop, so far as the array access is
concerned. It has converted 100 000 LOADs, 200 000 MULTns and
200 000 ADDs (800 000 store accesses) into just 100 000 ADDrs
(100 000 store accesses), which is a worthwhile saving. The object
program will run noticeably faster - if the machine has lights and
a loudspeaker, visibly and audibly faster!

When the same optimisations are performed with the the
enclosing loops in turn, code for the nest of loops might appear
as in figure 10.13. I assume that neither J nor K appear within
the body of the nest and therefore the code which controls
iteration of the middle and inner loops can do so by counting
iterations without altering J or K. The value of I is required (at
least in the assignment 't1:=I') and therefore the controlling
code for the outer loop is more conventional. I have assumed that

```
t1 := J*5 + I
t2 := 40*5
r2 := t1
DO 1 K = 1,
    ....
r1 := <expression>
r2 := r2+t2
A[r2] := r1

    ....
1 CONTINUE
```

Figure 10.12 Inner loop after strength reduction

t1, t2 and I itself can be allocated to registers. Note that this optimisation ensures that the code for the nest of loops does not alter the stored values of I, J or K, which is why the FORTRAN 66 standard insists that the value of a controlling variable is 'undefined' after the loop has finished.

Hardware Design and Optimisation

Many advances in hardware design have an effect on compiler design and in particular on optimisation. Some advances make optimisation less necessary, some make it more necessary, some make it harder and some make it easier. At the extremes of machine size, for example, code optimisation can be almost essential. Very small microprocessors demand very compact object code. (Optimisation is perhaps the wrong solution in this case since very small processors can be programmed with an interpreter which uses a very compact representation of the source program.) At the other extreme, some very large machines can execute programs with amazing efficiency provided that the object program makes careful use of the hardware to exploit its peculiarities and optimisation is essential to do this. The CRAY-1, for example, is a machine dedicated to vector-processing for which a compiler must generate vector-processing instructions if its expense is to be justified. A less extreme example is the use of multiple arithmetic units in the CDC 7600: code for this computer is most efficient when

---

Diagrammatic code: Actual code:

```
  t2 := 40*5                      LOADn   t2, 200
  DO 1 I = 1, 5                   LOADn   rI, 1
  t1 := I              %outer:    LOADr   t1, rI
  DO 1 J = 1, 40                  LOADn   1, 40
                                  STORE   1, %middlecount
  t1 := t1+5           %middle:   ADDn    t1, 5
  r2 := t1                        LOADr   2, t1
  DO 1 K = 1, 50                  LOADn   1, 50
                                  STORE   1, %innercount
     ...              %inner:     ...
  r1 := <expression>              r1 := <expression>
  r2 := r2+t2                     ADDr    2, t2
  A(r2) := r1                     STORE   1, <#A-204>(2)
  ....                            ...
1 CONTINUE                     1: DECSKP     , %innercount
                                  JUMP       , %inner
                                  DECSKP     , %middlecount
                                  JUMP       , %middle
                                  ADDn    rI, 1
                                  SKIPGTn rI, 4
                                  JUMP       , %outer
```

Figure 10.13 Code for nest of loops after optimisation

interlocks between arithmetic units are avoided, as figure 10.14 illustrates.

If some hardware designs make optimisation essential, some can make it less important. User-microprogrammable 'soft' machines or 'emulators' allow the compiler-writer in effect to design the object code of the machine on which the program will run. Much of the need for code optimisation arises because source language operations are difficult to specify in the object code of a machine which doesn't cater for them directly: by designing a machine with a convenient set of operations the compiler-writer can ensure a compact object program at least.   Even some 'hard' machines have special instructions which reduce the need for optimisation by taking over specialised tasks. For example the Manchester University MU5 has instructions which calculate the address of a row of a two-dimensional array, given the dope-vector and the row number.

Some other hardware designs take over tasks which have traditionally been carried out by compile-time optimisation. Global register allocation, for example, attempts to reduce the number of store accesses during execution of a program by holding important values in registers. This optimisation can be carried out automatically by hardware which includes an associatively addressed 'naming store' or 'cache memory'. Such hardware intercepts store accesses, shadowing those locations which are most frequently accessed in a super-fast associative memory. Such hardware optimises the program more effectively than any compiler, since the choice of locations which are selected for shadowing in the cache memory depends on the detailed behaviour of the object program. The behaviour of the program, and hence the use of the cache memory, may vary over time - even during execution of a single loop - and may depend on the data which the program reads in. By contrast a compiler must attempt to optimise every possible control path through the program at once, which means that no particular path can be optimally translated. The cache memory doesn't take over all the tasks of register allocation: deferred storage optimisation may still be worthwhile and redundant code elimination will certainly be useful.

Expression: a+b+c+d

minimum register use	maximum parallelism
(3 additions in sequence)	(3 additions but 2 in parallel)
r1 := a+b	r1 := a+b
r1 := r1+c	r2 := c+d
r1 := r1+d	r1 := r1+r2

Figure 10.14 Efficient use of multiple arithmetic units

Although the use of special hardware - 'soft' machines, special instructions, cache memories - can reduce the need for optimisation it cannot yet totally duplicate its effect. Special hardware may reduce the cost advantage of optimisation to such an extent, though, that for many users and many programs code optimisation isn't worth the time and effort.

Language Design and Optimisation

One view of programming, to which I subscribe, has it that the design of a program should be couched as a high-level description of the behaviour which a processor must imitate when it runs that program. This description can be broken down into simpler descriptions, which are then refined into still simpler descriptions, and so on until a description is produced which is sufficiently low-level to be transcribed into a programming language and executed on a computer. If a programming language has constructs which allow the text of the program to mimic the hierarchy of its design - recursive procedures, co-processing classes, **while** and **for** loops, **begin-end** bracketing of statements, etc. - then the activity of program design and the activity of programming in the language become almost the same activity. Furthermore the program can express its designer's intentions directly. Two examples: if the algorithm conceived uses conditional iteration then the program contains a **while** loop, if the algorithm breaks an action down into a number of sub-actions then the program uses **begin-end** bracketing of a sequence of recursive procedure calls.

Such so-called 'structured programs' are not only easy to read or to understand but are also easy to translate into relatively efficient code. A tree-walking simple translator can generate efficient code for a recursive procedure call, for example, while it would take quite an effective optimiser to generate efficient code for the same algorithm if the stack were simulated with an INTEGER array in FORTRAN. The example of optimisation of array access within a loop, shown in figures 10.10 to 10.13 above, could be directly expressed in ALGOL 68 by using identifiers in the inner loops of the nest to refer to 'slices' of the array: a similar improvement could be produced in any system programming language which allows the user to address the 'array' as a 5-element vector of (40-element vectors of (50-element vectors)).

This argument may take the 'programs should say what they mean' argument too far: it is unreasonable to expect programmers to be concerned with aspects of program efficiency which might just as easily be taken over by a compiler. In many cases, though, the demands of program clarity and the requirements of object program efficiency can be met with a single construct. The recursive procedure is one example of a construct which does this: another is provided by the **where** construct, illustrated in figure 10.15. This mechanism reduces the need for common sub-expression evaluation and for redundant code elimination by allowing the programmer to specify important (high-level) relationships between the values of expressions.

The message of this book is that a simple translator can produce acceptable code for a well-designed modern language, and I argue that much of the demand for code optimisation is caused by the widespread use of inappropriate programming languages. If the source language contains constructs which closely model the behaviours which the user wishes to describe, then programs in the language will be easier for humans to understand and easier for compilers to translate into efficient code. BCPL, for example, is a better system programming language than is FORTRAN so a straightforward BCPL compiler will generate better 'bit-pushing' code than any but the most sophisticated FORTRAN optimising compiler. It is easier to write and debug system programs in BCPL than in FORTRAN, because the language is designed for it. Similarly, COBOL is a better data-processing language than ALGOL 68, but a worse numerical programming language, and these facts will be reflected in the clarity of source programs and the efficiency of object programs in the two languages.

I argue, then, that designing a language so that users can specify the processor's behaviour directly yet at a high level leads to clear programs and to efficient code with a minimum need for expensive and complicated optimisation. A contrary view is that programming language design should move away from 'imperative' instructions to the 'declarative' description of a program's intended net effect: the task of the programmer is to specify the net effect and of the compiler to generate a program which produces that effect efficiently. In this view the program should contain little or no imperative 'control' information and the compiler should infer what it can from the declarative or functional specification of the program's net effect. There isn't yet a totally effective technology which allows us to program in this way: when one exists we shall be in a position to judge which of the two approaches to programming makes our programming life easier, more pleasant and more productive.

```
      B[x,y] := x*(y+2) where x = z+2, y = z-1
                        where z = A[i];

ALGOL 60:
   B[A[i]+2, A[i]-1] := (A[i]+2)*(A[i]+1)

FORTRAN:
   I1 = A(I)+2
   I2 = A(I)-1
   B(I1,I2) = I1 * (A(I)+1)
```

Figure 10.15 Use of the 'where' construct

Summary

Code optimisation increases the efficiency of object programs but
at the same time increases the cost of program development both by
increasing compilation time and by imposing restrictions on the
behaviour of object programs which can't be checked by the
compiler. No compiler can reasonably attempt all conceivable
optimisations and a few simple techniques can produce a large
fraction of the effect of more powerful mechanisms at a fraction
of their cost.

Optimisation proceeds by discovering the essential order of
computation within and between 'basic blocks' of statements, by
re-ordering and merging code fragments within a basic block and by
moving code between basic blocks. An optimiser can increase the
proportion of calculations which are carried out at compile-time.
By allocating values to be held in registers it can reduce the
number of store accesses required in the   evaluation   of
expressions. By moving code fragments out of loops it can increase
the speed of execution of the object program.

Hardware design can reduce or increase the need for code
optimisation. Modern language design tends to reduce the need for
optimisation although in the future 'functional' programming
languages may revive it. The simplest, and at present for many
users the cheapest way to optimise all programs in a computer
system is to buy a new computer!

Section III
Run-time Support

The procedure[1] is perhaps the most powerful program structuring
device so far invented and programmers should not be discouraged
from using the full power of procedural abstraction by an
inefficient or incomplete implementation of procedure call and
return. It is particularly important that language implementations
don't discourage the use of recursion. In practice
(Wichmann,1975) many implementations of recursive programming
languages have suffered adversely in comparisons of their
efficiency with that of FORTRAN, largely because of poor design of
the code fragments which handle argument passing, procedure call
and procedure return. Even on a conventional machine there is no
justification for such a large efficiency gap as occurs in
practice: chapters 11, 12 and 13 show how to minimise the gap in
efficiency; chapter 14 shows how the provision of special stack-
handling instructions can allow a modern recursive programming
language, such as PASCAL or ALGOL 68, to be implemented as
efficiently as FORTRAN. The recursive language is then doubly
desirable since FORTRAN implementations gain much of their fabled
speed by eliminating almost all of the necessary run-time checks,
for example on argument types at procedure entry; a compiler for a
modern recursive language can impose such checks entirely at
compile-time and then no run-time checking is necessary.

In addition to the code fragments generated from the
translation of expressions and statements, discussed in section
II, the object code of a compiled program contains a high
proportion of 'overhead' fragments. Some overheads have to do with
run-time error checking - for example checking that the object
program doesn't overstep the bounds of an array when attempting to
access it - but there are many others which have to do with
maintaining communication between the different blocks and
procedures of the program, with storage handling and so on. The
fragments which implement the source language operations of
argument passing, procedure call and return are run-time support
fragments, and the cost of executing them is part of the run-time
support overhead.

It's perhaps misleading to refer to the code fragments which
implement argument passing, procedure call/return and storage or
stack management as 'overhead' fragments since they are essential
to the operation of the object program as a whole. I prefer to
call them run-support or environment support fragments since they
produce and maintain the run-time environment within which other
code fragments can operate. Run-time support is rather like an
overhead, however, in that many users seem to be unaware of the
need for it and of its necessary cost! It's also convenient to
separate the cost of executing a procedure body from the cost of

---

1 Throughout this book the word 'procedure' is intended to
  include 'function': a function is merely a procedure which
  returns a result.

setting up and returning from the procedure call and in this book
I refer to the latter cost as the 'overhead' of the procedure
call.

The efficiency of run-time support fragments is crucial to the
efficiency of the object program as well as essential to its
operation. History has shown that inexperienced compiler-writers
often design disastrously inefficient code for run-time support,
in particular for the argument passing fragments discussed in
chapter 12. Because ignorance of the tasks of run-time support
seems widespread, chapters in this section concentrate upon "what
to do" - the design of the code fragments - rather than "how to do
it" - the design of procedures to generate such code - which is
the emphasis of the rest of the book. The code fragments are set
out in some detail: naturally the peculiarities of any particular
instruction set will affect the detail design of code fragments
and therefore the examples may need modification before they can
be implemented on any particular object machine.

Chapter 11 discusses the mechanism of procedure call, both for
non-recursive languages such as FORTRAN and for stack-based
languages such as ALGOL 60, PASCAL and ALGOL 68: it also
introduces a model of procedure call and return which is referred
to in later chapters. Chapter 12 concentrates on the translation
of procedure calls with arguments and in particular on the need to
check argument-parameter compatibility at compile-time. Chapter 13
deals with non-local data addressing, procedure values passed as
arguments and the implementation of ALGOL 60's call-by-name
facility. Chapter 14 discusses the effect which the provision of
special stack-handling instructions can have on the implementation
of procedure call and return, touches on the implementation of
system-programming languages and ALGOL 68, introduces the notion
of 'heap' storage and sketches the implementation of **class**es in
SIMULA 67.

Throughout this section I have assumed that the object program
uses the method of non-local data addressing called 'procedure-
level addressing' in which data frames are allocated to procedures
alone and the data frames of blocks nested within the procedure
are coalesced with that of the procedure. This mechanism has some
advantages and some disadvantages: I compare it with the
alternative mechanism of 'block-level addressing' in chapter 13.

In the examples below I assume that the object machine has a
large number of general-purpose registers available for stack
handling and procedure call. I've used a separate register for
each task and a single letter to identify each of the different
registers: 'F' (frame) for the register which points to the
current stack frame, 'L' (link) for the register which holds the
address for procedure return and so on. On a machine with fewer
registers a single register may have to carry out several tasks
but the run-time support fragments would still have to operate in

much the sort of way which I describe, although they would
naturally become longer and slower because of the need to
continually load and store the pointer values which are normally
held in separate registers.

Where there is a conflict between fast code and compact code in
the fragments described in this section, I have tended to prefer
fast code. On small machines compact code is essential and in such
cases it may be worthwhile to make standard fragments such as the
'prologue' and 'epilogue' fragments of chapter 11 into subroutines
which are called from relevant positions in the object program.
The program will then be smaller but slower - once again the
principles of operation of the run-time support fragments aren't
affected by such pragmatic adjustments.

11 Procedure Call and Return

This chapter discusses the design of code fragments which support procedure call and return in both recursive and non-recursive programming languages. To aid the discussion in later chapters it includes a model of procedure call and return based on the notion of a procedure activation record. A procedure activation is a special case of a 'micro-process[1]', and the same model can explain the operation of languages such as SIMULA 67 whose control structures are not restricted to simple procedure call and return. It also helps to explain how restrictions on the use of data and procedures in the source language can allow restricted (and therefore less costly) implementations of the general procedure call and return mechanism. The mechanism of procedure call and return in FORTRAN is briefly discussed: then I concentrate on the mechanisms of stack handling which are required to implement procedure call and return in a recursive language on a conventional object machine.

The Tasks of Procedure Call and Return Fragments

Each procedure body in the source program is represented by a section of instructions in the object program. When a procedure has been called, and before it returns, various items of information represent the state of the current procedure activation. The instruction pointer defines a position in the code, the contents of the data frame (see chapters 1 and 8) define the values both of the parameters and of any data objects owned by the activation, and an explicit or implicit collection of pointers defines the activation's <u>environment</u> - those non-local data frames which the current procedure activation may access. Note the distinction between the instructions of the procedure body, the data frame set up when the procedure is called and the procedure activation proper, which is defined by a position in the code

---

1 'Micro' process because a process in many languages can be made up of many micro-processes.

together with the contents of the data frame and linkages to other
data frames (activation records).

When execution of the procedure body reaches a point at which
the current procedure calls another procedure, or calls itself
recursively, the current activation is halted, the items of
information which record its state are saved and similar
information is set up for the newly created procedure activation.
In a recursive language the action of calling a procedure involves
the acquisition of space for the data frame of the new activation,
usually taken from a stack.

When execution of the new activation reaches a point in the
procedure body which corresponds to a procedure return, the stored
items of information which defined the state of the calling
activation are reloaded, and execution of that procedure's
instruction sequence continues from the point indicated by the
instruction pointer. In a recursive language the space acquired
for the data frame of the returning procedure activation must be

---

Call

1. Allocate space for the data frame (activation record)
   of the called procedure.
2. Prepare information about the arguments of the
   procedure call and place it in the parameter slots of
   the new data frame (or in some pre-arranged locations).
3. Set up environment pointers to allow the new activation
   access to other data frames (e.g. those of textually
   enclosing blocks or procedures in block-structured
   languages).
4. Save the current data frame/ environment/ instruction
   pointers and create new values for the new activation.
5. Stop execution of the current procedure activation and
   start that of the new (called) activation.

Return

1. Store the procedure result in a pre-arranged register
   or location.
2. Reload the calling procedure activation's data frame/
   environment/ instruction pointers.
3. Stop execution of the called procedure activation and
   resume execution of the calling activation.

Garbage Collection

1. Reclaim the space allocated for the data frame
   (activation record) of the called procedure.

Figure 11.1 Tasks of procedure call and return fragments

recovered at some stage - usually this means adjusting the stack during or after the sequence of instructions which implement the procedure return. Manipulating data frame pointers, acquiring and releasing data frame space are all part of the maintenance of the <u>Activation Record Structure</u> introduced in chapters 1 and 4.

The tasks which must be carried out during execution of procedure call and return are summarised in figure 11.1. Efficiency of execution comes not only from careful design of the individual code fragments which carry out these tasks but also from careful design of the source language to allow short-cuts in the execution of the object program. Restrictions on the source language may reduce its expressive power but can increase the efficiency of execution of object programs.

In FORTRAN, for example, the allocation of data space can be performed once and for all at load-time when the program is loaded and before it is run. Procedure call and return are then more efficient (although not so much more efficient as you might expect - see the examples below and in chapter 13) but the penalty is that FORTRAN programmers can't use the expressive power of recursion. You can't write in FORTRAN, for example, the sort of recursive procedures which are used in this book to illustrate the translation of a parse tree into object code.

Conventional recursive languages are also restricted, though less so than FORTRAN, in order that data frames can be allocated from a stack. In PASCAL and ALGOL 60 the type of result which can be returned from a procedure or assigned to a location is restricted so that there can be no pointers to a procedure activation's data frame when it returns; ALGOL 68 imposes similar restrictions but in a less severe form (see chapter 14 for a discussion of the problems this causes).

Only SIMULA 67 among the popular compiled languages uses the fully general call and return mechanism, as part of the implementation of **class**es, and as a result allows the most general form of programming. The cost of generality is relative inefficiency - simple programs tend to run slower in SIMULA than they might in, say, PASCAL - but the benefit of generality is that new ways of programming are made possible. In particular SIMULA 67 allows co-processing, which may prove as much of an influence on program design in the future as recursion has proved in the past.

Figure 11.1 does not include the checking of compatibility between arguments and parameter specifications (number of arguments, type, kind, etc.) as a task of the object program. Such checks are rarely necessary, are expensive to execute and are too often included in place of more convenient and more efficient compile-time checks. Chapter 12 concentrates on the topic of argument passing and on ways of avoiding run-time

argument/parameter checks in modern languages. FORTRAN is the
major language in current use which requires run-time
argument/parameter checks and yet in implementations of FORTRAN,
for the sake of efficiency, such checks are almost never included.

Layout of Procedure Call and Return Fragments

The number and complexity of the tasks set down in figure 11.1
suggest already that it takes more than a single JSUB instruction
to call a procedure and more than a single RETN instruction to
return to the calling procedure. The layout of code fragments in
the object program is illustrated in figure 11.2: the fragments in
the calling procedure would be generated as part of the
translation of an expression or a statement and the fragments in
the called procedure as part of the translation of the procedure
declaration.

   The cost of executing a procedure call is therefore the cost of
executing all the fragments shown in figure 11.2 - argument
preparation, precall housekeeping, JSUB, prologue, procedure body,
epilogue, RETN and postcall housekeeping. Minimising the cost of
a procedure call means minimising this total execution cost. In
most cases the cost is reduced by shortening and speeding-up the
operation of the run-time support fragments - the 'overheads' of
the procedure call - but it may occasionally be worthwhile to
increase the overhead cost in order to speed up the execution of
the procedure body. Examples in which this is so are given in the

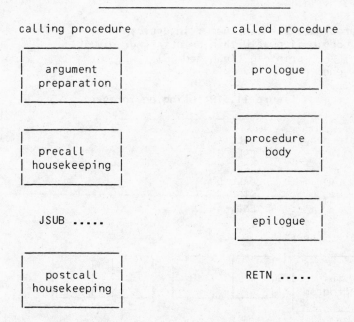

Figure 11.2 Layout of code fragments in procedure call

discussion below of 'call-by-result' in FORTRAN and in the discussion in chapter 13 of the relative merits of environment links and display vectors for non-local data addressing.

In order to minimise object program size, as many as possible of the tasks defined in figure 11.1 should be performed in the called procedure (i.e. in the prologue and epilogue fragments) rather than in the fragments which occur in the calling procedure. Since there are surely never more procedure declarations than there are procedure calls in the source program, shortening the procedure call at the expense of the prologue and epilogue must lead to a smaller object program.

Recursion and the 'Efficiency' of FORTRAN

There are many programming problems which have a 'naturally recursive' solution. An obvious example is the tree-walking translation mechanism used in section II: without recursive procedures it is much more difficult to write a bug-free translator. Another example is that of printing an integer, shown as a PASCAL procedure in figure 11.3. Given a 'printdigit' procedure which is capable of printing out the character representation of a single integer digit, the 'printint' procedure shown will print the character-string representation of any

---

```
procedure printint(num : integer);
   begin if num>10 then printint(num div 10);
         printdigit(num mod 10)
   end;
```

Figure 11.3 Printing an integer

```
main program:     CALL A
                  CALL B
                  CALL C
                  CALL D
                  STOP
                  END
```

data frames:

Figure 11.4 Space allocation at load time

positive integer[1]. As any programmer who has tried to write the corresponding non-recursive printing procedure will know, the recursive solution is simpler and easier to write. Ease of construction means fewer bugs, which means faster program development.

Problems with a naturally recursive solution, then, are harder to program in a non-recursive language such as FORTRAN, which means that FORTRAN solutions to such problems will be more expensive to develop than solutions written in a recursive language. Since the cost of developing a program often exceeds the cost of running it over its entire lifetime, ease of expression in the source language may be a better guide to overall cost than the raw efficiency of the object code fragments. Such 'efficiency' as is actually gained by eliminating recursion from a programming language is dearly bought.

Source: FRED(K1*K2, FRED(M, N))

```
Code:        LOAD    1, k1
             MULT    1, k2
             STORE   1, #t1    /* K1*K2 in #t1 */
             LOADa   1, argblock2
             JSUB    L, #fred
             STORE   1, #t2    /* FRED(M,N) in #t2 */
             LOADa   1, argblock1
             JSUB    L, #fred
                ....
argblock1:   #t1     /* address of K1*K2 */
             #t2     /* address of FRED(M,N) */
argblock2:   m       /* address of M */
             n       /* address of N */
```

Source: INTEGER FUNCTION FRED(I, J)

```
#fred:       STORE   L, #link
             LOAD    2, 0(1) /* first argument address */
             STORE   2, #i   /* store as first parameter */
             LOAD    2, 1(1) /* second argument address */
             STORE   2, #j   /* store as second parameter */

             .. procedure body ..

             RETNi   , #link
```

Figure 11.5 Possible code for FORTRAN procedure call

---

1 The **div** operator is defined to calculate the quotient of integer division, the **mod** operator calculates the remainder.

In the simplest implementations of FORTRAN each procedure is allocated data frame space when the program is loaded and no data frames share storage space. Space allocation at load time (so-called static allocation) is made possible precisely because FORTRAN prohibits recursive procedure calls. This technique of storage space allocation saves instructions in the procedure call and return fragments, but wastes storage space when compared with a stack allocation mechanism (see below) in which space for a data frame is allocated each time the procedure is called and is reclaimed each time it returns. Thus in figure 11.4 the main program calls subroutines A, B, C and D and, if none of these procedures calls any of the others, the object program contains storage for five data frames when no more than two are ever simultaneously required.

To counteract this waste of space, FORTRAN implementations often allow the user to specify 'overlaying' of procedure data frames. Subroutines A, B, C and D in figure 11.4 could then be made to share a single data frame area. In a more complicated program than that shown, however, the inter-procedure linkages may be difficult to discover and overlay allocation will then be difficult and prone to error. The penalty for error is disaster: if procedures A and B share a data frame area yet A calls B (indirectly through other procedures, say) the operation of B will overwrite the data frame of A. If it overwrites essential housekeeping information, such as the code address to be used on return from A, then the program will loop or go out of control.

As well as wasting space, the FORTRAN procedure call mechanism isn't as efficient as might be supposed. The design of the language makes compile-time checking of argument/parameter correspondences impossible since procedures are declared quite separately, yet most implementations omit the necessary run-time checks[1] in the cause of object program efficiency. All arguments must be passed by reference, which increases run-time efficiency because the addresses of many arguments can be computed at load time but the gain may be reduced in practice because of the need to move argument information into the data frame of a called procedure. Few implementations include a run-time check in the procedure prologue to ensure that a procedure isn't called recursively[2]; in the absence of such a check an accidentally recursive program will loop.

---

1 Load-time argument/parameter checking is possible, but rarely seems to be attempted.

2 It is possible to implement a (rather over-severe) load-time check, using Warshall's algorithm as described in chapter 15. I don't know that such a check is ever used in practice.

Figure 11.5 shows a fragment of a FORTRAN expression together with the code that might be produced. To execute the procedure calls shown takes twenty instructions in addition to two executions of the body of the procedure FRED. The twenty overhead instructions make thirty-six store accesses. This is a smaller overhead than that for recursive procedures using the same instruction set and the same example (at least twenty-six instructions and forty-two store accesses - see chapter 12) but it is worth remembering that FORTRAN's advantage is partly gained by 'streaking' (running naked without run-time checks!). Using a 'block move' instruction in the procedure prologue which transfers all the argument information in a single instruction would reduce the number of overhead instructions in the procedure call and return but would still require several store accesses to move the information across.

In figure 11.5 the 'return link' register is 'L', the procedure result is passed back in register 1. I won't explain the detailed operation of this code: it can be understood more easily after you have grasped the principles of operation of the stack-handling fragments discussed later in this chapter and the argument-passing fragments of chapter 12. Including a check against a recursive call of FRED would take an extra couple of instructions in the procedure prologue and epilogue; checking the number of arguments and their types would take two further instructions per parameter. With more complete run-time checks, therefore, the overhead cost of the procedure calls in figure 11.5 might rise to thirty instructions.

Although FORTRAN procedure call/return overheads are significant, FORTRAN programs are super-efficient in their manipulation of environments and non-local data objects. A procedure body may access only its own data frame and those of any COMMON blocks mentioned in the declaration part of the procedure. Because space for every data frame, including those of COMMON blocks, is allocated before the program runs, the loader can relocate each access to any variable and each such access therefore will take only a single instruction. By contrast, some environment access mechanisms used in recursive programming languages (see chapter 13) may take more than one instruction to access non-local variables. Note also that access to FORTRAN vectors is highly efficient, as chapter 9 shows, and that chapter 10 shows how access to FORTRAN arrays can often be effectively optimised.

Figure 11.5 illustrates a point about the trade-off between the cost of run-time support 'overheads' and the total cost of execution of a procedure call. Each access in the body of procedure FRED to the arguments which correspond to parameters I or J must, in the example shown, be indirect via the stored parameter addresses. This will involve an extra store access (compared with access to a local variable) even if the program uses an indirect-addressing instruction such as LOADi or STOREi: it will be still less efficient if the machine doesn't have indirect-addressing instructions. If the prologue copies the value of each argument into the called procedure's data frame, the procedure body operates directly on this local copy and finally the epilogue copies the (possibly altered) values back into the argument location then the execution time of the procedure body, and hence the total execution time of the procedure call, may be reduced although the 'overhead' cost is increased by about three instructions per parameter. The FORTRAN 66 standard contains some cryptic remarks designed specifically to permit this slightly more efficient 'call-by-result' mechanism as an alternative to the more normal 'call-by-reference'.

Overall the restrictions of the FORTRAN language make programming harder and therefore more expensive; the use of static allocation wastes space compared with stack allocation; the procedure call and return mechanism is only super-efficient when used without run-time checks. FORTRAN implementations gain efficiency, however, in the simplicity of access to vectors and to non-local variables.

Simple Stack Handling

In order to implement recursive procedure calls it is necessary to provide a more general space allocation mechanism than that described for FORTRAN above. A recursive procedure call means that the same procedure text is being scanned by two or more separate activations: they can share the same code but they can't share a data frame. At each recursive procedure call, therefore, the run-time support mechanisms must acquire space for the data frame of a new procedure activation; after the procedure returns the space may be reclaimed. Although the compiler could in principle distinguish between potentially recursive procedures and those which are definitely non-recursive, in practice it need not since a recursive procedure call is at worst only slightly less efficient than the non-recursive kind. In most implementations of recursive programming languages, therefore, every procedure call is treated as if it were recursive and all are handled by the same run-time support mechanism.

The data frame space for the procedure activation created by the execution of a procedure call is normally allocated from a stack on procedure entry and reclaimed at procedure exit. While the activation is running there must be some pointer to its data frame space so that it can access its parameter information, passed in the procedure call, and the other values which are stored in its data frame. I assume that an index register 'F' (for Frame) points to the current data frame. I assume also that an index register 'T' (for Top-of-stack) points to the first free location on the stack[1].

Accessing non-local data (for example variables in the data frame of an enclosing block) will require other index registers,

---

Before call, in procedure A:

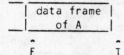

```
 __| data frame |
 __|   of A     |
    ^             ^
    F             T
```

After A calls B:

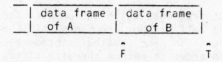

```
 __| data frame | data frame |
 __|   of A     |   of B      |
    ^             ^
    F             T
```

After B calls C and C calls A:

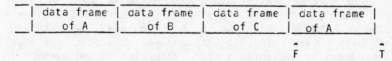

```
 __| data frame | data frame | data frame | data frame |
 __|   of A     |   of B     |   of C     |   of A      |
                              ^             ^
                              F             T
```

After A returns to C and C returns to B:

```
 __| data frame | data frame |
 __|   of A     |   of B      |
    ^             ^
    F             T
```

After B returns to A:

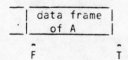

```
 __| data frame |
 __|   of A     |
    ^             ^
    F             T
```

Figure 11.6 Stack changes during a procedure call

---

1 This register is really only required when the source language allows the user to declare a data structure, such as an array, whose size is determined dynamically during entry to the block or procedure in which it is declared: in such a case it is impossible to calculate the total size of the data frame at compile-time. Chapter 14 discusses the implementation of languages which require only a single register to address the stack.

whose use is discussed in later chapters. No machine has an infinite supply of index registers and therefore the same collection of registers must be shared by all the procedures and blocks in the program: much of the cost of the procedure call and return, as hinted in figure 11.1, lies in the manipulation of the data frame pointer registers.

Figure 11.6 shows how the stack changes during a procedure call. When procedure A calls procedure B a new data frame is created on the top of the stack, at the position defined by the 'T' register. Similar things happen when B calls C and when C calls A - note how readily the stack mechanism implements the indirect recursion in procedure A. As each procedure returns, the previous values of the 'F' and 'T' registers are reset.

Figure 11.7 shows possible code fragments which manipulate the stack pointers during a procedure call without arguments. All the stack-handling tasks are carried out in the called procedure's prologue and epilogue fragments in order to reduce the size of the object program: there is no precall or postcall housekeeping. Note, however, that the stack-handling mechanism of figure 11.7 requires eight instructions to execute a procedure call and return with no arguments: compare this with the three instructions - JSUB, STORE, RETN - which would be required by FORTRAN. Efficiency isn't everything, though, and you shouldn't lose sight of the programming advantages of recursive languages: in particular the code fragments in figure 11.7 allow recursion and run-time calculation of array dimensions.

The fragments shown in figure 11.7 are designed using the assumption that a procedure activation's data frame space can always be reclaimed immediately the activation terminates (i.e. on

---

```
Source: joe()

Call:      JSUB  L, #joe

Source: procedure joe(); ...

#joe:      STORE  L, 0(T)   /* save return address */
           STORE  F, 1(T)   /* save old value of F */
           LOADr  F, T      /* point to new data frame */
           ADDn   T, data-frame-size /* allocate space */

           ... procedure body ...

           LOADr  T, F
           LOAD   F, 1(T)
           RETNi    , 0(T)
```

Figure 11.7 Stack-handling code fragments

procedure return). This simple garbage collection mechanism is only possible if the <u>source language</u> restricts the use of pointers (ALGOL 68 **ref**s) which may lead from one data frame to another. In 'ALGOL 60-like' languages such as PASCAL or ALGOL 60 itself, such pointers are used implicitly in passing arrays, procedures or labels as arguments. These values cannot be returned as the result of a procedure, or assigned to a memory location, since this might produce a pointer from an older data frame to a newer and this would preclude reclamation of the data frame which is pointed to when its procedure returns. PASCAL allows free use of pointers which lead to 'heap' storage, though, and ALGOL 68 goes further in allowing some use of pointers which lead from data frame to data frame. I discuss the problems caused by this feature of ALGOL 68 in chapter 14; in other languages the run-time support fragments in the object program need not check the use of pointers on procedure exit because the necessary restrictions can be enforced by the compiler.

Allocating space for vectors and arrays

The object description mechanism discussed in chapter 8 allocates the data objects declared in a block or a procedure to consecutive locations in the data frame. This caters for variables and for fixed-size data structures such as FORTRAN vectors or arrays but, as figure 11.8 shows, it is impossible to allocate space for 'dynamic arrays' in this way. In the "impossible" data frame layout shown the cell allocated to variable 'i' would be offset n+2 cells from the start of the data frame and the cell for variable 'h' would be offset n+m+7 cells. This would mean that access to most variables in the block would require run-time calculation of their address - which would be somewhat inefficient!

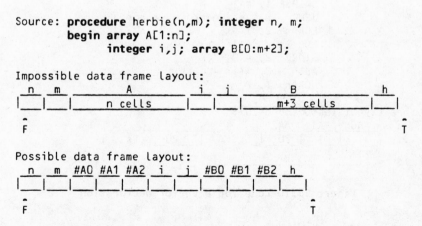

```
Source: procedure herbie(n,m); integer n, m;
        begin array A[1:n];
              integer i,j; array B[0:m+2];
```

Impossible data frame layout:
```
   n    m           A           i    j           B             h
 |___|___|     n cells     |___|___|     m+3 cells     |___|
   ^                                                           ^
   F                                                           T
```

Possible data frame layout:
```
   n    m   #A0  #A1  #A2   i    j   #B0  #B1  #B2   h
 |___|___|___|___|___|___|___|___|___|___|___|
   ^                                   ^
   F                                   T
```

Figure 11.8 Allocating space for vectors and arrays

```
let TranVecDecl(nodep) be
{ let vecname, lowerbound, upperbound =
                  nodep.first, nodep.second, nodep.third
  let addr = vecname.descriptor.address

  TranArithExpr(lowerbound, 1)
  Gen(STORE, 1, addr+1, F)   /* lower bound in #A1 */
  TranArithExpr(upperbound, 1)
  Gen(STORE, 1, addr+2, F)   /* upper bound in #A2 */

  Gen(SKIPGE, 1, addr+1, F) /* check upper >= lower */
  Gen(JSUB, L, vec-underflow-error)

  Gen(LOADr, 2, T)
  Gen(SUB, 2, addr+1, F)      /* r2 := T - lower bound */
  Gen(STORE, 2, addr, F)      /* address of A[0] in #A0 */
  Gen(ADDn, 2, 1, 1)          /* r2 := r2 + upper bound+1 */
  Gen(LOADr, T, 2)            /* extend top of stack */
}
```

Figure 11.9 Translating a vector declaration

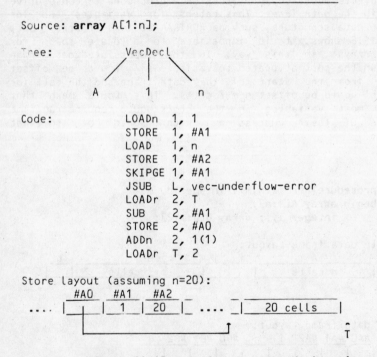

Source: **array A[1:n];**

Tree: VecDecl

                 A   1   n

Code: LOADn   1, 1
               STORE   1, #A1
               LOAD   1, n
               STORE   1, #A2
               SKIPGE 1, #A1
               JSUB   L, vec-underflow-error
               LOADr   2, T
               SUB   2, #A1
               STORE   2, #A0
               ADDn   2, 1(1)
               LOADr   T, 2

Store layout (assuming n=20):
     #A0   #A1   #A2
.... |_____|_1__|_20_|_ .... _|___20 cells__|
                                          ^
                                          T

Figure 11.10 Code for a vector declaration

The vector accessing mechanism described in chapter 9 allows the "possible" storage layout of figure 11.8. Each vector or array is allocated a fixed number of locations - in the case of a vector one each for base address, lower bound and upper bound - and thus the space required by the data frame at procedure or block entry can be calculated at compile time. The procedure prologue can be set up to allocate eleven cells to the data frame of the procedure shown in figure 11.8.

At some stage the space for the array or vector elements must be allocated. This can be done by a code fragment which is generated as the translation of the array declaration. Figure 11.9 shows a procedure which handles vector declarations and figure 11.10 shows an example of its operation. I have included a simple error-checking fragment which in practice would have to be more sophisticated because of the need to give a run-time error report which names the vector and gives values of lower and upper bounds. Error-checking code isn't really optional in this case, since without it an invalid declaration - a negative value of 'n' in figure 11.10, for example - would move the top-of-stack register downwards with almost certainly disastrous effects. Note that the space allocated for any vector or array in this way will be automatically reclaimed in the procedure epilogue of figure 11.7 when the top-of-stack register is moved to the base of the data frame.

The code fragment shown in figure 11.10 would run faster if it used the 'T' register for calculation rather than an intermediate register (register 2). For the purposes of run-time debugging, however, it is essential that the data frame registers are maintained correctly at all times - see chapter 20 for a fuller discussion. If the program can be interrupted for the purposes of run-time debugging and if the top-of-stack register ever holds an incorrect value, no matter how momentarily, an unfriendly universe will ensure that one day that will be the instant at which an interrupt occurs!

Summary

The operations required to implement procedure call are those required to create a data structure which describes a procedure activation and to link it into the Activation Record Structure which describes the state of execution of every procedure activation in the object program. The operations of procedure return are those required to remove an entry from the Activation Record Structure. By prohibiting recursion, FORTRAN allows the Activation Record Structure to be set up before the object program starts to run, and therefore FORTRAN procedure call and return fragments are relatively efficient in execution.

In the case of a procedure call in a recursive programming language, the object program must acquire space for each data frame (activation record) from a stack, and must return it to the stack when the procedure returns. This is more expensive than the FORTRAN operation when using the instructions discussed in this chapter. Chapter 14 discusses the effect of special stack-handling instructions on the efficiency of recursive procedure call and return. The use of a stack allows the allocation of space for 'dynamic arrays' - stack-borne data structures whose size is determined dynamically on block or procedure entry. Modern recursive programming languages allow full compile-time argument checking, which may make them preferable to FORTRAN even when they are slightly less efficient in execution.

12 Arguments and Parameters

The tasks set out in figure 11.1 of chapter 11 include the preparation of argument information - for example the value of an argument expression, a pointer to an argument variable or a pointer to an argument vector - and the placing of this information in a location within the new procedure activation's data frame. This chapter concentrates on this apparently insignificant aspect of run-time support in part because it is so often inefficiently implemented in practice and in part because compilers do not always perform all possible syntactic checks at compile-time.

Figure 11.1 does not include the run-time checking of the correspondence between argument type or kind and parameter declaration as a necessary task of the object program: this chapter shows that such run-time checks are <u>almost</u> <u>never</u> <u>necessary</u>. Deficiencies in the design of a language may cause a minimum of run-time checking - see the discussion of ALGOL 60 'parametric procedure calls' below - but in most modern languages argument/parameter correspondence checks can be performed completely at compile time.

Run-time argument/parameter checks are confusing to use because a program which the compiler passes as 'correct' can fail during execution due to an error which ought to be detected by the compiler. Perhaps an even greater drawback is that run-time checks are disastrously inefficient: they can impose a ten-fold increase in the number of 'overhead' instructions in a procedure call and return. Since procedural abstraction is such an important program structuring device in any programming language, this inefficiency can have a devastating effect on the overall usefulness of the language implementation. It may even encourage programmers to use a less convenient language merely because its implementation produces more efficient object code.

Different Kinds of Argument Information

Different languages employ different mechanisms of linking between
a procedure and the arguments in a procedure call. Such mechanisms
are often described from the point of view of the called
procedure, and when seen in this way there are a variety of
different mechanisms. These include 'call-by-value', 'call-by-
reference', 'call-by-result, 'call-by-name', 'call-by-need' and so
on and on. From the point of view of the language implementor,
though, the process of communication can be split into two parts:
first, some <u>argument information</u> is passed to the new procedure
activation; second, that activation makes use of it in one way or
another to implement the communication appropriate to the source
language.

   In practice there are only three different kinds of argument
information which can be passed to a procedure activation: they
are

  (i) <u>Value</u> information: the value of an expression.

  (ii) <u>Reference</u> information: the address of a data object, or
    the dope vector in the case of an object such as a vector
    or array.

  (iii) <u>Name</u> information: a mini-procedure which the called
    procedure can activate to find out either 'value' or
    'reference' information about the actual argument.

In theoretical terms there is no difference between (i), (ii) and
(iii) - an address is just a special kind of value, as is a
procedure - but when a procedure call is translated the code which
is generated to pass argument information will depend on which of
the three kinds of information is to be passed.

   The use of the argument information by the called procedure
body - or from its point of view the <u>parameter</u> information -
implements a particular 'call-by-X' mechanism. Chapter 11
discusses the difference between call-by-reference and call-by-
result in FORTRAN: each of these mechanisms is implemented by
passing 'reference' argument information which the called
procedure makes use of in different ways. In most implementations
of ALGOL 60 when a vector or array parameter is called-by-value
the argument information which is passed is the 'dope vector' of
the argument vector or array - i.e. 'reference' information. The
called procedure body then uses the reference to make a copy of
the argument vector or array in its own data frame space. The
difference between an ALGOL 60 **integer** parameter called-by-value
and an ALGOL 68 **int** parameter lies only in the way in which the
called procedure may manipulate the parameter: in each case the
argument information is an integer number stored in the data frame
of the called procedure activation but in ALGOL 68 that activation

may not assign a new value to the parameter or manipulate its address. The ALGOL 60 call-by-name mechanism and the newer call-by-need (and the still newer mechanism of 'lazy evaluation') are implemented by passing 'name' information which is used in different ways in the called activation.

This chapter concentrates on the passing of 'value' and 'reference' information for simple expressions and data objects. 'Name' information is discussed in chapter 13, where I also discuss the mechanisms required to pass a procedure value[1] as an argument in a procedure call.

Passing Argument Information

The tasks set out in figure 11.1 of chapter 11 include the storing of information about the arguments of a procedure call in the data frame of the called procedure activation. When using the stack-handling mechanism illustrated in figure 11.7, the new data frame space is allocated during execution of the procedure prologue: nevertheless it is possible for the calling procedure activation

---

```
Source: fred(m,n)

Code:           LOAD    1, m
                STORE   1, 2(T)
                LOAD    1, n
                STORE   1, 3(T)
                JSUB    L, #fred

Source: function fred(i,j: integer):integer; ...

#fred:          STORE   L, 0(T)
                STORE   F, 1(T)
                LOADr   F, T
                ADDn    T, data-frame-size

                ... procedure body ...

                LOADr   T, F
                LOAD    F, 1(T)
                RETNi    , 0(T)
```

Figure 12.1 Calling a procedure with two arguments

---

1 This is not the value produced as a result of calling a procedure, but a value which can be used to call the procedure. It consists of the code address of the procedure together with a representation of the 'environment' discussed in chapter 13. In chapter 13 I refer to this kind of value as a closure.

to store the argument information in locations above the current
top-of-stack, within the space which will eventually be occupied
by the data frame of the called procedure activation. This chapter
discusses the detailed implementation of this mechanism and
chapter 14 shows how specialised stack-handling instructions allow
simpler methods of passing argument information.

Figure 12.1 shows possible code for a procedure call with two
arguments, each passed as a value. I assume that the object
description phase has allocated the parameters 'i' and 'j' of
procedure 'fred' to locations 2 and 3 of the data frame, leaving
locations 0 and 1 to hold the pointers stored by the procedure
prologue. The body of procedure 'fred' can access its parameters
via the frame register 'F': for example the instruction
'LOAD reg, 2(F)' will load the value of parameter 'i'. Note also
that the prologue and epilogue of figure 12.1 are identical to
those of figure 11.7 since all argument passing is handled by the
calling procedure.

In the interests of execution efficiency, the mechanism
presented in figure 12.1 doesn't move the top-of-stack register
each time an argument is placed in position: thus the argument
information is in a sort of no-man's-land above the top of the
stack. It would be dishonest to conceal the fact that this

---

source: fred(k1*k2, fred(m,n))

tree:

```
                         ProcCall
                        /        \
                   fred        ArgList
                              /        \
                             *          ArgList
                            / \        /      \
                          k1   k2   ProcCall
                                    /      \
                                 fred     ArgList
                                         /    \
                                        m     ArgList
                                             /  \
                                           n
```

code: LOAD   1, k1
         MULT   1, k2
         STORE 1, 2(T)
            ADDn   T, 3
            LOAD   1, m
            STORE 1, 2(T)
            LOAD   1, n
            STORE 1, 3(T)
            JSUB   L, #fred
            SUBn   T, 3
         STORE 1, 3(T)
         JSUB   L, #fred

(code for procedure 'fred' is as shown in figure 12.1)

Figure 12.2 Code for nested procedure calls

mechanism is rather tricky to implement when procedure calls are
nested - i.e. when an argument to a procedure call contains
another procedure call. For example the source fragment shown in
figure 12.2 contains the fragment of figure 12.1 as an argument to
an enclosing procedure call. Before executing the code which is
the translation of 'fred(m,n)', the object program must move the
top-of-stack register to protect the value of the argument 'k1*k2'
of the enclosing procedure call. Specialised stack-handling
instructions make such trickery unnecessary, as I show in chapter
14.

Figure 12.3 shows part of a 'TranProcCall' procedure which is
capable of generating the code of figure 12.2. In this procedure
'arglist' is a list of argument nodes, 'paramlist' a list of
parameter descriptors and 'procname' a pointer to the symbol table
entry of the procedure to be called. The 'TranArg' procedure
discussed below, generates code for each of the arguments in turn
and the 'link' procedure inserts the address of the procedure
prologue or generates the necessary loader requests (see chapter
4) to link to the called procedure. The TranProcCall procedure
keeps a record in a global variable of the current data frame's
'stack extension', which represents the number of locations above
the top-of-stack register currently occupied by argument

```
let TranProcCall(nodep) be
{ let procname, arglist = nodep.first, nodep.second
  let paramlist = procname.descriptor.params
  let OldStEx = StackExtension

  if StackExtension \= 0 then
    Gen(ADDn, T, StackExtension)
  StackExtension := 0

  while arglist\=empty & paramlist\=empty do
  { TranArg(arglist.head, paramlist.head)
    StackExtension := paramlist.head.offset+1;
    arglist := arglist.tail
    paramlist := paramlist.tail
  }

  if arglist\=empty | paramlist\=empty then
    Error("wrong number of arguments")

  Gen(JSUB, L, link(procname))

  StackExtension := OldStEx
  if StackExtension != 0 then
    Gen(SUBn, T, StackExtension)
}
```

Figure 12.3 Translating a procedure call

information. Each time an argument is placed on the stack (by the
TranArg procedure) the stack extension is noted and whenever a
procedure call is translated the top-of-stack register is moved up
if necessary before the procedure call (ADDn) and down afterwards
(SUBn). The TranProcCall procedure checks that the number of
arguments in the procedure call matches the number of parameters
recorded in the symbol table descriptor of 'procname', whilst the
TranArg procedure must check that each argument is compatible with
the corresponding parameter.

The procedure call of figure 12.2 executes twenty-six overhead
instructions, which make a total of forty-two store accesses.
This compares with a twenty instruction, thirty-six store access
overhead required to execute the similar FORTRAN fragment shown in
figure 11.5. The gap in object code efficiency is 17%. This gap
isn't large, although it may increase with the inclusion in the
procedure prologue of the environment-manipulating instructions
discussed in chapter 13. If the prologue of procedure 'fred'
contains instructions to check that the stack limit isn't exceeded
(see below) the total overhead for the procedure calls shown in
figure 12.2 would rise to thirty instructions and forty-eight
store accesses.

Once again it is worth emphasing that the FORTRAN mechanism
gains much of its efficiency by omitting essential run-time checks
and that the mechanism of figure 12.2 allows for recursion, full
compile-time argument/parameter checking and variable-size
('dynamic') arrays at run-time. Extra expressive power in the
language means a slight loss of object program efficiency but I am
certain that it is worth the cost.

Generating Code for a Single Argument

In a two-pass compiler for a well-designed language the TranArg
procedure referred to in figure 12.3 is presented with a node
representing an argument of a procedure call - an expression or a
simple name - and a symbol-table descriptor for the corresponding
parameter. This means that the TranArg procedure can check at
compile-time that argument and parameter are compatible. Also it
means that TranArg can generate a code fragment which is designed
to pass precisely the information which the called procedure needs
to know about that particular argument given that particular
parameter specification - e.g. for a 'reference' parameter the
address of an argument variable but for a 'value' parameter merely
the contents of the relevant memory cell.

Figure 12.4 shows a TranArg procedure for a simple language in
which a name may identify a variable, a vector or a procedure and
in which argument information may be passed by 'value' or by
'reference' (vector arguments must be passed by 'reference').
Figure 12.5 shows some possible code. The code fragment which
passes the vector information is somewhat verbose: if the object

machine has a 'block move' instruction it can be used to improve
the operation of this fragment[1].

_____

```
let TranArg(argnodep, paramdescp) be
    if argnodep.kind=name &
       argnodep.descriptor.kind=procedure then
     { ... pass a closure - see chapter 13 ... }
    else
    switch paramdescp.sort into
     { case value:
         /* TranArithExpr will report if node does not
          * represent a valid expression
          */
         TranArithExpr(argnodep,1)
         if argnodep.atype\=paramdescp.atype then
           Error("wrong type of parameter")
         else Gen(STORE, 1, paramdescp.offset, T)
         endcase

       case reference:
         if argnodep.kind=name &
            argnodep.descriptor.kind=vector then
          { ... pass dope vector information ... }
         else
          { /* TranAddress (see chapter 7) will
             * report if node does not describe the
             * address of a data object
             */
            TranAddress(argnodep,1)
            if argnodep.atype\=paramdescp.atype then
              Error("wrong type of reference argument")
            else
             { Gen(LOADa, 1, Address, Modifier)
               Gen(STORE, 1, paramdescp.offset, T)
             }
          }
         endcase

       default: CompilerFail("invalid parameter descriptor")
     }
```

Figure 12.4 Translating a single argument

_____

1 For ease of explanation the 'stack extension' mechanism of
  figure 12.3 is simplified and won't properly protect the three
  parts of a vector reference argument. A possible remedy is to
  make the TranArg procedure calculate and return the necessary
  stack extension.

The TranArg procedure performs all necessary argument-parameter checking and can provide a useful error report for each of the possible mismatches - there is no need for run-time checking. In practical languages, which usually allow more varied kinds and types of arguments and parameters, the TranArg procedure will naturally become rather voluminous since it must be capable of generating a code fragment for each valid argument-parameter combination and an appropriate error report for each invalid combination. It is certainly worthwhile to attempt to clarify and simplify the operation of TranArg but it would be wrong to omit the argument-parameter checking entirely - imagine the confusion if an integer value argument is passed during execution of the object program, and accepted by the called procedure, when a vector reference parameter was specified!

Checking Stack Limits

The stack-handling fragments of figures 11.7, 11.9, 12.1 and 12.2 alter the stack-pointer registers F and T but don't check that in doing so the stack stays within the limits of the data space allocated to it. If the frame register or the top-of-stack register is altered so that it points outside this area then instructions which access the current data frame or pass argument information may overwrite data and program instructions, or may cause a processor interrupt if you are lucky enough to have an object machine with address-protection hardware. There may therefore be a case for the inclusion of instructions which check that the limits of the stack are not exceeded by a fragment which alters the pointer registers.

Possible code to check stack limits in either procedure prologue or array space allocation is shown in figure 12.6. The argument-passing mechanism described in figures 12.1 and 12.2, which stores argument information in the space above the current top-of-stack, makes stack-limit-checking a little less efficient

---

```
variable value:                 vector reference:
    LOAD    1, x                     LOAD    1, #A0
    STORE   1, n(T)                  STORE   1, n(T)
                                     LOAD    1, #A1
variable reference:                  STORE   1, n+1(T)
    LOADa   1, x                     LOAD    1, #A2
    STORE   1, n(T)                  STORE   1, n+2(T)

expression value:
    LOAD    1, y
    MULT    1, z
    ADDn    1, 3
    STORE   1, n(T)
```

Figure 12.5 Code which passes argument information

than it might otherwise be: the code must cater for the maximum
'stack extension' used by any argument-passing fragment in the
body of the procedure, which can be calculated by the TranProcCall
procedure of figure 12.3.

If the object machine has hardware address-protection then it
is tempting to omit any stack-checking code and to rely on the
hardware to detect stack overflow. Explicit stack-checking has an
advantage, though, because it separates stack overflow from all
other potential causes of addressing error and thereby gives the
object program an opportunity to do something about the error. The
'stackoverflow' procedure of figure 12.6, for example, may be able
to obtain more stack space from the operating system and in this
way the object program's stack space can grow to the actual size
required without explicit user intervention. If it is possible in
some other way to distinguish stack overflow from other errors -
for example from those caused by invalid array subscripting or
even those caused by the execution of incorrect code generated by
a faulty compiler - then hardware address-checking is preferable
because of its greater efficiency. Special stack-handling
instructions make the whole business of stack-limit checking much
easier, as the discussion in chapter 14 shows.

The Evils of Run-time Argument Checking

The argument translation mechanism illustrated in figures 12.3 and
12.4 assumes that a two-pass (or three- or four- or more-pass)
compiler is presented with the entire source program which it
converts into a tree, that the object-description phase scans the
tree of every block or procedure before it is translated and that
therefore the translation phase has available to it at any instant
a complete specification of the run-time object denoted by each of
the names which may validly be used. In particular this means
that the translation phase has a full specification of the
parameters of every procedure which may validly be called. There
are three situations in which a translator can be less well-
informed:

(i) when translating mutually recursive procedures in a
one-pass compiler, where sometimes use of a procedure must
precede its declaration;

(ii) when the language implementation allows the program to
be compiled in separate sections and the compiler does not
have access to the declarations in sections other than the

```
LOADa  1, extension(T)
SKIPLE 1, stack-limit
JSUB   L, stackoverflow
```

Figure 12.6 Stack-limit-checking code

one being translated;

  (iii) when translating certain languages (notably PASCAL and ALGOL 60) in which a parameter which is specified to be a procedure need not be completely described.

In all but the last case (incomplete specification of parametric procedures) there is <u>no</u> <u>need</u> for run-time checking of compatibility of argument information and parameter specification.

Run-time checking should be avoided because the compiler (or at worst the loader) should detect any errors which can validly be called 'syntax errors': it is not necessary to run the program to find out whether the arguments in every procedure call are compatible with the parameters specified in the procedure declaration. Run-time checking should also be avoided because it causes inefficiency - the voluminous TranArg procedure, which checks every possible combination of argument and parameter, must in effect be included in the object program and must process each argument every time a procedure call is executed. When run-time checks are employed the argument information passed to the called procedure must state the number of arguments and identify the type and kind of each argument so that the prologue fragment can check whether the information provided is acceptable to the procedure.

As well as checking that the argument is compatible with the parameter, when run-time argument checking is used the procedure prologue must be able to convert the argument information <u>actually</u> passed into that which <u>should</u> have been passed. This is necessary because the code fragment which passes the argument information has to pass the most general kind of information possible. In a language which allows a choice between 'reference' or 'value' arguments, for example, the procedure prologue can find a variable's value when given its address (reference) but cannot find the address when given its value - therefore, in the absence of any compile-time information about the parameters of a procedure, the argument passing fragments must pass the address of every argument. In the case of ALGOL 60, which allows a choice between 'call-by-name' and 'call-by-value', a compiler which doesn't check at compile time that arguments and parameters are compatible must pass every argument by 'name'. This means that those arguments which should have been passed by 'value' must be immediately evaluated in the called procedure's prologue, but

---

```
procedure A(i : integer, var j : integer);
   begin ... B(j, i-j); ... end;

procedure B(u,v : integer);
   begin ... A(u+v, u); ... end;
```

Figure 12.7 Mutually recursive procedures

evaluating a 'name' parameter can be an expensive business.

Mutually recursive procedures

Figure 12.7 shows two procedures A and B, each of which calls the other: it is impossible in such a case to order the procedure declarations so that the declaration of each procedure textually precedes the first call on that procedure. (In the simple case of two mutually recursive procedures it may be possible to put the declaration of one procedure inside the body of the other but in general there is no simple solution to the problem.)

If a one-pass compiler is presented with the source program fragment shown in figure 12.7 it must translate the call of B which occurs inside the body of procedure A before it has encountered the declaration of B and it would therefore be unable to check the number, type and kind of the arguments in the procedure call. This would compel it, in a language which includes 'value' and 'reference' parameters, to produce argument-passing fragments which pass the address of variable 'j' together with the value of the expression 'i-j', which identify the first argument as the address of an **integer** memory cell and the second as an **integer** value. At run-time the prologue of procedure B must first check that the number of arguments provided is correct (it is), that the arguments provided are compatible with the parameters specified in the declaration of the procedure (they are) and finally must load the value held in the memory cell (j) whose address is given as the first argument.

```
forward procedure A(i : integer; var j : integer);

procedure B(u,v : integer);
  begin ... A(u+v, u); ... end;

body A;
  begin ... B(j, i-j); ... end;
```

Figure 12.8 Separating heading and body

```
proc(int, ref int)void A;

proc B = (int u,v)void:
  begin ... A(u+v, u); ... end;

A := (int i, ref int j)void:
  begin... B(j, i-j); ... end;
```

Figure 12.9 Mutual recursion in ALGOL 68

A two-pass compiler doesn't have this difficulty, so the simplest solution to the problem of mutually-recursive procedures is to write a two-pass compiler! If you are forced to write a one-pass compiler - for example if the compiling machine's store is so small that it can't hold the parse tree of a reasonably-sized program section - then it is better to change the syntax of the source language than to introduce run-time argument checking. Figure 12.8 shows a possible syntax in which the heading of a procedure, which specifies the argument-parameter interface, is separated from the body, which specifies the actions of the procedure. This ensures that each procedure declaration textually precedes the first call of that procedure. The normal syntax of ALGOL 68 allows one-pass compiling if the user is prepared to use procedure variables (rather than procedure constants as is more normal) to help in the declaration of mutually recursive procedures. Figure 12.9 shows an example - it is essentially the same device as that used in figure 12.8.

Separately compiled sections of program

One of the simplest yet most important maxims of good program design is that a very large program should always be built up from a collection of relatively independent modules or sections. Programmers find it easier to handle the development and maintenance of a large program if the source is divided into separate sections kept in separate backing store files. The sections of source program are compiled (separately!) to produce separate object program sections, which the loader eventually combines into a complete object program. This introduces the problem that the objects declared in one section (say section X) can be referenced in the code of another section (say section Y), yet the sections have to be compiled separately and therefore the compiler will not have access to X's declarations during the translation of Y.

The problem is in effect the same as that of mutual recursion in a one-pass compiler, discussed above. The simplest solution to the problem is to require that each procedure is declared in every program section from which it is called. The extra declarations must state that the text of the procedure body occurs in another program section, perhaps by using the syntax

external procedure alpha(x : **real**);

Once again, therefore, there is no need for run-time argument checking since the symbol table descriptor for every procedure will be set up before a call to the procedure is encountered.

It is still necessary to check before the program runs that every 'external' declaration is operationally identical with the actual declaration of the procedure and this task can be left to the loader. If the system loader can't or won't make such a check, the object code of each section can contain a short sequence of instructions, executed before the object program proper, which checks that the actual declarations of all procedures called from that section match the external declarations which it contains.

A more elegant solution to the problem of separate compilation of program sections is provided if the compiler produces, as part of the translation output or as a separate file, information summarising the declarations encountered in a program section. The compiler can scan this information during the later compilation of other sections of program, which gives it access to the declarations within previously-compiled sections of the source program. Care must be taken over mutually-recursive procedures in different program sections and the mechanism still requires a load-time check to guard against user error because the declaration used when a section is translated may be altered before the separate sections are loaded together.

Incompletely specified parameters

The program of figure 12.10 shows a difficult compiling problem which arises in ALGOL 60 and in PASCAL. In specifying that the parameter 'f' of procedure 'apply' must correspond to a **real procedure** argument, the user need not - indeed in these languages cannot - specify anything else about the argument procedures. In particular it is impossible to specify the parameter interface (number of parameters, type and kind of parameters) which the argument procedures should possess. In the different calls of 'apply' shown, therefore, the procedures 'p1', 'p2' and 'p3' can have very different parameter specifications. Although figure 12.10 shows a pathological example of the difficulty, it illustrates a practical problem which arises in the translation of

---

```
begin ....
    real procedure apply(f,x);
      value x; real x; real procedure f;
        apply := f(x);

    real procedure p1(u); value u; real u;
        begin ..... end;
    real procedure p2(v); value v; integer v;
        begin ..... end;
    real procedure p3(w); real w;
        begin ..... end;
    ....
    print(apply(p1, 1.5)); print(apply(p2, apply(p2, 7.1)));
    print(apply(p3, 1/3));
    ....
end
```

Figure 12.10 Incomplete parameter specification in ALGOL 60

any language that doesn't demand full specification of 'parametric procedures'.

The only solution to the problem, unfortunately, is to use a run-time argument check in the prologues of procedures 'p1', 'p2' and 'p3'. It isn't sufficient to trust to luck, as in the FORTRAN example of figure 11.5. An ALGOL 60 argument can be passed by 'name' or by 'value' and the difference is operationally very important. The body of 'apply' must therefore call the procedure which corresponds to 'f' - its address will be part of the parameter information - with a single argument which is a variable passed by name. The prologue of each of the procedures shown must examine the parameter information supplied, to check that there is only a single parameter and that the information provided is compatible with the parameter specification. In each case the information provided will be valid, but procedure 'p1' must evaluate the parameter to produce a **real** value and procedure 'p2' must evaluate it and convert it to an **integer** value. Only procedure p3 can accept the argument information in the form in which it is provided. Checking the parameter information and converting one kind of parameter into another is expensive but in this case unavoidable.

Even in ALGOL 60, however, compile-time argument checking should be used wherever possible. Each procedure can be provided with two prologues: one 'normal' and one 'abnormal'. Each non-parametric procedure call can be linked to the 'normal' prologue, which would be like those described in this chapter, while the address of the 'abnormal' prologue, which performs run-time argument checking, could be passed as part of the information about a procedural argument. A sophisticated loader and careful use of loader directives can perhaps ensure that the 'abnormal' prologue is only included in procedures which actually require it.

Summary

The code which implements argument passing is part of the code of procedure call: its efficient implementation is therefore crucial to the efficiency of the object program. It is almost never necessary to employ run-time checks on the compatibility of arguments and parameters since compile-time checks are both more efficient and more convenient.

Different parameter-handling mechanisms can be implemented in every case by passing either 'value', 'reference' or 'name' information which can be manipulated in various ways. By inspecting the symbol table descriptor of a procedure the translator can discover the kind of information which is required for each argument in a procedure call and generate instructions which pass precisely that kind of information.

When argument passing is taken into account, the mechanism of recursive procedure call is only slightly less efficient than subroutine call in FORTRAN, even on a conventional object machine with a conventional instruction set.

13 Environments and Closures

In a block-structured language such as PASCAL, ALGOL 60, ALGOL 68, CORAL 66, PL/1 or SIMULA 67 the text of a procedure may refer to run-time objects or values declared in the current procedure or in textually-enclosing procedures[1] but the address of the data frames which contain these objects isn't known at compile-time or even at load-time. Thus it is difficult to provide single-instruction access to all data objects which may be accessed by a procedure, since it may be impossible to provide enough index registers to point at all relevant data frames on the stack. The problem of <u>environment addressing</u> is to provide a mechanism which allows efficient access to non-local data objects and which doesn't impose too great an overhead on procedure entry and exit, when the data frame pointers which define the environment must be set up.

When a procedure is being executed, the data frames belonging to its textually-enclosing procedures will always exist and be in place on the stack. To see why this is so, consider the program in figure 13.1. Each procedure in a block-structured language has a certain 'textual level' of operation. The outer block operates at the lowest level - I have called it textual level 0. Procedures declared in the outer block - f1 and f2 in figure 13.1 - operate at textual level 1, since the activation created when such a procedure is called can access its own data frame and that of the outer block. Similarly a procedure declared within a level 1 procedure - f1a, f1b, f2a and f2b in figure 13.1 - operate at textual level 2 since they can access values in their own data frame, that of the enclosing level 1 procedure and that of the outer block. To generalise - a procedure declared at level 'n' operates at textual level 'n+1'.

---

1 In the discussion here I consider only the mechanism of 'procedure-level addressing'. The addressing of data in blocks which are not the body of a procedure is discussed later in this chapter.

The block-structuring scope rules ensure that a procedure operating at textual level 'i' may normally call only procedures declared in blocks or procedures whose data frames it may access. In figure 13.1, for example, f1 may call f1 or f2 (declared in the outer block), f1a or f1b (declared within f1 itself) but it may not call f1a1 or f1a2 (declared within f1a, whose data frame it may not access), f2a or f2b (declared within f2, whose data frame it may not access). Thus the data frames which a called procedure activation can access are, apart from the data frame created during the procedure prologue, also accessible by the calling activation. This means that the 'environment of the called procedure activation - the collection of data frames which it can access, other than its own - is always present on the stack when

---

```
begin .... /* textual level 0 */
    procedure f1; .... /* textual level 1 */
        begin
            procedure f1a; .... /* textual level 2 */
                begin
                    procedure f1a1; ... /* textual level 3 */
                    procedure f1a2; ... /* textual level 3 */
                        ....
                end;
            procedure f1b; .... /* textual level 2 */
                begin
                    procedure f1b1; ... /* textual level 3 */
                    procedure f1b2; ... /* textual level 3 */
                        .. .
                end of f1b;
                ....
        end of f2;
    procedure f2; .... /* textual level 1 */
        begin
            procedure f2a; . .. /* textual level 2 */
                begin
                    procedure f2a1; ... /* textual level 3 */
                    procedure f2a2; ... /* textual level 3 */
                        ....
                end of f2a;
            procedure f2b; .... /* textual level 2 */
                begin
                    procedure f2b1; ... /* textual level 3 */
                    procedure f2b2; ... /* textual level 3 */
                        ...
                end of f2b;
                ....
        end of f2
        ....
end of the program
```

Figure 13.1 Textual levels of procedures

the activation is created. The environment is part, or all, of the environment of the calling activation and may include the data frame of the calling activation. The various possible environment changes during a 'normal' procedure call – i.e. one which isn't made via a procedural parameter – are summarised in figure 13.2.

An important fact about block-structured languages is that the number of data frames in the environment of an activation is <u>fixed at compile-time</u> and is not altered by any pattern of procedure calls. No matter how procedure f1a1 in figure 13.1 is called, for example, the procedure activation which is created can only access four data frames: its own, that of f1a, that of f1 and that of the outer block. When the program runs there may be many data frames on the stack – see figure 13.3, which shows the stack layout after the outer block calls f1 which calls f1a which calls f1a1 which calls f1 ... – yet the number of data frames in the environment of

---

(i) A procedure operating at textual level 'i' may call a procedure which will operate at the same level (e.g. f1 calls f1 or f2, f2a calls f2a or f2b in figure 13.1). In this case the environment of the called procedure is identical to that of the calling procedure.

(ii) A procedure operating at textual level 'i' may call a procedure which will operate at level 'i+1' (e.g. f1 calls f1a or f1b, f1a calls f1a1 or f1a2 in figure 13.1). In this case the environment of the called procedure is that of the calling procedure, plus the current data frame.

(iii) A procedure operating at textual level 'i' may call a procedure which will operate at textual level 'i-k' (e.g. f1a may call f1 or f2, f2b2 may call f2a, f2b, f1 or f2 in figure 13.1). In this case the environment of the called procedure is a part of the calling procedure's environment (it consists of levels 0 to 'i-k-1' inclusive).

Figure 13.2 Possible environment changes during procedure call

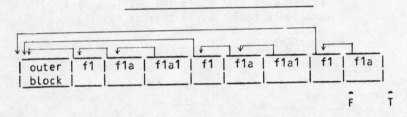

Figure 13.3 Environments during mutual recursion

each activation remains fixed. In figure 13.3 the environment is indicated by a pointer from each data frame to the data frame of the immediately enclosing block. Note that in this example the different activations of f1a1 access the data frames of different activations of f1a and f1.

The object-description phase's address allocation mechanism, discussed in chapter 8, allocates each data object to a location or locations within a particular data frame. The technique for handling declarations in a block-structured language, also discussed in chapter 8, ensures that the translator can easily find the symbol table descriptor for all objects whose declarations are currently 'in scope'. To access a variable, therefore, the translator must check the textual level of its definition and perhaps generate instructions which will make an index register point to the relevant data frame in the environment: then it can generate an instruction which accesses the relevant location within that data frame. Note that the stack-handling mechanism described so far allows single-instruction access to the current data frame, and that since the outer block's data frame is in a fixed run-time position references to data objects within it can be relocated and need not use an index register at all.

An Explicit Representation of the Environment

The example of figure 13.3 shows that the actual addresses of environment data frames cannot be fixed at compile-time. The environment data frames are all on the stack below the current data frame, however, and it would seem possible to access non-local data by searching down the stack for the data frames of textually-enclosing procedures. Each procedure prologue would have to store some identifying marker in its data frame, which would make the prologue less efficient, but the major inefficiency of this technique lies in the enormous overhead which it would impose on every non-local data access, especially in a recursive program.

Suppose, for example, that procedure f1 in figure 13.1 were to call procedure f1a, which then called f1a recursively twenty times. In order to access a value held in the data frame of f1, now, the twentieth activation of f1a must search through nineteen data frames before it finds the one it is looking for - at a cost of at least three instructions per frame inspected. Such a cost would make recursive programming languages vastly less efficient than FORTRAN in which access to any variable in the environment takes only a single instruction. It would clearly be more efficient to provide each procedure activation with pointers to its own environment data frames, thus eliminating stack searches entirely. I discuss two mechanisms below which do just this. Inefficiency is not the worst drawback of the 'search-down-the-stack' mechanism, however: it simply does not work in many situations, in particular in those situations created by the passing of a procedural value as an argument in a procedure call.

So far I have discussed only the simplest kinds of procedure calls, which refer to a procedure declaration currently 'in scope'. In most languages a procedure may be passed as an argument and may then be called, via the parameter, from a position where its declaration may be 'out of scope' and where its environment may not be a part of the current environment. Since the environment must have existed when the procedure was passed as an argument, it will still exist on the stack when the parameter is activated and therefore the problem is to <u>find</u> the environment when the procedure is called.

```
function searchmaze(i, goal : integer,
                function unexplored : boolean): boolean;
  var nexti : integer;
  function offmyroute (k : integer): boolean;
    begin if k=i then offmyroute := false
          else offmyroute := unexplored(k)
    end;
  begin
      if i=goal then ... found the route ...
      else
      for nexti := .. each neighbour location .. do
        if unexplored(nexti) and
          searchmaze(nexti, goal, offmyroute)
        then .. found it ..;
      ....
  end

function emptymaze(i:integer):boolean;
  begin emptymaze := true end;

begin
  searchmaze(1,100,emptymaze);
  ...
end
```

Figure 13.4a Use of a procedural argument

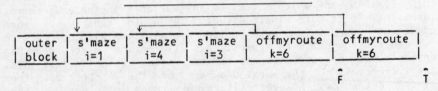

outer block	s'maze i=1	s'maze i=4	s'maze i=3	offmyroute k=6	offmyroute k=6

Figure 13.4b State of the stack in mid-execution

Any short example program which illustrates the problem will seem artificial, since the program could have been written some other way, but nevertheless I present figure 13.4a as a candidate example. The 'searchmaze' procedure shown could be part of a program which finds a route through a maze. Each position in the maze is numbered; the searchmaze procedure is provided with a position 'i' to explore, a position 'goal' to search towards and a **boolean** procedure 'unexplored' which can be given the number of a position and will return **true** if that position is so far unexplored. The 'searchmaze' procedure finds a route through the maze by a sequence of recursive calls, providing in each case the 'offmyroute' procedure which merely treats the current position as an explored position.

Figure 13.4b shows the state of the stack after positions 1, 4 and 3 have been occupied and whilst the searchmaze procedure is investigating location 6. To do this it calls its 'unexplored' parameter, which activates a version of the 'offmyroute' procedure in whose environment 'i' has the value 4. In turn this procedure activates an 'offmyroute' procedure in whose environment 'i' has the value 1. Note that for neither of these activations of 'offmyroute' is the relevant 'searchmaze' data frame the one on top of the stack - the 'search-down-the-stack' mechanism just wouldn't work. Part of the argument information passed by 'searchmaze', therefore, must indicate the actual data frames which can be accessed by the 'offmyroute' procedure when it is called.

The example of figure 13.4 shows that the information required when a procedure is passed as an argument has two components

(i) The code address of the procedure.

(ii) Information which defines the collection of data frames which can be accessed when the procedure is called - i.e. the environment to be used by the procedure activation when it is created.

This coupling of code with environment is called a <u>closure</u>. In effect the closure mechanism lies behind the implementation of SIMULA 67 **class**es. The value returned in an ALGOL 68 program when a 'procedure' is returned as the result of a procedure call is also a closure. There is some discussion in chapter 14 of the implementation of these features.

To summarise: a procedure activation should have links to its environment data frames, both for the sake of efficiency (to avoid searches through the contents of the stack) and also to cater for the case when a procedural value is passed as an argument. There is therefore a need to maintain some explicit representation of the environment of a procedure, in order that it can be passed as part of such an argument. Of the two techniques which I describe

below the 'environment link' or 'static chain' mechanism, which
uses a single environment pointer, is simpler to implement and
more efficient in its manipulation of closures, but the 'display'
technique is more efficient in the accessing of non-local data and
in simple procedure calls. Nevertheless I favour the 'environment
link' mechanism overall because of its simplicity and because I
believe that in modern languages the use of closures is becoming
more important.

The Environment Link Mechanism

In the stack handling fragments of figures 11.7, 12.1 and 12.2,

---

```
source: procedure f1 ....
          begin procedure f1a ...
              begin .... end;

              ... f1a(...) ...
          end

code for call of f1a:
          LOADr   E, F
          JSUB    L, #f1a


#f1a:     STORE   L, 0(T)   /* store return link */
          STORE   F, 1(T)   /* store frame pointer */
          STORE   E, 2(T)   /* store environment link */
          LOADr   F, T
          ADDn,   T, data-frame-size

          .. procedure body ..

          LOADr   T, F
          LOAD    F, 1(T)
          RETNi    , 0(T)
```

Figure 13.5 Creating the environment link on procedure call

```
Access to textual level 'j' from a procedure operating
  at textual level 'i' -

     (i)    j=i       LOAD reg, offset(F)
     (ii)   j=0       LOAD reg, offset+baseaddress
     (iii)  j=i-1     LOAD E, 2(F); LOAD reg, offset(E)
     (iv)   j=i-2     LOAD E, 2(F); LOAD E, 2(E);
                           LOAD reg, offset(E)
     (v)    j=i-n      n+1 instructions
```

Figure 13.6 Access to non-local data via environment link

each procedure is provided with a return address in the link
register L. If in addition it is provided with a pointer to the
data frame of the textually enclosing procedure in register 'E'
(for Environment) which it stores in its own data frame, a chain
of environment pointers will point from data frame to data frame
which can be followed to find all of the environment of any
procedure activation. Figure 13.5 shows code for a procedure call
from textual level 'i' to level 'i+1'. The procedure prologue is
extended by a single instruction, compared with figure 12.1 or
12.2, and there is a single instruction precall fragment (as I
show below, there may be more than one instruction in this
position). Use of the environment-link mechanism, therefore, would
increase the overhead of the procedure calls shown in figure 12.2
to thirty instructions and fifty store accesses compared with
twenty instructions and thirty-six store accesses for a similar
fragment in FORTRAN. This is a 35% efficiency gap, caused mostly
by the lack of instructions which help in the implementation of
recursive procedure call. The mechanism uses three stack-
addressing registers - F, E and T - and three 'housekeeping'
locations in every data frame.

Access to non-local data objects usually takes more than a
single instruction, as figure 13.6 shows. The figure for the
number of instructions required to access a non-local variable is
frightening at first, but reality isn't quite so grim. First,
access to data in the outer block - global data objects - is
immediate since references to that data frame can be relocated by
the loader. Second, the textual nesting of a program is rarely
very deep: figure 13.1, for example, has only four levels
including the outer block and so in the worst case, when a
fragment in the body of a procedure which operates at textual
level 3 accesses a data object declared in a textual level 1
procedure, non-local data addressing involves only (!) two
overhead instructions. In practice even the worst case can be
improved by careful code generation since the translator can avoid
reloading the 'E' register if it already points to the relevant
data frame or to a data frame at an intermediate level in the
environment: as a result the environment register isn't reloaded
very often.

A procedure operating at textual level 'i' calls one which
operates at level 'j':

```
(i)    j=i+1        LOADr E, F; JSUB L, ...
(ii)   j=i          LOAD E, 2(F); JSUB L, ...
(iii)  j=0          JSUB L, ...
(iv)   j=i-1        LOAD E, 2(F); LOAD E, 2(E); JSUB L, ...
(v)    j=i-n        n+1 precall instructions.
```

Figure 13.7 Environment link manipulation in procedure call

The efficiency of non-local data access is very important and for this reason the environment link mechanism is sometimes implemented in a form which is a kind of hybrid with the display mechanism described below. If each procedure prologue stores in the current data frame a pointer to each of the data frames which the current procedure activation can access - in effect each of the pointers in the environment chain - then every non-local data access takes a maximum of two instructions, and there is a single precall instruction in every procedure call fragment. You will find, however, if you examine the text of a program in a block-structured language that by far the majority of storage accesses refer to the current data frame, to the outer block or to that of the immediately enclosing procedure. If the translator remembers which data frame the environment register points at, there is rarely any occasion to reset it. The hybrid mechanism increases the cost of procedure call and perhaps may not increase the overall efficiency of the object program.

The preparation of environment information in the precall fragment, shown as a single LOAD instruction in figure 13.5, uses the stored environment links in the same sort of way as they are used for non-local data access. Figure 13.7 shows the instructions required in various cases. Note that a procedure declared in the outer block needs no environment pointer and that therefore the prologue of such a procedure need not store the value of the E register.

Passing a procedural value as an argument and using this information to call a parametric procedure is now extremely simple: figure 13.8 shows how the mechanism operates. Note in particular how easy it is to use the information when the parametric procedure is eventually called (if the parameter belongs to the current procedure then it is possible to use only two instructions to call it - 'LOAD E; JSUBi L' - rather than three). Similar manipulations can be used when a procedural value is returned as the result of a procedure call in ALGOL 68 and when manipulating procedural attributes of **class**es in SIMULA 67.

```
passing procedure as argument:
        {load E register as if to call the procedure}
        STORE   E, #param
        LOADa   1, prologue-address
        STORE   1, #param+1

calling the procedure via the parameter:
        LOAD    1, #param+1
        LOAD    E, #param
        JSUB    L, O(1)
```

Figure 13.8 Procedural argument using the environment link

The environment link mechanism, then, increases the overhead of simple procedure call and return and imposes an overhead on non-local data access. Its advantage is that it is simple to implement, uses only three registers and makes the manipulation of closures simple and obvious.

The Display Vector Mechanism

The environment link mechanism maintains what is essentially a list of data frames which can be accessed by the current procedure activation. The maximum number of data frames in such a list is limited by the textual nesting of procedures in the source program and, as mentioned above, procedures are rarely nested more than four or five deep. It is therefore possible to avoid the overhead of tracing through the environment list on each non-local data access if a separate index register is allocated to each textual level of the program (excluding the outer block, which doesn't need a register). All non-local data can then be accessed in a single instruction via the appropriate index register. Such a vector of registers is called a display. Most implementations which use a display have between five and eight registers in the display vector.

When calling a procedure whose declaration is currently in scope, the environment of the procedure activation which is created will already be a part of that of the calling activation. The new procedure activation will use one of the registers from the display vector to access data in its own data frame: therefore the prologue fragment must save this register and the epilogue fragment must reset it. Figure 13.9 shows the instructions required to call a procedure which operates at textual level 'j'. In storing the relevant display register the prologue fragment

---

```
source: edgar()

code:     JSUB   L, #edgar

source: procedure edgar() .....

#edgar:   STORE  L, O(T)
          STORE  F_j, 1(T)
          LOADr  F_j, T
          ADDn   T, data-frame-size

          .. procedure body ..

          LOADr  T, F_j
          LOAD   F_j, 1(T)
          RETNi  , O(L)
```

Figure 13.9 Procedure call and return with display vector

simultaneously performs all necessary environment and frame-pointer manipulations so that, unlike the environment link mechanism, the display imposes no overhead in addition to that of simple stack handling. Using the display mechanism, therefore, the overhead of the procedure calls in figure 12.2 would stay at twenty-six instructions, compared with twenty instructions for FORTRAN and thirty instructions using the environment link mechanism.

Access to non-local data via the display is super-efficient. Since a register points to each textual level of the current procedure activation's environment, access to local or non-local data takes a single instruction in all cases. Figure 13.10 summarises the technique.

The display vector mechanism is highly efficient, then, in simple procedure calls and in accessing non-local data. It uses a lot of registers to address the stack - between five and eight for the display, plus one for top-of-stack - and you should bear in mind that some registers will be needed for other purposes such as the evaluation of expressions. If the machine doesn't have sufficient registers it isn't worthwhile to implement a display vector in store, since it would be no more efficient than the more straightforward environment link mechanism. When the machine has enough spare registers, however, the display mechanism would seem ideal. Unfortunately it is far from ideal in the way in which it handles closures.

When a procedural value is passed as an argument it is necessary to include the environment in which the procedure activation will eventually operate as part of the argument information, as figure 13.4 shows. When using a display the environment is a vector of registers, which makes a procedural argument quite a bulky item. When the procedure is called via the corresponding parameter the display must be set up; it must be reset on the corresponding return. Figure 13.11 shows how the display could be manipulated by a collection of standard subroutines to produce the desired effect. The current contents of the display vector are placed in the parameter locations by the 'storedisplay' subroutine; when the parametric procedure is called the contents of the then current display are stored on the top of the stack by the 'stackdisplay' subroutine; the destination address is loaded, the parametric display is loaded by the

---

current data frame: LOAD reg, offset(F_i)

outer block: LOAD reg, offset+baseaddress

other textual levels: LOAD reg, offset(F_j)

Figure 13.10 Access to data using the display mechanism

'loaddisplay' subroutine; and finally the procedure is called. On return the contents of the display must be retrieved from the stack by the 'unstackdisplay' subroutine.

Calling a parametric procedure in this way is a complicated and inefficient activity when compared with that required by the environment link mechanism (see figure 13.8). It can be made slightly more convenient if the contents of the display are stored in each data frame during execution of the procedure prologue — then a pointer to the current data frame gives access to the current display. This means that a procedural value argument is more compact and can be passed more efficiently and also that parametric procedure call is very slightly simpler to implement. What such a 'refinement' actually does, though, is to make procedure entry less efficient than it is with the environment link mechanism — it has just spread the inefficiency of parametric procedure call throughout the object program!

If you make the assumption that parametric procedure calls are rare while simple procedure calls and accesses to non-local data are commonplace, then the display vector mechanism is certainly more efficient in operation than the environment link mechanism. The display is more complicated to implement, which means that you may make mistakes when you implement it! When compiling a language in which closures are manipulated freely, the display vector is extremely inconvenient to use.

One final reason why I prefer the environment link to the display is that the environment link makes interactive run-time debugging much easier to implement. If there are pointers from each data frame to the calling data frame and to the environment, as there are when using the environment link mechanism, it is easy to trace which procedure called which and to access any values in the data frame of any procedure activation or in the environment of any activation. Tracing through the stack in this way is much

---

```
passing the argument:
        LOADa  1, procedureaddress
        STORE  1, offset(T)
        LOADa  1, offset+1(T)
        JSUB   L, storedisplay

calling the parameter:
        JSUB   L, stackdisplay
        LOAD   1, offset(F_i)
        LOADa  2, offset+1(F_i)
        JSUB   L, loaddisplay
        JSUB   L, 0(1)
        JSUB   L, unstackdisplay
```

Figure 13.11 Procedural argument passing with a display

harder with the display, since there is only a pointer to the code
of the calling procedure in the data frame. (See chapter 20 for a
fuller discussion of the implementation of run-time debuggers.)

ALGOL 60's 'call by name'

Figure 13.12 shows an example of a procedure which uses call-by-
name in the operation of a summation procedure. One of the
arguments is an expression 'expr' and another is a variable
'subscr' (whose value is assumed to affect the value of 'expr').
SIGMA calculates a sum by varying the 'subscr' variable through an
indicated   range   and   evaluating   the parameter 'expr' for each
successive value. The syntax of ALGOL 60 prescribes that the lack
of a **value** specification for parameters 'expr' and 'subscr'
indicates that they are called by 'name': the semantics of call-
by-name are such that each time the value of a 'name' parameter is
required, the corresponding argument expression is re-evaluated.
Thus the argument corresponding to 'expr' is evaluated during each
iteration of the loop.

   The ALGOL 60 Revised Report defines the semantics of 'name'
parameter passing in terms of textual substitution but the only
practical means of implementation is the method of 'thunks'. I
don't want to give every detail of the implementation of call-by-

---

```
  begin
    integer procedure SIGMA(expr, subscr, lowb, incr, upb);
                  value lowb, incr, upb;
                  integer expr, subscr, lowb, incr, upb;
    begin integer answer;
       answer := 0;
       for subscr := lowb step incr until upb do
                answer := answer+expr;
       SIGMA := answer
    end of SIGMA procedure;

    integer array A[1:100, 1:100]; integer i,j;

    .....
    comment sum a row;
    print(SIGMA(A[i,1], i, 1,1,100));
    comment sum a column;
    print(SIGMA(A[1,i], i, 1,1,100));
    comment sum a diagonal;
    print(SIGMA(A[i,i], i, 1,1,100));
    comment sum top left hand corner;
    print(SIGMA(SIGMA(A[i,j], i, 1,1,25), j, 1,1,25)));
    ....
  end;
```

Figure 13.12 A procedure which uses call-by-name

name, but it is worth while to give a simple sketch. For most
'name' arguments, the translator constructs a simple procedure -
the thunk - containing a sequence of instructions which, when
activated, calculate the address and/or the value of the argument
expression. The argument information consists of the address of
the thunk procedure together with the current environment - i.e.
is a closure. When the value of a 'name' parameter is required,
the thunk can be activated in the same way as any other parametric
procedure.

I introduce call-by-name to make two points. The first point is
that in ALGOL 60 at least the use of procedural arguments is
commonplace, so that the display vector mechanism is less useful
than you might suppose. The second point is to re-emphasise the
need for compile-time argument checking: it is expensive to
evaluate a 'name' parameter when a simple value can be passed
instead with just a little care during translation. The call-by-
name mechanism is so expensive that modern languages have mostly
dropped it in favour of the semantically different, but
operationally more efficient, call-by-reference.

Block Structure and Data Frames

In the discussion so far I have ignored the declaration of data
other than at the head of a procedure. Block structuring proper
is a very powerful program-linguistic facility, however, and one
that is easy to implement with a minimum of execution overhead by
combining the data frame of every block with that of the procedure
which immediately encloses it.

Figure 13.13 shows an ALGOL 68 program with simple nested
blocks, and figure 13.14 shows the stack layout which would be
produced if every block was allocated a separate data frame in the
same way as a procedure. This technique is called "block-level
addressing" and has two drawbacks

- as figure 13.14 shows, the number of textual levels in the
  environment is increased sharply;
- each block entry and exit carries a stack-handling
  overhead similar to that of procedure call and return.

Increasing the number of textual levels makes non-local data
access the norm rather than the exception and would make the
environment link mechanism prohibitively expensive. Access from
block 2 in figure 13.13 to the parameters of procedure 'BS', for
example, would cost three instructions using the environment link
mechanism. The display vector mechanism doesn't do much better,
since increasing the textual nesting of the program makes it
unlikely that the machine will have sufficient registers to run a
display - blocks and procedures, considered together, are often
nested twelve or fifteen levels deep. Block-level addressing makes
block structuring expensive to use, by imposing an execution

overhead on block entry and exit, and therefore may tempt some
users to avoid using declarations other than at the head of a
procedure - i.e. it encourages an unnecessarily obscure
programming style.

   The solution to these problems is to combine data frames at
compile-time, in order to reduce the number of textual levels in
the program and to reduce the stack-handling overheads associated
with creating new data frames. The object-description phase of

```
proc BS = (int p1, p2) void:
   begin real x, y;
        .. block 1 ..
        begin int u,v,w;
           .. block 2 ..
        end;
        ...
        begin bool a,b;
           .. block 3 ..
        end
        ...
   end
```

Figure 13.13 Example block-structured program

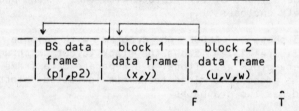

```
      |    |         |
   ___| BS data | block 1   | block 2    |
      | frame   | data frame| data frame |
   ___| (p1,p2) |   (x,y)   |  (u,v,w)   |
                                ^           ^
                                F           T
```

Figure 13.14 Stack layout using block-level addressing

```
let TranBlock(nodep) be
{ let odfs = dfsize

   newdeclare(declpart^node) /* object description */
   if dfsize>tidemark then tidemark := dfsize

   .. translate statements and declarations (chapter 7) ..

   newundeclare(declpart^node)
   dfsize := odfs
}
```

Figure 13.15 Combining data frames at compile-time

chapter 8 allocates data objects to locations within a data frame:
if it allocates those of a block to locations within the data
frame of the enclosing procedure then the number of textual levels
in the object program can be minimised.

Figure 13.15 shows a procedure which could be used, in a two-
pass compiler, to translate a node which represents a block. The
global variable 'dfsize' records the maximum offset within the
current procedure's data frame and 'tidemark' indicates its
highest level so far, throughout any of the blocks nested in the
current procedure. The 'newdeclare' procedure allocates data
objects to the current data frame, incrementing 'dfsize' as it
goes. After all objects have been processed, the value of
'tidemark' is altered if necessary. Whilst the statements are
translated the declarations are in force: any blocks nested within
this one will use locations above the position indicated by the
current value of 'dfsize'. When translation of the statements is
complete the descriptors allocated by 'newdeclare' are removed
from the symbol table by the 'newundeclare' procedure and the
value of 'dfsize' is reset so that the space used in this block
can be re-used in other blocks nested within the current
procedure.

Use of such a mechanism, given the procedure declaration in
figure 13.13, would produce a data frame layout like that in
figure 13.16. The first three locations shown contain the
'housekeeping' values needed by the environment link mechanism
(only two housekeeping locations would be needed with a display
vector). The maximum value of 'dfsize' is reached during the
translation of block 2 and the value of 'tidemark' would therefore
show that the procedure's data frame requires 10 locations. Access
to any value in the combined data frame now would take only a
single instruction no matter where the access occurs in the code
of the procedure body.

The procedure-level addressing mechanism imposes no stack-
handling overhead either on entry to and exit from a block which

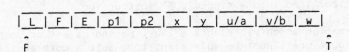

Figure 13.16 Stack layout using procedure-level addressing

```
entry:  STORE  T, #tblock

exit:   LOAD   T, #tblock
```

Figure 13.17 Block entry and exit overhead

is the body of a procedure (such as block 1 in figure 13.13) since
the prologue and epilogue fragments can perform all the necessary
stack-handling operations. For any other block there is likewise
no entry and exit overhead unless the block contains a declaration
of a 'dynamic' array. If a block does contain such a declaration
then, as figure 11.10 shows, the top-of-stack register is moved
after block entry to provide the space for the array. The space
should be reclaimed on exit from that block, rather than on exit
from the enclosing procedure, since otherwise repeated entry to
the block without exit from the procedure would move the top-of-
stack pointer inexorably upwards! There is thus a single
instruction overhead on entry to and exit from a block which
contains a declaration of a dynamic array, shown in figure 13.17.
The temporary location '#tblock' can be allocated to a location in
the current data frame in the same way as any variable declared
within the current block.

   Procedure-level addressing is preferable to block-level
addressing, then, because it makes access to non-local data more
efficient and because it almost entirely removes the execution
overhead of block-structuring. The only practical drawback of
procedure-level addressing is that it can waste stack space, since
the space for an inner block is claimed from the stack whether the
procedure is executing the code of that block or not. The smallest
waste of stack space can become important in a heavily recursive
program. In practice it may be worthwhile to treat all arrays as
if they were 'dynamic' arrays and to impose the block entry and
exit overheads of figure 13.16 on every block which declares any
kind of array. With this slight refinement I believe that the
procedure-level addressing scheme achieves a reasonable balance
between speed of execution and data space used.

Non-local 'goto' Statements

The stack manipulations required during procedure or block entry
and exit are structured: each exit removes the data space acquired
by the corresponding entry. A **goto** statement which crosses block
or procedure boundaries breaks through this structure, however,
and in an implementation of a recursive programming language few
gotos can be compiled into a single JUMP instruction.

   The information which represents a label passed as an argument
in a procedure call must be sufficient to enable a **goto** to that
label to restore the stack to the state it would be in if control
reached the label normally. This means that the argument
information must consist of the code address of the label, the
display or a pointer to the relevant data frame and the value of
the top-of-stack pointer which is valid in the procedure or block
that contains the label. A **goto** to a parametric label can use this
information to reset the stack-addressing registers just before it
JUMPs.

A **goto** to a non-parametric label which crosses only block boundaries must ensure that the top-of-stack register is reset to the correct value used by the destination block. One which crosses a procedure boundary as well must reset the F and T registers, or the display if one is used. Resetting these pointers will mean tracing down the stack to find the relevant values and resetting pointers on the way. The implementation of a non-local **goto** is complicated, then, and passing a non-local label as an argument is just as complicated to implement because the information which must be passed must be that required for a **goto** to that label. This is such a knotty problem that it is common to store the contents of the display and the value of the top-of-stack pointer in each data frame in order to make non-local **goto**s simpler to implement: the effect is to further depress the efficiency of procedure entry and exit.

Structured program design teaches (amongst other things) that Gotos are Harmful to the Brain: experience in language implementation shows that they are Hard to Implement and Not Particularly Efficient Either! You will probably find that you use **goto** statements much less frequently in your own programs once you appreciate the difficulty of translating them into efficient object code.

Summary

The fact that the code of a procedure body may refer to data objects other than those stored in the data frame of the currently executing procedure activation means that additional pointers are required to address data frames in the stack. The maintenance of an environment addressing mechanism during procedure call and return provides efficient access to non-local data and also allows 'closures' (procedure values, labels and 'thunks') to be manipulated and passed as arguments.

Of the two environment addressing mechanisms presented in this chapter, the 'environment link' (static link) mechanism imposes an overhead on procedure call and return and in the addressing of non-local data, but is efficient in its handling of closures. The 'display vector' mechanism imposes no such overheads but is more difficult to implement due to the difficulty of handling closures efficiently. Non-local **goto**s are inefficient using either mechanism.

It isn't necessary to allocate a separate data frame for each block: if the data frames of blocks are combined with those of the enclosing procedure then non-local data access is made more efficient because of the reduction in the number of textual levels in the program. This so-called 'procedure-level addressing' mechanism also reduces the overheads of block entry and exit to an insignificant level.

14 Efficiency, Heaps and Lifetimes

In the discussion in chapters 11, 12 and 13 I emphasise that a recursive programming language such as PASCAL, ALGOL 60 or ALGOL 68 can be implemented almost as efficiently as FORTRAN. In the case of system programming languages such as BCPL, BLISS or C 'almost as efficiently' isn't good enough: these languages must be implemented extremely efficiently, and certainly <u>more</u> efficiently than FORTRAN, in order to satisfy the demands of their users. In this chapter I discuss two ways in which efficiency can be improved. The first improvement involves the use of special stack-handling instructions which reduce the number of instructions required in procedure call and return. The second improvement relies on source language restrictions which enable the object program to address the stack with only a single register, thus reducing the register manipulations required in procedure call and return.

In implementations of modern languages which allow free manipulation of records and pointers to records it is necessary to provide a free-storage allocation and reclamation (garbage collection) mechanism which maintains a 'heap' area of off-stack storage. This chapter justifies the need for a heap and discusses the effect which the provision of a heap will have on the other run-time support mechanisms. The definition of ALGOL 68 contains certain provisions designed to reduce the use of heap storage by allowing some pointers to lead from data frame to data frame: this chapter discusses the compile-time and run-time checks required to police these restrictions. ALGOL 68 also allows a procedure (or indeed a block) to return a multi-word result: this chapter briefly discusses the implementation of procedure return in this case.

SIMULA 67 allows free use of pointers to 'block instances' or 'class instances' that are in effect activation records or data frames. These records cannot be allocated from a stack but must use a more general storage allocation scheme: this chapter touches on the run-time support mechanisms that this requires.

Procedure Call with PUSH and POP Instructions

The object machine assumed in earlier chapters is, in effect, a FORTRAN machine: it has instructions designed to help in the implementation of vector addressing and subroutine call or return, but no instructions to help with recursive procedure call and return. Many modern machines are more helpful in that they include special stack-handling instructions which enable the program to place a value on a stack (PUSH), remove a value (POP), call a procedure placing the return link address on the stack (PUSHSUB), and so on. Some machines go further still and include instructions designed to mimic the operations required in a particular implementation of a particular language: for example the Burroughs B6500 was designed to run ALGOL 60, the ICL 2900 series machines are descended from the University of Manchester MU5 whose design was heavily influenced by implementations of Atlas Autocode, the MIT 'LISP machine' is designed to run LISP. Some modern 'soft' machines go farther still – the Burroughs 1700 is an example – and allow users to define special microprograms so that the compiler-writer can, in effect, design the instruction set of the object machine to fit the operations of the source language. These more exotic possibilities are beyond the scope of this book, and I restrict discussion to the use of simple stack-handling instructions.

The use of PUSH and POP instructions on an otherwise conventional machine can reduce the procedure call and return overhead in an implementation of a recursive programming language. If the 'T' register used in earlier chapters is used as a true stack pointer register, the code for a procedure call with two arguments can be as shown in figure 14.1 (INCn and DECn are special instructions which are used to move the stack and simultaneously check against stack underflow and overflow). The code in this example would execute ten instructions and make eighteen store accesses (each PUSH makes three store accesses) rather than the twelve instructions and twenty store accesses of the more conventional fragment in figure 12.1. Figure 14.2 shows the storage layout produced by this code fragment: I assume that it is possible to address both above and below the 'F' pointer and that therefore the procedure addresses parameter 'i' as '-4(F)': if negative addresses aren't allowed a minor adjustment to the prologue and epilogue fragments would be needed.

Figure 14.1 assumes that the 'T' register is a true stack pointer, containing not only the pointer to the top of stack but also information about the upper and lower limits of the store area allocated to the stack. The PUSH, PUSHSUB and INC instructions can use this limit information to check against stack overflow and the POP, POPSUB and DEC instructions can use it to check against stack underflow. If the 'T' register is merely a normal index register, a combination of the mechanisms of figure 14.1 and 12.1 can further reduce the cost of procedure call and return - see figure 14.5 for an illustration - but the advantages of hardware stack-limit checking are lost.

The code for nested procedure calls is shown in figure 14.3. This code shows a twenty instruction procedure call and return overhead, which matches that of the FORTRAN example in figure 11.5, and would make thirty-eight store accesses, which is almost as good as the thirty-six required for FORTRAN. The more conventional stack-handling fragment of figure 12.2 takes twenty-six instructions and forty-two store accesses, so the fragment of figure 14.3 gains approximately 10% in execution. The fragment in figure 14.3 would require to include about four extra instructions, and make about eight more store accesses, if the environment-link mechanism of chapter 13 was implemented.

```
source:   fred(m,n)

code:        PUSH    T, m        /* first argument */
             PUSH    T, n        /* second argument */
             PUSHSUB T, #fred    /* call procedure */
             DECn    T, 2        /* reclaim argument space */

source:   function fred(i,j: integer): integer

#fred:       PUSHr   T, F        /* save old value of F */
             LOADr   F, T        /* set up new data frame */
             INCn    T, data-frame-size
                                 /* acquire data frame space */

          ... procedure body ...

             LOADr   T, F        /* reclaim data frame space */
             POPr    T, F        /* reset old value of F */
             POPRETN T,          /* return from procedure */
```

Figure 14.1 Procedure call with PUSH and POP

Before call:

```
| current data frame |
^                     ^
F                     T
```

After call:

```
| old data frame | i | j | link | F | new data frame |
                                  ^                   ^
                                  F                   T
```

Figure 14.2 Data frame layout using PUSH and POP

Specialised stack-handling instructions can therefore have a fairly dramatic effect on the efficiency of procedure call and return. The fragment of figure 14.3 will execute almost as fast as the corresponding FORTRAN fragment shown in chapter 11, and can utilise full compile-time argument checking and hardware run-time stack limit checking. The remaining difference in efficiency is caused by the fact that the recursive programming languages allows the declaration of 'dynamic arrays': if the language only permits FORTRAN-like arrays then the recursive language can be implemented as efficiently as, or perhaps more efficiently than FORTRAN, as the discussion below establishes.

Addressing the Stack with a Single Register

Most programming language designers attempt to strike a balance between efficiency and generality, providing only those language constructions which give rise to 'acceptably efficient' object programs. In the case of a system programming language the demands of efficiency are given more weight than they are in more conventional languages and the facilities provided are restricted in the interests of efficient implementation. The most effective restrictions are those which improve the operation of crucial code fragments such as the loading of the value of a variable, procedure call and return, and so on. BCPL, for example, doesn't allow access to non-local data, thus eliminating environment manipulation, turning closures into simple code addresses and ensuring that every data access can be a single instruction.

Most system programming languages demand, amongst other things, that vectors and arrays must have bounds which are fixed at compile-time. This restriction enables the compiler to calculate the total size of the data frame, including the space required for any arrays, before the program runs and means that only one of the stack-addressing registers is required, since the distance from

---

```
source:      fred(k1*k2, fred(m,n)

code:          LOAD    1, k1
               MULT    1, k2
               PUSHr   T, 1
                 PUSH    T, m
                 PUSH    T, n
                 PUSHSUB T, #fred
                 DECn    T, 2
               PUSHr   T, 1
               PUSHSUB T, #fred
               DECn    T, 2
```

(prologue and epilogue as in figure 14.1)

Figure 14.3 Nested procedure calls using PUSH and POP

base of data frame to top of stack is always known. It thus allows
extremely efficient procedure call and return and may remove the
need for block entry and exit overheads entirely. The same trick
will work for any language which demands that stack-borne data
structures are fixed-size: PASCAL is an obvious example.

Figure 14.4 shows the instructions required to implement a
nested procedure call in BCPL, from a procedure whose data frame
occupies N words. The code fragment could be generated by a
procedure which uses the 'stack extension' mechanism of chapter 3,
except that in the case of BCPL it isn't necessary to generate
instructions to adjust the position of the top-of-stack - it's

---

Stack before call:

```
___ | current data frame
  -
  F
```

During call of fred(m,n):

```
___ | old data frame     | k1*k2 | L | new data frame
                                  -
                                  F
```

Source: fred(k1*k2, fred(m,n))

Code: LOAD   1, k1
               MULT   1, k2
               STORE 1, N+1(F)   /* k1*k2 */
               LOAD   1, m
               STORE 1, N+3(F)
               LOAD   1, n
               STORE 1, N+4(F)
               ADDn   F, N+2   /* set up new data frame */
               JSUB   L, #fred /* call procedure */
               SUBn   F, N+2   /* reclaim space */
               STORE 1, N+2(F)   /* fred(m,n) */
               ADDn   F, N   /* set up new data frame */
               JSUB   L, #fred /* call procedure */
               SUBn   F, N   /* reclaim space */

Source: **let** fred(i,j) = **valof**

#fred: STORE L, 0(F)

           ... procedure body ...

               RETNi   , 0(F)
```

**Figure 14.4 Procedure call using only Frame register**
```

merely necessary to note the new size of the data frame. This code fragment executes only eighteen instructions, two less than the FORTRAN example of chapter 11, and makes only thirty store accesses, which is a 17% improvement over that example.

It is possible to produce a still more efficient code fragment by eliminating the base-of-frame register and addressing the data frame relative to the top of stack. The mechanism is a little more difficult to implement, since the relative address of values in the data frame changes each time anything is PUSHed or POPped, but with careful design it can be done. Figure 14.5 shows code for the familiar source example: it would execute only fourteen instructions, which is remarkably small, and would make only twenty-six store accesses, which is slightly less than the example in figure 14.4, and almost 30% less than the FORTRAN example of chapter 11. Note how each PUSH instruction alters the addressing of the variables in the current data frame: 'n' is initially addressed as '-1(T)' but by the time it is passed as an argument it has become '-3(T)'.

Unfortunately the mechanism of figure 14.5 is rather over-simplified. Most system-programming languages allow an indefinite number of arguments in a procedure call, no matter how many are

---

Initial stack layout:

```
| k1 | k2 | m | n |
                    ^
                    T
```

source: fred(k1*k2, fred(m,n))

code:
```
            LOAD     1, -4(T) /* k1 */
            MULT     1, -3(T) /* k2 */
            PUSHr    T, 1
            PUSH     T, -3(T) /* m */
            PUSH     T, -3(T) /* n */
            PUSHSUB  T, #fred
            PUSHr    T, 1
            PUSHSUB  T, #fred
```

source: **let** fred(i,j) = **valof**

#fred:
```
            ADDn     T, data-frame-size

            ... procedure body ...

            SUBn     T, data-frame-size + 2
            RETNi      , 2(T)
```

Figure 14.5 Procedure call using only Top-of-stack register

specified in the procedure declaration, yet the use of a SUBn instruction in the prologue in figure 14.5 is only possible if exactly two values are pushed onto the stack. If a postcall DECn or SUBn instruction is included after the PUSHSUB to remove the arguments from the stack and the arguments are pushed in the reverse of the normal order (i.e. the last argument is pushed on the stack first of all) then an indefinite number of arguments can be passed yet the overhead of procedure call and return is only sixteen instructions and twenty-eight store accesses - still much faster than FORTRAN.

The code of figure 14.4 also allows an indefinite number of arguments in the sense that they can be placed in position on the stack but, unfortunately, if more arguments are given than parameters are declared the called procedure activation will overwrite the excess parameters since they occupy locations in the data frame which are allocated to local values of the called procedure. The base-of-frame addressing mechanism has a slight advantage, however, in that it can use procedure-level addressing without wasting any stack space: the distance to top-of-stack is always just the sum of the sizes of the data frames of the current procedure and the blocks within it which are currently being executed. It is simpler also in its treatment of non-local **goto**s and in the manipulation of label values, since in no case is it necessary to move a top-of-stack pointer.

Heap Storage

The space allocation mechanism described in chapter 11 caters only for data structures whose lifetime is the same as that of the procedure activation in whose data frame the space is allocated. An ALGOL 60 array, for example, is defined by the contents of the 'dope vector' which is set up by the code described in chapter 11 and manipulated by the code described in chapter 9. The dope vector contains a collection of information about the array, including a pointer to the memory cells which make up the array proper. A dope vector, or a pointer to a dope vector, can be passed as argument information in a procedure call in order to give the called procedure access to an array: this gives no run-time garbage-collection problem because it merely creates a pointer from newer to older data frame, which is destroyed on procedure return.

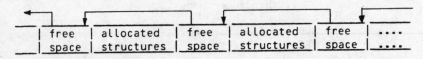

Figure 14.6 Fragmentation of free space in the heap

If it were possible to declare an **array procedure** in ALGOL 60 or PASCAL then it would not be sufficient for it merely to return a dope vector or a pointer to a dope vector since the memory cells to which it would point might be held in the data frame of the returning procedure, which is about to be destroyed. It would be necessary therefore to inspect the dope vector which is returned and if necessary copy the memory cells to which it points into the local data frame. This would be inefficient, but not disastrously so: copying in the reverse direction is already necessary when an array is 'passed by value'.

In the case of data structures which contain pointers to other structures, such as records, and composite values which include pointers to data frames, such as closures, there is no such simple remedy. The 'records' discussed in chapter 9, for example, are in effect vectors whose elements may contain pointers to other vectors. The useful lifetime of a record begins when it is created and lasts until there are no accessible pointers to it held either in pointer-type variables on the stack or in other accessible records: this lifetime has no relation whatsoever to the lifetime of the procedure activation which creates the record.

For this reason it is impossible - or at least impossibly inefficient - to allocate space for record-vectors from the stack unless the source language is heavily restricted to ensure that when a procedure activation returns there can be no pointers from any other data frame to the data structures held in its data frame[1]. If record-vector space were allocated from the stack without the imposition of such a restriction then each procedure return would have to invoke a full garbage collection and storage compaction process (see below) in order to move any accessible records out of the returning activation's data frame and to update any pointers to them held elsewhere in the stack!

For a language which allows the free manipulation of pointers to data structures it is therefore necessary to provide an off-stack storage area - called the <u>heap</u> in ALGOL 68 terminology - to contain those data structures which can be pointed at. There are two problems of heap maintenance

(i) allocation of space for a new structure

(ii) reclamation of space when the useful lifetime of a structure is over.

It would require a separate book to do justice to the topics of space allocation and reclamation: there are features of both,

---

1 ALGOL 68 does impose such restrictions, and I discuss below the compile-time and run-time checks which are required to enforce those restrictions.

however, which affect the run-time support mechanisms of the object program and which the compiler-writer ought to understand.

Space <u>allocation</u> is relatively straightforward. A library subroutine - the 'allocate' procedure called from the code illustrated in chapter 9 - can be used to allocate space from a list of 'free blocks' in the heap. The heap will start life as a single area of free space, but after some allocation and reclamation of space has occurred it will typically appear as in figure 14.6: a mixture of free space areas and allocated areas. As structure space is reclaimed it can be collected together into contiguous free space areas: when it is allocated there are are various algorithms which can be used to decide which of the free space areas should be depleted.

When the data structures which can be allocated aren't all the same size then <u>storage fragmentation</u> can result. The problem arises because structures are not necessarily reclaimed in the order in which they were allocated, or in any sensible order: thus after a sequence of partial reclamations and re-allocation of different-sized data structures the free heap space will tend to be divided up into separate, small, non-contiguous free spaces. A sophisticated storage allocation mechanism can slow the process of fragmentation, but the heap may eventually reach a state in which, when space is required for a new data structure, no single area of free space is large enough to hold it although in total there is plenty of free space available.

An apparent 'solution' to the storage-fragmentation problem is to allocate several different heaps, one for each size of structure which can be allocated. Even when this is possible it is rather unsatisfactory, because space in one of the heaps can become exhausted while there is space still available in some of the others. In effect the store is fragmented into several heaps! The only effective solution is to expand the heap or to invoke a <u>storage compaction</u> process, which is a garbage collection mechanism discussed below.

Space <u>reclamation</u> is the real difficulty, and the one which has most effect on the run-time support mechanisms of the object program. There are several possible mechanisms: the most reasonable are

(i) The user may be required to release structure space explicitly.

(ii) The program can invoke a <u>garbage collection</u> process when space is exhausted and more is required (or can invoke it at intervals or even continuously) in order to discover structures in the heap which are inaccessible, and can reclaim the space it finds.

If space is released explicitly by the user then allocation and reclamation of heap space, discounting the storage-fragmentation problem, imposes very little run-time overhead on the program. It may be difficult or impossible, however, for the user to release every data structure which ought to be released and it is possible that the user may accidentally release a record which is still in use (to which there is an accessible pointer). Such a user error will create a 'dangling' pointer which points to reclaimed space - in effect to space which will later be occupied by some other data structure. Subsequent use of the 'dangling pointer' will produce strange results: although garbage collection imposes a run-time overhead, it does at least prevent the creation of dangling pointers.

Every garbage collection mechanism consists of at least two phases: a <u>mark</u> phase and a <u>collect</u> phase. When the mechanism is invoked, it must first 'unmark' every structure in the heap, unless this is already ensured by the operation of previous garbage collections. It must know, or must discover, the value of every pointer which leads into the heap from outside: only the structures which are accessible via these pointers are accessible to the program. Taking each of these pointers in turn it can 'mark' the structure to which it points, the structures to which pointers held in that structure point, and so on. A recursive description of a mark algorithm is given in figure 14.7[1]. Once the marking procedure has marked all the structures which are accessible from each of the off-heap pointers, any structure which is still unmarked is clearly inaccessible. The 'collect' phase can then accumulate all unmarked structures for re-allocation and simultaneously unmark all marked structures ready for the next 'mark' phase.

The requirements which the garbage collector puts on the object program are at least

(i) that it should indicate the location of <u>every</u> off-heap pointer so that they can be used for marking accessible structures.

```
let mark (structurep) be
 if structurep \= empty & structurep.mark=0 then
 { structurep.mark := 1
    for each pointer-element in the structure do
        mark(structurep.element)
 }
```

Figure 14.7 Marking accessible structures

---

1 This procedure is given merely for illustration - there are many efficient non-recursive marking algorithms.

(ii) that each data structure in the heap should somehow be
tagged so that the mark phase can find which of its
elements are pointers and can trace the structures to
which they point.

The first of these requirements is quite severe: it implies that
every data frame on the stack should contain a map that indicates
which of the values in that data frame are pointers and which are
not, or perhaps in practice a pointer to such a map which can be
shared by all the data frames of a recursive procedure. The
procedure prologue must store the pointer to the map in the data
frame and it must initialise every location which can contain a
pointer to some neutral 'empty' value. If the program allocates an
array of pointers then the map must indicate this in some way and
each of the pointers in the array must be initialised.

When the garbage collector is invoked the mark phase can trace
down the stack from the current (topmost) data frame to the bottom
(outer block) data frame, inspecting the map in each frame and
marking via the pointers which it indicates. If there are any
pointers held in 'static' storage areas outside the stack then
there must be a map which indicates their location as well. All
the maps must be set up by the object-description phase and the
translation phase before the program runs.

The second requirement above implies that each structure in the
heap should contain a pointer map, or a value which identifies
such a map held elsewhere in the program. In most languages which
use heap allocation the user can invent new kinds and shapes of
records, so that the object-description phase must set up the maps
for the loader to link into the garbage-collection mechanism's
data space.

It all sounds very simple, but it is very tricky to implement
and there are all sorts of unexpected pitfalls: I give two
examples. First, the procedure-level addressing mechanism of
chapter 13 may allocate a pointer variable, declared in a
particular block within a procedure, to a location in the data
frame which is shared by a non-pointer variable declared in a
different block in the same procedure: this must be prevented
because it means that the pointer map of the data frame is valid
for only part of the execution of the procedure body. Second, if
the program can be interrupted in mid-execution for purposes of
debugging then the registers may contain pointer values: this can
cause severe problems for the garbage collector since these will
appear in none of the maps. The debugger must therefore ensure
that the program can only be interrupted in a 'clean' state.

One of the drawbacks of most garbage collection mechanisms is
that they make the program run in fits and starts because they are
invoked only when space is exhausted. Typically the program runs
for a time consuming heap space, then stops while some of the

space is reclaimed, runs again, stops, runs, stops, and so on. If the heap is perpetually almost full, the program will spend more time garbage collecting than running - the only remedy is to expand the heap. Modern research has shown how a garbage collector can be made to run continuously, perhaps on a parallel processor (Dijkstra et al.,1978), or how each space allocation can perform a corresponding amount of garbage collection (Baker,1978). In either case the program no longer runs in bursts but merely runs a little slower overall.

When storage fragmentation has reached an advanced stage then storage compaction may be necessary. This involves moving data structures in the heap so that the various small areas of free space can become a single large area. It also means that every location in the store which contains a pointer must be updated so that it shows the new position of the structure which it addresses. Storage compaction can be combined with the collect phase of the garbage collector: it uses the same maps as the mark phase, but in this case to locate the pointers which must be updated. It's more costly than a normal garbage-collection, so that storage compaction is normally avoided if possible.

When the heap space is exhausted, or so nearly exhausted that the program is too frequently garbage-collecting, the heap space must be expanded. On a multi-segment-addressing machine, or a paged (virtual storage) single-segment machine this presents no particular problem, but on an unpaged single-segment machine it may be necessary to move some other data areas to make more room for the heap. If the data area to be moved contains pointers of any kind, then the problem is the same as compacting the heap: perhaps the simplest solution is to buy a multi-segment machine!

ALGOL 68, Lifetimes and Pointers

The definition of ALGOL 68 permits relatively free use of values whose use is restricted in most other languages: closures, arrays, 'slices' of arrays, records, pointers to records, and so on. This freedom introduces at least two problems for the compiler-writer. First, the result returned by a procedure may often be a composite value (such as an array or a structure) which takes up more than one word and so cannot be returned in a single register: the code fragments which implement procedure return, developed in earlier chapters, will therefore need to be altered for an ALGOL 68 implementation. Second, when pointers (ALGOL 68 **ref**s), or values which contain pointers, are manipulated, various compile-time and run-time checks will be required to ensure that no 'dangling pointers' can be created. In particular it is important to note that a closure contains pointers to data frames in the form of an environment.

The basic restriction on the use of pointers in ALGOL 68 can be stated in implementation terms as follows

>   There must be no pointers which lead from an older data
>   frame to a newer. Pointers may lead from stack to heap but
>   not from heap to stack.

The restriction ensures that no program can ever reach a state in
which there is a pointer from some data frame, or from the heap,
to the data frame of a returning procedure activation: if the
restriction were contravened then 'dangling pointers' would be
created when the data frame space was reclaimed in the procedure
epilogue.

   The restriction is imposed in the interests of efficiency. Use
of the heap implies garbage collection, as the discussion above
establishes, but disciplined use of pointers in the stack imposes
a much smaller run-time overhead. For some source programs it is
possible to discover at compile-time whether the restriction is
obeyed or not: in such cases the use of pointers in the stack
imposes no run-time overhead whatsoever. (It is worth noting that
most system-programming languages allow stack pointers to be used
with even more freedom than in ALGOL 68. Users of such languages
are assumed to be knowledgeable enough to avoid the creation of
dangling pointers.)

   There are two aspects to the problem of dangling pointers: the

---

```
begin int a, b; ref int ra, rb;

   ra := a;     co #1 - valid oc

   begin int i,j; ref int ri, rj;
   bool x,y;

   ri  = i;  co #2 - valid oc

   rb := j;  co #3 - invalid oc
   rj := b;  co #4 - valid oc

   read((x,y));
   (if x then ra else ri fi) := (if y then a else i fi);
            co #5 - needs run-time check oc

   ri := ra; co #6 - valid oc
   rb := rj  co #7 - needs run-time check oc
   end
end
```

Figure 14.8 Checking the lifetimes of data objects

use of pointers to data objects and the use of closures[1], which contain pointers to data frames because they include an environment (see chapter 13). In the case of pointers to data objects, the problem is to identify the 'lifetime' of the object. The lifetime of a heap object is potentially infinite, that of an object on the stack is the same as the lifetime of the procedure activation in whose data frame it resides. No procedure activation can be permitted access to a pointer which leads to an object with shorter lifetime than itself. Older activations live longer than younger ones (it's a stack!) so the restriction is that no pointer must lead from an older data frame to a younger one. Lifetimes are easy to measure: at compile-time the higher the textual level (see chapter 13, figure 13.1) the shorter the lifetime; at run-time the higher the data frame address on the stack[2] the younger the data frame and therefore the shorter the lifetime.

The program in figure 14.8 contains a sequence of assignment statements. Statements #1 and #2 can be seen to be valid at compile-time because the textual levels (and therefore the lifetimes) of the left- and right-hand-sides are the same. Statement #3 can be seen to be invalid because the textual level of the right-hand-side is higher than that of the left-hand-side: if permitted it would give the outer block access to variable 'j' after execution of the inner block had finished. Statement #4 is valid because the lifetime of the left-hand-side is less than that of the right-hand-side.

It isn't always possible to determine the lifetime of the object or pointer denoted by an expression, but it is always possible to put lower and upper bounds on the lifetime. Call these bounds L and U: the restriction is then

- an assignment is <u>valid</u> if the left-hand-side object will certainly die before the right-hand-side object - i.e. if U(lhs) is shorter than L(rhs).
- an assignment is <u>invalid</u> if the left-hand-side object will certainly live longer than the right-hand-side object - i.e. if L(lhs) is longer than U(rhs).
- otherwise a run-time check is required

In figure 14.8 the upper and lower bounds of left- and right-hand-sides in statement #5 are the same, so the statement needs a run-time check. Statement #6 is valid because a lower bound on the lifetime of a pointer held in 'ra' is that of 'ra' itself:

1 On a point of terminology: I use the word 'lifetime' where ALGOL 68 uses 'scope'; I use 'closure' where ALGOL 68 uses 'routine denotation'.

2 Assuming that the stack starts at a low address and grows towards higher addresses.

statement #7 needs a run-time check.

Note that when a pointer to a data object which itself contains pointers (a **struct,** say) is manipulated it isn't necessary to inspect the pointers within the object since earlier applications of the restriction will have ensured that they don't point to other objects with shorter lifetimes.

If a procedure or block activation returns a pointer to a data object as its result, or a composite object which contains such a pointer, then the object pointed to must have greater lifetime than the activation itself. Upper and lower bounds can be placed on the lifetimes of values returned and they can be manipulated in the same way as those in the assignment statements discussed above.

Checking lifetimes connected with the use of closures — ALGOL 68 'routine denotations' — is a little more difficult than checking lifetimes of pointers. A closure consists of a procedure code address and a collection of data frame pointers, as chapter 13 established. Nothing can go wrong when a closure is passed as

---

```
begin proc counter = (int initial)proc(int)int counter:
        (int start := initial;
         proc update = (int incr)int: (mem := mem+incr);
         co result is closure of procedure update oc
         update);

        proc(int)int c1, c2;

        c1 := counter(100); c1(3); print(c1(0));
        c2 := counter(5); print(c2(-5));
        ....
end
```

Figure 14.9 Invalid use of closure as procedure result

```
begin real B;
        proc power = (real base)proc(int)real:
         (proc calc = (int power)real: (B^power);
          B := base;
          calc);
        proc(int)real s1, s2;

        s1 := power(2.0); print(s1(3));
        s2 := power(3.1); print(s2(1));
        ....
end
```

Figure 14.10 Valid use of a closure as a procedure result

an argument in a procedure call but when a closure is assigned to a memory cell or is returned as the result of a procedure then dangling pointers become possible. Figure 14.9 shows an artificial example. The procedure 'counter' attempts to return a closure of the procedure 'update': the environment of 'update' includes the data frame of 'counter' and thus a dangling pointer would be produced. In the same spirit as the restriction on the use of pointers to data objects, therefore, the youngest data frame in the environment part of a closure must be older than the procedure activation which is returning it.

In order that restrictions on the use of closures don't become too stifling, many ALGOL 68 implementations use a slightly different notion of 'environment' to that developed in chapter 13. It is possible to discover, by looking at the non-local names mentioned within the procedure and the blocks and procedures nested within it, the 'effective environment' of the procedure. (If the procedure calls other procedures, it is necessary to take account of those procedure's effective environments: the closure algorithm presented in chapter 15 can be used to compute the effective environment in this case.) Figure 14.10 shows an example which can be permitted since the 'effective environment' of the procedure 'calc' contains only the outer block. Note that it may be impossible to calculate 'effective environments' if procedure variables are used to enable one-pass compilation, as suggested in chapter 12.

This chapter has only touched on the difficulties introduced by the use of stack pointers in ALGOL 68. In the solution of some problems it is necessary to employ run-time checks, in others it is necessary to use the heap to store structures which otherwise could reside on the stack. It may not always be practicable to satisfy the requirements of the language definition, in which case it is essential that the implementation is over-cautious.

Multi-word results

A mechanism by which an array can be returned as the result of a procedure is discussed above: it involves the copying of the array from the data frame of the returning procedure activation into the data frame of the calling activation. The same mechanism can be used for any composite value: **struct**s, closures, etc. If a procedure is declared to return a multi-word result the prologue cannot reclaim the data frame space with a single instruction which resets the top-of-stack register, and there must be a more sophisticated postcall sequence. If the multi-word result is to be immediately assigned to a data object of the same size the postcall fragment can perform the assignment, then reclaim all the data frame space: otherwise it must 'collapse' the stack, preserving the result but removing the rest of the data frame. If the result returned is a composite value which can contain pointers, the lifetime of each pointer will have to be checked either at compile-time or at run-time.

There are many quite tricky problems in the implementation of ALGOL 68 and this chapter has only touched on a few. Most of them have to do with the handling of pointers: all of these problems can be avoided if every structure which can be pointed at is stored in the heap, as is the case in PASCAL for example. This mechanism increases the frequency of run-time garbage-collection and imposes an execution overhead on programs which at present don't require it, but at the same time it leads to a simpler and more reliable implementation. Unfortunately the integration of the **ref** notion into the substructure of ALGOL 68 makes it almost impossible to do this for a complete implementation of the language.

SIMULA 67 'classes'

The invention of the **class** in SIMULA 67 has sparked off a variety of interesting language developments. In particular the notion of 'abstract data type' is used in several modern languages [CLU, EUCLID, ALPHARD, MODULA, etc.] and the idea of 'co-processing' has been brought to the attention of the programming public. Essentially a **class** can be implemented rather like an ALGOL 60 **procedure,** except that the result returned when a **class** is activated by an expression

new <class name> (...)

is a pointer to the activation record itself[1], rather than any value which it calculates. This pointer can be used to access the values in the data frame of the class activation record, thus enabling SIMULA 67 **class**es to behave very like records in other programming languages. It can be used to **resume** the execution of the class activation from the point at which it left off via a **detach** statement, thus enabling SIMULA 67 classes to implement pseudo-parallel processing or 'co-processing'. In this latter case, the pointer returned from **new** is in fact a pointer to a collection of class and procedure activations one of which issued the **detach** and which will therefore continue its execution when the collection as a whole is **resume**d.

The fact that free use of pointers to class activation records is allowed means that a class activation can outlive the activation which originally created it. This in turn means that an implementation of SIMULA 67 can't use a data frame stack but that

---

1 Chapter 11 defines the procedure activation created by a procedure call as consisting of the data frame, a position in the code of a procedure and a collection of (pointers to) data frames which form the environment of that activation. A SIMULA class activation is almost identical in implementation.

all data frames must be allocated from heap storage. That single fact is almost all that need be said about the implementation of SIMULA 67: everything else follows.

There isn't sufficient space in this book to give a tutorial on SIMULA 67: there are many excellent introductory texts available. Figure 14.11 shows a simple example of the use of a **class** as a record. The result of **'new** intlist' is a pointer to a data frame, within which the values 'head' and 'tail' are accessible. The same data frame forms the environment of the procedure 'printlist', which is one of the attributes of every 'intlist' object.

Figure 14.12 shows an example of a **class** which uses the co-processing mechanism of SIMULA 67 to implement pseudo-parallel lexical analysis. In this case the pointer returned by **new** is used to define a co-process which 'sleeps' between items using **detach** and is 'reawakened' by **resume.**

SIMULA 67 is much more general in its application than ALGOL 68, in the sense that it allows more forms of control behaviour to be specified. These forms (for example co-processing) are outlawed by the 'lifetime' restrictions of ALGOL 68 - and indeed those of PASCAL or any other stack-based recursive language. The cost of generality is that data frames of **class**es must be garbage collected, just like the records of PASCAL and the 'global' objects of ALGOL 68. Note, however, that the data frame space of a SIMULA 67 **procedure** can be reclaimed immediately it returns, although it cannot be allocated from a stack because the use of **resume** and **detach** may mean that procedures don't return in the reverse of the order in which they were called. For similar programs in PASCAL and SIMULA 67, therefore, SIMULA will lose a little in efficiency because of the greater number of instructions which are required to allocate space from the heap on procedure call and to return it on procedure return. ALGOL 68 object programs can gain more efficiency still, but only if they are able

---

```
class intlist(head, tail);
    integer head;
    ref(intlist) tail;
  begin procedure printlist;
        begin print(head); newline;
            if tail=/=none then tail.printlist
        end;
  end;
ref(intlist) a, b;

a := new intlist(1,none); b := new intlist(3,a);
a.tail := new intlist(-1,a);
a.printlist; b.printlist;
```

Figure 14.11 Lists of integers in SIMULA 67

to perform their record processing entirely on the stack rather than in the heap.

Summary

Special stack-handling instructions can increase the efficiency of procedure call and return. Restrictions on the source language can increase this efficiency still further if they enable the stack to be addressed with only a single register. It is possible to implement recursive procedure call more efficiently than FORTRAN, given a suitably restricted language: if the object machine has instructions equivalent to PUSHSUB and POPRETN then recursive

---

```
character item[1:80];
integer itemtype, itemsize;

class LexAnalyse;
  begin character c; integer i;

    detach;

    c := readchar;
    for i := 0 while c /= endoffile do
      if alphabetic(c) then
        begin
            for i := i+1 while alphabetic(c) do
              begin item[i] := c; c := readchar end;
            itemtype := name; itemsize := i-1;
            detach
        end
      else if digit(c) then
        begin
            for i := i+1 while digit(c) do
              begin item[i] := c; c := readchar end;
            itemtype := number; itemsize := i-1;
            detach
        end
      else
        begin
            item[1] := c;
            itemtype := punctuation; itemsize := 1;
            detach;
            c := readchar
        end
  end

ref(LexAnalyse) L;

L := new LexAnalyse; ... resume L; ... resume L;
```

Figure 14.12 Pseudo-parallel lexical analysis

procedure call can be as efficient as subroutine call.

For a 'secure' implementation of heap storage allocation it is essential that the heap is garbage collected. Garbage collection is expensive at run-time and involves additional overheads even if it is never invoked: these are to do with the maintenance of the pointer maps which the garbage collector needs if it is to find all the pointers to heap structures which are held elsewhere in the program.

ALGOL 68 and SIMULA 67 differ in implementation in that one uses a stack of data frames and the other uses a heap. ALGOL 68 implementation is tricky because it is essential to police source language restrictions on the use of pointers which lead from one data frame to the other. SIMULA 67 implementation is simpler in principle but will in some cases produce very much less efficient object programs because of its use of the heap for record processing where ALGOL 68 can use the stack. For programs without record-processing (and of course without co-processing) SIMULA may be only marginally less efficient than more conventional programming languages.

Section IV
Parsing Algorithms

Books on compiler writing (and the lecture courses which follow them) tend often to concentrate on syntax analysis at the expense of other topics. Perhaps this is because the theoretical attention which this part of the subject has received makes it capable of a highly formal presentation. This makes it easy for academics like me to teach it and (very important!) easy for us to write examination questions about it. For the practical compiler-writer, however, syntax analysis is merely a means to an end. You need only know a reliable means of building a syntax analyser without necessarily understanding all the theoretical background. In this section chapters 16, 17 and 18 include descriptions of three useful mechanisms with explanations about how to use them to construct a practical syntax analyser, while there is enough background theory in chapter 15 to explain just how and why they work.

It would be wrong of me to give the impression that theoretical analysis isn't worthwhile or that the treatment of parsing algorithms in this section tells you all that you will ever need to know. I find that practical experience of writing syntax analysers gives many people a taste for the theory that lies behind them. You'll have to gratify such awakened appetites by reading any one of the worthwhile books which cover the field: in this book I concentrate mostly on getting you started.

Often it is necessary to build a syntax analyser without any automatic aid, apart from an existing compiler for the 'host' language in which you are writing your compiler. Of the various techniques which have been used in the past and are used at present, a combination of 'top-down', 'one-track' parsing[1] to process the statement and declaration syntax together with 'bottom-up', 'operator-precedence' parsing for the syntax of expressions provides the best and simplest solution to the problem. This combination of techniques is so convenient that until recently it seemed that automatic aids to the generation of a syntax analyser - called 'parser-generators' or 'compiler-compilers' - were a thing of the past. With the rise in popularity of automatic parser generators based on the LR(1) mechanism discussed in chapter 18 the compiler-compiler has made a come-back. It is still probably the case, however, that most syntax analysers are written by hand and it is too early to say whether or not the compiler-compiler will eventually become as universally accepted in compiler writing as is the system-programming language.

The combination of top-down parsing for statements and declarations with operator-precedence parsing for expressions complements the strengths and weaknesses of each technique.

---

1 Also known as LL(1) parsing, in the notation introduced in chapter 18.

First, the syntax of statements and declarations is highly redundant, in that a parser can largely predict what symbol ought to come next on the basis of the input already processed: a top-down parser can use this redundancy to good effect in producing clear and useful error reports. Problems associated with converting the grammar of a programming language into the special form required by a top-down parser are relatively easy to solve given the sparse nature of the syntax of statements and declarations. Second, within the syntax of expressions redundancy is much reduced and the error-reporting powers of the top-down analyser are less useful. Indeed it is possible to exploit the fact that an operator-precedence analyser can be made to overlook certain errors, particularly those associated with invalid combinations of operand types. The well-known drawback of operator-precedence parsing, which is that a parser may go well past an error and process much of the subsequent input before noticing that a syntax error is present, is once again relatively easy to overcome within the limited world of expressions.

In practice both one-track analysers and operator-precedence analysers can be generated by a compiler-compiler designed for the purpose: I touch on this topic briefly in chapters 16 and 17. The modifications required to turn a grammar into one suitable for top-down or operator-precedence parsing are complex, however, and the LR(1) mechanism discussed in chapter 18 is almost certainly a better bet for the compiler-compiler-writer.

Chapter 15 defines notation and introduces most of the theoretical ideas used in the later chapters. On first reading of this section it may be advisable to read only as much of chapter 15 as you find digestible and then to skip on to chapters 16, 17 and 18, returning to chapter 15 when you come across concepts which need explanation.

In chapters 16, 17 and 18 I devote a great deal of attention to the business of error detection, error reporting and error recovery, since it is the quality of error handling which distinguishes a good syntax analyser from a poor or average one. Efficiency isn't particularly important, provided the analyser never 'backtracks', and none of the techniques presented below involves backtracking. Therefore the compiler writer should choose the parsing mechanism (or combination of mechanisms) which provides the simplest, most convenient and most automatic route to a working syntax analyser and should concentrate upon providing good, clear, relevant, reliable and useful error reports to the user (that's you and me!) who submits a program which contains syntax errors. As I quoted in chapter 4 "any fool can write a compiler for correct programs", so we should all try to write syntax analysers which cater for human error!

The Dangers of Backtracking

All syntax analysers break down the problem of finding the structure of their input into a sequence of smaller and simpler sub-problems. In discovering the structure it must make an exhaustive search of all possible structures which might describe the input and, as we all know, exhaustive searches are prone to backtrack. Backtracking will occur when the analyser is faced with alternative ways in which the input might be analysed and has no immediate means of distinguishing which of the possible paths of analysis is the correct one. A conventional program can only follow one of the paths at a time and, if the path it chooses turns out to be the wrong one, it must eventually backtrack to the decision point where the alternatives presented themselves and attempt once more to find the right path.

To backtrack means to restore the state of the analyser to that which obtained when the alternative analysis paths were first encountered. The analyser must destroy any parts of the parse tree that may have been constructed during the now abandoned analysis path, 'rewind' the input to its previous position and erase (or 'unmake') any alterations which it made to the memory during that analysis. All of this is fairly easy to do, if somewhat inefficient: when the tree is built using the 'node' procedure of chapter 3 then resetting a single pointer will delete a section of the tree; if all the output from the lexical analyser is stored in the memory then rewinding it is a matter of resetting another pointer; if the syntax analyser is careful not to make any alterations to the memory (such as alterations to the contents of symbol table descriptors) then there will be no need to make any erasures.

Although backtracking makes the analyser less efficient than it might be, its most important drawback is that it prevents accurate error reporting. The syntax analyser can't produce an error report based on a path of analysis which it is abandoning when there are other as yet unexplored alternative paths and it cannot even produce a useful report when all alternatives have failed since it cannot be sure which of the paths were cul-de-sacs and which detected the true error. All it can do is to keep silent until all alternatives have been attempted and all have failed and then report that fact. Thus the classical backtracking analyser's error report is the "STATEMENT NOT RECOGNISED" of the early University of Manchester Autocode compilers, or the equally unhelpful "Statement syntax" and "Expression syntax" error reports of the current C compiler under the UNIX operating system. Faced with such a general condemnation of a section of the source program, even the most experienced programmer can be at a loss to decide how to find and correct the error.

Of the mechanisms presented in this section, only the top-down analysis technique presented in chapter 16 has been frequently used to produce a backtracking syntax analyser: the treatment in that chapter shows how to design and build a non-backtracking top-down analyser. Operator-precedence analysers, discussed in chapter 17, could be made to backtrack only with difficulty but they have other error-handling deficiencies which make them useful only in the restricted area of the analysis of programming language expressions. The LR(1) mechanism discussed in chapter 18 avoids backtracking first by allowing different paths of analysis to proceed in parallel and then by forcing an irrevocable choice between different analysis paths at the point where they would begin to build different parse-tree structures.

15 Notation and Formal Language Theory

The theory of formal languages, so far as it is applicable to compiler writing, covers only issues of <u>syntax</u>: it describes those arrangements of symbols which constitute executable (runnable) programs in a programming language. It isn't concerned at all with the <u>semantics</u> of those programs: what they 'mean' or what will be the effect when you run them. Sections II and III above assume an intuitive understanding of the semantics of languages such as PASCAL, FORTRAN, ALGOL 60 or ALGOL 68 and that's as far as this book goes in the discussion of programming language semantics.

<u>Syntax</u> <u>analysis</u>, or <u>parsing</u>, is a process of discovering whether a sequence of input characters, symbols, items or tokens constitutes an executable program in a language. In order to understand how this is possible it is necessary to grasp some of the simpler insights of formal language theory. This chapter introduces notation and ideas which are used in later chapters and defines various technical terms, set out in figure 15.1.

At the end of the chapter I give an example to show how you can sometimes turn a type 2 grammar - the form of grammar in which programming languages are usually defined - into a type 3 grammar, which can then be used as the basis for the construction of a lexical analyser. I also give a closure algorithm (Warshall's algorithm) which is useful in the computation of the FIRST+, LAST+ and 'follower' lists which are used in the discussion in chapters

---

sentence	type 0, 1, 2, 3 grammars
language	left recursion
grammar	right recursion
production	self-embedding
terminal symbol	ambiguity
non-terminal symbol	equivalence
sentential form	derivation, =>, =>+, =>*

Figure 15.1 Terms defined in this chapter

16 and 18. There is a short discussion about context-dependent syntax and the usefulness of two-level (van Wijngaarden) grammars.

Languages and Sentences

The formal language theory expounded below was inspired originally by the work of Noam Chomsky in the 1950s. Chomsky adapted the production systems of Emil Post (themselves developed in the 1930s) to the study of 'natural languages' such as English, Hindi, Mandarin, etc. Computer scientists rapidly adapted Chomsky's ideas to the study of programming languages (unnatural languages?) where they had an immediate and lasting impact, although the validity of Chomsky's ideas remains a matter for fierce debate in natural-language research circles.

The fundamental principle of the theory is that a language can be described in terms of how its sentences[1] may be built up: a generative description of the language. It is possible, as I show below, to use such a generative description to prescribe a parser for the language but generative description is not directly concerned with techniques of parsing. The first two definitions are

1.   A sentence is a string (a sequence) of symbols.

2.   A language is a set of sentences.

Programs, or sometimes statements and declarations, are the 'sentences' of programming languages. Languages usually contain an infinite number of sentences.

Note that these definitions say nothing about the way in which a language should be described and don't tie a language to any particular description: there may be several equally useful descriptions of a single language. This is important because most of the work in designing a syntax analyser lies in transforming the 'reference' or 'standard' description of the language, which is usually an unsuitable description of the language for the purposes of analysis, into one which can form the basis of a syntax analyser.

Note also that a language, according to the definition above, may exist independently of any useful definition of itself (as natural languages do, for example) and that therefore grammars can be said to describe languages rather than to define them. In compiler-writing, however, it is conventional to regard a grammar as defining the language which it describes.

---

1 The terminology of formal language theory comes from natural language usage – thus it has 'sentence' rather than 'program', it has 'alphabet', 'phrase' and so on.

Generating a Sentence

A description of a language is a <u>grammar</u> of the language. A grammar shows how a sentence may be built up by successive expansions of a string (sequence) of symbols. Figure 15.2 shows a sample grammar for a language which consists of simplified arithmetic expressions made up of 'i's, 'n's and arithmetic expression operators. The grammar is shown in the well-known 'Backus-Naur' notation (also known as Backus-Naur form or BNF for short) which was popularised by the definition of ALGOL 60. Figure 15.3 shows the same grammar in the more concise notation which is conventionally used for the description of formal grammars. In either notation it is necessary to distinguish phrase names, such as <term> or 'T', from symbols which can appear in the sentences of the language, such as 'i' and '('. In the BNF notation the phrase-names appear in angle brackets - e.g. <expression> - and in the conventional notation as single capital letters - e.g. 'E'. Figure 15.3 is not quite in the conventional form, in that it has borrowed the BNF shorthand for indicating alternative right-hand-sides. In the conventional notation each rule of the grammar is written on a separate line, as for example

$$E \rightarrow T$$
$$E \rightarrow E+T$$
$$E \rightarrow E-T$$

but the shorthand which shows alternative right-hand-sides on a single line, separated by a vertical bar, is clear and concise.

```
<sentence> ::= <expression> | +<expression> | -<expression>
<expression> ::= <term> | <expression>+<term>
               | <expression>-<term>
<term> ::= <factor> | <term>*<factor> | <term>/<factor>
<factor> ::= <primary> | <factor>^<primary>
<primary> ::= i | n | <function reference> | (<sentence>)
<function reference> ::= i(<argument list>)
<argument list> ::= <sentence> | <argument list>,<sentence>
```

Figure 15.2 Backus-Naur form (BNF) grammar

```
S -> E | +E | -E
E -> T | E+T | E-T
T -> F | T*F | T/F
F -> P | F^P
P -> i | n | R | (S)
R -> i(L)
L -> S | L,S
```

Figure 15.3 Grammar in conventional notation

Figures 15.2 and 15.3 define <u>rewriting</u> <u>rules</u> or <u>productions</u> which can be used to build up a sentence of the language in the way illustrated in figure 15.4. Starting with a string which consists only of the 'sentence symbol' S, each step of the process alters the string by using just one rule of the grammar. Each rule of the grammar shows how to replace the symbol which appears on the left-hand-side of the rule with the string of symbols which

Derivation of sentence 'i+(n*i)'

String	Production		String	Production
S => E	[S -> E]		=> i+(S)	[P -> (S)]
=> E+T	[E -> E+T]		=> i+(E)	[S -> E]
=> T+T	[E -> T]		=> i+(T)	[E -> T]
=> F+T	[T -> F]		=> i+(T*F)	[T -> T*F]
=> P+T	[T -> P]		=> i+(F*F)	[T -> F]
=> i+T	[P -> i]		=> i+(P*F)	[F -> P]
=> i+F	[T -> F]		=> i+(n*F)	[P -> n]
=> i+P	[F -> P]		=> i+(n*P)	[F -> P]
			=> i+(n*i)	[P -> i]

Figure 15.4 Derivation of a sentence

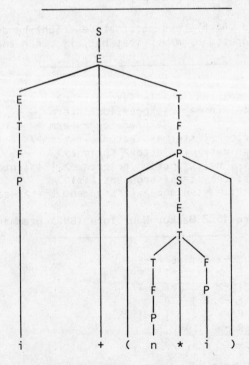

Figure 15.5 Derivation of a sentence shown as a tree

appear on the right-hand-side (or one of the alternative right-hand-sides) of that rule. The rewriting process stops when there are no more left-hand-side symbols in the string. The whole process, which is called a <u>derivation</u>, can also be illustrated by a tree as shown in figure 15.5.

Provided that you don't mind which sentence you finish up with it doesn't matter in what order you use the rules (although in the example I have expanded symbols in the string working strictly from left to right) nor does it matter which rules you choose at each stage. Whichever rules you choose, and in whatever order you use them, you still end up with a sentence, as figure 15.6 illustrates by using the rules of figure 15.3 to derive a more complicated sentence. In this figure I have contracted several steps of the derivation into one, using the notation '=>' for a single-step derivation, '=>+' for a multi-step derivation.

The derivation tree in its full form, as in figure 15.5, includes a node for each step of the derivation. When building a tree to show the result of syntax analysis, however, it is more normal to construct a contracted form of the tree such as that illustrated in figure 15.7 (in which steps that replace one left-hand-side symbol with another are omitted) or the form illustrated in figure 15.8 (which is the 'parse tree' of earlier chapters).

Although not every grammar is as simple as that of figure 15.2, the example serves to illustrate several points. When the left-hand-side of every production in the grammar is a single symbol then the derivation of a sentence can always be shown as a tree;

Derivation of sentence 'n+i*i(-i^n,i+(n-i))'

```
S =>    E                        [S -> E]
   =>    E+T                      [E -> E+T]
   =>+   n+T                      [E -> T -> F -> P -> n]
   =>    n+T*F                    [T -> T*F]
   =>+   n+i*F                    [T -> F -> P -> i]
   =>+   n+i*i(L)                 [F -> P -> R -> i(L)]
   =>    n+i*i(L,S)               [L -> L,S]
   =>+   n+i*i(-E,S)              [L -> S -> -E]
   =>+   n+i*i(-F^P,S)            [E -> T -> F -> F^P]
   =>+   n+i*i(-i^P,S)            [F -> P -> i]
   =>    n+i*i(-i^n,S)            [P -> n]
   =>+   n+i*i(-i^n,E+T)          [S -> E -> E+T]
   =>+   n+i*i(-i^n,i+T)          [E -> T -> P -> i]
   =>+   n+i*i(-i^n,i+(S))        [T -> F -> P -> (S)]
   =>+   n+i*i(-i^n,i+(E-T))      [S -> E -> E-T]
   =>+   n+i*i(-i^n,i+(n-T))      [E -> T -> F -> P -> n]
   =>+   n+i*i(-i^n,i+(n-i))      [T -> F -> P -> i]
```

Figure 15.6 Derivation of a longer sentence

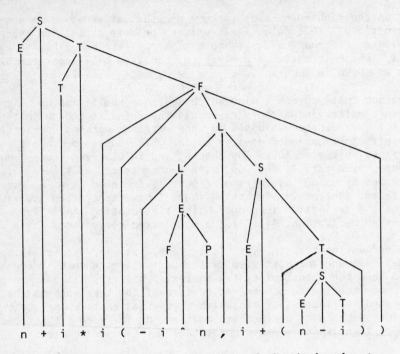

Figure 15.7 Contracted form of the derivation tree

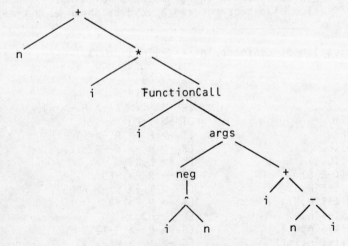

Figure 15.8 Simplified parse tree

symbols which never appear on the left-hand-side of a rule are called terminal symbols because they terminate the derivation (and therefore make up the sentences of the language); symbols which do appear on the left-hand-side of rules are called non-terminal symbols because their expansion isn't complete. Each of the strings in figures 15.4 and 15.6 is called a sentential form: the final sentential form, which contains only terminal symbols, is of course a sentence.

Grammars and Productions

In chapters 16, 17 and 18 I shall be dealing with grammars very like that in figure 15.3, which are known as type 2 grammars in the hierarchy of grammar-types defined below. It is necessary, however, to talk about grammars in more general terms at first, in order to understand the need for some of the changes which must be made to a grammar to make it fit the purposes of syntax analysis. Some further definitions

3. A grammar is a finite set of productions, which contain both terminal and non-terminal symbols. One of the non-terminal symbols is the sentence symbol of the grammar (in the examples in this chapter the sentence symbol is always "S").

4. A production is of the form
         A -> alpha
    where **A** is a non-empty string of non-terminal symbols and **alpha** is a string (possibly empty) of terminal and/or non-terminal symbols. A production expresses the assertion that wherever the string **A** occurs in a partially-derived sentence, it may be replaced by the string **alpha.**

Note that the definition of a production allows a more general form than any I have showed so far, with a string of symbols on the left-hand-side rather than a single symbol. The form of the productions in the grammar defines its position in the Chomsky hierarchy of grammar-types.

The Chomsky Hierarchy

In the Chomsky hierarchy the most general form of grammar is type 0, in which the form of the productions is unrestricted, while grammar types 1, 2 and 3 are categorised by increasing restrictions on the form of the productions. There are two well-known alternative definitions of both type 1 and type 3 grammars: in each case I give the one which I find most convenient.

5. A type 0 grammar contains productions of the form
         A -> alpha
    where **A** is a non-empty string of non-terminal symbols, **alpha** is a string of terminal and/or non-terminal symbols.

6. A <u>type 1</u> or <u>context-sensitive</u> grammar contains only
   productions of the form
   >   **A -> alpha**
   where **A** is a non-empty string of non-terminal symbols,
   alpha is a non-empty string of terminal and/or non-
   terminal symbols and the length of the right-hand-side
   string **alpha** is not less than the length of the left-
   hand-side string **A**[1].

7. A <u>type 2</u> or <u>context-free</u> grammar contains only
   productions of the form
   >   **A -> alpha**
   where A is a single non-terminal symbol and **alpha** is a
   string of terminal and/or non-terminal symbols.

8. A <u>type 3</u> or <u>regular expression</u> grammar contains only
   productions which are one of the forms
   >   A -> a
   >   A -> aB
   in which A and B are single non-terminal symbols, a is a
   single terminal symbol[2].

In the discussion which follows I shall restrict attention to
grammars without useless productions (productions which can't be
used in the derivation of any sentence) and circularities
(productions or collections of productions which can be used to
replace a string with an identical string).

In compiler-writing we are mainly interested in type 2 and type
3 grammars. Type 2 grammars define the syntax of statements,
declarations, expressions and so on while type 3 grammars define
the 'micro-syntax' of lexical items such as names, numbers and
strings. To determine the type of a grammar it is necessary to
look at the left-hand and right-hand-sides of every production.

If every left-hand-side is a single symbol the grammar is
type 2 or type 3: then if <u>every</u> right-hand side is one of
the type 3 forms it is a type 3 grammar, otherwise type 2.

---

1 In the alternative definition of type 1 grammars the
  productions are defined to be of the form
  >   **beta A gamma -> beta alpha gamma**
  where each production replaces a single non-terminal symbol in
  a particular context.

2 In the alternative definition of type 3 grammars the second
  form of production is A -> Cd - a left-recursive rather than
  right-recursive definition. A type 3 grammar must obey one
  definition or the other: if some productions are left- and
  some right-recursive the grammar is type 2.

If any of the productions in the grammar has more than one
symbol on its left-hand-side then the grammar is type 0 or
type 1: then if <u>every</u> production is in the restricted type
1 format it is a type 1 grammar, otherwise it is type 0.

The grammar-types form a hierarchy because type 3 is a
restricted form of types 0, 1 and 2, type 2 a restricted form of
types 0 and 1 and type 1 is a restricted form of type 0.
Corresponding to the hierarchy of grammars is a hierarchy of
<u>languages</u>. Some languages are simple enough to be described by a
type 3 grammar, some are too complex for type 3 grammars and
require a type 2 grammar, and so on.

The Parsing Problem

It is now possible to begin to make the connection between the
generation of a sentence from a grammar and the use of the same
grammar to parse, or syntax analyse, a sequence of symbols which
are given as the input to a syntax analyser. The clue is in the
restrictions which are put on type 1, 2 and 3 grammars. The
'parsing problem' may be characterised as follows

> Given a grammar and a particular sequence of symbols,
> either find how that sequence might be derived from the
> sentence symbol by using the productions of the grammar
> and display the derivation (i.e. show that the input
> sequence is a sentence) or else show that it couldn't be
> derived from the sentence symbol and therefore isn't a
> sentence.

Now if the grammar is type 1 it is possible to prove that the
parsing problem is decidable. This means that it is possible to
write a procedure which can decide in finite time whether any
input sequence is a sentence or not. Since type 2 and type 3
grammars are a restricted form of type 1 grammar, the proof
applies to types 2 and 3 as well as to type 1: it can be
informally summarised as follows

> The length of the input sequence is finite and the grammar
> contains a finite number of productions. In a type 1
> grammar the use of a production either lengthens the
> string or does not alter its length
> - since circularities are not allowed the string
>   must lengthen after a finite number of productions
>   have been used;
> - therefore there are only a finite number of ways
>   in which a sentence of given length can be
>   generated;
> - therefore there are only a finite number of
>   sentences which have the same length as the input
>   sequence and, by searching through all such
>   sentences, it is possible in finite (!) time to

> determine whether the input sequence is a sentence
> or is not.

It isn't necessary to generate every sentence during the search –
it would be sufficient to generate only those sentences whose
first symbol is the same as the first symbol of the input
sequence, and within that group only those sentences whose second
symbol is the same as the second symbol of the input sentence, and
so on. This is in fact the basis of the technique of <u>one-track</u>
analysis, discussed in chapter 16.

The proof presented above isn't quite as useful as it might
seem, however, because it breaks down if any production has an
empty (**null**) right-hand-side. In chapter 16 I show that one-track
analysis in practice demands a grammar with **null** right-hand-sides,
and in that case a modification to the proof is required to ensure
that the **null** symbol only occurs in particular contexts.

Derivations and Sentential Forms

In later chapters it will be necessary to use certain relations
between the symbols of a grammar. All of these relations have to
do with the way in which the productions of the grammar can be
used to produce, or <u>derive</u>, one string from another.

9. If the string **alpha** may be changed into a string **beta** by
    a single application of a single production then **beta** is
    <u>directly</u> <u>derived</u> from **alpha,** written

    alpha => beta

10. A <u>derivation</u> is a sequence of strings
     $alpha_0$, $alpha_1$, $alpha_2$, ... $alpha_n$
     such that $alpha_{i-1} => alpha_i$, $0<i<=n$.

11. If we know that there is at least one step in a
     derivation (n>=1) then $alpha_n$ is <u>eventually</u> <u>derived</u> from
     $alpha_0$, written

     $alpha_0 =>+ alpha_n$

12. If we know that there may be no steps in a derivation
     (n>=0) then $alpha_n$ is <u>derived</u> from $alpha_0$, written

     $alpha_0 =>* alpha_n$

13. A <u>sentential form</u> is a string which is derived from the
     sentence symbol – i.e. if S =>* **alpha** then **alpha** is a
     sentential form.

14. A <u>sentence</u> is a sentential form which contains only

terminal symbols[1].

The relations =>, =>+ and =>* express the assertion that you can get from one string to another in one step (=>), one or more steps (=>+) or in zero or more steps (=>*). In later chapters the use of these relations will become important.

   In the case of type 2 or type 3 grammars it is possible to define three important properties of a symbol which appears on the left-hand-side of a production

   15.   If A =>+ **alpha** A then the symbol A is <u>right-recursive</u>.

   16.   If A =>+ A **beta** then the symbol A is <u>left-recursive</u>.

   17.   If A =>+ **alpha** A **beta** then the symbol A is <u>self-embedding</u>.

Left recursion is particularly important when preparing a grammar to serve as the basis of a top-down analyser (see chapter 16) and self-embedding symbols are important when producing a lexical analyser (see below).

Equivalence and Ambiguity

For the rest of this chapter I discuss the properties of type 2 and type 3 grammars, since they are almost the only types of

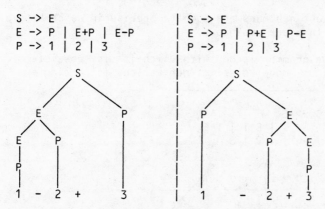

```
S -> E                    | S -> E
E -> P | E+P | E-P        | E -> P | P+E | P-E
P -> 1 | 2 | 3            | P -> 1 | 2 | 3
```

Figure 15.9 Equivalent grammars can define different trees

---

1 Note that this definition implies that a grammar defines the language, whereas above I took the view that a language is independent of any grammar which might describe it. It isn't an important point so far as the practice of compiler-writing is concerned.

grammar that compiler-writers use in practice. At the end of the chapter there are some brief remarks about two-level grammars of the kind used in the definition of ALGOL 68. Definitions and explanations are simpler, however, if they are restricted to grammars whose derivations can always be expressed as a tree.

A language may be described by any number of equivalent grammars. Trivially, we may produce a new grammar just by changing the letters which are used for the non-terminal symbols, but more realistically there may be several different grammars for a language, each of which describes it with a very different derivation of the sentences - i.e. with a different shape of derivation tree.

18. Two grammars are <u>equivalent</u> if they describe the same language - i.e. if they generate exactly the same set of sentences.

Figure 15.9 shows two equivalent grammars for a simple language, whose sentences consist of sequences of 1s, 2s or 3s separated by '+' and '-' signs. The two grammars are quite different so far as the compiler-writer is concerned, since if given to a tree-walker of the kind discussed in chapter 5, the left-hand tree would be treated as '(1-2)+3', which has the value '2', whereas the right-hand tree would be taken as '1-(2+3)' which has the value '-4'. So equivalence of two grammars in terms of the sentences which they produce is not the whole story - we must choose or invent a grammar which describes an appropriate shape of parse tree.

Not all equivalent grammars are equally precise in describing a language: some of them are ambiguous.

19. An <u>ambiguous</u> grammar is one with which it is possible to show two or more distinct derivations for a single

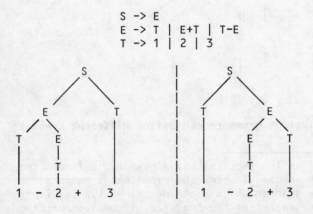

```
S -> E
E -> T | E+T | T-E
T -> 1 | 2 | 3
```

Figure 15.10 An ambiguous grammar

sentence - i.e. two or more distinct parse trees.

It only takes a single example sentence to prove that a grammar is ambiguous, although there are usually whole classes of sentence which have multiple derivations. Figure 15.10 shows a third grammar, equivalent to those in figure 15.9, which is capable of deriving two distinct tree structures for a sample sentence. Such a grammar would produce enormous confusion if used as the basis of a syntax analyser since users of the compiler would not know which out of the two possible interpretations the compiler would select given the input '1-2+3'.

Ambiguity is a problem, then, because of the confusion it introduces about the interpretation of a sentence. Given an ambiguous grammar as a description users may not be able to tell, in some combination of phrases A and B say, whether A is part of B or B is part of A. In practice the user may guess that one of the interpretations is 'obviously' correct when the compiler-writer has guessed that it is the other interpretation that is 'obvious'. The most famous ambiguity of this kind occurred in the original Report on ALGOL 60, which gave the structure of a <conditional statement> as in figure 15.11. The ambiguity which resulted is illustrated in figure 15.12, which displays two distinct parse trees (simplified derivation trees) for a single input. It is impossible to decide, given the syntax definition in figure 15.11, whether execution of statement S2 is under control of expressions E1 and E2 together (Tree1) or under control of E1 alone (Tree2).

The Revised Report on ALGOL 60 removed this confusion by changing the definition of a <conditional statement> to that shown in figure 15.13. An <unconditional statement> can't be a <conditional statement> but can be a <compound statement> so that the user must use **begin** and **end** to bracket potentially ambiguous constructions. Note that this definition doesn't resolve an ambiguity in the original grammar but <u>changes the language</u> so that input like that in figure 15.12 is invalid. The new definition forces the user to state clearly which of the two possible parse trees is intended, by giving one of the input sequences shown in figure 15.13. The original problem was only partly one of formal ambiguity of the grammar: the language designers had to produce a grammar which didn't allow 'visually ambiguous' constructions like that of figure 15.11. There are other solutions to the problem: ALGOL 68 uses **if - fi** bracketing to achieve a similar effect.

ALGOL 60 isn't the only language to suffer from ambiguity of definition. Closer to modern times, the published definition of BCPL contains a glaring ambiguity which is illustrated in abbreviated form in figure 15.14[1]. The syntax definition of a

---

1 This example is also referred to several times in chapter 16 - watch it carefully!

<command> which contains both **while** and **repeatuntil** commands is ambiguous: it is impossible to tell whether the **repeatuntil** command in figure 15.14 is inside the **while** (Tree1) or vice-versa (Tree2). In practice all BCPL compilers select the first of these interpretations - the 'right-recursive' or 'right-associative' version - which is a fact that many BCPL users have had to discover by trial and error! Although it is possible to construct a grammar which resolves this ambiguity (one is given in chapter

---

```
<statement> ::= ....  | <conditional statement> | ....

<conditional statement> ::= <if clause> <statement>
                          | <if clause> <statement> else <statement>
<if clause> ::= if <Boolean expression> then
```

Figure 15.11 Ambiguity in unrevised ALGOL 60

Input: **if** E1 **then if** S1 **then** S2 **else** S3

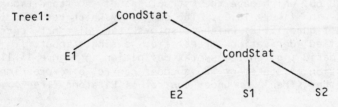

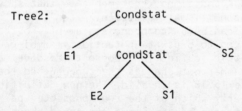

Figure 15.12 Two derivations of a <conditional statement>

```
<conditional statement> ::= <if clause> <unconditional statement>
                          | <if clause> <unconditional statement>
                                      else <statement>
```

Input to produce Tree1:
        if E1 **then begin if** E2 **then** S1 **else** S2 **end**

Input to produce Tree2:
        if E1 **then begin if** E2 **then** S1 **end else** S2

Figure 15.13 The <conditional statement> ambiguity resolved

16) I believe that it would be better to adopt the approach of the authors of the ALGOL 60 Revised Report and to outlaw 'visually ambiguous' input like that in figure 15.14 either by imposing strict rules for the bracketing of commands or by using additional kinds of statement brackets like those in ALGOL 68 (**if-fi**, **do-od**, etc.). An impeccably unambiguous grammar may be a joy to its inventor but usually languishes, unread by any user, in a distant appendix of the programming manual!

When is a grammar ambiguous?

Ambiguity is an undecidable property of a grammar: that is, it is impossible to construct a fool-proof procedure which can decide in finite time, given any grammar as input, whether that grammar is ambiguous or not. However all is not lost: there are some classes of grammar which are definitely <u>un</u>ambiguous: the one-track and one-symbol-lookahead grammars of chapter 16, the operator-precedence grammars of chapter 17 and the LR(1) grammars of chapter 18, for example, are practically useful classes of grammar which are provably unambiguous. It is relatively easy to decide whether any particular grammar falls into one of these classes.

When a real-life grammar is ambiguous it is usually for one of a small number of familiar reasons. Any grammar, for example, which contains a symbol which is both left- and right-recursive

A =>+ A **alpha**   and A =>+ **beta** A

will be ambiguous - the ambiguity of figure 15.10 and the BCPL ambiguity of figure 15.14 are examples of this. Any grammar which contains a symbol which is both self-embedding and left- or right-recursive such that

A =>+ **alpha** A **beta**   and   A =>+ **alpha** A   or   A =>+ A **beta**

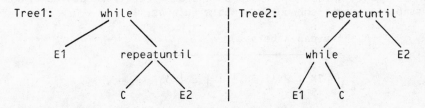

```
<command> ::= ....  | while <expression> do <command>
                    | <command> repeatuntil <expression>
                    | .....
```

Input: **while** E1 **do** C **repeatuntil** E2

Tree1:   while | Tree2:   repeatuntil
                                     |
  E1   repeatuntil | while   E2
                                     |
            C   E2 | E1   C

Figure 15.14 Ambiguity in BCPL command syntax

will be ambiguous - the ALGOL 60 ambiguity of figure 15.11 is an
example of this. Any grammar which contains circularities

        A =>+ A

is ambiguous (which is good enough reason not to consider such
grammars in the first place).

Lexical Analysis and type 3 grammars

Figure 15.15 shows a grammar which is equivalent to those in
figures 15.9 and 15.10. The grammar of figure 15.15 is a type 3
grammar, where the earlier examples were type 2: unlike the
grammar of figure 15.10, that of figure 15.15 is unambiguous.

As mentioned above, the micro-syntax of lexical items can
usually be specified in terms of a type 3 grammar. A language
defined by a type 3 grammar can be recognised by a finite-state
machine, in which there are states which correspond to the non-
terminal symbols and in which the state-transitions are determined
by the terminal symbols in the productions of the grammar.
Finite-state machines are easy to implement and highly efficient:
lexical analysers must be efficient so that type 3 grammars form a
suitable basis for lexical analysis.

It is perhaps surprising that sometimes a language described by
a grammar of a particular type may be described by a grammar of
simpler (more restricted) type. Whether this is possible or not
depends on the details of the particular language: some are too
complex for type 3 grammars, some too complex for type 2 and so
on. In the case of type 2 and type 3 grammars there is a simple
and useful test

  20. If a language is described by a type 2 grammar in which
      there are no self-embedding symbols then the language can
      also be described by a type 3 grammar.

Thus, for example, if the language had included bracketed
expressions - if the grammars of figure 15.9 had included a
production P -> (E), for example - it might not have been possible
to describe it with a type 3 grammar. Intuitively the reason for
the non-self-embedding condition is that finite-state machines
can't count unless they have a separate state for each numerical
possibility: self-embedding symbols such as

        A =>+ **alpha** A **beta**

```
S -> 1X | 2X | 3X | 1 | 2 | 3
X -> +S | -S
```

Figure 15.15 A regular expression grammar

impose a condition that each **alpha** in the input should be followed
by one **beta** and that the **alpha**s and **beta**s should be nested like
the brackets of an arithmetic expression. An analyser which can
police this condition must use recursion or at least possess the
ability to count, neither of which mechanisms is within the range
of action of a finite-state machine. The condition stated above is
sufficient but not necessary: it is easy to construct a trick
grammar with self-embedding symbols which describes a type 3
language.

Given a type 2 definition of the syntax of lexical items, then,
it is necessary to check that none of the non-terminal symbols is
self-embedding. This is usually simple to do, and merely involves
writing out the strings which can be derived from each symbol.
Taking the left-hand grammar from figure 15.9, for example, it is
immediately obvious that the "P" symbol isn't self-embedding.
Writing out those strings which can be derived from the "E" symbol
and which don't merely consist of terminal symbols, as illustrated
in figure 15.16, makes it clear that the "E" symbol isn't self-
embedding either.   The strings which can be derived from "E" can
be written as <u>regular expressions</u>

P { {+P} {-P} }*
or
P { [+|-] P }*
or
[1|2|3] { [+|-] [1|2|3] }*

in a fairly obvious notation in which {...} indicates optional
inclusion, '|' indicates alternative strings, [...] is used to
bracket alternative inclusions and '*' denotes repetition. From
the last of these expressions it is easy to define a finite-state
machine or a grammar - the most obvious grammars are shown in
figure 15.17.

The grammars are constructed by observing that the regular
expression specifies a sequence of states. In 'state' S (the
sentence-state or start-state) the input must be a 1, 2 or 3: this
either transfers the analyser into a second state or terminates
the input: in this second state (state A in grammar (i)) the input
must be a '+' or a '-' which transfers the analyser into a third
state: the third state is in effect the same as state S. Grammar
(i) defines a non-deterministic analyser - given a 1, 2 or 3 in
state S it can't decide whether to switch into state A or to
terminate - but the introduction of an empty right-hand-side in

---

```
in one step:    P E+P E-P
in two steps:   E+1 E+2 E+3 E+P+P E-P+P E-P+P E-P-P
in three steps: E+P+1 ... E+P+P+P E-P+P+P ... P+P+P P-P+P ...
```

Figure 15.16 Strings which can be derived from figure 15.9

grammar (ii) makes the analyser deterministic. Recognising that states V and S are identical gives grammar (iii).

Figure 15.18 shows a possible type 2 grammar for <numbers>, such as might be found in the syntax definition of a programming language, and a type 3 grammar which is equivalent to it. In the type 3 grammar I have used **d** as a terminal which is equivalent to any digit, in order to simplify the example. Given the type 3 grammar it is simple to construct a finite-state machine either as a program - figure 15.19 shows an example - or as a finite-state table - figure 15.20. Each of these examples shows only the recognition of numbers and not the <u>actions</u> with which the compiler-writer would need to augment the grammar in order to record information about the number which was read. The examples in chapter 4 show a lexical analyser, complete with actions, which uses a grammar very like that of figure 15.18.

Expression: [1|2|3] {[+|-] [1|2|3]}*

Grammars:
```
      (i)    S -> 1A | 2A | 3A | 1 | 2 | 3
             A -> +B | -B
             B -> 1A | 2A | 3A | 1 | 2 | 3

      (ii)   S -> 1U | 2U | 3U
             U -> +V | -V | null
             V -> 1U | 2U | 3U

      (iii)  S -> 1U | 2U | 3U
             U -> +S | -S | null
```

Figure 15.17 Grammars from a regular expression

Type 2 grammar:
```
      <number> ::= <integer> | <real>
      <integer> ::= <digit> | <integer><digit>
      <real> ::= <integer> . <integer>
                     | <integer> . <integer> e <integer>
                     | <integer> e <integer>
```

Type 3 grammar
```
      S -> dI
      I -> dI | .R | eE | null
      R -> dF
      F -> dF | eE | null
      E -> dX
      X -> dX | null
```

Figure 15.18 Syntax description of numbers

```
/* state S */
readchar(ch)
unless '0'<=ch<='9' do Error("no digit at start of number")

/* state I */
readchar(ch) repeatwhile '0'<=ch<='9'
if ch='.' then
{ /* state R */
  readchar(ch);
  unless '0'<=ch<='9' do Error("no digit in fraction part")

  /* state F */
  readchar(ch) repeatwhile '0'<=ch<='9'
}

if ch='e' then
{ /* state E */
  readchar(ch)
  unless '0'<=ch<='9' do Error("no digit in exponent")

  /* state X */
  readchar(ch) repeatwhile '0'<=ch<='9'
}
```

Figure 15.19 Finite-state machine represented as a program

---

state

input

	S	I	R	F	E	X
'0'..'9':	I	I	F	F	X	X
'.':	error	F	error	exit	error	exit
'e':	error	E	error	E	error	exit
other:	error	exit	error	exit	error	exit

Figure 15.20 Finite-state machine represented as a table

The program and table are constructed by observing that the production "A -> bC" means that in state A the input of a 'b' character will transfer the analyser into state C: that a production "D -> e" means that in state D the input of a 'e' character will terminate the sentence and that if the input doesn't match any of the terminal symbols in the productions which define the current state there is an error, except that the production "F -> **null**" defines a 'don't care' alternative which terminates the sentence without error.

The whole process is so trivial in practice that it is easy to write an automatic 'scanner-generator' or 'lexical-analyser-generator' whose input is a type 2 grammar like that in figure 15.18 and whose output is a program like that in figure 15.19 or a table like that in figure 15.20. Simple conventions allow the attachment of 'action procedures' to each state-change so that the analyser can accumulate information about the item being read or can print error messages when the analysis breaks down. Such aids to the compiler-writer are mostly to be found in compiler factories where the labour of building the generator program is repaid in the time saved during the construction of several compilers. If you can get access to this kind of program then use it - it will save you time[1] - but if you can't get access to one then don't bother to write your own unless you are certain that it will be used in the preparation of many generations of future compilers for many different languages.

Warshall's Closure Algorithm

Often the most useful information about a grammar is contained in the lists of symbols which can start a string, finish a string or follow a string derived from a particular symbol. Such lists enable you to check for indirect left-recursion and context-clashes (chapter 16) to construct tables of operator priorities (chapter 17) and to build an SLR(1) or LALR(1) analyser (chapter 18). There is a simple algorithm - Warshall's algorithm - which can be used to construct such lists by hand and which can be coded so that these lists can be computed efficiently in a parser-generator or compiler-compiler.

Perhaps it may seem difficult to construct such lists, because there are usually an infinite number of strings which can be derived from a single symbol. However there are only a finite number of symbols in the grammar and the productions define only a finite number of relations between them, so the problem is far from infinite. Figure 15.21 gives the algorithm in English for the

---

1 Another good way to save time is to copy an existing lexical analyser for the source language, or to adapt an existing analyser for a similar language. Writing lexical analysers is just plain boring and should be avoided whenever possible!

Initialisation:
> For each non-terminal construct a FIRST symbol list, containing the first symbol of each right-hand-side of every production in which that non-terminal is the left-hand-side symbol. For example, given the production
> E -> a... | B... | c... | E...
> the FIRST symbol list of 'E' will include 'a', 'B', 'c' and 'E'.

Closure:
> Take each non-terminal symbol in turn (the order doesn't matter) and look for it in all the FIRST symbol lists: add its own FIRST symbol list to any list in which it appears. For example, if 'A' appears in the FIRST symbol list of 'X', add the symbols from the FIRST list of 'A' to the FIRST list of 'X'.

That's all!

Figure 15.21 Constructing the FIRST+ list

Symbol	FIRST list	FIRST+ list
S	E + -	E + - T F P i n R (
E	T E	T E F P i n R (
T	F T	F T P i n R (
F	P F	F P i n R (
P	i n R (	i n R (
R	i	i
L	S L	S L E + - T F P i n R (

Figure 15.22 The FIRST+ lists for the grammar of figure 15.3

```
{ n = number of non-terminals, s = number of symbols }
procedure Warshall(var F: array [1..n] of set of 1..s);
    var sym, row : 1. n;
    begin for sym := 1 to n do
          for row := 1 to n do
              if sym in F[row] then F[row] := F[row]+F[sym]

    end
```

Figure 15.23 Warshall's algorithm in PASCAL

case of constructing the 'first symbol' or FIRST+ list. The same closure algorithm with a different initialisation phase will compute any of the other lists mentioned.

Formally, the algorithm takes a relation 'R' - in this case the FIRST relation - and constructs the transitive closure of the relation

$$R + R^1 + R^2 \ldots + R^n$$

Thus the example in figure 15.21 takes the FIRST relation, which relates the strings which can be derived from a symbol in one step, and constructs the FIRST+ relation, which relates the strings which can be derived from a symbol in any number of steps. Adding each non-terminal to its own FIRST+ list would produce the relation FIRST*, which relates the strings which can be derived in zero or more steps.

Figure 15.22 shows the result of applying the procedure of figure 15.21 to the grammar of figure 15.3. The result shows that all symbols are left-recursive except for "P" and "R", which is pretty obvious if you glance at the grammar, and also shows that a sentence can only start with the terminal symbols 'i', 'n' and '(', which is not quite such an obvious deduction.

Figure 15.23 gives a PASCAL version of Warshall's algorithm. The procedure is given a vector 'F' of **set**s, each of whose elements is initialised so that 'A **in** F[X]' is **true** if and only if the symbol 'A' appears in the FIRST list of the symbol 'X'.

Context Dependency and Two-level Grammars

I observed above that the syntax of programming languages is normally defined in terms of type 2 and type 3 grammars. This is true for most languages, with the notable exception of ALGOL 68, whose syntax is defined in a 'two-level' grammar. This type of grammar is also known as a 'van Wijngaarden' grammar after its inventor. Van Wijngaarden grammars overcome one of the well-known drawbacks of type 2 grammars, which can only describe context-free constructs although programming language definitions almost universally contain context-dependent elements. Context dependency enters most clearly in the treatment of declarations. In a block-structured language an identifier must be declared in every block in which it is used, or in an enclosing block or procedure, and must be declared only once in any particular block or procedure. The notion of 'textual scope' is itself a notion of context[1].

---

1 In the sense in which it is used in most language definitions, that is. 'Scope' in the sense in which it is used in the ALGOL 68 definition is equivalent to the notion of 'lifetime' used in chapter 14.

Figure 15.24 shows some examples of the syntax errors which can occur when context-dependent syntax rules are broken.

It is possible to prove that no type 2 grammar can handle the contextual dependencies which make each of the programs in figure 15.24 invalid. For this reason conventional programming language descriptions split the syntax definition into two parts: first a type 2, context-free, grammar which describes the phrase structure of programs, declarations, statements, expressions and so on; second some remarks in legalistic English (or some other quasi-natural language) about rules of context such as the necessity for consistency between declaration and use of each identifier.

The van Wijngaarden grammar of ALGOL 68, however, is able to give a more formal description of context-dependency and its adherents claim, not unreasonably, that this reduces confusion about the syntactic details of the language. Its opponents counter-claim that the two-level grammar is so large and complex that it increases rather than decreases the confusion in the minds of users of the language. The issue of whether van Wijngaarden grammars clarify or obscure syntax descriptions is a matter for current debate: what is certain is that up to now they haven't inspired any new kinds of parsing mechanisms which can use their undoubted powers of expression. Since this is so I haven't discussed them in detail in this book.

Parsing with a context-dependent grammar

The activity of parsing a program, then, is a three-stage process. First, the context-free 'shape' or 'superficial form' of the program is recognised by a syntax analyser which is based on a type 2 grammar, usually assisted by a lexical analysis subroutine which is based on a type 3 grammar. Second, the declarative information - the information on which context-dependent syntax checks can be based - is extracted from the output of the syntax analyser by the object-description phase, which records it in the symbol table. At the same time the object-description phase checks the contextual validity of each declaration, ensuring for example that that there is only a single declaration for each identifier in any block. Finally, the translation phase uses the information placed in the symbol table to check that each use of every name is consistent with the declaration then in force.

```
    double declaration                    missing declaration
   begin real x; integer x;              begin real a;
          x := 3;                               b := 0;
   end;                                  end;
```

Figure 15.24 Context-dependent syntax errors

Present theoretical understanding of the parsing of programming languages only encompasses restricted forms of type 2 grammars. The three-way breakdown of the parsing process, or at least the distinction between syntax analysis and later phases, is reflected in the distinction between context-free (type 2) and context-dependent (higher type) syntax description in the language definition. There may be error-handling advantages in the current approach: it enables us, for example, to separate messages concerning punctuation (produced by the syntax analyser) from those concerning contextual errors (produced by the object-description and translation phases). If newer parsing strategies are to prove more than a notional advance they must provide error recognition and error reporting performance at least as good as those which are possible at present.

Summary

This chapter has introduced some formal terminology, some notation and the closure algorithm of figures 15.21 and 15.23. Chapters 16, 17 and 18 use this framework to show how a practical parser can be built, starting from a type 2 grammar as the definition of the syntax of a programming language.

Programming languages in current use are too complicated to be completely described by a type 2 grammar and therefore the process of parsing a source program must be carried out in stages by the syntax analysis, object description and translation phases of a compiler.

16 Top-down Syntax Analysis

The most difficult task when writing a top-down syntax analyser is that of preparing a grammar which is suitable for top-down analysis. Once you have manipulated the grammar so that it possesses certain simple properties, which I describe below, it is trivially easy to write a syntax analyser as a collection of mutually recursive procedures, one for each non-terminal symbol in the grammar. Each procedure has the task of recognising and analysing a section of the input which represents a phrase described by its particular non-terminal symbol. It does so by checking the output of the lexical analyser, and by calling procedures associated with the non-terminals of the grammar, in the sequence defined by the production on which it is based.

In order to be able to give simple and concise descriptions of grammars used in top-down syntax analysis it is convenient to introduce an extension to the notation defined in chapter 15. Figure 16.1 shows how an optional alternative in a production can

---

Optional alternatives:

```
U -> A { +B | -C }
        is the same as
U -> A [ +B | -C | null ]
        which is the same as
U -> AV
V -> +B | -C | null·
```

Repetition:

```
Y -> Q { +R | -T }*
        is the same as
Y -> QZ
Z -> +RZ | -TZ | null
```

Figure 16.1 Optional alternatives and iteration

K

be indicated with braces '{' and '}', how a non-optional
alternative can be indicated with square brackets '[' and ']' and
how repetition of an alternative can be shown by following the
right brace or right bracket with an asterisk.

Unfortunately the grammar modification described by certain of
these abbreviations may introduce a hidden **null** symbol into the
grammar. Use of the **null** symbol introduces a problem, as the
informal proof about the 'parsing problem' given in chapter 15
shows - if the grammar contains a **null** symbol then use of certain
productions will shorten the sentential form and that proof will
break down. A grammar which contains a **null** symbol may be
unsuitable for top-down analysis because of so-called "context
clashes", whose detection and resolution is discussed below.
However a grammar which contains no context-clashes and which
satisfies certain other simple conditions can however be shown to
be unambiguous and to be a suitable basis for the construction of
a top-down analyser.

Figure 16.2 shows a procedure which analyses conditional
statements: the 'errorpoint' parameter is associated with error
recovery and its use is discussed below. The procedure illustrated
could form part of a 'one-symbol-look-ahead' syntax analyser and,
as I show below, the procedures in such an analyser either return

---

```
Production:
  <conditional statement> ::= if <expression> then <statement>
                              { else <statement> }


Procedure:
  let ParseCondStat(message, errorpoint) = valof
  { let expr, stat1, stat2 = empty, empty, empty

    if lexitem \= ifsymbol then Error(message, errorpoint)

    LexAnalyse()
    expr := ParseExpression("expression expected", errorpoint)
    if lexitem \= thensymbol then
      Error("'then' expected ", errorpoint)

    LexAnalyse()
    stat1 := ParseStatement("statement expected", errorpoint)
    if lexitem = elsesymbol then
    { LexAnalyse()
      stat2 := ParseStatement("statement expected", errorpoint)
    }

    resultis node(CondStatNode, expr, stat1, stat2)
  }
```

Figure 16.2 Analysing a conditional statement

a node describing the input or else call an error procedure: backtracking is never necessary.

Apart from the context-clashes mentioned above, the basic problems which have to be overcome in the design of a grammar which is suitable to form the basis of an analyser like that illustrated in figure 16.2 are backtracking and left recursion. I discuss methods for overcoming each of these difficulties below, along with some discussion of pragmatic solutions to well-known knotty problems such as the syntax analysis of labelled statements.

Factoring to Reduce Backtracking

The fragments of a grammar shown in figure 16.3 show how the combination of common portions of alternatives can reduce the incidence of backtracking. An analyser based on the original grammar of case 1, faced with input which matches "D;S" and attempting to find an instance of a "B" phrase, would analyse the "D;" portion of the input and then fail to analyse the "B". It would have to backtrack in order to attempt to analyse the input as "D;S" - which would mean re-analysing the "D;" portion of input before it can successfully analyse "S". Inspecting the alternative right-hand-sides in the opposite order - first "D;S" then "D;B" - won't help because the analyser would then backtrack if the input matched "D;B". The remedy, as figure 16.2 shows, is to factor the productions so that common portions at the left end of each alternative are checked only once[1].

Note that factoring by itself doesn't entirely eliminate backtracking. The analysis of a "B" phrase, using the first grammar from figure 16.3, might continue for some time and then

---

case 1: (grammar of Blocks, Declarations and Statements)

    original: B -> D;B | D;S
    factored: B -> D; [B | S]

case 2: (grammar of conditional statement):

    original: C -> i E t S | i E t S e S
    factored: C -> i E t S { e S }
    alternatively: C -> i E t S [e S | **null**]

Figure 16.3 Factoring to reduce backtracking

---

1 This is called left-factoring. A similar process known as right-factoring combines common portions at the right end of alternatives. Right-factoring reduces the size of the grammar but has no effect on backtracking.

fail: it seems that then the analyser, even when using the
factored version of the production, would have to backtrack to the
point at which it started analysis of "B" in order to attempt
analysis of the input as an "S" phrase. This form of backtracking
may occur because of conflicts between different non-terminal
symbols: if in this grammar

$$B =>* \textbf{ alpha } ... \quad and \quad D =>* \textbf{ alpha } ...$$

then the analyser might still backtrack because even after
discovery of an **alpha** string it cannot be sure whether it has
begun to discover a 'D' or an 'S' symbol.

In many cases the difficulty can be resolved by replacing one
of the conflicting non-terminals with the right-hand-side of its
defining production. This isn't always effective, but the example
of figure 16.4 shows how it can be done in many cases. When the
grammar is factored so that each alternative starts with a
different symbol it can be noted that the production for 'S'
requires further treatment because it chooses between 'A' and 'C'
yet C =>+ A=A. It is clear that the remedy in this case is to
replace 'C' by its definition in terms of 'D'. This still does not
resolve the difficulty but replacing 'D' by its definition in

---

```
Original grammar:
        S -> A | C
        A -> B | B+B
        B -> x | y
        C -> D | D&D
        D -> A=A


First factoring:
        S -> A | C
        A -> B {+B}
        B -> x | y
        C -> D {&D}
        D -> A=A

First replacement:
        S -> A | D {&D}

Second replacement:
        S -> A | A=A {&D}

Factored grammar:
        S -> A { =A {&D}}
        A -> B {+B}
        B -> x | y
        D -> A=A
```

Figure 16.4 Factoring of conflicting non-terminal symbols

terms of 'A' produces a grammar which doesn't specify backtracking.

The factoring of case 2 in figure 16.3 illustrates a more subtle difficulty in that it introduces a **null** symbol into the grammar. The **null** symbol is interpreted as "forget it": the analyser tries to analyse the input as "eS" but, if the analysis fails, merely backtracks (if necessary) to the point reached after analysis of "iEtS" and accepts the situation. It is imperative that the procedure which finds an instance of a "C" phrase checks for "eS" before it accepts **null**, since this is the only way in which the "iEtSeS" form of input can be analysed without re-awakening that procedure activation[1]. Even so, factoring may not eliminate backtracking if there is a "context clash" caused by the use of the 'e' symbol for some other purpose elsewhere in the grammar: I discuss the detection and elimination of context clashes below.

Removing Left Recursion

When the grammar has been thoroughly factored, it will almost certainly still contain left-recursive productions: productions in which the left-hand symbol appears at the left end of one of the right-hand-side alternatives. Such a production is illustrated in figure 16.5: because of factoring the right-hand-sides consist of

---

Production: S -> abc | def | Srx

Strings which can be derived
  - in one step: abc def Srx
  - in two steps: abcrx defrx Srxrx
  - in three steps: abcrxrx defrxrx Srxrxrx
  - in n+1 steps: abc{rx}^{n} def{rx}^{n} S{rx}$^{n+1}$

Iterative production: S -> [abc| def] { rx }*

Figure 16.5 Converting left recursion to iteration

Original production:
  <command-list> ::= <command> | <command-list> ; <command>

Right-recursive production:
  <command-list> ::= <command> { ; <command-list> }

Figure 16.6 Converting left recursion to right recursion

---

1 Which is not the same thing as calling the same procedure again, and would be impossible in a conventional system programming language.

just one left-recursive alternative ("Srx" in this example) together with one or more non-left-recursive alternatives. If the analyser tries the left-recursive alternative first it will attempt an infinite regression (to find an instance of an "S" phrase first look for an instance of an "S" phrase ...). If it tries the non-left-recursive alternatives first it must backtrack: the grammar is not properly factored since

              Srx => abc... and Srx => def.

and therefore the head of any input sequence which would match the left-recursive alternative would also match the head of the non-

---

```
Original production:
  <command list> ::= <command> | <command list> ; <command>

Iterative production:
  <command list> ::= <command> { ; <command> }*

Procedure (one-track):
let ParseCommandList(errorpoint) = valof
{ let listsofar = ParseCommand(errorpoint)

   if listsofar=empty then resultis empty

   while lexitem = ';' do
   { let second = empty

     LexAnalyse()
     second := ParseCommand(errorpoint)

     if second = empty then
       Error("command expected after semicolon", errorpoint)
     else
       listsofar := node(CommandListNode, listsofar, second)
   }

   resultis listsofar
}
```

Input: C1; C2; C3

Tree:

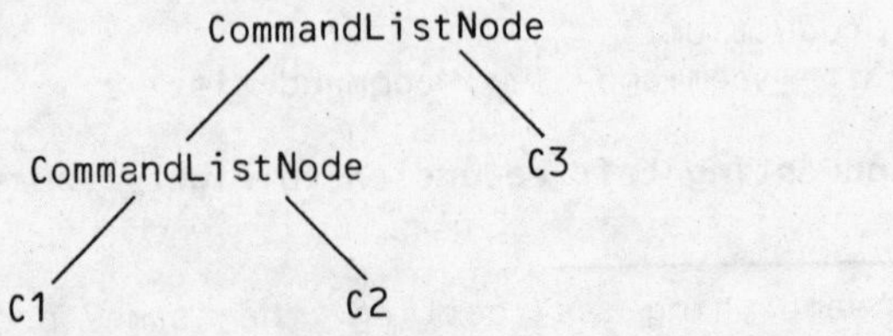

Figure 16.7 Building a left-recursive tree

```
Production:
  <command list> ::= <command> { ; <command> }*

Procedure (one-track):
let ParseCommandList(errorpoint) = valof
 { let start = topofstack
   let nodep = ParseCommand(errorpoint)

   if nodep=empty then resultis empty
   else
    { stack(nodep)
      while lexitem = ';' do
       { LexAnalyse()
         nodep := ParseCommand(errorpoint)

         if nodep=empty then
           Error("command expected after semicolon", errorpoint)
         else stack(nodep)
       }

      resultis NaryNode(CommandList, start, topofstack)
    }
 }
```

Input: C1; C2; C3

Tree: CommandList
                  / / | \
                3   C1   C2   C3

Figure 16.8 Building an n-ary node

_____

```
Original productions:
   S -> C | L | R
   L -> SrE | SruE
   R -> wEdS | iEdS | Lx

Combined production:
  S -> C | SrE | SruE | wEdS | iEdS | SrEx | SruEx

Production after removal of direct left recursion:
  S -> [ C | wEdS | iEdS ] { r [ E | uE ] {x} }*
```

Figure 16.9 Removing indirect left recursion

left-recursive alternative.

There is a simple trick, though, which transforms a left-recursive production into an iterative form. If the left-recursive production is expanded, as in figure 16.5, it is easy to see that all strings which can be derived from it eventually consist of an instance of one of the non-left-recursive alternatives followed optionally by one or more iterations of the tail of the left-recursive alternative. This immediately suggests that the production can be recast in an iterative form. The iterative form is illustrated in figure 16.5 for the "S" production, and expresses it as a choice between the non-left-recursive alternatives followed by an optional repetition of the tail of the left-recursive alternative. Use of iteration eliminates the left recursion entirely: note, however, that the alteration to the grammar has introduced an implicit **null** symbol, and that this may cause "context clash" problems later.

To resolve the problem by changing the production into a right-recursive form may be possible but, as discussed in chapter 15, the left-recursive form of the tree may be essential to the tree walker - for example it is important in most languages to analyse "4-2-2" as if it were "(4-2)-2" rather than "4-(2-2)". In some cases the left-recursive form may not be essential and the right-recursive form may be more convenient - the left-recursive production may then easily be changed into a right-recursive production, as illustrated in figure 16.6.

When a left-recursive production is converted into an iterative production, the iterative production defines an n-ary tree, whose use has been discussed in chapter 5 for the case of arithmetic expressions. If you want to build a left-recursive tree, so as to represent the phrase structure defined in the original grammar, then it is quite simple to do so. Figure 16.7 shows an example of a procedure which builds a left-recursive tree from an input sequence which contains <command>s: it does so by collecting together the current <command> node with the 'node list so far'. The procedure of figure 16.2 is of the one-symbol-look-ahead type in which each procedure need never report failure: that of figure 16.7 is of the one-track type in which each procedure can either call a syntax error procedure, signal failure to find a phrase by returning an empty tree (a special pointer value) or signal success by returning a pointer to a node which describes the input that has been analysed. Just as in the one-symbol-look-ahead case, the procedures in a one-track analyser need never backtrack.

The iterative form of the production can also be used to build an n-ary node, which is a more compact form of the tree and is in many ways a more convenient representation. Figure 16.8 shows an example procedure: the technique requires an auxiliary stack of nodes on which the results of each step in the analysis can be accumulated so that the procedure can eventually combine them into a complete n-ary node when analysis is complete.

Converting left-recursive productions into iterative productions only eliminates <u>direct</u> left recursion. It is possible to encounter <u>indirect</u> left recursion (left recursion which involves more than one derivation step) if there are mutually recursive productions in the grammar. Indirect left recursion is rare in practice[1] but usually extremely easy to eliminate when it does occur. It is discovered by constructing the FIRST+ list for each non-terminal, using the closure algorithm of chapter 15. (The FIRST+ list is usually needed in any case to check that the grammar satisfies the one-track or one-symbol-look-ahead condition and will not backtrack.) Once direct left recursion has been eliminated, construct the FIRST+ list: if any symbol is indirectly left-recursive it will appear in its own FIRST+ list. There will be more than one such symbol, since the grammar must contain, say, A -> B..., B -> C... and C -> A...

Indirect left recursion can usually be eliminated by removing the relevant symbols from the grammar, one-by-one, merely replacing each occurrence of each such symbol by its definition wherever it occurs, just as if you were factoring the productions. Figure 16.9 shows an (artificial) example. It is often necessary, as it is in this example, to be careful about the order in which symbols are eliminated. When all but one of the mutually left-recursive symbols have been eliminated, the resulting direct left recursion can be removed by the mechanisms discussed above. If this mechanical procedure produces long, confusing and unwieldy productions then the best remedy is to start again and to construct an equivalent grammar without the indirect left recursion which gave you the trouble in the first place.

One-symbol-look-ahead and One-track Analysers

When the grammar has been factored and left recursion has been removed then it may already be in a form which entirely eliminates backtracking in the syntax analyser. The simplest form of non-backtracking analyser is the <u>one-symbol-look-ahead</u> form, so called because the analyser can always decide which path of analysis to follow merely by looking at the current input symbol (current lexical item). In order to construct a one-symbol-look-ahead analyser you need a one-symbol-look-ahead grammar.

Ignoring the problem of **null** symbols, which will almost certainly have been introduced by factoring and the removal of left recursion, the one-symbol-look-ahead condition can be stated as follows

---

1 Outside the confines of the examination room!

If each alternative in every production in the grammar starts with a terminal symbol, and if the symbols which start competing alternatives are distinct, then the grammar is a <u>one-symbol-look-ahead</u> grammar.

Figure 16.10 shows a sample one-symbol-look-ahead grammar. Each of the competing alternatives in the production for the "S" symbol starts with a different terminal symbol - "i", **"goto"**, **"if"** or **"begin"**. The alternatives in the production for "C" start with ";" or **"end"**. An analyser based on such a grammar need only look at the current lexical item to decide which alternative to follow. Figure 16.11 shows a procedure loosely based on the "S" production of figure 16.10.

An informal argument shows that a one-symbol-look-ahead analyser need never backtrack

Since each alternative starts with a terminal symbol and competing alternatives always start with different alternative symbols, the analyser need never guess what to do but must always follow the alternative indicated by the current lexical item. If at any stage the analysis breaks down then there is no need to backtrack to an earlier position in the analysis since there is no position in the analysis so far at which the analyser could have followed an alternative path.

The analyser need never backtrack and therefore as soon as the

---

```
S -> i := E | goto E | if E then S else S | begin C
C -> S [ ;C | end ]
```

Figure 16.10 A one-symbol-look-ahead grammar

```
let ParseStatement(message, errorpoint) = valof
 { switchon lexitem into
   { case identifier:
           resultis ParseAssignment(message, errorpoint)
     case gotosymbol:
           resultis ParseGoto(message, errorpoint)
     case ifsymbol:
           resultis ParseCondStat(message, errorpoint)
     case beginsymbol:
           resultis ParseCompoundStat(message, errorpoint)

     default: Error(message, errorpoint)
   }
 }
```

Figure 16.11 Part of a one-symbol-look-ahead analyser

current line of analysis fails - i.e. as soon as the current
lexical item doesn't fit in the current production or doesn't
start any of the alternatives currently presented - the analyser
can produce an error report. The report can only indicate the fact
that the current lexical item doesn't match the current production
and it usually states that an expected symbol is 'missing' or that
an unexpected symbol has been found where another was 'expected'.
Careful phrasing can normally produce a clear and useful error
message (the error messages in the example procedures of this
chapter aren't particularly useful because they have been
compressed to save space on the page). Recovering from a syntax
error so as to search for further errors is never simple, however,
and is discussed below.

It isn't always possible or convenient to produce a one-
symbol-look-ahead grammar since in many cases the grammar
expresses a choice between non-terminal symbols in a production.
The class of one-track grammars, however, allows a choice between
non-terminals at the start of alternatives in a production and
still eliminates backtracking. Ignoring the problems of the **null**
symbol once more, the one-track condition can be stated as

If, in every production in the grammar, the FIRST* lists
of the symbols which start competing alternatives are
disjoint (have no symbols in common) then the grammar is a
one-track grammar.

The FIRST* list is just the FIRST+ list of a symbol augmented with
the symbol itself - note that one-symbol-look-ahead grammars are
just a special form of one-track grammar under this definition.
Figure 16.12 shows part of a one-track grammar and the FIRST*
lists of all the symbols within it (I have invented a FIRST* list

---

Grammar:
      S -> E := E | goto E | if E then S else S
              | begin B | D<error>
      B -> D;B | C
      C -> S [;C | end]
      D -> let i [= E | be C]

Symbol   FIRST* list
    E   E i (+ -
    S   S E i (+ - **goto if begin**
    B   B D **let** C S E i (+ - **goto if begin**
    C   C S E i (+ - **goto if begin**
    D   D **let**
    goto   **goto**
    if   **if**
    (etc.)

Figure 16.12 An example of a one-track grammar

for the "E" symbol and I have ignored for the moment the
"D<error>" alternative, which I shall discuss below). The
competing alternatives in each production have disjoint FIRST*
lists. The "S" production chooses between "E", **"goto"**, **"if"** and
"begin": an "E" cannot start with a **"goto"**, an **"if"** or a **"begin"**
and therefore the production for "S" satisfies the one-track
condition. The symbols which can start a "D" are different from
those which can start a "C", which makes the "B" production one-
track. The only alternatives in the grammar depend on a choice
between two terminal symbols in the "C" and "D" productions and
therefore the entire grammar is one-track. Figure 16.13 shows a
procedure based on the "S" production of figure 16.12.

An informal argument shows that a one-track analyser also need
never backtrack

> When the analyser is faced with a choice between
> alternatives in a production the current lexical item will
> be in the FIRST* list of only one of the alternatives (or
> none of them if there is an error): therefore whenever
> analysis breaks down midway through an alternative there
> is no reason to backtrack to try one of the other
> competing alternatives: since this is so for each of the
> productions used so far there is no reason whatsoever to
> backtrack since there is no point in the analysis so far
> at which the analyser could reconsider its choice.

```
let ParseStat(errorpoint) = valof
{ switchon lexitem into
   { case gotosymbol:
           resultis ParseGoto(errorpoint)
     case ifsymbol:
           resultis ParseCondStat(errorpoint)
     case beginsymbol:
           resultis ParseBlock(errorpoint)

     default
       { let nodep = ParseExpression(errorpoint)

         if nodep \= empty then
         resultis ParseAssignment(nodep, errorpoint)
         elsf ParseDeclaration(errorpoint) \= empty then
         Error("declaration found in statement position",
                        errorpoint)
         else resultis empty
       }
   }
}
```

Figure 16.13 A procedure from a one-track parser

Just like a one-symbol-look-ahead analyser, therefore, a one-track analyser can produce an error message as soon as analysis breaks down. Note, however, that where a non-terminal symbol appears as the first symbol of an alternative ("E" or "D" in the production for "S" in figure 16.12, for example) the analyser must investigate whether a phrase derived from that non-terminal is present or not - if no such phrase is present there is no error but the analyser must try another alternative. Therefore the procedures of a one-track analyser must be able to signal whether a phrase instance is present or not - in figures 16.7, 16.8 and 16.10 the procedure returns a node if all is well, returns the value 'empty' if none of the symbols which start a right-hand-side is present and calls the 'Error' procedure if analysis breaks down in any other way.

The procedures of a one-track analyser are constructed from the grammar in the same way as those of a one-symbol-look-ahead analyser except that, where a production is a choice between alternatives, the procedure tests the first symbol of each alternative in turn (by looking at the current lexical item or by calling the relevant non-terminal procedure). If none of the first symbols is present then the procedure returns the 'empty' value to signal that no instance of the phrase can be found: if one of the first symbols is present then analysis can continue by following that alternative. Should analysis break down subsequently then an error procedure can be called immediately: error recovery is just as difficult as in a one-symbol-look-ahead analyser and error messages can likewise only inform the user that a particular symbol or phrase was expected but not encountered in the input.

One-track analysers allow more flexible use of the grammar than can one-symbol-look-ahead analysers. First, it is not always convenient to produce a grammar in which every alternative starts with a terminal symbol: in most modern programming languages, for example, a procedure call may appear as a statement and the left-hand-side of an assignment statement may be a fairly complicated expression rather than just a simple identifier. In such cases it is natural that at least one of the alternative productions for the <statement> non-terminal will start with the <expression> non-terminal and it would be very difficult and inconvenient to factor the grammar so as to construct a one-symbol-look-ahead analyser. Second, it is possible (with care) to augment the grammar with 'unnecessary' alternatives such as the "D<error>" alternative of figure 16.12 in order to check for and report upon commonly encountered syntax errors. It would be a laborious task to factor the grammar when such error-checking alternatives are included.

The "D<error>" alternative included in the "S" production of figure 16.12 shows an example of the kind of specialised error detection that is a major strength of the one-track mechanism. Provided that the alternatives in the "B" production are tested in

the order shown - first "D" then "C" - the additional alternative
in   the   "C" production allows the   analyser   to   test   for   a
particularly common error and to produce a special error message
on encountering it. Using such an analyser users will be told that
it is an error to place declarations in the statement part of a
block and, furthermore, will be informed of any syntax errors
which occur in the erroneously-placed declaration. Without such a
special alternative in the "S" production the analyser can only
produce a generalised error message such as "Statement expected
but not found".

Context Clashes and Null Symbols

Figure 16.14 shows a grammar - a simplified version of the ALGOL
60 block syntax - which, when left recursion is removed from it,
appears to satisfy the   one-symbol-look-ahead   or   one-track
conditions but in fact doesn't do so because of a context clash.
An analyser based on the converted grammar would backtrack given
any valid input because of the context clash between the semicolon
symbols in the "B" and "D" productions. Figure 16.15 illustrates
the difficulty by showing the first stages of processing of some
sample input. The problem is caused by the use of the ';' symbol
for the purposes both of separating 'd' items in the "D"
production and separating the "D" phrase from the "S" phrase in
the "B" production - the symbol appears in two conflicting
contexts and hence the problem can be described as a <u>context</u>

```
Original grammar:
  B -> begin D ; S end
  D -> d | D;d
  S -> s | S;s

Converted grammar (not one-track):
  B -> begin D ; S end
  D -> d { ;d }*
  S -> s { ;s }*
```

Figure 16.14 Context clash due to multiple use of semicolon

Input: **begin** d; d; s; s **end**

1: B finds **'begin'**, reads next symbol
2: B calls D
   3: D finds 'd', reads next symbol
   4: D finds ';', starts iteration and reads next symbol
   5: D finds 'd', terminates iteration and reads next symbol
   6: D finds ';', starts iteration and reads next symbol
   7: D <u>does not</u> find 'd', yet there is no error ...

Figure 16.15 Backtracking due to a context clash

clash. The context clash causes backtracking because the analyser cannot decide, merely by looking to see if the current symbol is a semicolon, whether to start the iteration in the procedure which represents the "D" production or to return from that procedure. In the absence of certain knowledge it must guess which way to jump - and if it guesses wrongly it must backtrack later.

In order to remove context clashes, so as to eliminate backtracking and to satisfy the one-symbol-look-ahead or one-track condition, it is necessary to look at the symbols which can follow the null symbol in any sentential form which can be generated from the grammar. The situations which must be checked can be stated as in figure 16.16. The cause of the problem which arises in case (i) is easily shown by rewriting an example production

$$A \rightarrow B\{Cd|E\}F \;\; ==> \;\; A \rightarrow B[CdF|EF|F]$$

which shows immediately why the FIRST* symbols which can start an option must be disjoint from those which can follow it: the cause of the problem in case (ii) can as easily be shown by rewriting one of the productions from figure 16.14

$$B \rightarrow \textbf{begin} \; d \; \{ \; ;d \; \}* \; ; \; S \; \textbf{end}$$

The detection of context clashes depends on the calculation of the follower list of each non-terminal symbol: a list of those symbols which can follow an occurrence of that symbol in any

---

(i) If there is a production which contains an option or a repetition

$$A \rightarrow \; ... \; \{ \; \textbf{alpha} \; ... \; \} \; \textbf{beta} \; ...$$
$$\text{or}$$
$$A \rightarrow \; ... \; \{ \; \textbf{alpha} \; ... \; \}* \; \textbf{beta} \; ...$$

then the FIRST* symbols of **alpha** must be disjoint from those of **beta**.

(ii) If there is a production which ends with an option or a repetition

$$B \rightarrow \; ..... \; \{ \; \textbf{gamma} \; ... \; \}$$
$$\text{or}$$
$$B \rightarrow \; ..... \; \{ \; \textbf{gamma} \; ... \; \}*$$

then the FIRST* symbols of **gamma** must be disjoint from those which can follow B in any sentential form which can be generated from the grammar.

Figure 16.16 Causes of context clash

sentential form which can be produced from the grammar. The basic
process of computing the follower list has four stages and is
summarised in figure 16.17a.

Each option or repetition in the grammar introduces a hidden
null symbol and makes the determination of follower lists a little
more intricate. Figure 16.17b shows the additional stages needed
to cope with this complication. If the grammar were to contain a
production which could generate the **null** symbol alone (the empty
string) then there are still more refinements to the process of
computing the follower list: I shan't consider this possibility
since it isn't introduced by the mechanisms for factoring and
removal of left recursion which I have described.

Once the FIRST*, LAST* and follower lists have been computed it
is possible to check for context clashes. Figure 16.18 shows a
grammar which exhibits context clashes. The productions which
include a hidden **null** symbol are those for "C" and "A" - there are

---

(i) Prepare the FIRST* list of each non-terminal symbol. If
there is a production

    U -> A ... | B ... | c ...

then the FIRST list of 'U' contains 'A', 'B' and 'c'.
From the FIRST list, compute the FIRST+ list as in
chapter 15: add each symbol to its own FIRST+ list to
make the FIRST* list.

(ii) Prepare the LAST* list of each symbol similarly: if
there is a production

    V -> ... X | ... Y | ... z

then the LAST list of 'V' contains 'X', 'Y' and 'z'.
From the LAST list, compute the LAST+ list using the
closure algorithm of chapter 15: add each symbol to its
own LAST+ list to make the LAST* list.

(iii) The FIRST* and LAST* lists of each terminal symbol
consist of the symbol itself alone.

(iv) Prepare the follower lists: if there is a production

    W -> ... alpha beta ...

then the FIRST* symbols of **beta** must be included in the
follower list of each of the LAST* symbols of **alpha**.

Figure 16.17a Computing the follower list

no context clashes involving "A". Although there is no production
in which "C" is followed directly by **repeat** or **repeatuntil**, "C"
appears in the LAST* list of "L", and "L" <u>is</u> followed by those
symbols in the "C" production itself: therefore there is a context
clash (case ii from figure 16.16) and the grammar isn't one-track.

   Unfortunately there is no simple way to remove context clashes
once you have discovered them. In simple cases a little thought
will enable you to juggle with the grammar to avoid a trivial
difficulty - figure 16.19 shows how the problem of figure 16.14
may be overcome - but often the context clash is a symptom of a
deeper problem. As shown in chapter 15, the grammar of figure
16.18 is ambiguous, and this fact has eventually shown itself in
the form of a context clash. I believe that the syntax of figure
16.18 would be improved if it were changed to

> R -> **do** C [**repeat** | **repeatuntil** E]

which would remove the ambiguity both visually and formally.
Compiler-writers aren't usually empowered to change the form of
the source language, however, and it is normally necessary to
prepare an unambiguous grammar. Figure 16.20 shows a possible
grammar, which permits only the right-recursive interpretation (of
the two interpretations permitted by the grammar of figure 16.18)
for a statement involving both **while** and **repeatuntil**. It isn't

---

(ii.b) If a production ends with an option or a repetition

> P -> ... alpha { ... beta }
> or P -> ... alpha { ... beta }*

then the LAST list of P includes both alpha and gamma.

(iv.b) If a production contains an option

> Q -> ... alpha { beta ... gamma } delta ...

- the FIRST* symbols of both beta and delta may
  follow the LAST* symbols of alpha
- the FIRST* symbols of delta may follow the LAST*
  symbols of gamma.

The same applies if a production contains a repetition

> Q -> ... alpha { beta ... gamma }* delta ...

but in addition the FIRST* symbols of beta can follow
the LAST* symbols of gamma.

Figure 16.17b Follower list with option and repetition

easy to invent such a grammar: even when it is published it may escape the naive user's attention that the grammar of figure 16.20 is unambiguous where that of figure 16.18 is not, and in practice many users will continue to read the 'wrong' interpretation into the grammar of figure 16.20.

```
Original grammar:
  C -> E() | E(A) | goto E | L | R
  L -> if E then C | while E do C
  R -> C repeat | C repeatuntil E
  A -> E | A,E

Converted grammar:
  C -> [ E( [)|A)] | goto E | L ]
                { repeat | repeatuntil E }*
  L -> if E then C | while E do C
  A -> E { ,E }*
```

Symbol	FIRST* list	LAST* list
E	E i (+ -	E i)
C	C E goto L i (+ - if while	C) E L repeat i
L	L if while	L C) E repeat i
A	A E i (+ -	A E i)

Symbol	Follower list
E	(repeat repeatuntil then do ,)
C	repeat repeatuntil
L	repeat repeatuntil
A	,)

Figure 16.18 Context clashes in BCPL command syntax

```
Original grammar:
  B -> begin D ; S end
  D -> d | D;d
  S -> s | S;s

Converted grammar (one-track):
  B -> begin D S end
  D -> d; { d; }*
  S -> s { ;s }*
```

Figure 16.19 Removing simple context clashes by rewriting

```
C -> L | U
L -> if E then C | while E do C
U -> [ E( [)|A)] | goto E ] { repeat | repeatuntil E }*
```

Figure 16.20 Unambiguous BCPL statement syntax

A One-track Grammar is Unambiguous

A grammar which displays context clashes may be ambiguous but luckily the converse is true: if a grammar satisfies the full one-track condition (the FIRST* symbols of competing alternatives are distinct and there are no context clashes) then it is unambiguous. The following informal argument establishes this result

> Starting from the sentence-symbol "S" and expanding the left-most non-terminal symbol at each step there is only one way to produce a sentential form which has the same first symbol as a given sentence, since at each choice-point we must follow the alternative whose FIRST* list contains that symbol. Taking the first non-terminal in the resulting sentential form, there is only one way to produce a sub-string whose first symbol matches the corresponding terminal in the given sentence - and so on for all non-terminals in the sentential form. Since there is only one expansion there is only one tree: therefore the grammar is unambiguous.

The absence of context clashes means that the order of expansion is irrelevant - if there __are__ context clashes in the grammar then the argument breaks down because there may be more than one way of generating a particular sub-string.

Error Detection and Processing

The example of figure 16.12 shows how extra alternatives in a production ("D<error>" in that example) can be used to improve error reporting in a one-track analyser. By including alternatives which test for commonly-encountered errors, the compiler is able to produce special messages designed for just those errors. Such a message can be phrased to give the user more information than could the more conventional "X expected but not found" message. Examples of the sort of errors which are commonly encountered and can be handled in this way are summarised in figure 16.21. The fact that one-track analysis allows this kind of flexibility in error detection is a major strength of the technique. Writing an analyser becomes more than ever like programming in 'BNF'. Time spent in special error detection doesn't slow down the processing of 'correct' programs since all the processing involved takes

---

  (i) Declarations used in the middle of statements.
 (ii) Semicolon inserted between a statement and a following
      'else' symbol.
(iii) Blocks which don't contain a statement.
 (iv) Too many **begin** or **end** symbols in the input.

Figure 16.21 Syntax errors which can be anticipated

(i) Abandon the compilation forthwith.
(ii) Delete part of the program so that the error
     disappears.
(iii) Insert extra symbols into the program so that the
     error disappears.

Figure 16.22 Forms of error recovery

```
let Error(message, savedstate) be
{ print(message); jumpto savedstate }

let ParseCommandList(errorpoint) = valof
{ let start = topofstack
  let nodep = ParseCommand(errorpoint)

  if nodep=empty then resultis empty
  else
  { stack(nodep)
    while lexitem=';' do
    { Lexanalyse()

    tryagain:
      nodep := ParseCommand(label(recover))
      if nodep=empty then
      { Error("statement expected", label(recover));
      recover:
        until lexitem=';' or lexitem=endsymbol or
              lexitem=beginsymbol do
          Lexanalyse()

        if lexitem = beginsymbol then goto tryagain
      }
      else
      { stack(nodep);
        unless lexitem=';' or lexitem=endsymbol
          Error("Possibly semicolon omitted?",
                          label(tryagain))
      }
    }

    resultis bignode(CommandList, start, topofstack)
  }
}
```

Figure 16.23 Error recovery in a one-track analyser

place when an error message would be produced anyway.

Transforming the grammar into one-track form is a fairly mechanical process and transcribing the grammar into a program in a system-programming language is even more mechanical. The only interesting bits of the work, I believe, are to do with error handling. Indeed many users will find the compiler useful in direct proportion to the quality of your error handling! Good error detection plays an important role in error handling, and the discussion above shows how a one-track analyser can be given exceptionally good error-detecting abilities.

Error recovery is much more difficult than error detection and the implementation of an error recovery mechanism requires careful design. Error recovery is necessary because the compiler should attempt to find as many syntax errors as possible in a single run: it is difficult, however, because a partial or ineffective recovery is likely to cause 'secondary' errors. In effect recovery can take one of three forms, detailed in figure 16.22 - the first form is unacceptable so that one of the other forms of error recovery must be attempted.

'Recovery' must always be tentative: on detecting an error a compiler should note that the program is faulty and should not normally allow it to be executed. Error correction, when the compiler assumes that its error recovery strategy has produced the source program which the user would have preferred to write, is rather dangerous since the 'correction' may produce the wrong program, with quite different behaviour to that expected by the user.

The simplest error recovery mechanism is to ignore (and thus effectively to delete from the input) the rest of the phrase in which the error occurred and if possible to continue processing as if a valid phrase had been encountered in that position. In line-based languages, such as FORTRAN, a compiler will normally ignore any line in which an error occurs but in most modern languages it is necessary to be a little more sophisticated. Figure 16.23 shows a possible example procedure, in which an error encountered during analysis of a statement causes the rest of that statement to be ignored. The mechanism assumes that each procedure in the analyser is passed an 'errorpoint' argument, which is a label value[1] to which control should be transferred on encountering a syntax error. In figure 16.23 the processing after the label 'recover' consists of ignoring input until a symbol is encountered which signals the end of the statement (';' or **end**) or the start of the next statement (**begin**).

---

1 As chapter 11 shows, label values of this kind must include a pointer to the data frame of the procedure activation which is to be resumed when control is transferred to the label value.

The careful treatment of **begin** and **end** symbols in the error recovery mechanism of figure 16.23 attempts to minimise the incidence of secondary errors. If the error recovery mechanism was to ignore a **begin** symbol, for example, the effects would be that any declarations at the head of the block which it opens would be treated as if they were erroneously placed in the statement list of the enclosing block - also the analyser would misunderstand the **begin-end** bracketing of the rest of the program.

No matter how carefully the error recovery mechanism is designed, however, secondary errors will result if the parts of the program which are ignored contain any declarative information. If the mechanism of figure 16.23 ignores a statement label then all references to that label will produce the error message "Label not declared". If a similar mechanism in a procedure which analyses declarations ignores part of a variable declaration, say, then any names declared in that part of the declaration will provoke an error message each time they occur elsewhere in the program - figure 16.24 shows a possible example. This kind of secondary error is unavoidable in practice and as a result many compilers produce the error message "Identifier X not declared" only once per identifier no matter how many times that identifier is encountered, on the assumption that secondary errors are more likely than consistent mis-spelling!

If error recovery which ignores input is prone to produce secondary errors, error recovery which assumes that a symbol is missing (and thus in effect inserts an extra symbol into the input) is just as difficult to implement and perhaps even more likely to produce secondary errors. The ParseCommandList procedure

---

```
Input: .... real a, b* c, d, e; .... c := d*e; ....
              ^               ^     ^ ^
              1               2     3 4
```

```
Errors: 1. Comma expected in declaration
        2. Identifier not declared
        3. Identifier not declared
        4. Identifier not declared
```

Figure 16.24 Secondary errors due to ignoring input

```
Input: .... ; i := 4 if j<0; ...
                 ^    ^
                 1    2
```

```
Errors: 1. Possibly semicolon missing?
        2. 'then' expected in conditional statement.
```

Figure 16.25 Secondary errors due to inserting symbols

of figure 16.23 checks, after finding a valid statement, that the
next symbol is either a semicolon or an **end** and, if neither symbol
is found, produces an error message which enquires "Possibly
semicolon missing?" and proceeds as if a semicolon had been
present. Figure 16.25 shows a small example of the confusion which
can result when the input insertion is misguided.

Syntax error recovery is in practice a rather messy and ad-hoc
activity. The basic mechanism of jumping to an error label which
attempts some primitive recovery seems to be the only workable one
in a recursive-descent analyser, although a more automatic
mechanism can be used when the analyser works from a syntax graph
(see below). The users of your compiler will derive enormous
benefit from good syntax error handling, however, and it is
worthwhile to expend a great deal of effort to produce a compiler
which accurately locates and clearly reports upon syntax errors.
In order to measure the performance of your compiler in this
respect, it can be useful to collect a large number of programs
which contain known syntax errors against which to pit its error
handling mechanism[1], and to pay close attention to the
difficulties which early users of your compiler find in
understanding its carefully-phrased error reports!

Reporting a syntax error

Error reports should always contain, or be directly related to,
the region of the source program text which provoked the report.
In a two-pass compiler designed for off-line (batch) processing it
is normal to produce a line-by-line listing as the lexical
analyser and the syntax analyser read through the program: the
natural thing to do is to print the error messages immediately
after the line on which they occur. If possible there should be
some mark which indicates the position on the line at which the
error was noted, and where the message refers to some particular
item in the input then the message should quote that item - for
example "Identifier FREX not declared". Messages should <u>always</u> be
in plain language - to print an error number which indexes a
message in a manual is to shift a data-processing load from
machine to human. Indeed, confronted with an error number without
accompanying text, hurried users are prone to guess what the
corresponding error message might be, wasting precious time when
they guess wrongly.

In on-line compiling, or whenever a listing isn't produced, the
error report should consist of the current input line (assuming
that input is read in line-sized chunks, as suggested in chapter
4) together with the error message, and perhaps a line number to
further identify the line. It's fairly easy to suppress the

---

1 It pays to increase your collection at regular intervals, just
  to stave off complacency!

listing of the line in subsequent error reports about the same
line. The line number alone isn't sufficient as an identification
of the error because it makes the user work to find the error
context which the compiler can perfectly easily display: users
often work from partially out-of-date listings, for example, and
their idea of the line number may not correspond to the
compiler's. If error numbers are offensive, error numbers indexed
by line numbers are doubly so and are likely to antagonise even
the friendliest of users!

Pragmatics and Tricks

It isn't always trivial to convert a grammar into one-track form.
Figure 16.26 shows a situation which commonly arises when a
language permits use of identifiers as statement labels. An <L-

```
<statement> ::= <identifier> : <statement>
              | <L-expression> := <R-expression>
              | <procedure call> | ...
```

Figure 16.26 A grammar which isn't one-track

```
let ParseStatement(errorpoint) = valof
{ ....
   switchon lexitem into
    { case ifsymbol: ...
      case gotosymbol: ...
            ... etc. ...

       default:
         { /* first look for an expression of any kind */
           let firstitem = lexitem
           let nodep = ParseExpression(errorpoint)

          if nodep\=empty then
           { if nodep.type=firstitem=identifier & lexitem=':' then
               ... /* process a labelled statement */
             elsf lexitem=assignsymbol then
               ... /* process an assignment statement */
             elsf nodep.type=ProcedureCall then
               ... /* process a procedure call */
             else
               Error("expression out of context", errorpoint)
           }
           else resultis empty
         }
    }
}
```

Figure 16.27 Pragmatic solution to labelled-statement problem

expression> (the left-hand-side of an assignment statement) may
start with an identifier, as may a <procedure call> - indeed in
many modern languages an <L-expression> may itself consist of a
procedure call. This makes it difficult or impossible to factor
the grammar of figure 16.26 so that it is usable in a one-track
analyser, and even if it were possible to factor it the resulting
grammar would be confusing and difficult to use as the basis of a
system of recursive-descent procedures. A possible formal solution
could be to use two-symbol-look-ahead to recognise a label - but
that doesn't solve the problem of recognising the difference
between an <L-expression> and a <procedure call>.

A pragmatic solution to the 'label' problem is shown in the
procedure of figure 16.27. A statement label is treated as a
special kind of expression, recognised because it consists of a
single identifier (not surrounded by brackets - the procedure is
careful to check that the first lexical item of the expression is
an identifier). Any expression will do as an <L-expression>
provided it is followed by an assignment symbol: otherwise the
expression should be a procedure call. If none of these
alternatives is satisfied, the error message can be printed - it
is rather lame as error messages go. If the form of an <L-
expression> is more restricted than that of an expression in
general then, as discussed in chapter 2 and in section II, the
translator may be entrusted with the task of ensuring that the
expression on the left-hand-side of an assignment statement is of
the correct form.

Error detection of the kind proposed in figures 16.12 and 16.13
is also a useful trick to overcome the difficulties of error
recovery. By accepting invalid input yet producing an error report
the analyser removes the need for error recovery in that situation
and thus reduces the incidence of secondary syntax errors.

Perhaps the most important pragmatic observation which should
be made about top-down analysis is that neither one-symbol-look-
ahead nor one-track analysers are particularly good at the
analysis of expressions. The grammar of figure 16.28 illustrates
why this is so: an analyser based on this grammar and presented
with input such as

           (if a then b else c)(d()+g^f, 100)

would spend a great deal of time in unnecessary procedure calls
and would inspect each operator symbol a great many times. It
would check the then symbol in this example seven times: first to
see if it is a '(' symbol, then to see if it is '^', then to see
if it is '*', then to see if it is '/', then to see if it is '+',
then to see if it is '-', and finally to see if is 'then'. This
kind of activity indicates that the one-track analyser cannot use
its error-detection or error-recovery strategies usefully in
handling syntax errors in expressions - if the symbol encountered

is none of those which could have been expected then it is
difficult to guess which symbol ought to have occurred. Consider
the case of an expression which contains too many right brackets -
for example

    while a+b) d+e(f) **do** ...

A simple one-track ParseExpression procedure would not detect the
error (although it would notice if an expression contained too few
right brackets) and would return to the procedure which called it
without analysing all of the 'expression' between the **while** and
the **do.** Faced with a ')' symbol in the input, the calling
ParseWhile procedure would have to report **'do** expected', which is
not a very useful diagnostic in the circumstances.

There are many other examples which could be given of the
ineptness of a top-down analyser when faced with an expression:
there are, luckily, other methods of syntax analysis which can be
used instead. In practice the best solution to the problem is to
write (or use a parser-generator to construct) an operator-
precedence analysis procedure which analyses expressions and to
call that procedure whenever an expression is expected in a
statement or declaration. As the example in chapter 17 shows it
is possible to cater for the case when, as in BCPL, an expression
can contain a statement if the ParseExpression procedure can call
the ParseStatement procedure, which can call the ParseExpression
procedure, and so on.

```
Original grammar:
  S -> E | if S then S else S
  E -> +A | -A | A
  A -> T | A+T | A-T
  T -> F | T*F | T/F
  F -> P | P^F
  P -> i | n | (S) | P() | P(L)
  L -> S | L,S

Grammar in one-track form:
  S -> E | if S then S else S
  E -> +A | -A | A
  A -> T { +T | -T }*
  T -> F { *F | /F }*
  F -> P { ^F }
  P -> [i | n | (S)] { ( {L} ) }*
  L -> S { ,S }*
```

Figure 16.28 Expression grammar in one-track form

Interpretive Top-down Analysis

Figure 16.29 shows a graph which represents a simple grammar. Each
node in the graph consists of a tag and two values:

- when the tag is 'a' (for alternative) each of the two
  values is a pointer to a node, giving two alternative
  routes for parsing.
- when the tag is 'n' (for non-terminal symbol) the first
  value is a pointer to a node (the position in the graph
  which represents the production for that symbol).

Grammar:
  S -> E := E | **goto** E | **begin** B
  B -> S [;B | **end**]
  E -> i { +i }* | (E)

Graph:

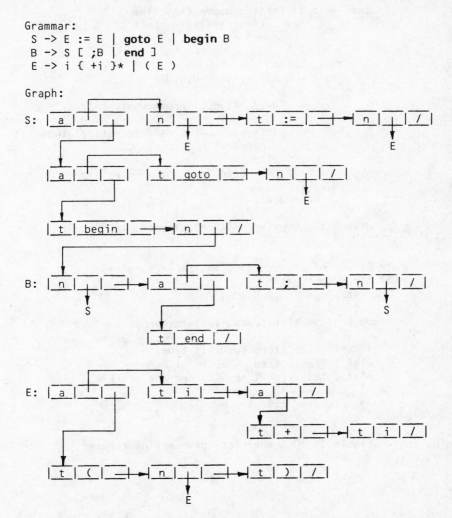

Figure 16.29 An analyser represented as a syntax graph

```
let Interpret(nodep, controlstack) = valof
{ let lexcount = 0

  push(-1, empty, 'finish')

  while true do
   { switchon nodep.tag into
     { case 'a': push(lexcount, nodep, 'alternative')
                 nodep := nodep.first; endcase
                 /
       case 'n': push(lexcount, nodep, 'call')
                 nodep := nodep.first; endcase

       case 't': if lexitem=nodep.first then
                  { LexAnalyse(); lexcount :=+ 1
                    nodep := nodep.second
                  }
                 else
                  { let l,n,t = 0,0,0

                    do pop(l,n,t) repeatwhile t='call'

                    if l=lexcount & t='alternative' then
                      nodep := n.second
                    else
                      Error(nodep.first, "item expected");
                  }
                 endcase

       default:  CompilerFail("invalid node in graph");
     }

     /* at end of production simulate 'return' */
     if nodep=empty then
      { let l,n,t = 0,0,0

        do pop(l,n,t) repeatwhile t='alternative'

        if t='finish' then resultis true
        elsf t='call' then nodep := n.second
        else CompilerFail("invalid control stack")
      }
   } /* end of outer loop */
}
```

Figure 16.30 A one-track grammar-interpreter

- when the tag is 't' (for <u>t</u>erminal symbol) the first value
  is a lexical item code.

In both 'n' and 't' nodes the second value is a pointer to the
next node in sequence - the node to be inspected if the current
node matches. An empty pointer means that a right-hand-side of a
production has matched successfully. Thus the first row of figure
16.29 defines the right-hand-side "E:=E" while the sixth and
seventh rows define the right hand side "i{+i}*". A simple
interpreter - see figure 16.30 - can follow the graph and simulate
the operation of a recursive-descent parser. To 'call' a phrase it
stacks the current lexical item count, the current graph pointer
and a 'call' marker: when the phrase is recognised it unstacks the
graph pointer and continues. To process an alternative it stacks
the current lexical item count, graph pointer and an 'alternative'
marker: when the current lexical item doesn't match that in an 'a'
node the analyser unstacks back to the preceding alternative (if
any) and attempts to continue from that point. Since it is a one-
track analyser it will not backtrack the input - hence the check
on the value of 'lexcount' at this point.

The graph and interpreter of figures 16.29 and 16.30 define a
recogniser: with the addition of 'action' nodes to the graph, each
of which contains a procedure address and causes the interpreter
to call that procedure, it is possible to define a complete syntax
analyser in the form of a graph. Particular action procedures can
be used to manipulate the contents of a 'node stack', thus
allowing the analyser to build a tree; other action-procedures can
call the Error procedure and perform the kind of error recovery
discussed above. More flexible node formats would allow the graph
to specify arguments to action-procedures, thus allowing the
compiler-writer to use the graph as a programmable machine. It is
possible to use a top-down analyser, defined as a syntax graph,
together with an operator-precedence analyser for expressions -
merely replace each occurrence of the <expression> non-terminal by
a call on a 'ParseExpression' action-procedure, which action-
procedure performs operator-precedence analysis of expressions.

The graph itself can be defined in some data-structuring
language - even in assembly code perhaps - but the simplest way of
creating a graph is to use a parser-transcriber. This is a program
which takes a grammar as input and produces a graph which follows
the specifications of that grammar. Sophisticated parser-
transcribers can check that the grammar obeys the one-track
condition: when using such a program to build a syntax analyser
you really are 'programming in BNF'. The output of the parser-
transcriber will be designed to be processed by some pre-defined
interpreter, so that all the compiler-writer has to do is to
prepare the grammar and design the action-procedures.

When using a graph and interpreter, the syntax analyser can be
expected to be a little slower than the hand-built version, but

the difference will be slight: in any case, as chapters 1, 4 and 8 emphasised, the syntax analyser's speed of operation isn't particularly important. The graphical representation saves a great deal of space compared with the procedures of a recursive-descent analyser, and is often preferred for this reason alone.

One possible advantage of the graph and interpreter is that a measure of <u>automatic</u> error recovery is possible. The control stack gives the state of the analyser in a form which an error recovery procedure can use in deciding whether to delete or to insert symbols after finding a error. This procedure can use the pointers in the current node of the graph, and the stored pointers in the 'alternative' and 'call' entries on the stack, to determine whether a symbol appears to be 'missing' - i.e. whether the current lexical item appears to continue the analysis correctly if the current node were ignored - or whether a symbol ought to be deleted - i.e. whether the next lexical item would be acceptable to the current node.

Shortage of space precludes a full description of such a technique here: one was proposed by Irons (Irons,1961) in the very early days of the development of top-down analysis and is described by Gries (Gries,1971). The mechanism only works really well with input which is 'almost correct'. Faced with a really garbled program, any automatic technique gets very confused and will produce a mountain of secondary error reports - which is why they aren't very much used.

Automatic Generation of Top-down Analysers

In the discussion above I have concentrated on the manipulations which you must carry out in order to produce a grammar suitable for one-track analysis. The transcription of the grammar into a working syntax analyser is then so mechanical that it can in fact be entrusted to a a parser-transcriber program. The manipulations on the grammar are themselves fairly mechanical, and it is possible to write a parser-generator (or compiler-compiler) which will perform them for you and produce the analyser direct from the reference grammar. Input to a parser-transcriber or a parser-generator must specify the actions of the analyser (tree building, error handling, etc.) as well as the phrase structure of the source language: figure 16.31 shows a possible grammar which could be given to a parser-transcriber for one-track grammars.

```
<CompStat> ::= [ <statement> | <error("missing statement")> ]
              [ ; <CompStat> <buildnode(CSnode,2)>
               | end
               | <error("semicolon or end expected")> ]
```

Figure 16.31 Possible input to a parser-transcriber

Use of a parser-generator to perform the factoring, removal of left recursion and elimination of context clashes discussed earlier in this chapter might seem to be the ideal way of building a top-down syntax analyser. In practice the manipulations required to turn a reference grammar for a real programming language into one suitable for a one-track analyser are too often outside the capabilities of such a program. Modern parser-generators are usually based on the LR(1) mechanism discussed in chapter 18, which is more suitable as a basis for automatic construction of syntax analysers because it requires less modification to the reference grammar and often no modification at all.

If you have access to a one-track parser-generator, though, you should certainly use it rather than writing the analyser in a system programming language. Use of a parser-generator will save you precious time and effort and allow you to get on with the more interesting work of designing the object code fragments and writing the translator. Likewise if you have access to a parser-transcriber then you should use that. It isn't worthwhile to write either a parser-generator or a parser-transcriber to help in the construction of just one compiler, but in compiler factories they can be extremely useful.

Summary

The simplest way to generate a syntax analyser is to use a top-down-parser generator. If you don't have access to a parser generator, the next best thing is to use a parser transcriber – if you can't use a parser transcriber you must write your own analyser by hand, preferably using the techniques described in this chapter and in the next.

It is relatively simple to transform the grammar of the statements and declarations of a language so that they satisfy the one-track condition: when it is difficult (as for example with the conflict between labels which are identifiers and left-hand-side expressions in assignment statements) a 'fudged' solution to the problem can usually be constructed. Given a one-track grammar, it is simple to write a recursive-descent analyser as a system of recursive procedures or (if a parser-transcriber program is available) to prepare a syntax graph which can drive a grammar-interpreter.

The grammar of expressions is less suitable for top-down analysis. It is therefore usual to construct an operator-precedence analysis procedure which is called from the procedures of the recursive-descent analyser or by the syntax graph interpreter.

Error handling is an important part of any syntax analyser's task. The one-track mechanism provides good error-detection, good error-reporting and acceptable error-recovery facilities.

17 Operator Precedence Analysis of Expressions

The bottom-up syntax analysis algorithm of chapter 3 handles a subset of programming language arithmetic expressions using a system of numerical priorities. This is the basis of the operator-precedence mechanism. It is one of the oldest forms of syntax analysis, now less popular because it is not as flexible or as good at error detection as the one-track technique nor applicable to as many grammars as the LR(1) technique described in chapter 18, but still very useful in practice in the analysis of expressions of a programming language. It is useful in part because of its efficiency and in part because an operator-precedence analyser can usually be generated direct from the unmodified 'reference' grammar for expressions. Its error-processing performance is deficient in theory but with care and some simple pragmatic adjustments it can be made acceptable, given the simple syntactic structure of programming language expressions.

Operator-precedence analysis is a kind of bottom-up analysis, and like all bottom-up parsing mechanisms it depends upon the recognition of phrase-patterns in the input. When a phrase-pattern is recognised it is replaced by the symbol on the left-hand-side of the corresponding production: this action is termed reducing the input phrase. Figure 17.1 shows a pseudo-BCPL description of the mechanism. There isn't space here to go into all the theory which lies behind bottom-up parsing in general and operator-precedence parsing in particular, so the description in this chapter should be taken as a simplified description of 'how to do

---

```
until input is a single symbol do
  { find position of leftmost phrase-pattern in input;
    find phrase-pattern in list of productions;
    reduce phrase-pattern to a single symbol
  }
```

Figure 17.1 Stages in bottom-up analysis

it' rather than 'what to do in the general case'.

In operator-precedence parsing the phrase-patterns are located by checking the <u>precedence</u> or <u>priority</u> of adjacent terminal symbols in the language. The terminal symbols are called 'operators' but it isn't necessary to restrict attention to arithmetic expression operators such as '*' or '+'. Precedences must be assigned in such a way that

   (i) the operators at either end of a sub-phrase have
       priority over the operators in the phrase which surrounds
       them
   (ii) adjacent operators in a complete phrase are of equal
       precedence.

If this can be done consistently then the leftmost complete phrase can be recognised merely by scanning the input from left-to-right to find the first sequence of equal-precedence operators surrounded by lower-precedence operators. Figure 17.2 gives a pseudo-BCPL version of the algorithm.

```
until input is a single symbol do
  { start at left end;

    /* look for right-hand-end of phrase */
    until precedence[CurrentOp, NextOp] = '>' do
        move to the right;
    RightEnd := current position;

    /* find left-hand-end of phrase */
    until precedence[PreviousOp, CurrentOp] = '<' do
        move to the left;
    LeftEnd := current position;

    ReducePhrase(LeftEnd, RightEnd)
  }
```

Figure 17.2 Operator-precedence analysis

```
push(emptysymbol)

until TopStackOp=empty & InputOp=empty do
    if precedence[TopStackOp, InputOp] = '>' then
        ... reduce phrase on top of stack ...
    else
    { push(InputOp); read(InputOp) }
```

Figure 17.3 Operator-precedence analysis using a stack

In fact the algorithm can be even simpler than that shown in figure 17.2, because the reduction of a phrase to a single non-terminal symbol never alters the precedence relationships between the operators to the left of the phrase so reduced (how could it?). Therefore the algorithm can always start 'moving right' from the position at which the last phrase was found: therefore it can use a stack on which to store partially-analysed input. Figure 17.3 shows a more realistic version of the algorithm of figure 17.2 which uses a stack in just this way. Using either version of the algorithm the input starts out as a sequence of terminal symbols and, by successive reductions, is converted into a sequence of terminal and non-terminal symbols and eventually into a single non-terminal symbol.

The essence of the operator-precedence technique is that the analyser only looks at the <u>terminal</u> symbols - the 'operators' - to determine what to do. In order that the first and last operators in the expression can be handled correctly, the mechanism assumes that a notional 'empty' operator precedes the first symbol and follows the last symbol in the expression. This operator has the lowest priority of any, so that the first operator in the expression will always be placed on the stack correctly and so that all operators still held in the stack are reduced when the end of expression is reached.

Determining the Precedence of Operators

In order that the analyser should always be able to determine the positions and the relative priorities of adjacent phrase-patterns merely by looking at the terminal symbols which they contain, it is necessary that the grammar should be an <u>operator grammar</u>: one in which no sentential form (partially-reduced input) can contain adjacent non-terminals. A necessary and sufficient condition for this to be so is that no production should contain a right-hand-side which contains adjacent non-terminals: then by induction it is easy to show that it is impossible to produce adjacent non-terminals from the sentence symbol using the productions of the grammar. If the reference grammar contains productions which contravene this restriction, then they must be rewritten - see figure 17.4, for example. Rewriting the productions is always trivial in practice (and usually clarifies the grammar as well!).

Original:
  E -> I E **else** E | ...
  I -> **if** E **then**

Rewritten:
  E -> **if** E **then** E **else** E | ...

Figure 17.4 Constructing an operator grammar

Given an operator grammar the operator-precedence relations can be determined from the 'first operator' and 'last operator' lists as shown in figure 17.5. This process builds a matrix of precedence relations between the terminal symbols of the language. The FIRSTOP+ list is just a list of the terminal symbols which can

---

(i) For each non-terminal symbol construct a FIRSTOP list which includes the first terminal symbol in each right-hand-side of a production for that terminal, and also the first symbol if it is a non-terminal. For example, if there is a production

$$X \rightarrow a \ .. \ | \ Bc \ ..$$

include 'a', 'B' and 'c' in the FIRSTOP list of 'X'.

(ii) Construct a LASTOP list for each non-terminal symbol which includes the last terminal symbol in each right-hand-side of a production for that terminal, and also the last symbol if it is a non-terminal. For example, if there is a production

$$Y \rightarrow \ .. \ u \ | \ .. \ vW$$

include 'u', 'v' and 'W' in the LASTOP list of 'Y'.

(iii) Compute the FIRSTOP+ and LASTOP+ lists using the closure algorithm of chapter 15 (after this stage the non-terminal symbols can be removed from the lists if you wish).

(iv) Produce a matrix of operator-precedence relations from the productions of the grammar, the FIRSTOP+ and LASTOP+ lists.

- for every production U -> .. aB ..
  put 'a < alpha' for each terminal symbol 'alpha' in the FIRSTOP+ list of 'B'
- for every production U -> .. Bc ..
  put 'beta > c' for each terminal symbol 'beta' in the LASTOP+ list of 'B'
- for every production U -> .. aBc .. or
  U -> .. ac ..
  put 'a = c'.

(v) Put 'empty < gamma' for each terminal symbol 'gamma' in the FIRSTOP+ list of the sentence symbol 'S'; put 'delta > empty' for each terminal symbol 'delta' in the LASTOP+ list of 'S'.

Figure 17.5 Computing the operator precedence relations

appear first in any of the strings which can be derived from a non-terminal and the LASTOP+ list contains the terminal symbol which can appear last in any of those strings. The assignment of precedence relations ensures that when a phrase is to be reduced its subphrases will be reduced first because the operators which they contain will have precedence over the operators in the phrase itself. Figure 17.6 shows the precedence matrix for a simple expression grammar - '%' indicates the 'empty' symbol. The grammar of figure 17.6 doesn't include unary operators - they can introduce difficulties, for the resolution of which see the discussion of the 'input state' mechanism below.

Entries in the matrix which are either <, = or > indicate the relative priorities of adjacent operators; blank entries indicate an error since there is no sentential form in which those two operators can be adjacent. The grammar of figure 17.6, for example, doesn't allow an 'i' symbol to be followed by a '(' symbol and therefore there is a blank space in the matrix at position ['i', '(']. In larger grammars, with larger matrices, you can expect a larger proportion of the entries to be blank. The blank entries will only pick out a small proportion of the possible syntax errors, however, and further errors will be noticed when a phrase-pattern which is indicated by the precedence relations must be reduced to a single phrase.

```
Grammar:
  S -> A
  A -> T | A+T | A-T
  T -> F | T*F | T/F
  F -> P | P^F
  P -> i | n | (A)
```

Symbol	FIRSTOP+	LASTOP+
S	A T + - F * / P ^ i n (	A T + - F * / P ^ i n)
A	T A + - F * / P ^ i n (	T + - F * / P ^ i n)
T	F T * / P ^ i n (	F * / P ^ i n)
F	P ^ i n (	P ^ F i n)
P	i n (	i n)

	%	(	)	i,n	^	*,/	+,-
%		<		<	<	<	<
(		<	=	<	<	<	<
)	>		>		>	>	>
i,n	>		>		>	>	>
^	>	<	>	<	<	>	>
*,/	>	<	>	<	<	>	>
+,-	>	<	>	<	<	<	>

Figure 17.6 An example operator precedence matrix

Figure 17.7 shows a sequence of reductions using the algorithm of figure 17.3 and the matrix of figure 17.6. Note that in making a reduction, the phrase-pattern always includes the non-terminal symbols (if there are any) at the extreme end of the sequence of operators which is selected by the precedence relations. There is no need for the analyser to decide whether to reduce 'N2+N5' or to reduce '+N5', even when using a grammar which does include unary '+' operators, since to reduce '+N5' would produce adjacent non-terminals in the stack, which is impossible given an operator grammar.

Figure 17.8 shows the output which could be produced if each phrase symbol contains a pointer to a tree node and if every reduction of a phrase-pattern to a single symbol constructs a pointer to a tree node containing the symbols and pointers in the phrase-pattern which was reduced. This bottom-up means of building the tree shows clearly how the method of representing the analyser output as 'triples' or 'quadruples' (see chapter 4) is no

Stack	Input
%	a*b*c+d^(e+f)^g%
% a	*b*c+d^(e+f)^g%
% P1 *	b*c+d^(e+f)^g%
% P1 * b	*c+d^(e+f)^g%
% P1 * P2	*c+d^(e+f)^g%
% N1	*c+d^(e+f)^g%
% N1 *	c+d^(e+f)^g%
% N1 * c	+d^(e+f)^g%
% N1 * P3	+d^(e+f)^g%
% N2	+d^(e+f)^g%
% N2 +	d^(e+f)^g%
% N2 + d	^(e+f)^g%
% N2 + P4	^(e+f)^g%
% N2 + P4 ^	(e+f)^g%
% N2 + P4 ^ (	e+f)^g%
% N2 + P4 ^ (e	+f)^g%
% N2 + P4 ^ (P5	+f)^g%
% N2 + P4 ^ (P5 +	f)^g%
% N2 + P4 ^ (P5 + f	)^g%
% N2 + P4 ^ (P5 + P6	)^g%
% N2 + P4 ^ (N3	)^g%
% N2 + P4 ^ (N3)	^g%
% N2 + P4 ^ N3	^g%
% N2 + P4 ^ N3 ^	g%
% N2 + P4 ^ N3 ^ g	%
% N2 + P4 ^ N3 ^ P7	%
% N2 + P4 ^ N4	%
% N2 + N5	%
% N6	%

Figure 17.7 Sample operator-precedence analysis

different from the tree representation. If the nodes are written out in the order in which they are generated, they can be viewed as triples; but in effect the last triple is the root of the tree!

Numerical Operator Priorities

The operator precedence matrix is the most general means of indicating the relations between symbols. It doesn't take up much space, even for largish grammars, since each entry needs only two bits to indicate one of the four possibilities. Therefore the matrix of figure 17.6 would take only 48 bits of store. It can sometimes be convenient, though, to collapse the matrix into a system of numerical priorities, as illustrated in figure 17.9. Two priorities are required for each operator, since an operator may be either left-associative - e.g. '*'>'*' - or right-associative - e.g. '^'<'^' in figure 17.6, which is also the case in PL/1 and many FORTRANs - and because of the directional

---

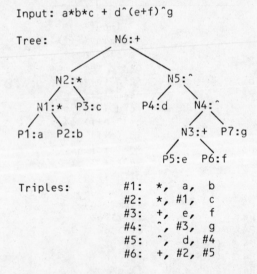

Input: a*b*c + d^(e+f)^g

Tree:

Triples:
```
#1:  *,  a,   b
#2:  *,  #1,  c
#3:  +,  e,   f
#4:  ^,  #3,  g
#5:  ^,  d,   #4
#6:  +,  #2,  #5
```

Figure 17.8 Output of the operator-precedence algorithm

Symbol	Rightprec	Leftprec
%	0	0
(	0	6
)	6	0
i,n	6	5
^	4	5
*,/	4	3
+,-	2	1

Figure 17.9 Numerical operator priorities

priorities of brackets.

The numbers can be calculated by an iterative process, starting either from the matrix or from the grammar together with the FIRSTOP+ and LASTOP+ lists: initially all the numbers are the same (I chose 0 in this example). The first step is to read through the matrix (or the grammar) and to check that the numerical relations are consistent with the operator precedences. If there is an inconsistency, increase the smaller of the numbers in the relationship

- if a>b but rightprec(a)<=leftprec(b), increase
  rightprec(a)
- if a=b but rightprec(a)\=leftprec(b), increase the lesser
  of the two values
- if a<b but rightprec(a)>=leftprec(b), increase leftprec(b)

The process is repeated until there are no further inconsistencies between the grammar (or the matrix) and the numerical priorities. Only the relative magnitudes of the numbers is important, so that it isn't necessary to start at any particular value: indeed it is reasonable to guess the priorities initially and to use this procedure to adjust any minor inconsistencies if necessary.

In some cases it isn't possible to prepare either the matrix or the numerical priorities because the grammar doesn't allow unique assignment of operator-precedence relations. Often the difficulty arises because the grammar is ambiguous, although it is perfectly possible to specify a reasonable grammar which isn't an operator-precedence grammar (for example see the discussion about the treatment of unary operators below). The syntax of FORTRAN 66, for example, specifies

$$T \rightarrow F \mid T+T \mid T-F$$

which implies both '+'<'+' and '+'>'+'. The problem was caused (presumably) by the language definers' desire not to prescribe an order of evaluation of sequences of '+' operations. The difficulty is overcome, and the ambiguity removed, if the production is recast as

$$T \rightarrow F \mid T+F \mid T-F$$

As with context clashes in top-down analysers, an inconsistency in operator-precedence relations sometimes reflects a deeper problem such as an ambiguity in the grammar, and the resolution of such problems cannot always be automatic.

In some pathological cases it is possible to construct the matrix but impossible to construct a consistent system of numerical priorities, due to some circularity of relations such as a<b, c>b, c<d, a>d. In practice, given the simplified nature of

expression grammars, you shouldn't encounter this difficulty. If
you do come across it then it may be worthwhile to question the
design of the programming language grammar: one which contains
such a circularity is almost certainly confusing to the user who
is programming in the language and if it is confusing then it
ought to be changed.

A deficiency of the numerical priority system is that blank
entries in the matrix can't be represented. Thus, although in
figure 17.6 the entry [')','('] is blank, the numerical priorities
of figure 17.9 imply that ')'>'('. Error detection can be more
difficult when using numerical priorities than when using the
matrix, therefore, although the mechanism of 'input states'
suggested below solves the problem in most cases.

Reducing a Phrase-pattern to a Single Symbol

Consider the grammar, input and sequence of reductions shown in
figure 17.10. Formally the input contains a syntax error, as you
can see if you trace the sequence of reductions (I leave it as an
exercise to compute the precedence matrix or the numerical
priorities to check that the actions of the analyser will be as

---

```
Grammar
   E -> B | A
   B -> R | B or R | B and R
   R -> A=A | (B)
   A -> P | A+P | A-P
   P -> <identifier> | (A)

Input: a+b or c=d

Stack                          Input
  %                            a+b or c=d%
  % a                          +b or c=d%
  % I                          +b or c=d%
  % I +                        b or c=d%
  % I + b                      or c=d%
  % I + I                      or c=d%
  % A                          or c=d%
  % A or                       c=d%
  % A or c                     =d%
  % A or I                     =d%
  % A or I =                   d%
  % A or I = d                 %
  % A or I = I                 %
  % A or R                     %

     - syntax error: A or R is not a phrase
```

Figure 17.10 Formal detection of invalid phrase-patterns

shown). The operator-precedence matrix merely serves to indicate the position of phrase-patterns in the input and, strictly speaking, a phrase-pattern can only be reduced when there is a symbol in the grammar from which that phrase-pattern can be derived. Thus 'I + I' in figure 17.10 can be reduced to 'A', but 'A or R' cannot be reduced since there is no symbol in the grammar from which it could be derived.

Although it is simple to construct an algorithm to decide when a pattern is reducible (is a valid phrase) or is not, the best solution to the problem is to ignore it and to treat all non-terminal symbols as equivalent. If this is done the input of figure 17.10 will be analysed into the tree of 17.11, which will eventually provoke a translation error because the subnodes of the **or** node are not both **Boolean** operation nodes or **Boolean** primaries. The error report can be of the form

'a+b' is not a valid **Boolean** value

If the syntax analyser doesn't ignore the error it must produce a report such as

a+b **or** c=d
    ^
Invalid phrase

or, if it is a top-down analyser, a report such as

a+b **or** c=d
      ^
Relational operator expected

Neither of these is to be preferred to the translation error report, which has the merit of at least seeming to explain the cause of the error. In the case of input such as 'a=b=c', which is also invalid given the grammar of figure 17.10, the translator might even inform the user that the input ought perhaps to have been 'a=b **and** b=c'. The final advantage for the compiler writer in ignoring errors which arise from invalid combinations of sub-

---

Input: a+b **or** c=d

Tree which might be produced:

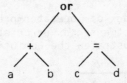

Figure 17.11 Some syntax errors should be ignored

phrases is that this reduces the incidence of error recovery in the syntax analyser,• and hence the incidence of secondary error reports.

There are diagnostic advantages, then, if the syntax analyser ignores errors which are caused by invalid combinations of phrases and leaves the translator to detect the error as one of invalid combination of sub-nodes. Luckily, there are operational advantages as well - the operator-precedence analyser is easier to construct if it ignores the difference between all non-terminals and simply reduces phrase-patterns depending on the operators which they contain. The fact that the grammar is an operator grammar already means that the boundaries of each phrase are clear - in a sequence

$$\ldots \; op_0 \; P_0 \; op_1 \; \ldots \; op_n \; P_n \; op_{n+1} \; \ldots$$

where $op_0 < op_1 = op_2 = \ldots = op_n > op_{n+1}$, the phrase to be reduced runs from P_0 to P_n - any other possibility would produce adjacent non-terminals in the stack, which is impossible given an operator grammar. Ignoring differences between non-terminals means that reducing a phrase is a very simple business indeed.

An Operator-precedence Grammar is Unambiguous

Like a one-track grammar, an operator-precedence grammar can be unambiguous. The argument which shows this depends upon the fact that an operator precedence analyser need never backtrack if, whenever a phrase-pattern is located, there is only one symbol to which it can be reduced. An operator-precedence analyser which makes no distinction between non-terminals clearly fulfills this requirement, since it reduces all phrase-patterns to the same <phrase> symbol. This makes the grammar effectively unambiguous, although it may be formally ambiguous. Thus in ALGOL 60, for example, an expression which consists of a single identifier might be reduced either to a <Boolean expression> or to an <arithmetic expression> and thus the grammar is ambiguous[1]: if the analyser takes note of the difference between the two kinds of phrase then it may have to backtrack. If it ignores the differences between phrases, however, backtracking is never necessary.

Input States, Error Detection and Unary Operators

The most important drawback of operator-precedence analysers is that they may not detect a syntax error at the earliest possible point. Figure 17.12 illustrates the confusion that can result: an

---

1 The ambiguity only arises if the sub-grammar of ALGOL 60 expressions is considered in isolation: in the grammar as a whole the effect of declarations removes the 'ambiguity'.

analyser using the precedence matrix of figure 17.6, or the numerical priorities of figure 17.9, will pass over a blatant error in the sequence 'a+*' and only much later, when it has analysed the phrase which follows the '*' operator, will it discover that '*P' isn't a reducible pattern. A one-track or an LR(1) analyser would detect the error immediately the '*' symbol was read. Reporting on the error long after the point in the input at which it should have been noticed is very confusing for the user, and for this reason (among others) operator-precedence analysis has fallen into general disrepute and disfavour.

```
    Stack                    Input
    ...                      a+*(b+c)^d+ ...
    a                        +*(b+c)^d+ ...
    P                        +*(b+c)^d+ ...
    P +                      *(b+c)^d+ ...
    P + *                    (b+c)^d+ ...
    P + * (                  b+c)^d+ ...
    P + * ( b                +c)^d+ ...
    P + * ( P                +c)^d+ ...
    P + * ( P +              c)^d+ ...
    P + * ( P + c            )^d+ ...
    P + * ( P + P            )^d+ ...
    P + * ( P                )^d+ ...
    P + * ( P )              ^d+ ...
    P + * P                  ^d+ ...
    P + * P ^                d+ ...
    P + * P ^ d              + ...
    P + * P ^ P              + ...
    P + * P                  + ...

    - syntax error: '*P' is not a phrase
```

Figure 17.12 Late detection of errors

Grammar:
```
E -> A | +A | -A
A -> T | A+T | A-T
T -> F | T*F | T/F
F -> P | P^F
P -> <identifier> | <number> | (E)
```

States:

	+	-	*	/	^	i	n	(	)	%
0	1	1				2	2	0		
1						2	2	0		
2	1	1	1	1	1				2	2

Figure 17.13 Input states in arithmetic expressions

Given the restricted syntax of programming-language
expressions, however, there is a simple solution to the problem of
early detection of errors. Using the FIRST* and LAST* lists it is
easy to compute which terminal symbols can follow which in the
input: given this information you can calculate a number of 'input
states' in which the analyser can find itself, each of which
effectively specifies the kind of symbol which is expected in the
input. Figure 17.13 shows the states, and the permissible
transitions between them, for a simple grammar (which in this case
does contain unary '+' and '-' operators). Conceptually state 0
corresponds to 'start of expression', state 1 'after an operator'
and state 2 'after an operand'. Blanks in the matrix indicate an
input error - thus for example the sequence 'a+*' will be detected
as an error immediately the '*' symbol is read, since the analyser
will be in state 1 after the '+' symbol is processed. In most
cases checking the permissible state transitions means that the
operator-precedence analyser will not read past the position of an
error which it would later detect[1].

Unary expression operators

An operator-precedence analyser using the input-state mechanism to
check the input as it is read can be based on the grammar of
figure 17.13. The first production implies '+'<'+' while the
second production implies '+'>'+'[2]. This can be viewed as a kind
of context clash: the '+' and '-' operators are being used for two
purposes in different contexts in the grammar. The analyser can
tell the difference between the contexts by using the input state
- a '+' or '-' symbol read in state 0 is a unary (monadic)
operator, while one read in state 2 is a binary (diadic) operator.
The different kinds of operator can be treated separately and
given different entries in the matrix or different numerical
priorities.

Implementing the input-state mechanism

The input-state mechanism can be implemented in a number of ways.
In the most obvious implementation the analyser calls an 'input

---

1 The trick of ignoring differences between non-terminals so
  that some errors aren't detected until translation time might
  be thought to be a drawback of the same kind as that in which
  the analyser reads past an error and later has to come back to
  report on it: however I believe the former behaviour to be a
  strength of the operator-precedence analysis mechanism.

2 In some modern languages, such as ALGOL 68, the unary
  operators have 'maximal priority'. In effect the operators are
  introduced at the level of expression primaries - P -> +P, say
  - and the difficulty of handling unary operators doesn't
  arise.

filter' procedure which remembers the input state and produces an error message if necessary. A more sophisticated implementation is to use a <u>transition matrix</u>. A third possible implementation is to use a combination of operator-precedence and top-down techniques as in the BCPL compiler example discussed below.

The matrix of figure 17.6 gives no information to the analyser other than 'start of pattern' (<), 'part of pattern' (=), 'reduce' or 'end of pattern' (>) and 'error' (blank). The state-transition matrix of figure 17.13 gives little more assistance. The two matrices can be combined into a larger matrix, in which each entry indicates the action to be taken if a particular input symbol is encountered in a particular analyser state with a particular operator on top of the stack, together with the new analyser state to be entered. The resulting 'transition matrix' can provide some advantages over the normal operator-precedence matrix.

First, the 'error' entries in the operator-precedence matrix can be replaced with actions in the transition matrix which print out an appropriate error message, thus improving the error-handling performance of the analyser. Second, the 'reduce' entries in the operator-precedence matrix can be replaced with action entries in the transition matrix which specify the number of symbols that make up the phrase-pattern, thus removing the need to examine relations between symbols near the top of the stack in order to find the beginning of the phrase-pattern. The transition matrix is an efficient and flexible means of building an operator-precedence analyser.

```
let ParseExpression(priority) = valof
{ let lhs = ParsePrimary()

  if lhs = empty then resultis empty

  while IsOperator(lexitem) & priority<=leftprec(lexitem) do
  { let op = lexitem
    let rhs = empty

    /* use priorities as in figure 17.9 */
    LexAnalyse()
    rhs := ParseExpression(rightprec(op))
    if rhs=empty then Error(...)
    else lhs := newnode(op, lhs, rhs)
  }

  resultis lhs
}
```

Figure 17.14 A recursive operator-precedence analyser

Recursive operator-precedence analysis

Figures 17.14 and 17.15 show a simplified version of a BCPL
compiler's expression analysis procedures. The ParsePrimary
procedure is a top-down, one-track procedure which analyses
'primaries' of expressions, including in this case unary
operators, bracketed expressions and function calls (the form of a

```
let ParsePrimary() = valof
 { let nodep = empty

   switchon lexitem into
    { case name:
      case number:
            nodep := node(lexitem, lexvalue); LexAnalyse();
            endcase

      case '(':
         { LexAnalyse(); nodep := ParseExpression(0)
           if lexitem=')' then
           { LexAnalyse(); endcase }
           else Error("right bracket missing", ...)
         }

      case '+', '-', '\', ...
            { let op, primary = lexitem, empty

              LexAnalyse(); primary := ParsePrimary()
              if primary=empty then Error(...)
              else nodep := node(op, primary)
            }

      case 'valof':
            LexAnalyse(); nodep := ParseStatement()
            if nodep=empty then Error(...)
            else nodep := node(ValOfNode, nodep)

      default: resultis empty
    }

   /* analyse function calls */
   if lexitem='(' then
   { LexAnalyse()
     if lexitem=')' then
     { LexAnalyse(); resultis node(FunctionCall, nodep) }
     else
     { .. analyse arguments with ParseExpression ... }
   }
 }
```

Figure 17.15 A top-down analyser for expression primaries

function call primary is 'P()' or 'P(arguments)' - see the grammar in figure 16.28). It is called by the ParseExpression procedure, which is a bottom-up, operator-precedence analyser used as a subroutine of the top-down procedures in the rest of the analyser. The ParseExpression procedure uses recursion to implement the conventional operator stack. The interplay of bottom-up and top-down mechanisms is intricate: when the ParsePrimary procedure recognises a **valof** symbol it calls the ParseStatement procedure, which may then call the ParseExpression procedure, which may call the ParseStatement procedure, and so on.

The use of ParsePrimary implements the 'input state' mechanism discussed above. The two procedures treat the expression as a sequence of <operand>s separated by <operator>s: <operand>s and unary <operator>s are recognised by ParsePrimary, binary <operator>s by ParseExpression.

Summary

An operator-precedence analyser can normally be constructed from the unmodified reference grammar for expressions. It is efficient, its error-handling is no worse than that of a one-track analyser working on expressions and with careful design its error-handling can be made acceptable.

If you can't gain access to a parser-generator or a parser-transcriber then it is possible to build an operator-precedence analysis procedure by hand. The best basis for a hand-built analyser is a transition matrix or a recursive procedure like that in figure 17.14. The operator-precedence analysis procedure can usefully form one of the procedures in a one-track recursive-descent analyser.

18 LR(1) Syntax Analysis

Theoretical studies of the properties of programming language grammars and of algorithms for syntax analysis have always been partly motivated by the search for a truly automatic means of constructing a syntax analyser. In the early 1960s so called 'compiler-compilers' were popular. One of the earliest was developed at the University of Manchester (Brooker et al.,1963): it included a parser-transcriber which took a syntax description and without alteration transcribed it into a top-down syntax analyser[1]. Foster's SID (Foster,1968) was the first of many parser-generator programs which went further so far as syntax analysis was concerned: its input was a type 2 grammar, on which it performed most of the operations discussed in chapter 16 to produce a one-symbol-look-ahead grammar, which it finally transcribed into an ALGOL 60 program. The transformations required to make a grammar one-track or one-symbol-look-ahead aren't always simply mechanical, however, and in practice a top-down parser-generator like SID often fails to complete its task. Parser-generators for top-down analysers were little used, therefore, and most syntax analysers were written by hand using the techniques discussed in earlier chapters.

Developments in bottom-up analysis also gave rise to work in parser-generators. The analysis techniques used were essentially developments of the operator-precedence mechanism discussed in chapter 17: Wirth's 'simple precedence' (described in (Gries,1971)), for example, gives a priority to every symbol in the grammar rather than just to the terminal symbols. Although some of the techniques which were developed required less hand-modification of the grammar than do top-down parser-generators, the analysers that were produced had inferior error-handling performance to, and were sometimes less efficient than a well-

---

1 The program was a compiler-compiler proper, in that it also associated each node-type in the tree with the procedure which was intended to translate that type of node.

designed one-track analyser.

Until relatively recently, therefore, it seemed that the best available practical means of building a syntax analyser was to use the mechanisms proposed in chapters 16 and 17 - 'best' because the transformations required to the grammar are fairly easy to understand, the analyser that is produced is efficient and, most important of all, the analyser has excellent error-detection and error-reporting performance. Now, however, the compiler-writing public is beginning to understand the mechanism known as LR analysis, originally described by Knuth (Knuth,1965) and later explained by various authors (Aho and Johnson,1974), (Aho and Ullman,1978), (Horning,1974). The mechanism has many advantages, not least of which is that it can be used as the basis of a parser-generator which can accept a much larger range of grammars than was hitherto possible. The error-handling performance of an LR(1) syntax analyser is as good as that of a one-track analyser. Its only possible drawback is that the method of producing a analyser is so intricate that in practice you <u>must</u> use a parser-generator to produce one[1].

Although the LR mechanism is suitable for automatic generation of a syntax analyser, some problems remain. The state-tables required to control analysis can become uncomfortably large and some effort has to be spent in encoding the information which they contain so as to reduce the size of the analyser. The simple parser-generators currently available may not always exploit the full power of the technique, and the error messages which they produce when problems arise in the generation of the analyser are sufficiently obscure that the the compiler-writer needs a clear understanding of the theory of LR analysis in order to understand them. This last is the reason for including a chapter on LR syntax analysis in this book.

At present the balance of advantages appear to be in favour of the use of a parser-generator for an LR(1) analyser over all other methods (but see the discussion at the end of this chapter) merely because it makes the writing of a syntax analyser partly automatic. If you can't get access to such a program you will just have to spend more effort in writing the analyser: a one-track syntax analyser with an operator-precedence subroutine for expressions will be as efficient and produce as good error reports as its LR(1) rival.

---

1 Cynics argue that parser-generators are popular in the early days of the introduction of a new syntax analysis technique. As soon as everybody really understands the technique, they start to write analysers by hand again!

Notation and etymology

The one-track analysis mechanism described in chapter 16 is good
at error detection because it never backtracks and never reads
past the point at which an error might first be detected. It is
good at error reporting because it is 'goal directed', which means
that it can give a report related to the goals of its analysis
when an error is detected. The goals which it has at any stage -
for example to find an expression within a conditional statement
within a procedure declaration within a block - are determined by
the input which it has analysed so far. In Knuth's notation the
results of analysis so far are termed the left context and it is
clear that any analyser which doesn't backtrack and which
determines each step of the analysis in part by examining the left
context will share the one-track analyser's error handling
advantages. LR analysers can use the left context in this way:
operator-precedence analysers can't and therefore in general have
inferior error detection and error reporting performance.

   Historically bottom-up analysers were distinguished from top-
down in that they recognise phrases by inspecting the entire
phrase together with some symbols to its right and some symbols to
its left. Top-down analysers have the much harder task of
recognising a phrase by looking only at its first symbol(s): they
can solve this problem only because they use the current left
context to cut down the number of possible phrases which might
occur. LR analysis is like bottom-up analysis in that it
recognises the whole phrase and inspects the symbols which follow
it but is like top-down analysis in that it uses the left context
to decide which phrases it should look for.

   An LR(k) analyser inspects 'k' input symbols after the phrase
in order to recognise it: in practice 'k' is always either 0 or 1.
Few analysers use the full power of the technique: practical
techniques, in order of increasing generality of application, are
LR(0), SLR(1), LALR(1) and LR(1) itself.

   The etymology of the term LR, and the associated term LL which
is used to describe top-down analysis, is simple but not
particularly illuminating. A left derivation of a sentence is one
in which at each step the leftmost non-terminal symbol in the
sentential form is expanded. Conversely a right derivation is one
in which the rightmost non-terminal symbol is expanded at each
stage. In a top-down analyser the order in which the goals are
selected when a sentence is analysed (for example, the order in
which the procedures are called in a recursive-descent analyser)
is identical to the order in which symbols are expanded in a left
derivation of that sentence. Hence top-down analysers are dubbed
'LL' because they use Left context and are guided by a Left
derivation. The order in which the phrases are recognised in a
bottom-up or LR analyser is the exact reverse of that in which
symbols are expanded in a right derivation: hence the term LR

since the analyser uses Left context and produces a Right
derivation in reverse.

The distinction between analysis mechanisms isn't as clear as
this notation tries to make it appear. The order in which the
nodes of the parse tree are built in a top-down analyser is just
the same as in a bottom-up or LR analyser - a reverse right
derivation - and an LR analyser is guided by a left derivation
held in the stack of analyser states. The real difference between
the mechanisms is more important than notational quibbles:
fundamentally it boils down to the fact that an LR analyser
doesn't decide on the identity of a phrase until it has seen it
all, while an LL analyser must decide on the basis of the first
symbols at the left-hand-end of the phrase.

LR(1) languages

If a grammar satisfies the one-track condition developed in
chapter 16 it is suitable to form the basis of a one-track
analyser and the grammar is a one-track, or LL(1) grammar.
Similarly, any grammar from which an LR(1) analyser can be
constructed is an LR(1) grammar. There are many more LR(1) than
LL(1) grammars: any LL(1) grammar is automatically an LR(1)
grammar but not vice-versa. Figure 18.1, for example, shows a
grammar which is LR(1) as it stands yet requires substantial
modification in order to be used as the basis of a one-track
analyser. This shows a major advantage of the LR(1) technique: it
requires substantially less modification to put a grammar into LR
form than into LL form. This illustrates a major advantage of the
LR(1) technique: it usually requires substantially less
modification to put a grammar into LR form than into LL form.

A more subtle point is that there are more LR(1) languages than
there are LL(1). Just as there are languages which can be
described by a type 2 grammar but not by a type 3 grammar, so
there are languages which can be described by an LR(1) grammar but
not by an LL(1) grammar. It can be proved that this is so but
whether the fact has any implications in practice is doubtful:
certainly there is no example of a useful programming language
which is LR(1) but not LL(1). It may be that such a language would
be confusing to use and that therefore we would voluntarily
restrict ourselves to the class of LL(1) languages.

Analyser States and the Stack

Consider the grammar of figure 18.1, a version of the grammar from
figure 16.14 of chapter 16. This grammar is not LL(1) even when
left recursion is removed because of context clashes: as we shall
see the LR mechanism has no such difficulty with this grammar. As
in any other bottom-up mechanism, the grammar is augmented with a
production which inserts a special 'empty' symbol at the end of
the input. Figure 18.2 shows an LR(0) state table for this grammar

(I deal below with the mechanism with by which this table can be
built). Figure 18.4 shows some sample input together with the
trace of its analysis. Figure 18.5 shows the tree which might be
produced as a record of the analysis.

During LR analysis the stack contains a sequence of states and
symbols. The state on top of the stack selects a row of the table

```
0.    S -> P empty
1.    P -> begin D ; C end
2.    D -> D ; d
3.    D -> d
4.    C -> C ; c
5.    C -> c
```

Figure 18.1 An LR(0) grammar

	begin	;	end	d	c	empty		P	D	C
1.	S2							12		
2.				S4					3	
3.		S5								
4.	R1,D	R1,D	R1,D	R1,D	R1,D	R1,D				
5.				S8	S7					6
6.		S10	S9							
7.	R1,C	R1,C	R1,C	R1,C	R1,C	R1,C				
8.	R3,D	R3,D	R3,D	R3,D	R3,D	R3,D				
9.	R5,P	R5,P	R5,P	R5,P	R5,P	R5,P				
10.					S11					
11.	R3,C	R3,C	R3,C	R3,C	R3,C	R3,C				
12.						H				

Figure 18.2 LR(0) state table

In state **s** (with state **s** on top of the stack) and with input
symbol **i** (**i** may be the 'empty' symbol), examine entry [**s**,**i**]

- a blank entry indicates an error: input symbol **i** should
  not be encountered in state **s**
- an 'H' entry means <u>halt</u>: the analysis has finished
- an 'S**n**' entry means <u>shift</u>: push symbol **i** followed by
  state **n** onto the stack and read a new input symbol –
  i.e. read input and change to state **n**
- an 'R**j**,**k**' entry means <u>reduce</u>: pop the top **j** symbols and
  states from the stack, uncovering state **m**, say. Push
  symbol **k** onto the stack, followed by the state indicated
  in entry [**m**,**k**] – i.e. reduce **j** symbols to one and change
  state.

Figure 18.3 Actions of an LR parser

and the current input symbol selects one of the entries in that
row. Entries in the table are blank, 'H', 'S' or 'R' entries.
Figure 18.3 summarises the actions which each kind of entry
prescribes. The action carried out during a reduction could build
a node of the parse tree and replace the symbols removed by a
pointer to that node, rather than by a non-terminal symbol.

Figure 18.4 shows the stages of analysis and figure 18.5 shows
the tree which would be built. Note the similarities first to
bottom-up analysis, in that phrases are reduced from the top of a
stack, and to top-down analysis, in that the history of analysis
determines the state and hence determines whether a particular
input symbol is acceptable in a particular context. Note also how
sparse the table of figure 18.2 is: it's a feature of the LR
mechanism that most entries in the table are blanks, and indeed
the table of figure 18.2 could be made still more sparse by using
the SLR(1) mechanism discussed below.

```
       Stack                              Input
1                                  begin d; d; c; c end
1 begin 2                          d; d; c; c end
1 begin 2 d 4                      ; d; c; c end
1 begin 2 D₁ 3                     ; d; c; c end
1 begin 2 D₁ 3 ; 5                 d; c; c end
1 begin 2 D₁ 3 ; 5 d 8            ; c; c end
1 begin 2 D₂ 3                     ; c; c end
1 begin 2 D₂ 3 ; 5                c ; c end
1 begin 2 D₂ 3 ; 5 c 7            ; c end
1 begin 2 D₂ 3 ; 5 C₁ 6          ; c end
1 begin 2 D₂ 3 ; 5 C₁ 6 ; 10     c end
1 begin 2 D₂ 3 ; 5 C₁ 6 ; 10 c 11  end
1 begin 2 D₂ 3 ; 5 C₂ 6          end
1 begin 2 D₂ 3 ; 5 C₂ 6 end 9    'empty'
1 P 12                            'empty'
```

Figure 18.4 Stages of LR(0) analysis

Input: **begin** d; d; c; c **end**

Tree:

Figure 18.5 Results of LR(0) analysis

It will be worth your while to study the table of figure 18.2, the actions of figure 18.3 and the example of figure 18.4 in detail. All LR analysis mechanisms discussed in this chapter - LR(0), SLR(1), LALR(1), LR(1) itself - use states and a table in just the manner described in figure 18.3. Differences between the mechanisms are merely to do with the choice of positions in the table which contain 'S' (shift) and 'R' (reduce) entries.

Why It Works: Non-deterministic Syntax Analysis

I believe that it isn't enough merely to present instructions on how to construct the states, resolve conflicts and represent the tables of an LR analyser. It's important also to construct an explanation which gives an intuitive insight into what is going on while an LR analyser is operating. The best such explanation, I believe, shows the links between LR analysis and top-down or bottom-up analysis by viewing an LR analyser as a non-deterministic or parallel program: one which, when presented with a choice between two alternative paths of analysis, is capable of following both of them at once. In order to justify this position it is necessary to re-examine the treatment which was given to the topic of top-down analysis in chapter 16.

The grammar modifications detailed in chapter 16 attempt to create a _deterministic_ top-down analyser: one which at every stage knows which of several analysis paths to follow, simply by examining the current input symbol. Backtracking is merely one of several possible implementations of _non-deterministic_ syntax analysis. If a backtracking analyser is presented with a choice between analysis paths it follows one of them, storing information about its current state so that if analysis breaks down along the chosen path it can restore that state in order to try one of the alternatives. It is possible to imagine a 'parallel' implementation of a non-deterministic top-down analyser which, when presented with a choice, splits or 'forks' into a number of identical independent analysis processes, each dedicated to analysis along one of the possible paths. After a time, therefore, the analyser program may consist of several analysis processes working in parallel.

As each input symbol (input item) is read, each of the analysis processes examines it and either proceeds to the next step of its analysis, if the symbol is what it currently expects to find, or 'dies', if the input symbol doesn't allow its path to continue. At the end of the program, provided the grammar is unambiguous, there will be only one analysis process 'alive': if there is a syntax error then all of the processes will 'die'. Note that the parallel implementation of non-deterministic analysis, unlike the backtracking implementation, doesn't prevent good error detection. Whenever a state is reached in which none of the current analysis processes can accept the current input symbol an error message can be produced immediately, phrased in terms which depend upon the

'goals' of all the current 'live' processes. In practice it might
be hard to devise a comprehensible message and error recovery
would be frighteningly difficult but at least the compiler
wouldn't report 'Statement not recognised' in the manner of a
backtracking analyser.

This sort of non-deterministic top-down analysis could be
implemented. It isn't an ideal mechanism because it isn't very
efficient if implemented as I have described it and because it
doesn't work if the grammar contains left-recursive symbols. Left
recursion produces an infinite expansion in the number of analysis
processes because after each input symbol has been processed, each
live analysis process continues processing up to the point at
which it is ready to examine the next input symbol, calling
phrase-procedures, forking because of alternatives and so on. An
analysis process which is searching for an instance of a directly
left-recursive symbol would fork into several processes, at least
one of which would search for an instance of that symbol and
therefore would fork ... and so on and on. Factoring isn't
necessary, though, because the analyser will happily follow more
than one path and context clashes give no difficulty since each
option or optional iteration merely causes an analysis process to
split into two otherwise identical processes, one of them a
process which examines the option and the other a process which
ignores it.

Left recursion can be handled by introducing an element of
bottom-up analysis into the non-deterministic mechanism. A
bottom-up analyser recognises an instance of a left-recursive
symbol - for example the "C" symbol defined in productions 4 and 5
of figure 18.1 - by first recognising a simple instance of the
symbol and reducing it to a single symbol - reducing 'c' to 'C',
for example - then finding and reducing a longer instance which
contains the recursive symbol - reducing 'C;c' to 'C', for example
- and so on. The non-deterministic analyser can mimic this
behaviour, and thereby handle left recursion, if the 'forking' of
an analysis process takes place only <u>after</u> each instance of a
phrase has been recognised.

LR analysis can now be seen as an alternative mechanism of
non-deterministic syntax analysis, which contains elements of both
bottom-up and top-down mechanisms. It controls the 'forking' of
analysis processes, and thereby handles left recursion, by
maintaining a 'pool' of top-down analysis processes, to which it
will not add multiple copies of a single process. Each of the
processes is a 'micro-analyser' based on a single production in
the grammar, whose task is to find an instance of the phrase
described by that production at a particular position in the
input. Micro-analysers are identical if they have reached the
same position in the same production and started from the same
position in the input. The number of distinct micro-analysis
processes is finite, because there are only a finite number of

productions in the grammar and a finite number of input positions
in the sentence being analysed.

At each step of analysis each of the micro-analysers in the
pool can be in one of three states: it may be expecting a
particular input (terminal) symbol, it may be expecting a
particular phrase (non-terminal symbol) or it may have recognised
an instance of its particular phrase. In the first case it can
inspect the current input symbol and either move on to the next
symbol in its production, if the symbol is what was expected, or
'die', if the symbol doesn't match. When expecting a phrase (a
non-terminal symbol in its production) the micro-analyser can
simulate a procedure call: it enters a 'suspended' state, first
adding micro-analyser processes to the pool based on each of the
productions for that non-terminal symbol. The suspended process
takes no further part in analysis until an instance of the phrase

Input position	Pool	Input
N(i):	#1(O,a): **begin** D ; . C **end**	c ; c **end**
N(ii):	#1(O,s): **begin** D ; . C **end**	c ; c **end**
	#2(N,s): . C ; c	
	#3(N,a): . c	
N+1(i):	#1(O,s): **begin** D ; . C **end**	; c **end**
	#2(N,s): . C ; c	
	#3(N,a): c .	
N+1(ii):	#1(O,s): **begin** D ; . C **end**	; c **end**
	#2(N,s): . C ; c	
	#1a(O,a): **begin** D ; C . **end**	
	#2a(N,a): C . ; c	
N+2:	#1(O,s): **begin** D ; . C **end**	c **end**
	#2(N,s): . C ; c	
	#2a(N,a): C ; . c	
N+3(i):	#1(O,s): **begin** D ; . C **end**	**end**
	#2(N,s): . C ; c	
	#2a(N,a): C ; c .	
N+3(ii):	#1(O,s): **begin** D ; . C **end**	**end**
	#2(N,s): . C ; c	
	#1b(O,a): **begin** D ; C . **end**	
	#2b(N,s): C . ; c	
N+4:	#1(O,s): **begin** D ; . C **end**	'empty'
	#2(N,s): . C ; c	
	#1b(O,a): **begin** D ; C **end** .	

Figure 18.6 Parallel syntax analysis

is recognised. Each of the processes which it adds to the pool
either expects a particular terminal symbol - in which case it
inspects the current input - or expects a non-terminal symbol, in
which case it also becomes suspended and adds new processes to the
pool. Note, however, that new micro-analysers cannot add an
identical copy of a process which is already present and that
therefore left recursion will not lead to an infinite expansion of
the pool.

Consider, for example, productions 1, 4 and 5 from the grammar
illustrated in figure 18.1. Figure 18.6 shows the stages of
analysis assuming that the input is "c ; c **end**", that the current
input symbol is number N in the current sentence and that there is
a single micro-analysis process in the pool, whose task is to
recognise an instance of the "P" phrase and which has reached the
stage in production 1 where it expects an instance of a "C"
symbol. In figure 18.6 the stage which each micro-analyser has
reached is shown by displaying a dot '.' at the point which it has
reached in its particular production. The input position at which
each process started work is shown in brackets, and the process is
shown as 'active' (a) or 'suspended' (s).

At the first stage of the analysis shown in figure 18.6,
micro-analyser #1 suspends itself, adding two new processes to the
pool whose task is to find "C;c" (process #2) and "c" (process #3)
at input position N. Micro-analyser #2 immediately suspends
itself, but cannot add any new processes to the pool because #2
and #3 are already present. Micro-analyser #3 inspects the
current input symbol, finds it is "c" as it expects (or as it
hopes?) and has completed its task: it therefore signals that an
instance of a "C" phrase has been recognised starting at input
position N.

At this point (input position N+1) the bottom-up mechanism
alluded to above takes over. Each of the process #1 and #2 is
waiting for an instance of the "C" phrase starting at position N:
each now 'forks' into two processes, one of which (#1, #2) waits
for a longer instance of the phrase and the other of which (#1a,
#2a) accepts the current instance and proceeds to the next step of
analysis. Micro-analyser #1a looks for an **end** symbol in the
input, fails to find it and 'dies'. Micro-analyser #2a finds a
";" symbol followed by a "c" symbol and therefore signals once
more (input position N+3) that a "C" phrase has been found
starting at input position N. Once again micro-analysers #1 and
#2 fork into two: this time #1b finds an **end** symbol while #2b
fails to find a ";" symbol. Micro-analyser #1b signals that a "P"
phrase has been found, the input is seen to be empty and analysis
is successfully completed.

By maintaining a pool of analysis processes, not adding
multiple copies of a single process to the pool and forking only
after a phrase has been recognised, the non-deterministic analyser

can handle left recursion. Note that it could produce an error
message, just like a one-track analyser, as soon as the current
input doesn't satisfy any of the current processes and that, like
a one-track analyser but unlike the operator-precedence analyser
of chapter 17, it will never read past the position at which an
error can first be detected.

Efficient implementation

The implementation described above would be enormously inefficient
because of the way the pool of processes is organised. Each of the
micro-analyser processes would need to keep its own record of its
analysis so far, in the form of a partially-built tree. A
suspended process should be removed from the pool when it has no
remaining 'children': in the example above processes #1 and #2 are
suspended at the end of analysis of the "P" phrase yet there are
no processes in the pool which can re-awaken them. Thus the pool
of processes would appear to need garbage-collection (which is
expensive!) to remove dead processes and the trees which they have
partially constructed.

A true LR analyser, therefore, maintains efficiency by forcing
determinism each time an instance of a phrase is recognised and a
tree node is built: it always decides whether to recognise a
phrase (whether to reduce) or not and it always decides which
phrase to recognise. If this can be done consistently then all the
current micro-analysis processes will agree that the single record
of analysis which is kept in the stack is the correct one. When a
phrase is recognised at a particular position all suspended
processes that are waiting for an instance of a phrase which
starts at a later position can be abandoned, since that instance
can now never be recognised. In such an analyser garbage-
collection is never required.

The problem of constructing such an analyser is to ensure that
it can decide, whenever an instance of a phrase is recognised,
whether to accept that instance and to abandon all other paths of
analysis or to ignore that instance and to continue with the other
paths. LR analysers choose whether to 'shift' or to 'reduce', and
choose which reduction to perform when there is a choice, by
looking at the current input symbols.

If the properties of the grammar are such that there can only
ever be one active micro-analyser when any phrase is recognised,
as is the case with the grammar in figure 18.1, then the analyser
is LR(0) because it need never look at the current input symbol to
decide whether to reduce or not. In most cases, however, it will
be necessary sometimes to inspect at most k input symbols in order
to decide and the analyser is then LR(k): in practice only LR(1)
is a useful mechanism. Often the properties of the grammar are
such that is impossible to produce a LR(1) analyser, either
because in some situations it could not decide whether to reduce

or not (a <u>shift-reduce</u> conflict) or because it could not decide which of several possible reductions to perform (a <u>reduce-reduce</u> conflict). If an LR(1) analyser can be constructed from the grammar using the mechanism which is set out below, then the grammar is LR(1).

For further efficiency, LR analysers don't represent the pool of analysers as a complicated data structure, but identify a number of <u>states</u> of analysis. Each state encodes the information that a particular set of micro-analysers is active, shows the particular stage which each has reached and also identifies those micro-analysers in the pool that have reached a position at which they are about to become suspended. By stacking each state on the stack which holds the results of analysis so far, the analyser represents the position in the input at which a process was invoked and also handles the suspension of processes. By removing states from the stack when a reduction is performed (see figure 18.3) it eliminates suspended processes which can never be re-awakened.

The number of <u>accessible states</u> of the pool of processes – the number of combinations of micro-analysers that can actually occur, taking account of the properties of the grammar – may be large but is very much smaller than the number of combinations of possible separate micro-analyser processes. In the case of an LR(0) analyser the number of accessible states is large enough but in an LR(1) analyser each micro-analysis process is further distinguished by the symbol which it expects to find after an instance of its phrase and the number of accessible states can be enormous. The SLR(1) and LALR(1) mechanisms, given a suitable grammar, can use the same number of states as an LR(0) parser yet use the LR(1) information to resolve shift-reduce and reduce-reduce conflicts.

Building an SLR(1) Analyser

The first stage in the construction of any LR analyser is to compute the <u>accessible states</u> of the analyser. I show first how to compute states and produce a table which defines an LR(0) analyser, like that illustrated in figure 18.2, and then how an

```
0. S -> P empty
1. P -> begin D ; C end
2. D -> D ; d
3. D -> d
4. C -> I
5. C -> I ; C
6. I -> c
7. I -> P
```

Figure 18.7 An SLR(1) grammar

enhancement to the mechanism can resolve some <u>shift-reduce</u>
conflicts, producing a so-called SLR(1) (Simple LR) analyser. The
example grammar is shown in figure 18.7 - it is a slightly more
complicated grammar than that in figure 18.1, in that the "P"
symbol can occur as part of a "C" phrase. Also the "C" symbol is
right-recursive rather than left-recursive, introducing a shift-
reduce conflict into the LR(0) table whose resolution is discussed
below.

_____

Closure

If a state contains an item (a partial parsing) which is
positioned immediately before a non-terminal symbol in
its production, include an item <i,0> for each of the
productions 'i' which define that non-terminal. Repeat
until there are no more items which can be added to the
state.

Successor states

If a state contains items (partial parsings) which are
positioned immediately before a particular symbol in
their productions, make a new state which contains only
those items positioned immediately after that symbol.
Compute the closure of that state and include it in the
accessible states of the analyser.

Figure 18.8 LR(0) closure and successor algorithms

_____

```
    Simple state          Closure
1.  {<0,0>}               {<0,0> <1,0>}
2.  {<0,1>}               {<0,1>}                  /* 1 + P */
3.  {<1,1>}               {<1,1> <2,0> <3,0>}      /* 1,6,13 + begin */
4.  {<1,2> <2,1>}         {<1,2> <2,1>}            /* 3 + D */
5.  {<3,1>}               {<3,1>}                  /* 3 + d */
6.  {<1,3> <2,2>}         {<1,3> <2,2> <4,0>
                            <5,0> <6,0> <7,0>
                            <1,0>}                 /* 4 + ; */
7.  {<1,4>}               {<1,4>}                  /* 6 + C */
8.  {<2,3>}               {<2,3>}                  /* 6 + d */
9.  {<4,1> <5,1>}         {<4,1> <5,1>}            /* 6,13 + I */
10. {<6,1>}               {<6,1>}                  /* 6,13 + c */
11. {<7,1>}               {<7,1>}                  /* 6,13 + P */
12. {<1,5>}               {<1,5>}                  /* 7 + end */
13. {<5,2>}               {<5,2> <4,0> <5,0>
                            <6,0> <7,0> <1,0>}     /* 9 + ; */
14. {<5,3>}               {<5,3>}                  /* 13 + C */
```

Figure 18.9 LR(0) accessible states of figure 18.7

Each state of the analyser represents a collection of micro-
analyser positions or partial parsings. Each partial parsing,
called an <u>item</u> in the LR literature[1], defines a position in a
production and corresponds to an assertion that the analysis so
far is consistent with the use of that production up to that
position. Following Aho (Aho and Ullman,1978) I describe an item
either by displaying the production with a dot indicating the
position which has been reached or by a pair of numbers which
define the production and the number of symbols which have been
recognised within that production. Thus an LR(0) item can be shown
as

> either   **<begin** D <u>.</u> ; C **end>**
> or   <1,2>

The initial state of the analyser contains only the item

> <<u>.</u> P **empty>**   or   <0,0>

and its final state contains only the item

> <P <u>.</u> **empty>**   or   <0,1>

A <u>state</u> of the analyser is a collection of items. The
<u>accessible</u> <u>states</u> of the analyser are calculated starting from the
initial state. The <u>closure</u> of each state is computed, and new
(successor) accessible states are added by computing the state
which can be reached by the recognition of a particular input
symbol or a particular phrase. The closure of a state corresponds
to the suspension of micro-analysers and the adding of new
processes to the pool.

Closure and successor algorithms which calculate the accessible
states of an LR(0) analyser are shown in figure 18.8. An
efficient closure algorithm could easily be constructed but for
the examples in this chapter the closures will be simple enough to
compute by hand. Figure 18.9 shows the accessible states which are
produced by applying the closure and successor algorithms of
figure 18.8 to the grammar of figure 18.7.

The initial state of the grammar is {<0,0>} and the closure of
that state is {<0,0> <1,0>}, since the first symbol in production
number 0 is "P" which is defined in production number 1. The
initial state has two successors: state 2 (the final state) when a
"P" phrase has been recognised and state 3 when a **begin** symbol is
read. State 3 can also be reached when a **begin** symbol is
encountered in state 6 or state 13. Each state in figure 18.9 is

---

[1] An LR 'item' should not be confused with a 'lexical item'. I
use the phrase 'input symbol' in this chapter, rather than
'lexical item', in order to reduce confusion.

marked to show which state or states it succeeds.

The states show very clearly the non-deterministic nature of LR
parsing, at least up to the point at which a reduction is
performed. State 6 is reached when a ";" symbol is read after a
declaration: the situation which would show a context clash in a
top-down analyser based on this grammar. From state 6 the analyser
reaches state 8 if a "d" symbol is read, state 10 if a "c" symbol
is read. Thus the analyser is in effect carrying forward two
possible lines of analysis when it encounters the semicolon: in
the simple case shown the alternatives are resolved as soon as the
next input symbol is read, but in more complicated cases it may
take longer.

Having constructed the LR(0) states, the next stage is to
construct the table. The table contains a row for each state, a
column for each terminal and non-terminal symbol in the grammar.
The entries in the table are computed as shown in figure 18.10 -
this is the procedure which produced the table of figure 18.2. A
completed item specifies a micro-analyser which has reached the
end of its production, such as

$$<D ; d \underline{.}> \quad \text{or} \quad <2,3>$$

(i) If state **i** is reached by recognition of input symbol **x**
in state **j**, entry [**j,x**] must show 'S**i**'.

(ii) If state **k** is reached by recognition of a phrase
(non-terminal symbol) **Y** in state **l**, entry [**l,Y**] must
show '**k**'.

(iii) If state **m** contains a completed item **<a,b>**, where
production number **a** defines non-terminal symbol **A**,
entries [**m,n**] must show 'R**b,A**' for all terminal symbols
'**n**'.

(iv) If state **p** contains the item <0,1> then entry
[**p,empty**] must show 'H'.

Figure 18.10 Constructing the LR(0) table

(iii) If state **m** contains a completed item **<a,b>**, where
production number **a** defines non-terminal symbol **A**,
entries [**m,n**] must show 'R**b,A**' for all terminal symbols
'**n**' which may follow **A** in any sentential form.

Figure 18.11 Adding SLR(1) reduce entries

The first rule corresponds to the operation of moving a micro-analyser forward on recognition of an input symbol, the second to the 'forking' operation, the third to the recognition of a phrase and the fourth to the completion of analysis.

If the rules of figure 18.10 produce a table without conflicts - i.e. a table in which each entry shows only a single action - then the grammar is an LR(0) grammar which can be analysed by an LR(0) analyser.

More often than not the rules of figure 18.10 fail to produce an analyser because of the rule which prescribes the placing of 'R' entries. In the case of the states shown in figure 18.9, for example, state 9 exhibits a <u>shift-reduce</u> conflict: rule (i) specifies that entry [9,";"] should show 'S13' while rule (iii) specifies that it should show 'R1,C'. The conflict can be resolved by observing that in the grammar of figure 18.7, from which the states were derived, a "C" phrase can only validly be followed by an **end** symbol. Therefore the reduction corresponding to "C -> I" should only take place when the next input item is an **end** symbol and otherwise the 'I' symbol must form part of the phrase "I ; C". By using the 'follower list' whose construction was discussed in chapter 16 (figure 16.17), it is possible to build an SLR(1) analyser which decides whether to shift or to reduce by inspecting the current input symbol. The modified rule for the placement of 'R' entries in the table is shown in figure 18.11 and the table which results is shown in figure 18.12.

The SLR trick doesn't always work: the grammar in figure 18.14, for example, requires a more sophisticated placement of reduce entries. Some grammars aren't SLR(1), LALR(1) or LR(1) at all: figure 18.13 shows a grammar which is not LR(1). An analyser could not tell whether to reduce "d" to "D" or not because in both cases

	begin	;	end	d	c	empty	P	D	C	I
1.	S3						2			
2.						H				
3.				S5				4		
4.		S6								
5.		R1,D								
6.	S3			S8	S10		11		7	9
7.			S12							
8.		R3,D								
9.		S13	R1,C							
10.		R1,I	R1,I							
11.		R1,I	R1,I							
12.		R5,P	R5,P			R5,P				
13.	S3				S10		11		14	9
14.			R3,C							

Figure 18.12 SLR(1) table for the grammar of figure 18.7

the next input symbol expected is a semicolon. It is interesting
that while top-down analysers experience difficulty with left-
recursive symbols, LR analysers sometimes have difficulty with
right-recursive symbols. Top-down analysis has no advantage in
this case, though: any grammar which isn't LR(1) won't be LL(1)
either and the LR conflicts will show up as LL(1) context clashes,
as they do in the grammar shown in figure 18.13.

Constructing an LALR(1) Analyser

The SLR(1) mechanism handles a variety of simple grammars but in
practice many real grammars aren't SLR(1) because of conflicts
which that mechanism can't handle. The problem is that sometimes
the 'left context' - the state of analysis so far - provides
information about the action which should be taken on different
followers of a particular symbol. The true LR(1) mechanism uses
some contextual information but requires a much larger number of
states: for most grammars the LALR(1) (Look-Ahead LR) mechanism
can use the LR(1) contextual information to resolve conflicts yet
uses no more states than LR(0) or SLR(1).

In true LR(1) analysis each item (each micro-analyser in the
pool) is distinguished by a lookahead set of input symbols which
must follow an instance of its phrase if the instance is to be
recognised. Conflicts are resolved because a reduce ('R') entry is
only placed in the table at the positions determined by the
lookahead set of a completed item, which are usually fewer than
the positions defined by the follower symbols of the reduced
phrase. Figure 18.14 shows a grammar which isn't LR(0) or SLR(1)
because of a reduce-reduce conflict. It describes a simplified
version of the BCPL assignment statement syntax: the grammar
restricts the form of the left-hand-side expression to a subset of

---

```
P -> begin D ; C end
D -> d | d ; D
C -> c | c ; C
```

Figure 18.13 A grammar which isn't LR(1)

```
0. S -> A empty
1. A -> V := E
2. V -> i
3. V -> P!E
4. E -> @V
5. E -> P
6. E -> P!E
7. P -> i
8. P -> n
```

Figure 18.14 An LALR(1) grammar

the expressions which can appear on the right-hand-side. The first
few LR(0) states of the grammar are shown in figure 18.15.

State 4 in figure 18.15 shows a reduce-reduce conflict: the
conflict becomes clearer when the state is shown in its
alternative form

          {<V -> i .> <P -> i .>}

This state is reached when an identifier is read at the beginning
of an assignment statement. You can see if you examine the

---

1. {<0,0> <1,0> <2,0> <3,0> <7,0> <8,0> }
2. {<0,1>}   /* 1 + A */
3. {<1,1>}   /* 1 + V */
4. {<2,1> <7,1>}   /* 1 + i */
5. {<3,1>}   /* 1 + P */
6. {<8,1>}   /* 1 + n */
   ....

Figure 18.15 LR(0) states of grammar from figure 18.14

---

1. {<1,0,[empty]> <2,0,[:=]> <3,0,[:=]>
   <7,0,[!]> <8,0,[!]>}
2. {<0,1,[empty]>}   /* 1 + A */
3. {<1,1,[empty]>}   /* 1 + V */
4. {<2,1,[:=]> <7,1,[!]>}   /* 1 + i */
5. {<3,1,[:=]>}   /* 1 + P */
6. {<8,1,[!]>}   /* 1 + n */
7. {<1,2,[empty]> <4,0,[empty]>
   <5,0,[empty]> <6,0,[empty]>
   <7,0,[empty,!]> <8,0,[empty,!]>}   /* 3 + := */
8. {<3,2,[:=]> <4,0,[:=]> <5,0,[:=]>
   <6,0,[:=]> <7,0,[:=,!]>
   <8,0,[:=,!]>}   /* 5 + ! */
9. {<1,3,[empty]>}   /* 7 + E */
10. {<4,1,[empty]> <2,0,[empty]>
    <3,0,[empty> <4,0,[empty]>
    <5,0,[empty]> <6,0,[empty]>
    <7,0,[empty,!]> <8,0,[empty,!]>}   /* 7 + @ */
11. {<5,1,[empty]> <6,1,[empty]>}   /* 7 + P */
12. {<7,1,[empty,!]>}   /* 7 + i */
13. {<8,1,[empty,!]>}   /* 7 + n */
14. {<3,3,[:=]>}   /* 8 + E */
15. {<4,1,[:=]> <2,0,[:=]> <3,0,[:=]>
    <4,0,[:=]> <5,0,[:=]> <6,0,[:=]>
    <7,0,[:=,!]> <8,0,[:=,!]>}   /* 8 + @ */
    ....

Figure 18.16 LR(1) states of grammar from figure 18.14

grammar that the reduction to "V" should be made when the next
symbol is ":=", to "P" when the next symbol is "!". The SLR(1)
mechanism won't resolve this conflict because V can be followed
either by ":=" or by 'empty', while P can be followed by either
":=", "!" or 'empty' in some sentential form. Other SLR(1)
conflicts also exist, not shown in figure 18.15 for reasons of
space.

The inference that different reductions ought to be made in
different contexts is the basis of LR(1) analysis. Figure 18.16
shows some of the LR(1) accessible states of the grammar from
figure 18.14. In this example the lookahead set is shown in
square brackets. These states were computed using the closure
algorithm shown in figure 18.17 – the successor algorithm is
identical to that in figure 18.8. The LR(1) rule for placing
reduce entries uses the lookahead set: the rule is shown in figure
18.18. Thus the conflict in state 4 from figure 18.15 is resolved
by the use of lookahead sets: state 4 of figure 18.16 shows that
if the input symbol is ":=" reduce to "V", if it is "!" reduce to
"P".

The LR(1) closure algorithm introduces an enormous number of
new states: in figure 18.16, for example, states 10 and 15 are
identical except for the lookahead sets of the items. The LALR(1)
mechanism uses the LR(1) lookahead sets to distinguish between
reductions in a single state, but merges all states which are
identical except for the lookahead sets of the items which they

---

Closure
  If a state contains an item
      <A -> **alpha** . B **gamma**, ls>
  with lookahead set **ls**, include an item
      <B -> . **beta**, nls>
  for each production which defines symbol B. If the
  string **gamma** is empty, the lookahead set **nls** of the new
  item is **ls**; otherwise the lookahead set **nls** contains the
  terminal symbols in the FIRST* list of **gamma**. Items in a
  state with identical analysis positions but different
  lookahead sets must be merged into a single item which
  has the union of the lookahead sets of all the items.

Figure 18.17 LR(1) closure algorithm

(iii) If a state contains a completed item <a,b,ls> where
      production number **a** defines symbol **A**, entries [m,n] must
      show 'Rb,A' for all symbols n in the lookahead set **ls**.

Figure 18.18 Placing LR(1) 'reduce' entries

contain. Thus it uses the same number of states as an LR(0) or
SLR(1) analyser but can resolve reduce-reduce conflicts with the
power of an LR(1) analyser. It is possible to construct
pathological grammars which are LR(1) but not LALR(1), in which
reduce-reduce conflicts are introduced because of merges like the
following

                  merge: {<A -> .xyz, [;]> <B -> .abc, [!]>}
                  and: {<A -> .abc, [!]> <B -> .xyz, [;]>}

but such situations are rare in real life grammars. In effect the
LALR(1) mechanism merges states, which correspond to the search
for a phrase in widely differing contexts, into a single state.

Encoding the state table

Even though an LALR(1) table is smaller than an LR(1) table it can
still be uncomfortably large: some hundreds of states and some
tens of input symbols. There are all sorts of ways in which the
space requirement can be reduced. The table is extremely sparse
and the most obvious encoding is to represent each row as a list
of <symbol,action> pairs or each column as a list of
<state,action> pairs. The table information can be represented as
a kind of program, in which the 'shift' entries are listed state-
by-state and the 'reduce' entries symbol-by-symbol.

    Just as the construction of the table is best left to a
parser-generator, so also it is best to leave the compaction of
the tables to the same program. Parser-generator writers need to
study the various compaction algorithms: the rest of us must trust
to their mercy.

It doesn't always work!

It should be emphasised that published programming language
grammars are not always LR(1). That of PASCAL is LL(1) and
therefore LR(1) but that of ALGOL 68 is neither LL(1) nor LR(1)
(Hunter et al.,1977). Hand-modification of the grammar may
therefore still be required to resolve shift-reduce and reduce-
reduce conflicts: the grammar of figure 18.13 shows a simple
example. Just as in the case of one-track analysis the removal of
LR conflicts requires insight into the aims of the language
designers: it should be obvious, for example, that the right
recursion in the grammar of figure 18.13 is used merely as a
device to describe lists of declarations and statements and that
it could therefore be replaced by left recursion without danger,
producing the LR(0) grammar shown in figure 18.7.

    An LR(1), LALR(1), SLR(1) or LR(0) grammar is unambiguous. The
proof is straightforward and depends on the facts that the
analyser never backtracks and always chooses a single reduction on
the basis of the current input symbol and the contents of the

table. therefore if the table can be built without conflicts, the grammar is unambiguous. The converse is not always true: if the table contains conflicts it may be that the grammar is ambiguous or it may be, as is the case with the grammar in figure 18.13, that the LR(1) mechanism can't handle this particular grammar even though it is actually unambiguous.

Error Detection and Tree-building Actions

The LR analyser, like the one-track analysers of chapter 16 but unlike the operator-precedence analysers of chapter 17, never reads past the position at which a syntax error might first be detected[1]. If a symbol doesn't match with any of the current paths of analysis then an error can immediately be signalled. The message produced will depend on the analyser's state: the shift and reduce entries in the current row of the table will show the symbols which were 'expected' and the compiler-writer can use information about the way in which this state can be reached to deduce the context and to construct a relevant error message. Errors in state 3 of the analyser shown in figure 18.12, for example, might state "declaration expected after begin"; errors in state 6 might state "declaration or statement expected after semicolon".

A measure of automatic error recovery is possible, using the stacked states and the table in much the same way as Irons' top-down error recovery mechanism (Irons,1961), (Gries,1971). The shift and reduce entries can be examined to find whether the current input symbol would be acceptable in one of the states which can be reached from the current one - i.e. whether a symbol appears to be missing - or whether the analysis could continue if the current symbol were ignored - i.e. whether an extra symbol appears to have been inserted in an otherwise valid program. Just as with automatic error recovery in top-down analysis, the mechanism has its drawbacks and it would tend to multiply the incidence of secondary error reports in certain situations.

Each reduction action indicated in the table corresponds to the removal of states and symbols (both input symbols and non-terminals) from the stack and their replacement by a single non-terminal symbol. It is clear that instead of non-terminal symbols the stack could contain pointers to nodes of the tree and that each reduction could build a node containing those symbols and pointers which it removes from the stack. The node need not contain all the symbols which are unstacked: the action taken on any reduction can be designed to build an abbreviated representation of the parse tree, rather than the full derivation tree which would be built if every reduction were to produce a

---

1 Which is the point at which a left derivation can't be constructed to explain the current input symbol.

tree node. In particular the reductions which replace one non-terminal by another - e.g. "C -> I" in the grammar of figure 18.14 - need do nothing other than change the analyser's state[1].

If each reduction is specified as an action-procedure, indexed by an entry in the table, it is clear that arbitrary actions can be included in the analyser by adding productions to the grammar which cause dummy reductions and which each have an attached action. Thus, for example, the productions

```
<block> -> begin X C end
X     -> D
D     -> <declaration> ; | D <declaration> ;
```

enable an action to be attached to the reduction "X -> D", which is performed after the last declaration in a block has been processed. Care is required when inserting dummy productions: the productions

```
<block> -> begin X ; C end
X     -> D
D     -> <declaration> | D ; <declaration>
```

include a shift-reduce conflict and aren't LR(1).

Sophisticated error detection via the inclusion of extra alternatives, as illustrated for one-track analysis in figure 16.12, is also possible for LR(1) analysers. The grammar of figure 16.12 is neither LL(1) nor LR(1): it is only possible to use it as the basis of a recursive-descent analyser if you are very careful about the order in which procedures are called. Since an LR(1) analyser effectively pursues several lines of analysis in parallel this simple trick isn't possible and a more explicit grammar is required, like that in figure 18.19, which distinguishes between the first statement and subsequent statements in a block. The reduction "X -> D" can trigger an action which prints a special error message, pointing out that a declaration has been found following the first statement in a block.

---

1 LR analysers can be made more efficient in operation if chains of such reductions are collapsed into a single state-change. Thus in simple arithmetic expression grammars like those discussed in chapter 17, reductions such as
  P -> <identifier>, F -> P, T -> F, E -> T
might be collapsed into a single state-change performed when an <identifier> is encountered followed by a '+' or a '-' sign.

Error Recovery

The error recovery mechanism described in chapter 16 passes an 'errorpoint' label to each of the procedures in a recursive-descent analyser. Control should be transferred to this label when a syntax error is detected: the code there will attempt error recovery. Essentially the same mechanism can be used for error recovery in an LR analyser, to be invoked when more general and automatic error recovery mechanisms have failed. It involves the placing of "marks" in the stack at positions where error recovery should be attempted. When error recovery is required the stack is stripped down to the nearest mark and an action procedure, indicated by the mark, is invoked.

The marks on the stack correspond very closely to the errorpoint labels in a recursive-descent analyser. A mark would be inserted by a micro-analyser (a production) whose task is to recognise some especially significant structure in a program, such as a list of statements or a list of declarations, and the action procedure which performs error recovery would typically discard input until a symbol is encountered which allows analysis of that structure to continue.

What are the True Advantages of LR(1) Analysis?

The grammar of figure 18.14 is LALR(1), but not LL(1). The grammar of figure 18.20 is both LL(1) and LR(0). It is, of course, a major advantage of the LR technique that it can more often be used to transform the reference grammar of a language into an efficient working syntax analyser, or that it can do so with the minimum of alteration to the grammar, but is worthwhile to question the wisdom of always doing so.

Not all grammatical modifications are forced upon the compiler-writer by the deficiencies of an analysis mechanism. Some alterations are desirable because they help the compiler to produce clear and meaningful error reports. The grammar of figure 18.21 might be more suitable to form the basis of a syntax analyser, by this criterion, than either the grammar of figure 18.14 or that of 18.20. This grammar is both LL(1) and LR(0), but that's a minor point: what is important is that it describes a

---

```
S -> E := E | goto E | if E then E else S | begin B
B -> D ; B | C
D -> let i = E | let i be S
C -> S V
V -> ; W | end
W -> C | X V
X -> D
```

Figure 18.19 Unnecessary alternatives to enhance error detection

different language so that the syntax analyser will accept input, like that shown in figure 18.22, which is prohibited by the earlier grammars. The translation phase of a compiler is quite capable of detecting and reporting upon the errors which are contained in the example statement: a number cannot have an address, an address expression cannot form the left-hand-side of an assignment statement. It is capable also of picking up an error which is not prohibited by the grammars of either figure 18.14 or 18.20: the expression '6!3' isn't particularly meaningful[1]. Use of the more permissive grammar in figure 18.21 allows the compiler-writer to defer error detection until the stage of compilation at which error reporting can be clearest. This mechanism also has the pragmatic advantage that it reduces the incidence of error recovery, and therefore the incidence of secondary error reports, in the syntax analysis phase of compilation.

Some general lessons can be drawn from the example grammar of figure 18.21. First, no automatic error recovery procedure can do as much, given a grammar which prohibits input like that in figure 18.22, as a translation phase can do given the output from a syntax analyser which permits this kind of input. Second, if the input doesn't make any sense at all to the analyser then error recovery is difficult. Third, the use of syntactic constraints to outlaw certain constructions in particular contexts is useful in that it transmits information about language restrictions to the human user, but should not necessarily be copied slavishly into the design of a compiler which has to process programs that will disobey the rules of the language in various ways. Many programs will be syntactically invalid because they contain valid phrases in an invalid context: as far as possible the compiler should be designed to detect such errors in the translation phase, which is naturally concerned with contextual questions.

In the case of BCPL it is possible to give a further example in favour of pragmatic changes to the grammar which leave syntactic checks as late as possible. The syntax of a multiple assignment statement is such that the first left-hand-side expression is associated with the first right-hand-side expression, the second left-hand-side with the second right-hand-side and so on - that is

$$a, b, c := A, B, C$$

is (almost) the same as

$$a := A; b := B; c := C$$

---

1 Actually it _is_ meaningful in BCPL: it means 'take the contents of location number 9'. However a compiler might at least query its validity.

There must, of course, be the same number of expressions on each side of the assignment symbol, but the type 2 grammar which seems to express this, shown in figure 18.23, shows the 'wrong' phrase structure, in that the first left-hand-side expression seems to be associated with the last right-hand-side.

It is provably impossible to construct a type 2 grammar which describes the 'correct' phrase structure in this case, although it would be possible to build an extremely convoluted translation procedure which used the 'wrong' structure as defined in figure 18.23. A pragmatic solution to the problem, which is easily incorporated into a one-track analyser or an LR(1) analyser, is to treat both left-hand and right-hand-sides as a list of expressions and to check (either when the tree is built or when it is translated) that the number of expressions is the same in each list. This gives the minimum requirement for error recovery in the syntax analyser and the maximum amount of information for the user who makes a simple syntactic error.

```
A -> V := E
V -> i | i!E | n!E
E -> aV | P!E
P -> i | n
```

Figure 18.20 LL(1) version of figure 18.14

```
A -> E := E
E -> P | P!E
P -> i | n
```

Figure 18.21 Alternative grammar for assignment statement

Input: a5 := 6!3

Tree: assign
              /   \
        address   subscript
           | /   \
           5   6   3

Figure 18.22 Statements which might be analysed without error

---

Formal but 'wrong':   A -> V := E | V , A , E

Pragmatic: A -> E {,E}* := E {,E}*

Figure 18.23 Syntax of a multiple-assignment statement

The SLR(1) and LALR(1) mechanisms have an advantage, then, in that they can often be applied to the published 'reference' grammar of the language. This 'advantage' is in fact a drawback if it means that the compiler-writer stops viewing the syntax analyser as a device which helps users to find errors in their programs. Many of the conflicts which make a grammar not suitable for one-track analysis are introduced in an attempt to specify contextual requirements in the same breath as the requirements of punctuation. A syntax analyser should be more permissive than the reference grammar: the compiler as a whole performs the task of 'parsing' the program and there is no operational reason why quite a lot of the task should not be given over to the translation phase.

Devising the grammar which forms the basis of such a permissive analyser requires more than mechanical transformation of the reference grammar: it requires sensitivity to user's requirements and experience of the behaviour of an analyser in the face of syntactically invalid programs. Producing a syntax analyser with a satisfactory behaviour is one of the compiler-writer's main tasks and beside it the task of coding the algorithm – transcribing the grammar into an analyser – is relatively trivial. The advantages of automatic syntax-analyser generation, which are enhanced by the use of LR techniques, are real but should be seen as an aid to compiler-writing rather than as a final solution to our problems. It is the compiler-writer's care and insight which make the difference between a compiler which can handle only 'correct' programs and one which operates satisfactorily in the 'real world'.

Summary

LR(1) analysis, and the efficient implementations of it known as SLR(1) and LALR(1) analysis, provides a means by which a syntax analyser may be automatically produced from a formal specification of the grammar of a language. The method requires less hand-modification of the grammar than one-track analysis and is therefore more suitable to form the basis of an automatic parser-generator. The error-handling and tree-building procedures of the analyser must still be prepared 'by hand', however, and the grammar must be augmented with actions in a way which doesn't impede the analysis mechanism.

Error detection and error reporting in an LR(1) analyser are as effective as in a one-track analyser. This, together with the labour-saving advantages of automatic generation of the analyser, make it an attractive choice for the compiler-writer. The grammar on which a syntax analyser is based, however, should specify a 'reasonable' response to simple syntax errors. The automatic generation of an analyser from the reference grammar which defines a programming language may not produce an acceptable analyser and hand-modification may therefore still be necessary.

Section V
Interpreting and
Debugging

Compilers were invented at a time when machines were enormously costly and human effort seemed relatively cheap: almost anything which seemed to provide effective utilisation of the expensive machine was welcomed. In particular the time during which a program is developed was seen as a short prelude to a relatively much longer lifetime during which the program would run on a computer and provide useful services to the user community. The ideal means of programming was that which led to the most efficient object programs: programming in assembly codes and machine codes was justified by pointing to the close control over the allocation of instructions and data space within the object program which they provide.

Programming in machine code or assembly code is difficult, though, and the programs which are produced tend not to work as they should. Programming in 'high-level' languages which are processed through compilers was at first an attempt to make 'coding' easier and less error-prone, to provide programs which had fewer bugs and therefore a longer useful life. Some inefficiency in the object program could be tolerated because of its relative freedom from bugs but for large important system programs, such as operating systems and compilers themselves, careful coding in assembly code or machine code was at first still seen as necessary in order to produce an efficient program.

As computers became cheaper and more widely available users began to notice that the cost of developing a program, which includes both human and computer effort, seemed to depend only on the length of the program and not on the language in which it is written. A thousand-line assembly code program takes ten times as long to develop - to bring to the stage at which its useful life begins - as does a one-hundred line program, written in a high-level language such as FORTRAN to perform the same task. For many programs calculation shows that the costs of development exceeds the total cost of the machine resources consumed by the program throughout its useful life and the excess costs of assembly code programming far outweigh the execution advantages of the assembly code program. Programming in high-level languages was increasingly seen as cost-effective and 'coding' began to be called 'programming'.

Users in general still remain dedicated to execution efficiency. A compiler is seen as the only practical language processing system and the best compiler is the one which produces the fastest object programs[1]. Error-checking code and run-time

---

1 The raw efficiency of the object code can be the means by which users choose between languages: as section III suggests, the too prevalent mis-implementation of recursive programming languages may be a major reason for the continuing popularity of FORTRAN.

debuggers are seen as expensive frills, helpful only to the novice, which degrade execution efficiency. Interpretation is not considered to be a practical tool because of the enormous gap in execution speed between compiled and interpreted programs.

It should be obvious from the tone of these paragraphs that I take an opposite view. I believe that computers exist to serve humans and to save human time. I believe that extra computer effort expended during the development and execution of a program is worthwhile if it saves precious human time and effort. I believe furthermore that this strategy is cost-effective: for many years it has been cheaper for most users to buy a new machine than to recruit and pay a couple of extra programmers. The advent of cheap microprocessors means that in the future the cost of computer power will become relatively less and less important, while savings in costly human effort will become more important. I would argue, as I do in chapter 19, that in many cases the use of interpretation can save even on the amount of <u>computer</u> time required to develop a program: however the chapters in this section concentrate on the advantages which interpretation and run-time debugging bring to the user.

Chapter 19 deals with mechanisms of interpretation and also discusses some of the problems of designing an interactive programming language, with particular reference to LISP. It discusses mechanisms by which interpretation and compilation together can combine ease of program development and efficient execution. Chapter 20 deals mainly with the problems of run-time debugging in a compiled implementation of a programming language - providing error reports, trace information, panic dumps and so on. It also justifies the assertion that the best run-time debugger for a compiled program is based on an interpreter.

Compilation has its advantages: interactive or on-line programming is a mixed blessing for the computer user. Weizenbaum (Weizenbaum,1977) has colourfully characterised the kind of programming behaviour which is encouraged by the use of an interpreter in an interactive environment - people often become so involved with the use of their computer terminal that they rarely leave it except for meals and sleep! One real advantage of off-line programming is that it encourages reflection: when the program is running the user is away from the computer and has a chance to think about other things, including perhaps the program's design. When the results of an off-line computer run are returned the user can often diagnose and correct several bugs at once while the interactive user tends to fix the bugs one at a time. Off-line users seem more ready to redesign and reconstruct their programs in order to overcome difficult problems while on-line users seem tempted to patch them over - in slang to 'hack' their way round a problem.

It is likely that in the future the provision of better means
of interacting with computers and better means of altering a
program, such as editors which are more user-oriented and more
language-specific, may help to make interactive programming more
effective. Even without such advances, though, the balance of
advantages is already with interactive programming. Programs can
be developed much faster when you are on-line to a computer,
particularly if you can resist the temptation to type something on
the terminal each time the computer invites it!

19 Interpreters and Interpretation

An interpreter is simply a device which takes some representation
of a program and carries out the operations which the program
specifies - i.e. it mimics or simulates the operations which a
machine would carry out if it were directly capable of processing
programs written in that language. A compiler takes a similar
representation of a program and produces instructions which, when
processed by a machine, will carry out the operations which the
program specifies. The difference between an interpreter and a
machine under this definition is not very great: the microprogram
of a computer is an interpreter which reads a machine code program
and imitates the behaviour that a 'real' machine would express
given that program.

   It's possible to imagine an interpreter which would read a
program written on paper or even scribbled on an envelope and
would interpret it directly. Present-day interpreters, though,
work with a representation of a program held in the store of a
computer: as a sequence of characters, a sequence of items or as a
parse tree. The parse tree is the most convenient representation
because on the one hand the interpreter doesn't have to parse a
statement in order to execute it and on the other hand a readable
version of the source program can be re-created from the tree
which is being interpreted, which makes run-time error reporting
and debugging of the source program relatively simple.

   Since the microprogram of a computer is an interpreter, it is
simple to understand the operation of hybrid systems in which a
compiler translates a program into some 'intermediate' pseudo-
machine code which is then processed by an interpreter. Although
the program will run more slowly than one which was compiled into
'real' machine code, the pseudo-machine code can be designed so
that object programs are extremely compact. Because the program
is already linearised, interpretation from the pseudo-machine code
will be faster than interpretation from a tree. Modern 'soft
machines' and 'emulators' allow the user to define the
microprogram which will interpret the object program, thus

allowing the design of 'real' object machine codes which are both
compact and efficient in execution.

Interpreting the parse tree

In this chapter I discuss the implementation and the advantages of
interpreters which work from a parse tree and a symbol table
similar to those which are used by the translation phase of a
compiler.   Such an interpreter is very like a tree-walking
translator but, instead of generating instructions which will have
a particular effect when the program runs, an interpreter carries
out actions which have that effect directly and immediately.   If
the program which is being interpreted is to be debugged, however,
an interpreter will have to act rather differently from a
recursive   tree-walker: I   discuss   the   differences between
'imitative' and 'linearising' interpreters below.

   The main advantage of working from the parse tree and a symbol
table, rather than from a linear pseudo-machine code program, is
that the tree is a direct and understandable representation of the
source program.   A 'pretty-printer' program can be written which
will produce a readable version of the source program given the
parse tree and the symbol table. The program which it produces
will be identical to the original except for the use of newlines,
tabs and spaces in the layout of the source program on the page.
(A good pretty-printer will produce a representation of the
program which is tidier and more readable than the original -
hence the epithet 'pretty'.) Since both the user and the
interpreter are working on essentially the same representation of
the source program, the program can be altered at any stage to add
new statements, to add new declarations, to add new procedures, to
rewrite procedures and so on. This makes run-time debugging
marvellously easy and often means that a program can be developed
in stages by a process of refinement which can be guided by
experience of executing the unrefined program.

   The major language which is used in this way is LISP. Modern
implementations   of   LISP,   such   as INTERLISP, have extensive
facilities with which a user can monitor a running program, take
action on run-time errors, edit a (halted) program in mid-
execution, and so on. The design of the LISP language is
interesting: many of the ways in which it differs from more
conventional languages can be justified by the demands of
interactive conversational program development. I discuss some of
the difficulties of LISP implementation below and touch on the
issues of the design of interactive languages.

The costs of interpretation

Every programmer knows that run-time interpretation takes longer
than the execution of compiled code for the same program. The
efficiency gap can be huge and even the best LISP interpreters

take at least twenty times as long to interpret a program as it would take to execute a compiled version of the same program. For many interpreters and for some programs the gap is larger still, which would seem to rule out interpretation as a useful mechanism for all but the super-rich.

Interpretation or execution of a program are only part of the story, though, because every program must be developed and debugged. When a programmer finds a bug in a compiled program it is normally necessary to abandon the current execution of the program, to edit and recompile at least one section of the source program, to reload all the sections into a complete object program and finally to execute the new program, at least up to the point at which the bug was discovered. This process can be very costly, not least because the process of loading a program will typically take almost as long as it would to compile it. If the first alteration to the program doesn't fix the bug then the whole cycle must be repeated until you get it right (run-time debuggers like those discussed in chapter 20 can help you to diagnose bugs more accurately, but we all make mistakes sometimes!). Often the bug only shows up when the program has been running for some time, which makes it very expensive to test whether or not a particular 'fix' has properly eradicated a bug.

Run-time debugging using an interpreter is much more straightforward. The program runs (is interpreted) up to the point at which a bug appears. The bug can then be fixed and the program can continue to run: there is certainly no need to reload the program and usually no need to restart it. All the run-time debugging facilities discussed in chapter 20, which enable you to inspect the state of the program, run procedures in isolation and so on, are simple to provide in an interpreter - indeed it is difficult not to provide them.

The actual cost of finding and fixing several bugs in a program may actually be less when using an interpreter than when using a compiler because the interpreter avoids all those expensive recompilations, reloads and restarts. When developing a program as large and complex as a compiler, for example, it is difficult to fit in more than three or four reloads and restarts in an hour's session at an interactive terminal connected to a medium-sized machine. During much of the time the user is merely waiting for the latest compilation or program load to finish: using the same amount of machine time to interpret the program can often be more effective and certainly the user's hour can be better spent than in staring at a computer terminal waiting for something to happen!

In an environment where program design is constantly changing, where programmers are experimenting with the design of programs or where people are simply learning to program, an interpreter certainly saves human time and effort because it permits more effective interaction with the object program than is possible

when the program is compiled. A language implementation which
allows a program to contain both compiled and interpreted modules
can give some of the advantages of both approaches. Debugging will
be easier than with a fully-compiled interpretation, particularly
if it is possible to replace compiled modules with interpreted
ones when bugs are discovered. The execution efficiency of the
program will increase as more and more of the modules are debugged
and compiled, eventually to rival that of a fully-compiled
program.

Imitative Interpretation

Figure 19.1 shows some fragments of an interpreter which mimics
the operations carried out by the statements of a source program
by directly executing those operations itself. The procedures
shown imitate the operation of a program without block structure
or declarations. Each entry in the symbol table represents a run-
time object directly: in the case of a variable it contains a
value, in the case of a procedure it contains a pointer to the
node of the parse tree which represents the body of the procedure.
If arguments to procedure calls and declaration of parameters are
to be included then some explicit representation of the current
environment is required, for which see the discussion of 'virtual
machine' interpreters below.

As Reynolds points out (Reynolds,1972), this simple imitative
mechanism has two major disadvantages. First, when presented with
a program which loops without producing any output or changes in
the store, such as the program

while true do a := a

the interpreter itself also loops without producing any output or
changes in the store. If it is forcibly interrupted then there is
no data structure, other than the data frame stack of the
interpreter itself, which says what was going on and why.
Therefore in order to debug the program which is being interpreted
it is necessary to use a run-time debugger on the interpreter
itself!

The second disadvantage is that the imitative interpreter can
only provide facilities which are available in the language in
which the interpreter itself is written. It is impossible to write
an imitative interpreter for SIMULA 67 in ALGOL 68 or BCPL, for
example, because neither ALGOL 68 nor BCPL has anything equivalent
to the SIMULA **class** mechanism. You couldn't write an imitative
ALGOL 68 interpreter in SIMULA 67 because SIMULA doesn't allow a
procedure to return an array as its result, and so on.

Imitative interpretation doesn't allow flexible debugging,
then, and usually only allows interpretation of a language very
like that in which the interpreter is written. An imitative

interpreter can still be useful as part of a run-time debugging
package which operates with compiled programs. As chapter 20
shows, such a package should allow the user to inspect memory
locations, evaluate simple expressions, call procedures in the
program being debugged and so on. An imitative interpreter is easy
to write, can be compact and, provided that the range of

```
let InterpretStat(nodep) be
  { ....
    switchon nodep.type into
     { case IfStat:
         if InterpretExpr(nodep.first) then
           InterpretStat(nodep.second)
         else InterpretStat(nodep.third)
         endcase

       case WhileStat:
         while InterpretExpr(nodep.first) do
           InterpretStat(nodep.second)
         endcase

       case ProcCall:
         InterpretStat(nodep.descriptor.body)
         endcase

       ......
     }
  }


let InterpretExpr(nodep) = valof
  { ....
    switchon nodep.type into
     { case PlusNode:
         resultis InterpretExpr(nodep.first) +
                        InterpretExpr(nodep.second)
       case OrNode:
         resultis InterpretExpr(nodep.first) -> true,
                        InterpretExpr(nodep.second)

           ....

       case name:
         resultis nodep.descriptor.value

       case number:
         resultis nodep.value

           ....
     }
  }
```

Figure 19.1 An imitative interpreter

facilities which it offers is limited, can serve as a useful interface to a program during run-time debugging.

The original definition of the semantics of LISP 1.5 (McCarthy et. al.,1965) was couched in the form of an imitative interpreter. It is interesting to look at this definition for the insight which it can give into the mechanics of interpretation and of imitative interpreters in particular.

Linearising or Virtual-machine Interpreters

Section III describes sequences of machine instructions which implement recursive procedure call and return, using an object machine which doesn't have recursive instructions. The activity of procedure call and return in a compiled program is normally carried out by a sequence of discrete instructions which operate on a data structure - the stack of data frames - to produce state changes. Only part of the program's state is represented by the contents of registers and a position in a sequence of instructions: most of its state is represented by the contents of data frames and, in particular, by pointers from one data frame to another and from data frames to positions in the sequence of instructions. Even the special 'stack-handling' instructions such as PUSH or POP don't implement recursion directly and are useful merely because they carry out a stack-handling operation which would otherwise require a short sequence of separate instructions.

An interpreter can also represent the state of the program as a data structure. This allows interpretation of programs which call upon facilities not directly provided in the interpreter's language itself. Furthermore the use of data structures to represent the state of the program allows run-time debugging: if the program is forcibly interrupted the contents of the data structure can be investigated to find out exactly what is going on. If the interpreter 'linearises' the program as it goes along, breaking down the operation of complicated constructs in the program (**if, while** or procedure call statements, for example) into a sequence of simple steps, then interruption of a program can give information about what was going on and why.

The most usual form of an interpreter, therefore, is a program which maintains a representation of the Activation Record Structure very like that which would be maintained by a compiled version of the same program. In effect both compiled and interpreted program are simulating the operation of a 'virtual machine' which is capable of executing the operations of the language: an ALGOL 68 machine, a SIMULA 67 machine, a PASCAL machine and so on. Ideas about such machines can be traced back to Landin's SECDM machine (Landin,1965) and are described in (Reynolds,1972). I describe the mechanism in terms which I believe emphasise its essential characteristics.

Linearising the program

Figure 19.2 shows how the interpreter carries out a sequence of
simple operations, during each of which it either breaks down a
complicated operation into a sequence of simpler operations or

---

```
while control stack isn't empty do
 { let nodep = popC()

   switchon nodep.type into
    { case IfStat:
        /* push the substatements on the stack, then
         * evaluate the test expression
         */
        pushC(newnode(IfStatA, nodep.second, nodep.third))
        pushC(nodep.first)
        endcase

      case IfStatA:
        /* after the test, select one of the sub-statements */
        if popV() then pushC(nodep.first)
        else pushC(nodep.second)
        endcase

        ....

      case WhileStat:
        /* remember the statement and sub-statement on the
         * stack, then evaluate the test expression
         */
        pushC(newnode(WhileStatA, nodep.second, nodep))
        pushC(nodep.first)
        endcase

      case WhileStatA:
        /* look at result - if true push the 'while'
         * statement back on the stack for iteration but
         * execute the sub-statement immediately - if false
         * just forget the whole thing
         */
        if popV() then
         { pushC(nodep.second)
           pushC(nodep.first)
         }
        endcase

        ....
    }
 }
```

Figure 19.2a Part of a linearising interpreter

carries out a primitive operation such as loading the value of a variable. The interpreter works with a 'control stack': when the stack is empty then execution of the program, or at least the current procedure, is complete. The procedures 'pushC' and 'popC' manipulate this stack. An associated 'value stack' is manipulated by 'pushV' and 'popV'.

Figure 19.2a shows how the interpretation of structured statements can be broken down into a sequence of simpler operations. In the case of a conditional (**if**) statement, for example, the interpreter pushes a node onto the control stack whose tag is 'IfStatA' and which contains the two sub-statement trees from the conditional statement node; it then pushes the

---

```
case PlusNode:
  /* evaluate both operands, then come back to PlusOp */
  pushC(newnode(PlusOp))
  pushC(nodep.second); pushC(nodep.first)
  endcase

case PlusOp:
  /* add the results */
  pushV(popV()+popV())
  endcase

....

case OrNode:
  /* evaluate the first operand, then come back to OrA */
  pushC(newnode(OrA, nodep.second))
  pushC(nodep.first)
  endcase

case OrA:
  /* if the first operand came out true report
   * true, otherwise evaluate the second
   * operand
   */
  if popV() then pushV(true)
  else pushC(nodep.first)
  endcase

....

case name: pushV(lookup(nodep, mPSD)); endcase

case number: pushV(nodep.value); endcase
```

Figure 19.2b Linearising expression evaluation

expression tree onto the control stack for immediate evaluation[1].
When the expression has been evaluated its value will be on top of
the value stack and the 'IfStatA' node will be on top of the
control stack again. At this point the interpreter examines the
value produced by interpretation of the expression and selects
either the first or the second sub-statement of the node for
further interpretation. The linearisation of a **while** statement is
similar, except that in this case when the value of the expression
turns out to be **true,** the original statement node is pushed onto
the stack for re-interpretation after the sub-statement has
completed execution.

Expressions can be linearised in a very similar way to that
shown for statements: figure 19.2b shows as an example how '+' and
'or' nodes can be treated. The difference between the two nodes
is that while both sub-nodes of the '+' node are always evaluated
(interpreted), the interpretation of an **'or'** node follows the
conditional interpretation discussed in chapter 6.

Representing the environment

The simplest form of an expression is a constant or a name. In the
case of a constant the value can be simply pushed onto the value
stack; in the case of a name it is necessary to look up the value
associated with the name in the current environment. Although it
is possible to check the type of each expression before
interpretation starts, as in a translator, the design of
interactive programming languages and the demands of flexible
debugging make it more reasonable in most cases to associate a
type with each value and to check that the type produced by
interpretation of an expression is consistent with the context in
which the expression appears. Thus each value on the value stack
would be tagged with its type and the interpretation of an **if**
statement, for example, could take account of this type as shown
in figure 19.3.

```
case IfStatA:
  { let v = popV()

    if v.atype = Boolean then
      pushC( (v.value -> nodep.first, nodep.second) )
    else Error("non-Boolean expression in if statement)
  }
  endcase
```

Figure 19.3 Run-time type checking

----

1 The interpreter would of course be more efficient if it didn't
  push a node onto the control stack in order to immediately pop
  it at the start of the next cycle!

The 'current environment' which determines the value which is associated with a particular name in the program is very similar to that which is maintained by a compiled program, as discussed in section III. It consists of a number of data structures, each of which describes information about one of the 'micro-processes' in the program, linked together to form a Process Record Structure[1]. The fundamental notion is that of a 'micro-process state descriptor' or mPSD for short. Each mPSD represents the state of a micro-process and contains, initially, a control stack which contains only (a pointer to) the procedure body, an empty value stack[2], a list of names of parameters and their corresponding values, a pointer to the mPSD which 'called' it and some pointers to other mPSDs which make up its enclosing environment.

The names and values held in the mPSD correspond to the data frame of section III; the pointers to other mPSDs to the 'return link' and 'environment link' or 'display'. Figure 19.4 shows a procedure which looks up the value associated with a name, assuming that each mPSD contains a pointer like the environment link of chapter 13. The 'locals' of a micro-process are a list of <name,value> pairs and the lookup procedure searches for a particular name in that list. If it is found then the result of

---

```
let lookup(name, mPSD) = valof
{ until mPSD = empty do
    { let locals = mPSD.params

      until locals = empty do
       { let pair = locals.head

         if name=pair.namepart then resultis pair.valuepart
         else locals := locals.tail
       }

      mPSD := mPSD.environment
    }

  Error("name not declared")
}
```

Figure 19.4 Looking up a value in an environment

---

1 A procedure activation is a special case of a micro-process, the Activation Record Structure a special case of the Process Record Structure. One reason for maintaining this data structure in the interpreter is to allow inter-process control behaviours that are more general than simple recursive procedure call and return.

2 It may be convenient to represent the 'stacks' as lists.

the search is the associated value: if not then the search is repeated in the environment mPSD. If a name is found nowhere in the environment then it is not declared (is not bound) and the interpreter should halt. Although it would be possible, given a block-structured source language such as ALGOL 68, to determine the position of each value in the environment before the program runs, this isn't possible for most languages designed for interpretation and in any case would make run-time editing of the program more difficult.

Setting up the environment

The actions required to call a procedure are set out in chapter 11. Compiled code for simple recursive programming languages can implement a simplified version of these actions, as can an interpreter for such a language. In general, though, an interpreter must carry out the actions in full. To call a procedure it must

(i) evaluate each argument.
(ii) check that the number of arguments and their type is what is expected by the called procedure.
(iii) create a new mPSD.
(iv) create a <name,value> list which contains the names of the parameters and the values of the arguments and store it in the new mPSD.
(v) link the new mPSD to the current one (the return link).
(vi) link the new mPSD to its environment.
(vii) place the procedure body statement in the control stack of the new mPSD.
(viii) switch to interpreting the new mPSD

Procedure return is extremely simple: switch to interpreting the mPSD indicated by the return link (and, if the source language allows it, reclaim the data space of the returning mPSD). Note that the interpreter need not be a recursive program in order to implement recursion, nor need it be capable of executing directly any of the control behaviours which can be carried out by the manipulation of mPSDs in the interpreted program.

There are many ways of implementing the mechanism described here: this explanation has concentrated on the principles of interpretation and has ignored questions of efficiency. Bundling up various values and pointers and describing them collectively as a 'micro-process' makes it easier to see how they can be manipulated as objects in the source language. A closure is simply a kind of mPSD, for example, as is a label value or a co-process. This makes it easier to see how to implement exotic language facilities, such as co-processing, non-deterministic evaluation, lazy evaluation, forking and so on and on. A full discussion of the implementation of such mechanisms would take a great deal more space than this book can spare.

The Design of Languages for Interpretation

Interpretation and interactive computing go together. Although in principle programs in any language can be interpreted or compiled, there are noticeable differences between those designed mainly for batch processing and for compilation, such as ALGOL 68, PASCAL or SIMULA 67, and those designed mainly for interactive processing and interpretation, such as LISP, POP-2[1], or APL. In particular the first group of languages is block-structured and compile-time typed, while languages in the second group don't demand nesting of procedures and use run-time typing.

The force which determines most of the characteristics of interactive languages is that programs are developed experimentally and interactively, in small relatively independent pieces[2]. Each piece is normally a single procedure, perhaps because it would be hard to manipulate nested function declarations as a single unit. Some means other than block-structuring must be found to allow a procedure to access objects other than those which are declared within the procedure itself. The LISP, POP-2 and APL convention is that the environment of a micro-process (procedure activation) is normally the calling micro-process. This so-called <u>dynamic binding</u> convention[3] has many purely linguistic repercussions which cannot be discussed here, but also has an enormous effect on the efficiency of execution of programs in the language.

'Deep' and 'shallow' dynamic binding

Chapter 13 shows how the use of an explicit representation of the environment of a procedure in a block-structured language allows a micro-process (a procedure activation) to access non-local values without searching down the stack to find a particular data frame. Such a search would be particularly expensive in a heavily-recursive program. In the case of languages which use dynamic binding it is obligatory to search the stack to find a particular

---

1 POP-2 is in fact 'compiled' into an object program which largely consists of subroutine calls. The effect is more linearisation than translation.

2 There is some argument as to whether piecemeal development is a good idea or not. For the purposes of this book, however, I take it that interpreter-writers must satisfy programmers' desires.

3 The convention used in block-structured languages is called <u>static binding</u>, in which each procedure declaration in effect creates a closure.

data frame and, since the layout of the environment may be
different each time the procedure is called, each data frame must
contain a list of <name,value> pairs which must be searched to
find a particular name. This is the so-called <u>deep binding</u>
implementation of the dynamic binding mechanism: it is a very
inefficient mechanism of accessing the current environment but it
allows the free manipulation of environments since an environment
can be represented by a pointer to a particular mPSD.

An alternative implementation of the dynamic binding mechanism
is known as <u>shallow binding</u>. In this implementation each name is
associated with a memory location in static (off-stack, out-of-
heap) storage: in LISP it is on each atom's property list, which
is equivalent to the symbol table descriptor. These memory cells
are used rather like a 'cache memory' to represent the current
environment. The association of names with run-time objects
changes on each procedure call and return: therefore on each
procedure call the values held in the memory cells associated with
the parameter names are saved on a stack and the argument values
are assigned to these cells. On procedure return the old values
are retrieved from the stack and assigned to the relevant memory
cells. Thus the contents of the static memory cells always
represents the current environment, provided the program only
performs simple procedure call and return, and there is no need to
search through data frames or mPSDs to find the current binding of
a particular name.

Static binding is then highly efficient for simple programs and
gives rapid access to the environment at the cost of a slightly
more complicated procedure and return mechanism. It makes more
sophisticated kinds of programming almost impossible, however,
because it is difficult to represent the environment. The
environment is defined by the contents of all the memory cells
together with the contents of the stack of stored bindings and
therefore it is very difficult to manipulate it - for example to
construct and to use a closure. Some modern implementations of
LISP have sacrificed the efficiency of shallow binding and
returned to the deep binding mechanism because it does not
restrict the control behaviour of programs. There is constant
effort to develop hybrid mechanisms which can provide relatively
efficient execution of simple programs yet don't prohibit the
manipulation of environments and therefore will allow more
sophisticated forms of program behaviour.

Debugging with an Interpreter

A program which is being interpreted may halt due to an error -
say for example the value associated with an expression is of the
wrong type for the context in which the expression occurs, a name
whose value is required isn't declared in the current environment
or a procedure is called with the wrong number of arguments. The
user may forcibly interrupt the interpretation of a program at any

time, or may have requested the interpreter to pause after a particular source program statement is processed, or when a particular procedure is called, or on any one of a variety of conditions. The language which the interpreter accepts must allow the user to request such debugging interrupts, but it is more important to consider the range of actions which the user can perform when an debugging interrupt occurs.

The conventional means of communicating with an interpreter is to type an expression, a statement or a declaration. The. interpreter analyses the input to produce a parse tree. It then interprets that tree to produce a response which it types to the user - in the case of an expression the response is the value of the expression, in the case of a statement or declaration some message which indicates that the input has been processed. Apart from the fact that this allows the interpreter to be used as a sophisticated desk-calculator, it makes it trivially easy to find the current value associated with a particular name: just type the name (which is a simple expression) and the interpreter will respond with the value, or with an error message if that name isn't declared in the current environment. Thus it is possible to examine the state of variables in the current environment during a debugging interrupt, merely by typing expressions which contain the names of those variables. Typing the name of a procedure will cause the interpreter to respond with some representation of the value of the procedure (which is typically a closure): if the interpreter is helpful this may be a 'pretty-printed' version of the procedure declaration.

This means of communication between user and interpreter doesn't restrict operation to simple one-line programs. If an expression or a statement typed to the interpreter contains a procedure call then interpretation of the input will cause that procedure to be called. If that procedure in turn calls other procedures then it can play the role of the 'main program' or 'outer block' of a program and can cause the entire program to be interpreted.

When interpretation of the program is interrupted for any reason the user can be invited to type expressions, statements and declarations as usual. Sometimes information about the values of variables and expressions can be enough to locate the cause of a bug in a program: more often it is necessary to ask about the current control state (state of execution) of the program in order to find which statement has been reached in the current procedure, which procedure called this one, and so on.

The interpreter can provide facilities which explain the contents of its various data structures in terms of the source program and of stages of execution by printing out the current statement or expression and its context in the current procedure body. For simplicity these debugging commands can be expressed as

procedure calls: thus typing 'tellstate()' might produce a
response which explains the state of execution of the current
procedure body; 'tellparams()' could print out the names and
values of the parameters of the current micro-process. If there
are debugging commands which allow the user to switch
environments, so as to examine the state of other micro-processes
in the program, quite complicated examinations of the program's
state become possible.

Run-time editing

At some point during a debugging interrupt the user will decide
that a bug has been found and may wish to change the program to
eradicate it. Sometimes the best course of action is to abandon
the current execution, go back to the 'top-level' of
interpretation, edit parts of the program and restart it. Often it
is more convenient to make some minor alteration to the program or
to the values contained in some data objects and to continue the
current interpretation. The simplest changes to the program
involve adding a new procedure declaration (thus correcting an
'undeclared procedure' bug) or altering the value of some
variable. Sometimes when the error has to do with a procedure
declaration the user may not wish to edit the declaration or to
add a new one: the interpreter may then be instructed to ignore
the procedure call, or perhaps to carry on as if that procedure
call had taken place and had produced a value specified by the
user.

When a more substantial error is found in a part of a procedure
which is currently being interpreted then recovery cannot be quite
so simple. It isn't sufficient to type in a modified declaration
of the procedure or even to use an editor to produce a new version
which is then associated with the procedure name, since that will
not affect the section of parse tree on which the interpreter is
currently working. To eradicate the bug and to continue the
interpretation it is necessary to alter the actual parse tree.

In many cases the alteration consists merely of overwriting one
node with another. Say, for example, the interpreter encounters
the procedure call statement 'p(x,y)' and finds that the procedure
'p' specifies three parameters. It should start a debugging
interrupt, first placing itself in a state in which it is ready to
re-interpret the procedure call after the interrupt. During the
interrupt the user can edit the declaration of 'p', if that is
what caused the error, or can tell the interpreter to replace the
offending statement with an alternative version. A possible syntax
employs a **use** keyword followed by a source program phrase which is
to replace the phrase which caused the interrupt. Thus the user

may type

```
use p(x,y,x+y)
        or
use g(x,y)
        or
use x := p(x,y,1)
```

to specify the desired alteration. Deleting statements from the parse tree is also relatively simple.

Correcting errors which affect the block or statement structure of a procedure - e.g. errors of **begin-end** bracketing - is by no means so simple. In order to make such a change it is essential to understand the structure of the parse tree so that you can be sure of the effect which any alteration will actually produce. In most languages the structure of the parse tree isn't part of the definition of the language and indeed different implementations may represent the same source program text with very different tree structures.

In the case of LISP, however, the text of the source program is a transparent representation of the parse tree (which is a binary tree) and some LISP implementations therefore include a 'structure editor' which allows the user to manipulate the parse tree directly, moving nodes around the tree, deleting parts of nodes, duplicating nodes and so on. The commands provided are typically very 'low level' in that they simply regard the tree as a list structure.

A 'high level' structure editor would need to be capable of executing commands which treat the program as a structure of statements, declarations and expressions. The user should be able to specify transformations in source-language terms - 'put that statement here', 'swap the operands of that operator with those of this one', 'put this group of statements inside that loop', 'sorry, I meant this loop down here', and so on. Although it is possible to conceive of such an editor I know of no useful example. The problem seems to be that different requirements conflict: on the one hand the transformations which can be specified should leave a parse tree which the interpreter can continue to process and, on the other hand, transformations should be expressible in source language terms and should be adequate to allow the correction of any error. A 'low level' structure editor, in the hands of an experienced user, is an adequate tool but cannot be instructed in source language terms.

Combining Interpretation and Compilation

Direct execution of compiled code is faster than interpretation from the parse tree not only because a microprogram runs faster than an interpreter but also because the compiler can perform once

and for all, at compile-time, operations which the interpreter
usually performs over and over again at run-time. These actions
are: first, decoding and linearising the tree; second, determining
the position of data objects in the environment. Given a suitable
language there is no reason why interpreted and compiled modules
of a program should not be intermingled but there are some
difficult problems associated with environment handling.

The problem is that once a module is compiled it contains a
'frozen' representation of its environment at the time of
compilation, yet part of that environment may be provided by
interpreted modules which may be altered at any time. If all
compiled modules were re-compiled each time an interpreted module
is changed there would be no environment-handling problem, but
that would defeat the main object of mixing interpreted and
compiled modules, which is to provide the twin benefits of easy
development and debugging of the interpreted modules with
efficient execution of the compiled modules.

The first aspect of the environment-handling problem has to do
with procedure call. The discussion in section III assumes that
the translator has full information about the procedure referenced
by a procedure call. In particular it assumes that the code
address of the called procedure is fixed and is either known by
the translator or can be supplied by the loader. In a mixed
implementation the procedure which is called might either be
interpreted or compiled and, even when already compiled, might
later be replaced by an alternative interpreted or compiled
version. In order to link to a called procedure, therefore, the
compiled code must call the interpreter, which must find the
relevant procedure definition and either interpret it or start its
execution. The overhead of procedure call is therefore much
greater in a mixed implementation than in a totally-compiled
program.

It is possible to alter the actual procedure call code sequence
during program execution, when it is discovered that the procedure
to be called is another compiled procedure. LISP systems often
allow this in order to gain extra execution efficiency but the
gain is at the expense of flexibility in debugging since once made
it is difficult to break the link between compiled procedures, say
to include an updated version of one of them. Major efficiency
gains can also be made by translating calls to some standard
system functions - particularly EQ, CAR and CDR which manipulate
LISP lists - into short sequences of 'in-line' instructions which
perform the operation without calling the system function at all.
This is acceptable provided that the user never re-declares these
functions (for debugging purposes, say): if they are re-declared
then all interpreted procedures in the program will use the new
definition yet all compiled procedures will continue to use the
old 'hard-compiled' definition.

The second aspect of the environment-handling problem has to do with the accessing of non-local data. Much of the efficiency of programs written in a conventional language and compiled into machine code derives from the fact that the compiler can determine the position of a data object in a data frame and can determine the position of a data frame in an environment, thus eliminating the need for run-time searches of the environment. In order to use this mechanism the environment must be fixed at compile-time. In a mixed interpreted-compiled implementation of a block-structured language it might be thought desirable to allow an interpreted procedure to form part of the environment of a compiled procedure, which would mean that changes to the declarations in the interpreted procedure could change the layout of the compiled procedure's environment. This would make it difficult to compile efficient code, though, and the simplest solution to the problem is perhaps to decree that only complete 'nests' of function definitions which don't make any access to non-local data objects can be compiled.

In languages which employ dynamic binding (i.e. don't use block structure) the 'shallow binding' mechanism discussed above allows rapid access to the environment, but each such access must allow for the possibility that the name which is searched for doesn't denote any object (isn't declared or isn't bound) in the current environment. Such access is so much less efficient than access to an object on the stack that LISP compilers typically employ a particular trick with the parameters of a compiled procedure. The trick is to keep the values of all parameters on the stack or even in registers, rather than in the static memory cells, and thus these values will not be part of the environment of any procedure which the current procedure may call. If strictly instructed that a particular name is 'special' the compiler will ensure that the values of any parameters with that name are handled by the normal mechanism and will form part of the environment of other procedures.

LISP, then, is an example of a language for which 'compilers' exist that can produce superbly efficient object code only by making flagrant assumptions about the way in which that code will be used. These compilers make assumptions about the environment in which a procedure will operate and also about the environment which it will provide for other procedures that it calls. A LISP compiler is a sharp tool for use by sophisticated programmers who think they know what they are doing: such people can't complain if they are cut when the tool slips.

Summary

Interpretation is a mechanism by which the user can effectively develop and debug a source program without translation into object machine code. The execution efficiency of an interpreted program is lower than that of a compiled program but interpretation has the advantage that run-time alteration of the source program is possible, which makes run-time debugging much simpler and more effective.

Imitative interpretation is possible but relatively inflexible, both in the range of facilities which an interpreter can offer and in the ease with which the user can examine and interrogate the state of the interpreted program. A linearising interpreter allows the execution of the program to be broken down into a sequence of short steps, each of which takes a finite time and between which the interpretation can be interrupted and the state of the program interrogated. If the interpreter maintains a representation of the virtual machine on which the source program 'runs' then it can provide facilities dramatically different from those which are provided in the host language in which it itself is written.

It is possible to mix interpreted and compiled modules in a single program but it is difficult to produce compiled code which will execute as fast as that in a totally compiled implementation unless severe restrictions are placed on the ways in which compiled and interpreted modules can communicate.

20 Run-time Debugging Aids

A program presented to a compiler is not written for the purpose of being compiled. Compilation is a means to an end and the compiler is just an aid to programming in the original source language. Once a program has been compiled it would be wrong to expect that the user should debug the actual instructions of the object program, because that would view the compiler as an 'auto-coder' which merely helps in the business of programming in machine code. The source program prescribes a sequence of actions which the machine must carry out: when the object program behaves unexpectedly the cause is a <u>source program</u> error. Run-time debugging aids must therefore help to find source program errors: only the compiler-writer should be concerned with the possibility that there are errors in the object program which make it other than a faithful representation of the user's expressed intentions.

What every programmer hopes for is a run-time debugger that could point out errors in the source program and explain the way to fix them. Pending such miracles, the best debuggers relate run-time events to the source program structures which give rise to them. If the debugger is to be able to do this, the compiler must provide it with information which connects source program fragments with object code fragments and run-time objects with source-program names. The debugger must be able to communicate information about the state of execution of a program and must be able to receive instructions from the user. The necessary information structures can be constructed at compile-time by the object-description and translation phases, using the contents of the symbol table, and can be linked in to the instructions of the object program by the loader. Communicating with the user requires some simple command interpreter and perhaps a simple imitative interpreter (see chapter 19) so that the user can investigate the values of expressions, test individual procedures, and so on.

Run-time debugging isn't an 'add-on extra', to be designed only when the rest of the compiler is operating satisfactorily. When designing a compiler and in particular when designing object code fragments it is important to bear in mind the need to provide assistance to a run-time debugger. The need to detect run-time errors will affect the detail design of code fragments, as the discussion of vector-space allocation code in chapter 11 shows. More exotic requirements, such as the need to be able to modify the object code of a program in order to plant break-points, may affect the design of code fragments. Often there may be several otherwise equivalent code fragments which might be generated in a particular situation and the needs of run-time debugging may influence the choice between them. If the debugger is designed only when the rest of the compiler is complete then it may be too late to influence the design of any code fragments and it may therefore be difficult to construct an adequate run-time debugging system.

Assembly Code Debuggers

Compilers produce machine code and compiler writers make mistakes. Finding the mistakes means looking at machine code instructions. This task is made easier if the machine code is printed out in some imitation of assembly code format, with mnemonic operation codes and symbolic names rather than run-time addresses. 'JSUB 3, FRED' certainly reads better than '0074002373'.

Some operating systems contain debuggers which do just this: the DDT program provided on various DEC machines is an example. They accept information about source program data structures, labels and procedures, either using tables generated by the compiler or else using the information generated by the loader when it fixes up references between separate sections of program (see chapter 4). Using this information the debugger can 'de-translate' quite a proportion of the machine code program into readable pseudo-assembly-code form.

An assembly code debugger may be useful to the compiler writer but it is not an acceptable debugging aid for the users of a compiler. It is unreasonable in any case to expect a general purpose debugger to contain facilities matched to the way that a particular compiler manages the store - so as to enable the user to examine the contents of stack locations via their source program names, for example. It would be unreasonable to expect it to help in the business of matching source program structures to code addresses (though it might help in the matter of source program line numbers, perhaps). For the author of a compiler, though, these are minor considerations. If you know your compiler well, if it is well designed, then when using an assembly code debugger you are in the position of any programmer reading through their program's output to find the symptoms of an error.

The advantage of interactive assembly code debugging is probably minor. An assembly code dump of the object program - if you can afford it and if you can get hold of it it quickly - can

often provide more information than an interactive search through
suspected regions of the program and use of such a dump may waste
less of your precious time than interacting with the debugger on-
line. After all, you aren't interested in debugging the actual
machine code but rather the compiler which generated it.

Source Language Debugging

There are two rather distinct ways of using debugging aids: in off
line or batch mode, when users cannot be expected to inform the
debugger of what they want to know; and in on line or interactive
mode, when they can't be expected to read vast volumes of output
but must be allowed to select and interrogate. When you submit a
program to a batch processor - perhaps by post or courier - you
can't usually say in advance what to do in case of an error. You
need comprehensive information when the program breaks down, so as
to avoid expensive and annoying reruns to trace elusive bugs.
Sitting at a console, on the other hand, you want a minimum of
initial information but the facility to discover those parts of
the entire picture that you find relevant.

Off-line debugging and the panic dump

Programs which are run in off-line mode must be assumed to be
running correctly until they cause some sort of processor
violation or unless some fragment of error detecting code calls an
error subroutine. Interaction with the operating system should be
organised so that processor violation causes re-entry to an
error-handling section of the object program - i.e. it calls the
run-time debugger.

    In order to locate and correct the source program error which
caused a run-time error, the user must be provided with all the
symptoms of the run-time error. First, the debugger should say
what happened.   The error subroutine should give a clear message
identifying the error; in the case of processor violations such as
'ADDRESS OUT OF RANGE' it is necessary to design code fragments so
that only a small number of source program constructions can cause
it to occur and the error message should indicate what these are -
say 'array subscript error' or 'recursion too deep' or whatever.

    Saying what happened isn't enough to indicate why it happened.
The best off line aid is the panic dump, which gives exact details
of what the program was doing when the error was detected. Merely
by using information from the compile-time symbol table and a
table giving line-number/code-address correspondences it   is
possible to print out the name of the procedure that was active,
the line number that the procedure had reached and the values of
all its local variables. Then the debugger can print out the name
of the calling procedure and the calling line number together with
all its local values; and so on until it has described the state
of all currently active procedures. Figure 20.1 gives an example

of a panic dump of this kind, adapted somewhat[1] from the output of
the UMRCC ALGOL 60 in-core compiler.

Such a printout gives a part of the history of the program. It
tells which procedure called which in the recent past, and in most
cases this information together with the internal states of these
procedures is sufficient to indicate the source of the error.
Trace output - discussed further below - is less useful to the off
line programmer than the panic dump.

The use of panic dumps has no effect on the speed of the object
program (until an error is detected, of course!). The tables
needed to describe the layout of data frames in the object program
occupy space, as does the table which specifies a correspondence
between instruction addresses and procedure names, label names or
source program line numbers. If space in the object program is at
a premium, these tables may be kept in backing store until they
are required.

The use of special error-checking code fragments which help to
pinpoint the cause of an error can be especially useful in off-
line working. In the compiler which produced figure 20.1, each
variable in every block was initialised to a standard value at
block entry - this is the 'undefined' value referred to in the

---

```
**** RUN **** TIME **** ERROR ****

Arithmetic Overflow

Error detected in library procedure EXP

EXP called from line 2 in procedure TRAP
    L       is undefined or illegal REAL number
    M       is undefined or illegal REAL number

TRAP called from line 3 in procedure INTEGRAL
    A       0.0
    B       5.0
    E       1.0E-3

INTEGRAL called from line 8 in outer block
    L       is undefined or illegal REAL number
    M       is undefined or illegal REAL number
```

Figure 20.1 Format of a panic dump

---

1 I have to admit that the real output of this compiler, which I
   wrote, wasn't quite up to the standard illustrated here. In
   particular, it didn't name procedures but relied on 'block
   numbers'.

example. The value used was a binary bit pattern with only the most significant bit set (equivalent to $-(2^23)$ on a 24-bit machine). This bit-pattern happened to be an invalid **real** number and also was only just a valid **integer** number - if the object program negated this value or subtracted anything from it the processor set the 'arithmetic overflow' condition[1].

Interactive debugging

When running a program interactively programmers demand more information than can reasonably be contained in a panic dump. In addition they require to be able to restart their programs, continue execution after errors, alter particular memory cells, ask for execution up to a particular point and so on and on. In order to provide such facilities it may be sufficient if the run-time information structures contain the same information as for off line debugging, with perhaps a finer grain of resolution in the code address/program section table and perhaps also some cross reference from instruction addresses to the actual text of the original source program.

The most important requirement of interactive debugging is that the debugger must be able to interpret the programmer's requirements. This implies some input language or other for the various requests which a user can make. The most flexible form of input language would be a programming language. Why not use the original source language? - if the debugger is based on an interpreter for the source language the user can interrogate the value of variables, test the value of expressions and call object program procedures. A further advantage in using the source language as the debugging language is that the user doesn't have to learn two separate languages, one for programming and one for debugging.

As well as interrogating the object program state and testing out parts of the object program, the debugger's input language must allow the user to control the execution of the source program. Some of the most useful controls can be specified in the source language itself - 'execute this statement 100 times', for example, may be expressed as a normal iterative statement. Others require special debugger-specific commands - 'run the program up to this point' or 'interrupt each time this procedure is called', for example. Implementation of such controls requires the placing of break points in the object code, which are discussed further

---

1 On the ICL 1900 series computers on which this compiler operated, the only useful means of comparison between two integers is to subtract one from the other and to inspect the sign of the result - so by a happy accident there was a good chance that use of an uninitialised variable would cause a detectable run-time error.

below.

Run-time event tracing

If the object program makes a note each time some important kind of event occurs - say each time any procedure is called or each time any label is passed - then the list of events may give important clues to the program's history. Tracing the execution of the program affects its execution speed, though. It is necessary also for the compiler (or the loader) to insert special event tracing code fragments into the object program.

The most prevalent kind of tracing is that which keeps a buffer of the **N** most recent events - **N** is usually about 100 or so - which is printed out after a run time error. Such a trace is very little use in practice because information about what the program just did is worthless without corresponding information about why it did it. Just saying that a procedure was called, or that it returned, without giving the values of parameters or the result when it returned is also insufficient, but accumulating and storing information about arguments and results on every procedure call is extremely expensive.

A still more expensive form of tracing, useful in programming languages which rely heavily on the procedure as a control construct, is to trace the execution of user-nominated procedures by printing out the argument values each time they are called and the result value each time they return. Such tracing implies some means of nominating the procedures to be traced and also perhaps some means of controlling the information that is printed out on entry and exit. Controls can vary from the very simple - the user might set a 'trace level' on a nominated procedure - to the extremely sophisticated - the user might specify a program in the debugger's language which specifies action on each entry to and exit from the nominated procedure.

Break points

The user must be able to influence the course of the program's execution via debugger commands. One of the most powerful tools in interactive debugging is the <u>break</u> <u>point</u>. The user asks the debugger to run the program up to a particular point (ideally specified by reference to the text of the source program) and then to interrupt execution so that the user can decide on further action. Essentially implementation of a break-point facility depends on altering the instructions of the object program which correspond to the indicated section of source program, so that they transfer control to the debugger instead of carrying out their original function. Before continuing execution of the program after the break point the debugger must simulate the action of the instructions it has altered.

Using the same basic mechanism, it is possible to set
conditional break points to interrupt execution at a certain point
in the program only when a specified expression evaluates as **true**,
or iterative break points to interrupt execution only after a
certain section of program has been executed a specified number of
times.

Break points are most conveniently set at noticeable source
program positions - at entry to or exit from a procedure, at the
beginning or end of a source program line, at entry to or exit
from a loop. Procedure entry break points are often particularly
useful, since many errors occur after a procedure has been called
with some unexpected combination of parameter values and a
conditional break-point set on the entry to that procedure can
halt the program just before the error becomes a disaster.

Producing Debuggable Code

As well as generating the information structures which cross
reference object and source programs, the translator can help the
debugger mainly by ensuring that it has a uniform framework to
operate within. The use of the store should be a particular
concern. Important registers such as the 'F' and 'T' registers
discussed in section III should always be in the correct state, as
far as is possible, so that the debugger can provide accurate
information about the state of the program. If the stack-pointer
registers can occasionally provide confusing information about the
current data frame then sooner or later (probably sooner) the
debugger will be confused and be unable to help in the debugging
of an object program. The code for a vector declaration given in
chapter 11, for example, is careful not to alter the T register
except in a way which preserves the integrity of stack addressing,
even at a cost of an extra instruction in the code fragment which
allocates the space for a vector.

Code fragments which must necessarily alter the state of
important registers need specially careful design, and the
debugger must be prepared to take special action if the program is
interrupted during such a sequence. The procedure call and return
sequences discussed in section III are a good example of this - if
the program is interrupted during one of these sequences then the
debugger must recognise the situation and take appropriate action
to set the stack-pointer registers to a reasonable value.

The contents of the data frame stack will be used by the
debugger in order to report on the state of the object program. It
will use this information when it produces a panic dump or when it
investigates the contents of data frames under the interactive
control of the user. The display mechanism discussed in chapter 12
doesn't do this very conveniently, for example, and it may be
worthwhile to depress the efficiency of procedure call and return
sequences to provide the equivalent of a 'frame link' which will

help the debugger to find its way around the Activation Record Structure.

Doing Without the Debugger

A major element in the cost of almost every program is the cost of its development.   Run-time debugging aids help to reduce the cost of development. The focus should therefore be on the _benefits_ of debugging, rather than on their cost. Nevertheless, there does come a time in the life of many programs when they must outgrow the development stage and when the user may expect the incidence of run-time errors to decrease dramatically.

Certain debugging aids slow the execution of the object program, and so it is conventional to abandon them when a program is believed to be 'working'. An example of a debugging aid that is often abandoned is the use of error-checking fragments to check the validity of array accesses. The point at which such aids can be abandoned comes often surprisingly late in a program's life, perhaps even after it has been used 'in anger' for some considerable time.

Run-time debugging aids which impose no execution penalty ought _never_ to be abandoned. Except on the smallest machines, the space occupied by the information structures which cross-reference between object and source programs is usefully occupied and these structures should be kept throughout the program's useful life. Without them, how could you debug a very old and very useful program which has suddenly shown an unexpected run-time error?

Summary

A run-time debugger is a program that relates run-time events to source program commands and run-time objects or values to the source programs names which were used to denote them. It requires information about the source program to do so: in particular it must be able to convert from instruction addresses to source program text positions and from data addresses to source program names.

The design of object code fragments must take account of the debugger, both in order to avoid the possibility that the object program may be interrupted at inconvenient moments and to ensure that break-points may be placed in the code by replacing particular instructions.

For off-line debugging the simplest acceptable debugging aid is the panic dump; for on-line debugging interactive interrogation of the state of the object program is essential.

Appendix A The BCPL Language

I've used BCPL as the language of illustration throughout most of this book because it is designed as a system-programming language and is especially suited to the special problems of compiler-writing (a recurrent joke is that BCPL is designed as a language in which to write the BCPL compiler!). It is suitable for this purpose mainly because of the ease with which the program can manipulate pointers. In addition it is untyped - all BCPL values are merely treated as 'bitstrings' - so that the program can do just about anything that you might require to do with a pointer. Recursion is efficient in BCPL (see chapter 13).

I have taken many liberties with BCPL syntax in examples, mainly inspired by the need to compress complicated algorithms into the space of a single page. I have used **if-then-else** in place of BCPL's **test-then-or** for no other reason than the first construction will be more familiar to many users: I have used **elsf** because it abbreviates the programs. I have used dot-suffix notation 'nodep.x' rather than 'nodep!x' or 'x^nodep' because I believe it will be more familiar to many readers. Apologies to BCPL fanatics (and to BCPL's designer), but I defend myself by saying that my task is to explain compiler algorithms, not the syntax of BCPL.

In what follows I explain only those portions of BCPL (and pseudo-BCPL) which I have used in examples. The language is much more powerful and elegant than I have made it seem - I commend its use to all readers.

Statements

BCPL provides several forms of iterative and conditional statements. In general, if there are two uses for a statement, BCPL provides two different syntaxes - hence **while, until, repeatwhile, repeatuntil** and **repeat** are all provided in BCPL. Semicolons aren't usually needed to separate statements, although I have used them where one statement follows another on a single line. The **then** or **do** symbol is usually unnecessary, but I have

generally included it to avoid confusing those readers unused to
the language.

1. Assignment statement:
        <lhs-exprlist> := <exprlist>

    The <lhsexpr>s can be

        <name>
        <expr>!<expr>
        !<expr>
        <name>.<name>

2. Procedure call:
        <expr>()
        <expr>(<exprlist>)

    - BCPL makes you indicate parameterless procedures by showing
    an empty parameter list; there is only call-by-value.

3. Iterative statements:
        while <expr> **do** <statement>
        until <expr> **do** <statement>
        <statement> **repeat**
        <statement> **repeatwhile** <expr>
        <statement> **repeatuntil** <expr>

    Test is either before execution of <statement> (**while, until**)
    or after execution of statement (**repeat, repeatwhile,
    repeatuntil**).

4. Selection of cases:
        switchon <expr> **into** <statement>

    The <statement> must contain **case** labels of the form
    case <constant>:   or   **case** <constant> .. <constant>:   or
    default:.

5. Conditional statement (not strict BCPL):
        if <expr> **then** <statement>
        if <expr> **then** <statement> **else** <statement>
        if <expr> **then** <statement> **elsf** <expr> **then** ...

6. Compound statements:
        { <statement>* }
        { <declaration>* <statement>* }

7. Control statements:
        break   - exit from current iterative statement
        loop   - end present iteration of current iterative
                        statement
        endcase - exit from current **switchon** statement

Declarations

8. Variable declarations:
       let \<namelist\> = \<exprlist\>

9. Procedures and functions:
       let \<name\>() **be** \<statement\>
       let \<name\>(\<namelist\>) **be** \<statement\>
       let \<name\>() = \<expr\>
       let \<name\>(\<namelist\>) = \<expr\>

Note that the \<expr\> in a function declaration is usually a **valof** expression.

Expressions

There are many kinds of BCPL operator, both binary and unary. I have assumed that all unary operators have the highest priority, that arithmetic operators come next with their conventional priorities, relational operators next, and finally logical operators. In cases of confusion I've used brackets. Conditional expressions have the lowest priority.

In translation examples I have used an invented operator: the '++' operator which takes a string and appends a character. It is quite unrealistic, but I hope you see what it means.

10. Value of a statement:
       valof \<statement\>

The \<statement\> must contain a **resultis** \<expr\> statement

11. Unary operators:
       @\<name\>   /* address-of */
       !\<expr\>   /* contents-of */
       +\<expr\>, -\<expr\> /* unary integer arithmetic */
       \ \<expr\>   /* logical 'not' */

12. Function calls:
       \<expr\>()
       \<expr\>(\<exprlist\>)

13. Binary operators:
       \<expr\>!\<expr\>   /* subscript operator */
       \<expr\>.\<name\>   /* field-select operator */
       +, -, *, /, **rem**   /* integer arithmetic */
       <, <=, =, \=, >=, >   /* integer relations */
       &, | /* logical 'and' and 'or' */
       ++   /* string concatenation */

'V!n' is similar to V[n] in most other languages, 'P.a' is

similar to SIMULA 67's P.a, PASCAL's P^.a and ALGOL 68's a of P.

14. Conditional expressions:
$<expr_0> \rightarrow <expr_1>, <expr_2>$

If the value of $<expr_0>$ is **true** then $<expr_1>$ is evaluated; otherwise $<expr_2>$ is evaluated.

Appendix B Assembly Code Used in Examples

I have been consistent in using a single-address, multi-register
machine as my illustration in examples. The code format is:

      <operation-code> <register-number>, <address>
    - where an address is either a <number> or <number>(<register>)

    Examples: JUMPFALSE 1, 44
                 ADD   1, 3217(7)
                 ADDr   5, 2

Any register may be used as an address modifier or as an
accumulator.   There are a fixed number of registers (the exact
number doesn't matter).   Sometimes (e.g. JUMP) the register
doesn't matter and is omitted, sometimes (e.g. FIXr) the address
is omitted

    I find it best to divide instructions into different groups
distinguished by a lower-case letter at the end of the operation
code.   This makes logically different operations, which on many
real machines are implemented by widely differing instructions,
visually distinct. The suffixes are:

- no suffix means a store-to-register operation (except
  STORE, which is of course register-to-store)
- 'r' means register-to-register
- 's' means register-to-store
- 'n' means the <address> part is to be interpreted as a
  number
- 'a' means the <address> part is to be interpreted as an
  address - this may seem just like 'n' but on some machines
  it isn't!
- 'i' means indirect addressing - the memory cell addressed
  contains the actual address to be used in the instruction.

Examples of the differences:

```
ADD  1, 2      means add the contents of store location 2
                  to register 1
ADDr 1, 2      means add the contents of register 2
                  to register 1
ADDs 1, 2      means add the contents of register 1 to
                  store location 2
ADDn 1, 2(4)   means add the number which is formed by adding
                  2 and the contents of register 4, to register 1
ADDa 1, 2(4)   means add the address which is formed by
                  combining 2 and the contents of register 4,
                  to register 1
```

I hope the instruction-names are fairly indicative of their operation. In the examples I've mostly used LOAD, STORE, JSUB, SKIP?? and the arithmetic operations. Here is a table which may clarify matters:

Instruction	Explanation
LOAD	place a value in a register
STORE	place a value in a memory cell
INCRST	add one to store location
DECRST	subtract one from store location
STOZ	set all bits in store location to zero
STOO	set all bits in store location to one
INCSKP	increment store location; skip next instruction if result is zero
DECSKP	decrement store location; skip next instruction if result is zero
ADD	add two values
SUB	subtract one value from another
NEGr	negate value in register
MULT	multiply two values
DIV	divide one value by another

(I have used fADD, fSUB etc. to denote the floating-point analogue of these instructions. Likewise xSUB, xDIV etc. denotes the 'exchanged' or 'reverse' variant - see chapter 5)

FIXr	convert floating point number in register to fixed-point
FLOATr	convert fixed point number in register to floating point

```
SKIP              jump over the next instruction
SKIPLT            jump over the next instruction if register
                    value is less than (LT) store value
SKIPLE            ditto, but relation is 'less or equal'
SKIPNE            ditto, but relation is 'not equal'
SKIPEQ            ditto, but relation is 'equal'
SKIPGE            ditto, but relation is 'greater or equal'
SKIPGT            ditto, but relation is 'greater than'

JUMP              transfer control to indicated address
JUMPLT            transfer control only if register value
                    is less than (LT) zero
JUMPLE            ditto, but if less than or equal to zero
JUMPNE            ditto, but if not equal to zero
JUMPEQ            ditto, but if equal to zero
JUMPGE            ditto, but if greater than or equal to zero
JUMPGT            ditto, but if greater than zero
JUMPTRUE          transfer control if register contains special
                    TRUE value
JUMPFALSE         ditto, but for FALSE value

JSUB  L, a        transfer control to indicated address, storing
                    address of next instruction (return address)
                    in register
RETN     , a      return to indicated address

PUSH  p, a        transfer contents of address a to top of stack
                    indicated by register p, increase p
POP   p, a        decrement stack pointer p, transfer contents of
                    top of stack to address a

PUSHSUB, POPRETN
                  analogous to JSUB, RETN but link address is on
                    the stack rather than in a register.

INC   p, a        add contents of location a to stack register p
                    and check that p is not outside bounds of
                    stack space
DEC   p, a        subtract contents of location a from stack
                    pointer and check limits of stack.
```

Some of the instructions in this list may seem to have the same effect as others, but I have in general included an instruction for each simple machine-code operation which I have needed to illustrate. Using such a large instruction set makes my task easier than it would otherwise be, of course, but some real machines have larger sets still (e.g. the DEC PDP-10). I've never yet seen a machine with a SKIPTRUE or a JUMPTRUE instruction, given that TRUE is to be represented as a specific non-zero bit pattern, but I have felt the need for it in practice!

Bibliography

The most important item in a compiler-writing bibliography isn't referenced here: it is a compiler, which should be written in a system programming language to compile some language which you know fairly well. Reading such a compiler will clarify many of the points which are made in this book. If you can get hold of the source code of any compiler on your machine then don't be ashamed to read it and don't be ashamed to copy algorithms from it if that will save you time. A good compiler to look out for is that for BCPL: most versions of the BCPL compiler are based on the original written by Martin Richards.

Books and papers referenced in the text above are:

Aho A.V., Ullman J.D. (1978) "Principles of Compiler Design", Addison-Wesley.

Aho A.V., Johnson S.C. (1974) "LR parsing", Computing Surveys 6, 1, pp 99-124.

Baker H. (1978) "List Processing in Real Time on a Serial Computer" Comm. ACM 21, 4, pp 280-294.

Brooker R.A., MacCallum I.R., Morris D., Rohl J.S. (1963) "The compiler-compiler", Annual Review of Automatic Programming 3, pp 229-275.

Dijkstra E.W., Lamport L., Martin A.J., Scholten C.S.and Steffens E.F.M. (1978) "On-the-Fly Garbage Collection: An Exercise in Cooperation", Comm. ACM 21, 11, pp 966-975.

Foster J.M. (1968) "A Syntax Improving Device", Computer J, 11,1, pp 31-34.

Geschke C.M. (1972) "Global Program Optimizations", Ph.D. thesis, Carnegie-Mellon University

Gries D. (1971) "Compiler Construction for Digital Computers", John Wiley, 1971.

Horning J.J. (1974) "LR parsing", in Bauer et al., "Compiler Construction - An advanced course", Springer-Verlag.

Hunter R.B., McGettrick A.D., Patel R. (1977) "LL versus LR parsing with illustrations from ALGOL 68", SIGPLAN notices 12, 6, pp 49-53.

Irons E.T. (1961) "An error-correcting parse algorithm", Comm. ACM, 4,1 pp 51-55.

Knuth D.E. (1971) "An Empirical Study of FORTRAN programs", Software - Practice and Experience, 1, 2, pp 105-133.

Knuth D.E. (1965) "On the Parsing of Languages from Left to Right", Information and Control 8, 6, pp 607-639.

Landin P.J. (1965) "A Correspondence between ALGOL 60 and Church's Lambda-Notation", Comm ACM 8,2 and 8,3, pp 89-101 and 158-165.

McCarthy et al. (1965) "LISP 1.5 Programmer's Manual", MIT Press, 1965.

Rohl J.S. (1975) "An Introduction to Compiler Writing", MacDonald and Janes, 1975.

Reynolds J.C. (1972) "Definitional Interpreters for higher-order programming languages", Proc 27th ACM National Conf, 717-740.

Steele G.L. (1977) "Arithmetic Shifting Considered Harmful", SIGPLAN notices, 12, 11, pp 61-69.

Weizenbaum J. (1977) "Computer Power and Human Reason", Freeman, San Francisco.

Wichmann B.A. (1975) "Ackermann's function, a study in the efficiency of calling procedures", National Physical Laboratory report.

Wulf W., Johnsson R.K., Weinstock C.B., Hobbs S.O. (1973), "The design of an optimizing compiler", Computer Science Dept. Technical Report, Carnegie-Mellon University (published in modified form under the same title by American Elsevier, 1975).